MW01001784

THE PUBLISHER AND THE UNIVERSITY OF CALIFORNIA PRESS FOUNDATION
GRATEFULLY ACKNOWLEDGE THE GENEROUS SUPPORT OF THE PETER BOOTH WILEY
ENDOWMENT FUND IN HISTORY.

A PEOPLE'S GUIDE TO
NEW YORK CITY

UNIVERSITY OF CALIFORNIA PRESS
PEOPLE'S GUIDES

Los Angeles

Greater Boston

San Francisco Bay Area

Orange County, California

New York City

Forthcoming

Richmond and Central Virginia

New Orleans

About the Series

Tourism is one of the largest and most profitable industries in the world today, especially for cities. Yet the vast majority of tourist guidebooks focus on the histories and sites associated with a small, elite segment of the population and encourage consumption and spectacle as the primary way to experience a place. These representations do not reflect the reality of life for most urban residents—including people of color, the working class and poor, immigrants, indigenous people, and LGBTQ communities—nor are they embedded within a systematic analysis of power, privilege, and exploitation. The *People's Guide* series was born from the conviction that we need a different kind of guidebook: one that explains power relations in a way everyone can understand, and that shares stories of struggle and resistance to inspire and educate activists, students, and critical thinkers.

Guidebooks in the series uncover the rich and vibrant stories of political struggle, oppression, and resistance in the everyday landscapes of metropolitan regions. They reveal an alternative view of urban life and history by flipping the script of the conventional tourist guidebook. These books not only tell histories from the bottom up, but also show how *all* landscapes and places are the product of struggle. Each book features a range of sites where the powerful have dominated and exploited other people and resources, as well as places where ordinary people have fought back in order to create a more just world. Each book also includes carefully curated thematic tours through which readers can explore specific urban processes and their relation to metropolitan geographies in greater detail. The photographs model how to read space, place, and landscape critically, while the maps, nearby sites of interest, and additional learning resources create a resource that is highly usable. By mobilizing the conventional format of the tourist guidebook in these strategic ways, books in the series aim to cultivate stronger public understandings of how power operates spatially.

A PEOPLE'S GUIDE TO
NEW YORK CITY

Carolina Bank Muñoz   Penny Lewis   Emily Tumpson Molina

University of California Press

University of California Press
Oakland, California

The *People's Guides* are written in the spirit of discovery and we hope they will take readers to a wider range of places across cities. Readers are cautioned to explore and travel at their own risk and obey all local laws. The author and publisher assume no responsibility or liability with respect to personal injury, property damage, loss of time or money, or other loss or damage allegedly caused directly or indirectly from any information or suggestions contained in this book.

Library of Congress Cataloging-in-Publication Data

Names: Bank Muñoz, Carolina, author. | Lewis, Penny, author. |
    Molina, Emily Tumpson, author.
Title: A people's guide to New York City / Carolina Bank Muñoz, Penny
    Lewis, Emily Tumpson Molina.
Description: Oakland, California : University of California Press, [2022] |
    Includes bibliographical references and index.
Identifiers: LCCN 2020055876 (print) | LCCN 2020055877 (ebook) |
    ISBN 9780520289574 (paperback) | ISBN 9780520964150 (ebook)
Subjects: LCSH: New York (N.Y.)--Guidebooks. | New York (N.Y.)—Description
    and travel.
Classification: LCC F128.18 .B26 2022 (print) | LCC F128.18 (ebook) | DDC
    917.47/104--dc23
LC record available at https://lccn.loc.gov/2020055876
LC ebook record available at https://lccn.loc.gov/2020055877

Designer and compositor: Nicole Hayward
Text: 10/14.5 Dante
Display: Museo Sans and Museo Slab
Prepress: Embassy Graphics
Indexer: Rob Saute
Cartographer: John Emerson
Printer and binder: Sheridan Books, Inc.
Manufactured in the United States of America

30   29   28   27   26   25   24   23   22
10   9   8   7   6   5   4   3   2   1

Contents

Maps

Introduction

No subways take you directly to its doors. But leave any station on 34th Street (33rd on the east side) and you will find, towering above you and dominating the nearby skyline, perhaps the most iconic of New York City's skyscrapers, the Empire State Building. New York elites who sank their millions into this construction project at the outset of the Great Depression did so as a symbolic assertion of the power of capital to rise again.

The Empire State Building sits on property formerly owned and developed by the Astor family, New York's first real estate moguls. At their height, Astor family holdings included properties on eleven Manhattan avenues and at least ninety-eight streets, including the entirety of what is now the west side of Times Square, from 42nd to 51st Streets west of Broadway. Little surprise that the Astor name lives on across the city—at Astor Place in Manhattan's East Village, along Astor Row in Harlem, and in the neighborhood of Astoria, Queens.

Construction on the Empire State Building began in March of 1930 and was completed on International Workers Day, May 1, 1931. Built in fourteen months under the direction of New York's former governor and 1928 Democratic presidential candidate Al Smith, the Empire State Building represented, in Smith's words, the "brains, brawn, ingenuity, and the muscle of mankind." In the building's lobby, above the doors, are platter-size brass medallions that salute the building's "Masonry," "Heating," and "Electricity" that were the marvels of the age. Its difficulty finding tenants in the Depression's first years earned it the nickname "the Empty State Building"; the 1933 film *King Kong*, which featured the giant ape climbing to the top of the radio tower, helped turn its fortunes around. Soon hundreds of businesses, many of them connected to the fashion and garment industries whose base was in the neighborhood, located to the building.

Formerly the Wigwam bar, now a beauty salon, 2021.
CREDIT: CAROLINA BANK MUÑOZ

1

New York City

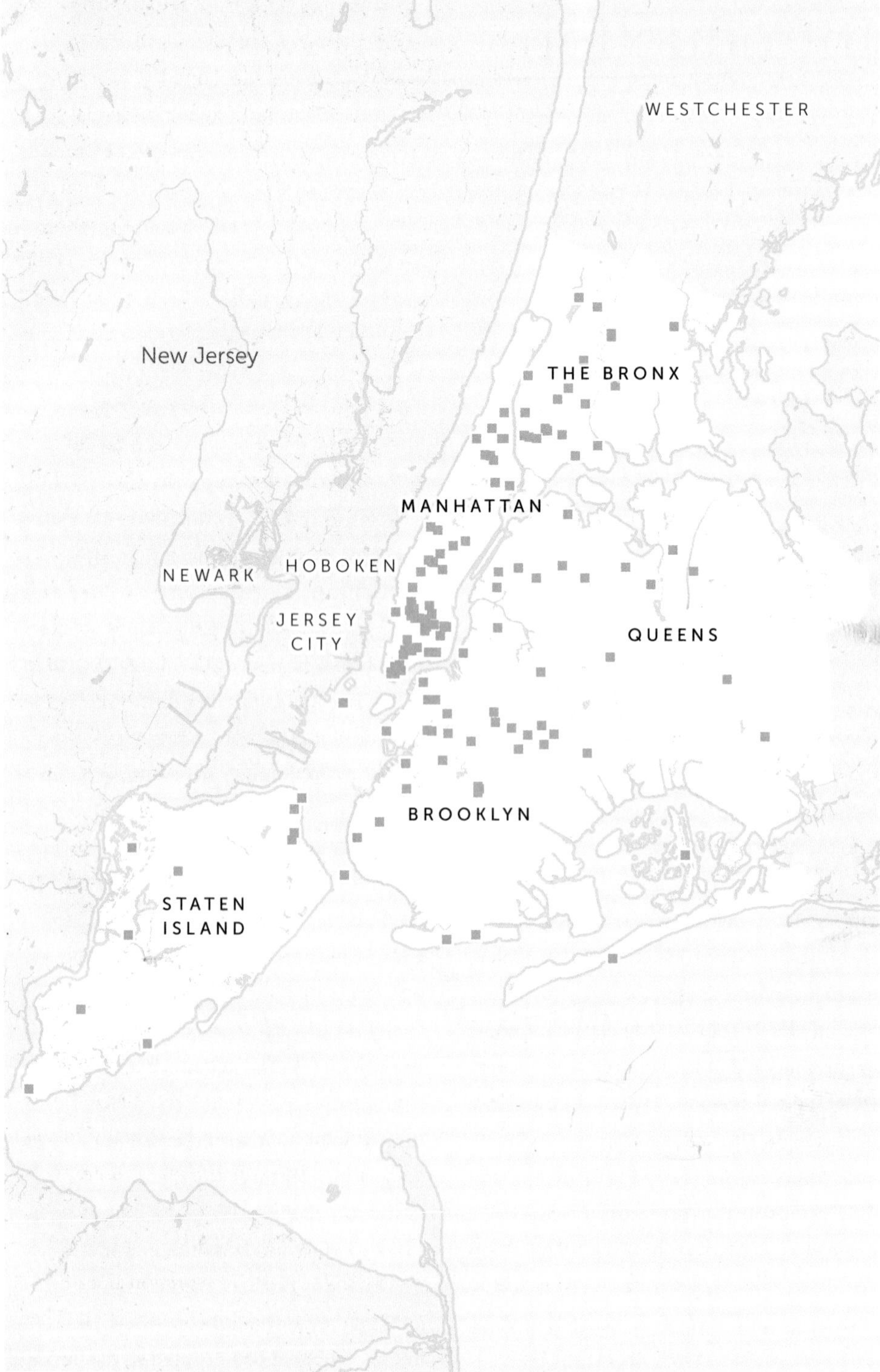

WESTCHESTER

New Jersey

THE BRONX

MANHATTAN

NEWARK   HOBOKEN

JERSEY
CITY

QUEENS

BROOKLYN

STATEN
ISLAND

But who built this soaring tower? Thousands of workers piled millions of bricks, hauled tons of steel, limestone, and marble, and installed miles of pipes and wires. Their frenetic pace surely helped contribute to the five official deaths recorded during construction, but as one worker recalled decades later, they were "glad to have the work" in those grim years.

And among the thousands of European immigrants and their children who formed the core of the construction workforce were hundreds of Mohawk ironworkers who immigrated to the city from Kahnawake, a reservation town outside of Montreal, Canada. These "skywalkers" were the riveters, also known as the connectors: they bolted the steel beams together after they had been put in place. Working with portable furnaces, red hot rivets, and heavy mallets, theirs was the highest, hardest, and most dangerous work in construction, and also the best paid. Mohawk ironworkers had come to New York during the building boom of the 1920s, and over the following years hundreds made the journey. They helped to build not only the Empire State Building, but Rockefeller Center, the United Nations, and, later, the Verrazzano-Narrows Bridge and the World Trade Center. Today, there are still around two hundred Mohawk ironworkers in New York, comprising around 10 percent of the workforce.

To consider the lives these ironworkers led in mid-twentieth-century New York, you could take a train from the west side (the 2 or 3) or the east side (the 6 to the 4 or 5) to Nevins Street, Brooklyn. Nevins Street begins at the edges of Brooklyn's ever-expanding downtown, heading south off Flatbush Avenue. For a few blocks, it would barely qualify as a commercial strip. The large buildings that line these blocks show their backs here, opening their freight entrances and little else. Yet as Nevins approaches Atlantic, you will notice a quick change in the character of the street. Suddenly you will come across two- and three-story residences, smaller shops, honey locust trees, and the occasional Callery pear.

75 Nevins Street, between State and Atlantic, is a hair salon today. Over half a century ago, it was a bar called the Wigwam Club. Here, and in the streets to the south, you are in what was once the heart of "Little Kahnawake." For a few decades, most of the Mohawk ironworkers in the city settled in the ten square blocks of Brooklyn known then as North Gowanus, today as Boerum Hill. Surrounding the Gowanus Canal, it was an industrial area, described in 1949 by the writer Joseph Mitchell as "old, sleepy, shabby," but it was also filled with red brick and brownstone residential buildings. The ironworkers moved there for its proximity to their union hall on nearby Atlantic Avenue, Local 361 of the International Association of Bridge, Structural, Ornamental, and Reinforcing Iron Workers. The hall served as a community center for the Mohawks and other ironworkers in the area, where they could find jobs and travel quickly—on the train you just left, which was only a nickel until 1948—to the construction sites of downtown and midtown Manhattan. Their wages assured them a decent living, and

many moved their families to Brooklyn or married local neighbors; Mitchell observed that the Kahnawake lived "in the best houses on the best blocks." A Presbyterian minister on Warren Street learned enough of the Mohawk-Oneida language to translate the Gospel of Luke and to preach to his Native Canadian immigrant parishioners once a month. The Nevins Bar and Grill, a neighborhood bar, became the Wigwam, where walking in one could find tomahawks and feather headdresses, and a sign over the door that read "The Greatest Iron Workers in the World Pass Thru These Doors."

Like weeds, condominiums and new office towers have sprung up to the north, west, and east of what was once the Wigwam. But from across Atlantic Avenue, looking north, you can still see the top of the Empire State Building rising above the midtown skyline in the distance. As you contemplate this symbolic center of the Big Apple from afar, you might consider some defining social contrasts that help to make sense of New York, stories concealed in the footprint of the tower and in the steel beams that help it fly to the sky.

You will likely encounter mention of the Empire State Building and the Astor family elsewhere in your journey to New York City, and many other guidebooks will draw attention to their prominence and legacy. But if you know where to look, and how to listen, different stories can be found as well. We can see soaring evidence of fortunes piling on fortunes, how city investments help the wealthy increase their wealth. Yet with some imagination, as you walk the quieter Brook-

lyn streets, you might still hear the communities formed by immigrant First Nation workers. And certainly, all around the city, we can see the fruits of their labor.

A People's Guide to New York City is the fifth in a series of books that seek to create a "deliberate political disruption" of the ways we know and experience the urban environment. As the authors of *A People's Guide to Los Angeles* observed in their introduction, "Guidebooks select sites, put them on a map, and interpret them in terms of their historical and contemporary significance. All such representations are inherently political, because they highlight some perspectives while overlooking others. Struggles over who and what count as 'historic' and worthy of a visit involve decisions about who belongs and who doesn't, who is worth remembering and who can be forgotten, who we have been and who we are becoming."

As told by most guidebooks, the story of New York City lingers on the stories of people like the Astors, or celebrities and artists who made their fortunes here and shared their fame with the city itself. The everyday citizens of New York are not necessarily forgotten in these guidebooks. Indeed their diversity and hardiness, their capacity for invention and overcoming adversity, their toughness, tolerance, and fast-talking hustles are often celebrated. New York is a global city, an immigrant city, a rags-to-riches city, a mecca for money and artistry. New York has created or refined dozens of cultural motifs that leap beyond its boundaries, and fortunes that span the world as well. Even the radicals agree. Leon Trotsky noted in his autobiography, describing his brief 1917 residence in New York: "Here I was in New York, city of prose and fantasy, of capitalist automatism, its streets a triumph of cubism, its moral philosophy that of the dollar. New York impressed me tremendously because, more than any other city in the world, it is the fullest expression of our modern age."

Over a century later, New York City continues to represent, in many respects, the fullest expression of our modern age. That is, it is a city of intensive and uneven capital investment; tremendous labor power, employed and not; vaunting ambitions and crippling inequality; and a myriad of peoples struggling to get by, creating communities, and establishing their very right to the city they live in. Guidebooks will often narrate aspects of this city of contrasts. But in capturing such contrasts as spectacle, such accounts do not make sense of the manifold relationships between the glitz and the glamour on the one side and the grit of the people and the grime of the streets on the other. Guidebooks, by their very nature, must freeze dynamic urban processes at a point in time.

A People's Guide to New York City makes the straightforward proposition that the life and landscape of New York are products of social power and its attendant struggles. The streets, the buildings, the institutions, the people, tell a story of movement and countermovement. It is often a story of the prerogatives of great wealth; a story of government invention, intervention, and repression; a story that is also of people's demands, creativity, and self-organization. It is

a story of standoff and of compromise; battles won, lost, avoided, celebrated, forgotten.

To see this, you have to see the whole of the city. As such, *A People's Guide* brings you to the five boroughs. We present them from north to south, and we also organize our sites from north to south and by neighborhoods, moving from Montefiore Hospital in the Bronx to the Lenape Burial Ridge in Staten Island. We selected sites that tell different parts of the stories of the people of New York City over time and today; not just who they were and are, but how they have made and remade the city around them. Our sites should change how you view the city itself—its physical landscape and the places that are most significant in its history and ongoing development. By making visible the invisible social dynamics that undergird the city, we hope to shift how the reader determines what and who are important to the Big Apple.

The Past and the Present

Like the ironworkers of Gowanus, *A People's Guide to New York City* is necessarily a story of disappearances. With its limited space, large crowds, real estate profiteering, and constant need for an edge, the built environment and streetscapes of New York are always under erasure. The writer Colson Whitehead observed that you become a New Yorker when, as you walk around the city, you begin to say "That used to be . . ." He explains, "You are a New Yorker when what was there before is more real and solid than what is here now."

To many, New York today is in fact haunted by *what was there before*, as the dizzying city we witness at this writing, with its hyper-gentrification and skyscraper homes for the world's billionaires, eclipses a scrappy city where, if you could "make it there," you'd "make it anywhere." Jeremiah Moss, an astute observer of the city, has described a *Vanishing New York*, in a popular blog and book by that name. Natives and more recent transplants wonder whether the transformations of the first decades of the twenty-first century—the explosion of high-end development and big-box stores; the closing of hundreds of small cafes, bars, theaters, galleries, and all kinds of mom-and-pop storefronts; the presence of a vast police force and other visible security measures—represent a moment when the sheer *quantity* of change augurs a true *qualitative* change to the very nature of the city. The devastation of the COVID-19 pandemic and the concurrent economic crisis promise still more upheaval, in directions that continue to unfold. Behind the changes to the buildings and their street-level occupants lurks a greater injustice: the mass displacement of middle- and lower-income residents from neighborhood after neighborhood, most often people of color or ethnic minorities, due to rising real estate costs and the city's un- and underemployment. Those living in New York City neighborhoods are no strangers to residential transformation. But such churn is never a "natural" process. Social forces push people out and pull people away; others draw people in; and sometimes others compel them to stay when they might otherwise leave.

The sites in this book tell many tales of the whys and wherefores of such neighborhood transformation. "Booms" lure job seekers and "busts" forcefully expel them. Employment and opportunity are constants in New York's push-pull, but the laws, investments, decisions, and costs surrounding real estate are perhaps the overriding determinants of the city's physical and social landscapes. In the twentieth century, racially discriminatory "redlining" devalued homes in multiethnic, interracial communities and encouraged racist mortgage lending practices, further spurring segregation and white flight from the city. Urban renewal and "slum clearance" displaced hundreds of thousands of New Yorkers, frequently leaving shattered neighborhoods or undersupported housing in its wake. Continually, bohemians and artists lay claim to cheap housing or abandoned industry, building galleries and creating new "hip" areas, and, wittingly and not, as geographer Neil Smith observed, often serving as shock troops for gentrification, which in turn can displace the very artists who helped begin the process. Anti-gentrification activists call this "artwashing" and are urging that community residents in places like Bushwick, Brooklyn, and in the South Bronx push back to "decolonize the hood."

Twenty-first-century displacements are widespread and, seemingly, as permanent as the titanic shifts of the past. Laws limiting rent increases were radically weakened in the early 1990s, and since that time to this writing New York City has lost close to half a million units of affordable housing. Aggravating this problem, since the financial crisis of 2008, a swarm of predatory investors in rental housing, seeking profits beyond what legal rents would bring, have tried to drive away renters who pay below-market rates by harassing tenants and neglecting buildings. Home values have doubled and tripled and more, again depending on the neighborhood. Were it not for public housing and other subsidies, overcrowded living spaces, and the remaining rent control and stabilization laws, Manhattan would not have any working-class or poor residents. All the boroughs are growing more expensive. Adding to the flux and churn, the COVID-19 pandemic has unsettled real estate patterns, with economic instability promising evictions and foreclosures at the same moment that the city itself becomes a less desirable place for many whose jobs have been lost, or who are concerned with the medium-term viability of office districts and dense, urban centers. The gulf between the "haves" and "have-nots," always profound, continues to foreshadow a future where a city organized around the needs and wants of the rich might fully eclipse the vibrant city of the people.

To a degree, *A People's Guide* shares this perspective. We draw attention to many of these vanished sites and peoples, highlighting their ongoing importance to what the city and its people have become. Many of the stories related in this guide touch upon the shutting out and shutting down of the people's city, and highlight those losses that mark erosions of community power, or that stifle and derail the bottom-up creativity and expression of the city's citizens.

But we don't think that vanishing is the whole of the story of New York. In *A People's Guide*, we also make visible the ongoing presence and assertion of the city's people to claim their city, build and defend neighborhood institutions, and make the streets and homes their own. Throughout its history, despite the larger social forces that buttress the city, the people of New York have inscribed and re-inscribed their own meanings on the places that make it up, and have asserted their rights to continue to live here. In fact, it is that ever-unfolding, persistent tug of possibility that helps to attract and retain so many for whom New York is otherwise such a difficult place to live. Today, when the city is once again in the grips of profound uncertainty, we have seen dozens of neighborhoods self-organize to help their neighbors; businesses retool to provide essential sustenance, products, and services for the city's common good; and communities create safe and playful opportunities for their residents to connect and come together. In times of crisis, the people's city emerges again after hiding in plain sight.

Many "baked-in" structural factors contribute to New York's capacity for renewal. Cramped living spaces, the relative availability of public transit and public space, and the density of commercial districts have all contributed to much of New York City life being lived outside, creating a constantly innovating street culture. Certainly, developers, marketers, landlords, city planners, and the police play outsized roles setting the structural parameters, prices, and tone of the city. But neighborhoods also change from the bottom up, revitalized by new migrants and immigrants who create new businesses, art, homes: again, it is New York's peoples that continually reimagine it. Such revitalization is repeated across time and across the city, and offers the possibility of a home, at least for a while, for new and thriving neighborhood cultures.

At the same time, people's movements have demanded and won rent control, public and other affordable housing, access to public space and more of it, housing subsidies, and sustainable urban planning. In fact, the very rent laws weakened in the 1990s were given new life and expanded in 2019 after years of concerted pressure from dozens of housing and community groups and thousands of tenants across the city and state. Time and again, the public and private spaces of this city have been contested turf. Apartments and all kinds of buildings, parks, streets, and schools are designed with one social class in mind and then inhabited by another. Such back and forth has always happened, and what we see around us is a landscape still shaped by class and cultural struggles. Despite the great power of real estate and the city's new financial princes, this story will continue.

City of Contradictions

Beyond New York's bottom-up creation and often obscured urban processes, the sites and tours of the *People's Guide* highlight dynamic tensions that take their own peculiar shape in this city. By drawing attention to these shifting contrasts that have shaped and continue to shape the city, it is our hope that even as the city changes around us, the very few sites we've chosen will still help to reveal and explain the very many possible sites that could be in this book, as well as potential sites that have yet to emerge.

New York's earliest days were similar to other North American territories seized by the Europeans. Early colonizers killed and displaced the Native American peoples who lived across the five boroughs through fortified occupation of their lands, disease, and a century of warfare. The Lenape were the most extensive group to be "bought" and forced out of what became New York City, among others including the Wappinger in the north, the Matinecock in the east, and the Carnarsie in the southern parts of what is now the city; further east and south, the Merrick and Rockaway tribes met similar fates. By 1800, none of New York's local tribes maintained settlements within the confines of what was to become the city.

The shorthand story of the eviction of native people was taught to every New York schoolchild: the Dutch West India Company "purchased" what was called "Mannahatta" from the Lenape for sixty Dutch guilders—popularly described as twenty-four dollars—in 1626. The first dynamic tension we trace thus lies with the social geography of the city itself and the history of its settling and growth: from the start, the story of New York affirms the prominence of the narrow island of Manhattan. But here we note that the classic urban relationship of core to periphery has long been a complicated one in New York City.

What eventually established the five boroughs of "Greater New-York" (as the press described it in the years leading to its creation) was the uniting of New York City (by that point, Manhattan and the Bronx) with Brooklyn, most of Queens County, and Staten Island in 1898. Using language of benevolent colonial expansion, in 1894 the *New York Times* imagined a glorious future for this soon-to-be vast territory:

> If Greater New-York becomes an established fact, it will be in a position to increase in value and population to rank with the greatest city in the world within a few years. Its increase will be greater than that of any cities of the Old World, as it will have facilities for developing its wealth such as no city now commands. . . . It will include within its limits a waterfront such as no city in the world has or can by any possibility ever obtain. It will have land for manufacturing interests, with cheap homes for employes [sic] far from the tenement districts, that will develop a stronger, healthier, and more industrious manhood than it is possible to develop in the closely-packed sections of the city where cheap homes only are now obtainable. The many obvious advantages that New-York will derive from the annexation of this territory were undoubtedly recognized by her voters. The advantages that she will derive will be fully offset by those that she will confer upon those whom she accepts as her citizens under the consolidation plan.

From the beginning, there was little room for doubt about which part of the city would be considered "central" and which would be considered "outer." Of the five boroughs that make up the whole of the city, Manhattan has the most documented and celebrated history. It has the highest population density and the greatest concentration of the city's landmarks, wealth, and famous cultural attractions. More people—a million and a half—commute into Manhattan every day than into any other place in the country. And more people leave the boroughs of Queens, Brooklyn, and the Bronx each day than any other place in the country, while Staten Island has some of the country's longest commuting times. Even within New York City, Manhattan is usually referred to as "the city." This idea of a center was in fact also at the heart of the city's own tourist marketing, guidebooks, and maps, which for many years provided visitors with maps and advice that took you only as far north as 96th Street in Manhattan, excluding uptown along with all of the other boroughs. The twentieth century hollowing-out of the urban core, typical of many other United States cities, never quite affected this vertically dense borough to the same extent.

Yet the urbanization of the New York area has, like other cities, produced additional "centers" beyond Manhattan's downtown and midtown, including some like downtown Brooklyn and Long Island City, Queens, that are within the city itself. Real estate prices in north and west Brooklyn, western Queens, and even parts of the city's poorest borough, the Bronx, are approaching Manhattan's stratospheric heights, as are many of the new buildings. As locals say, these areas are becoming "Manhattanized."

At the same time, the "outer boroughs," as they are referred to, are still separate counties in New York State and once contained their own towns—in the case of Brooklyn, its own large bustling city. Unifying Greater New York into one city in 1898 was a political struggle, not a foregone conclusion—for example, Brooklyn's Republican Protestants were concerned about losing their political autonomy, especially to Manhattan's Democratic Catholic immigrants. Staten Island is still not sure whether it was a good idea to join "the city," voting to secede as recently as 1993 (the popular will of the borough was ignored). Today, the city's immigrants live in the outer boroughs in much greater numbers than in Manhattan. The boroughs, differently and unevenly, have maintained and further developed their distinct characters, customs, accents, and even sports teams (the 1957 departure of the Brooklyn Dodgers for Los Angeles notwithstanding). The more you know the city, the more difficult it is to see it as "revolving around" a center.

Meanwhile, if the thesis of a "vanishing New York" can be anywhere decisively proven, it is along many streets of Manhattan. There, eclectic neighborhoods, as well as decades, even centuries, of cultural accumulation have been resettled or bought out or torn down and rebuilt. In some areas, walking past the chain stores, upscale malls, bank branches, and uninspired architecture of vast stretches of Manhattan, one could be in nearly any North American city. To find "authentic New York," one increasingly looks to the outer boroughs. In fact, in this century, the upsurge in global tourism encouraged NYC & Company, the city's official marketing arm, to begin promoting the "outer boroughs" and their neighborhoods, emphasizing ethnic enclaves and hip-hop, to attract tourists from diverse national and cultural backgrounds.

So while the "core" of the city merges with its periphery, the "periphery" more often retains its own unique identity (and has never fully been only peripheral). We urge our readers to see the places in this city through this taut balance—a center that is not fully or only a center, an outer ring that is arguably more often expressive of the city's historic essences and possible future dynamism.

Another tension we would draw attention to, following historian Josh Freeman, is New York's contradictory cultures of cosmopolitanism and provincialism. In strange contrast to their renowned worldliness, New Yorkers' outlooks and attitudes are often bounded by much more local experiences and allegiances.

Since its founding, New York has played a role in global commerce, first as a trading post for the Dutch West India Company and, later, as a valuable port for the British. By the middle of the eighteenth century, enslaved Africans comprised nearly a fifth of all New Yorkers. After the American Revolution, New York (and Brooklyn) families who had grown wealthy from trade and agriculture started New York's banks, and the city became a center of finance and trade, a center for dry goods, and a site of increasing property values and real estate speculation.

Despite the abolition of slavery in New York State in 1827, New York fortunes remained deeply integrated in financing and insuring the sea voyages that propelled the slave trade, while the city continued to buy, store, process, and distribute the raw goods and commercial products made possible through slave labor. New York was a manufacturing city for over a century, stretching from the nineteenth century through the first half of the twentieth, and as late as World War II fully a third of its workers were connected to the production or transportation of goods, with garment reigning supreme but joined by many other industries well-served by New York's density and location. Its global importance only increased as the tide turned more aggressively toward financial and other services in the postwar era. Today, New York City's position as a leading stock market and corporate headquarters, as well as a capital of media, marketing, and a burgeoning tech economy, continues to elevate it to the status of the leading global city in the United States.

From its earliest days, then, New Yorkers gathered by choice and by force from all over the world. Fostering a sophistication that crossed social classes, the ships and sailors visiting from all ports brought the news, fashions, and cultures of the world to New York. And New York has been the world's foremost "city of immigrants" for most of its history. Nineteenth century waves of immigration swelled the city from small town to major metropolis in a matter of decades. Remittances from and connections to new arrivals helped more families to come—for example, emptying Irish villages during the potato famine and Jewish shtetls and cities in the Pale of Settlement and other parts of Eastern Europe—joining thousands from dozens of nations who came to New York's shores fleeing oppression and seeking economic opportunities.

Today, at over 3 million, there are more foreign-born residents within New York City than any other city in the world except London; as a metropolitan region, New York outranks the world's diverse regions by a margin of over 1 million. Hundreds of languages are spoken within the city's limits. The Dominican Republic, China, Mexico, Jamaica, Guyana, Ecuador, Haiti, Trinidad & Tobago, Bangladesh, India: the leading countries of origin for NYC's contemporary immigrant population give some sense of its diversity. New York expressions and accents were born with the transmission of Dutch names and words ("stoop"; "boss"; possibly even "Yankee") learned by the British, who "taught English to," by speaking with, the Dutch, enslaved Africans, free Blacks, Irish, and Germans, who in turn introduced New York's English to Italians and Jews from across Eastern Europe and Russia, who then worked with Hungarians and Poles and Ukrainians who . . . and so it goes on to this day. The neologism "Nuyorican" developed in Puerto Rico to describe their compatriots who came and stayed in New York, and today it is both used to describe the culture of New York Puerto Ricans and the "Spanglish" spoken by thousands across the city.

And yet for all its global integration, melding, and worldliness, it is a city of neighborhoods and enclaves, including millions of people who rarely leave their borough and even more rarely the city itself. For some New Yorkers, New York, or their part of it, is the world, and they don't need to know much more than what they learn here, thank you very much. Its diversity even lends itself to neighborhood-specific insularity: as you walk in Queens past the sari shops and jewelers along 74th Street in Jackson Heights, or by the dim sum houses and Chinese supermarkets of Flushing, or alongside the manicured lawns and spacious houses of Forest Hills, you could be worlds, not subway stops, apart. These neighborhoods are an essential part of identity and culture for many New Yorkers. One might identify as being from New York but just as often refer to smaller geographic areas: I'm from Brooklyn; I'm from Williamsburg; I'm from Los Sures (the Southside of Williamsburg). In some places, such identification spans generations, and is taught to newcomers—along with neighborhood or borough-based accents, dialect, and slang. Such insularity is sometimes chosen, as communities choose to live close to others who share a common language, history, or culture. Other times, through both "top-down" institutional mechanisms (housing covenants; bank-lending practices), or "bottom-up" community attitudes and intimidation, the common identities, insularity, and segregation that typify many neighborhoods are forced. Rather than a "melting pot," communities are often divided from each other by power, race, background, or culture. In all, the sites we describe display the ways in

which daily life within New York's borders is made porous to events around the world, punctuated by and responsive to global crises and far-flung events. New Yorkers' reputation for tolerance and multicultural fluency are certainly earned. At the same time, segregation and clannishness abound; subcultures and enclaves are constructed and enforced. Some of this makes for deep ties, traditions, and rooted cultures; some of this makes for deep suspicion of difference, fear of the "strangers" who live across the avenue or down the street, racist and xenophobic stereotyping, and, at times, violence.

Another contradictory tension that is perhaps, for the United States, uniquely expressed in this city, is between the competing powers of the private and public sectors. As one of the wealthiest large cities in the country, the economic power that New York elites wield to shape the city is nearly unparalleled, and the voice of the private sector is constant. For the first twelve years of this century, the city was governed by its richest citizen, Mayor Michael Bloomberg. From the names emblazoned on the buildings of the city's leading cultural institutions to every square inch of the subways and buses festooned with advertisements, wherever you look you find reminders of the reigning "moral philosophy of the dollar." The workers of New York City have experienced the brunt of the dollar's power, too, from New York's early days as a center of slavery, through its sweatshops and dockside shape-ups, to today's underpaid service economy of dishwashers, home health aides, and retail clerks. Official poverty in the city has remained a dismal constant at around 20 percent, with 1.7 million of its over 8 million inhabitants qualifying for food subsidies in 2018, and the fallout from more recent crises as yet unknown.

At the same time, more than other US cities, New York is defined by a robust public sector. This is the result of the successful organizing by its people. New York has always been a union stronghold, and as of this writing is the country's most union dense city, with nearly a quarter of its citizens in labor unions. New York has housed and helped grow the country's radical movements, with strong traditions of socialism, anarchism, and communism. In the 1960s and 1970s, civil rights, Black nationalist, and Black Power groups asserted local power, alongside their Puerto Rican and Chinese activist neighbors. The modern gay rights movement blossomed here, and women's rights and radical feminism had no larger platform or participation than in New York. In the twentieth century these movements forged powerful labor, identity, and community organizations that won sweeping, even at times radical, reforms in public policy. As just one of many examples, by state constitution, dating from the Great Depression, the state is responsible for "the aid, care and support of its needy," and New Yorkers have a right to shelter and health care. Today's city continues to display the inheritance of the social democratic regime established during the heyday of "working class New York," as historian Freeman has described it. A vast health-care system and decent health and benefit plans for city workers; access to free and relatively low-cost higher education in the City University system for all high school graduates; the country's largest concentration of public housing, and other public policies protecting affordable housing and extensive housing subsidies; public access to numerous cultural institutions, free and low-cost recreation facilities, and fairly robust public spaces; extensive mass transit—the city retains much of the publicly oriented infrastructure won here through decades of struggle, even as much of it crumbles from decades of neoliberal austerity. A dense network of community-based organizations buttresses the relatively vibrant public sector. Ironically, one of the great eruptions in the contest for public space to take place in this century, Occupy Wall Street, began in one of the strange hybrids created by the (un)balanced interests of public and private in this city, Zuccotti Park, which is a "privately owned public space," or POPS. Many of the plazas and courtyards of Manhattan are such contradictory amalgamations of public access and private ownership, rules and responsibility. Similarly, the area outside of Brooklyn's Barclays Center (home of the Brooklyn Nets basketball team) became a central gathering space for the Black Lives Matter protests of 2020. Overall, a strange, contradictory, and generative admixture of private and public power dictates much of the action of the people's New York.

Occupy Wall Street and Black Lives Matter are just some of a number of movements that typify the final contrast we will highlight here, which is the uneasy strain between freedoms and repression found in this city. "In New York you can be your own man," as the Broadway musical *Hamilton* argues—or woman, genderqueer, genius, lunatic, freak. It's an open, explosively creative, "anything goes" city, famous for radical self-invention. Part of this can be traced to the anonymity a big city provides, but it also rests in its strenuous embrace of a liberatory individualism and widespread tolerance. You can do your own thing, as long as you're not bothering anyone else, and sometimes even if you are. This has meant that New York has long been a global center of all kinds of political, artistic, and cultural innovation. Some such New York characters prowl these pages—Coney Island locals, Thomas Paine, Mabel Hampton, Andy Warhol; the New York punk scene; DJ Kool Herc, Grandmaster Flash, and the birth of hip-hop. These freedoms extend across citizenship status too. All New Yorkers regardless of citizenship can qualify for official city ID and in-state college tuition and state financial aid; recently, in the face of rampant and dangerous xenophobia, New York joined hundreds of others in declaring itself a "sanctuary city," pledging refusal to cooperate with federal officials seeking to deport undocumented immigrants, fellow New Yorkers.

Yet for all of the freedom of expression, assembly, and action manifested by its citizenry and purportedly celebrated by its political leadership, New York is also the most heavily policed city in the United States. There are over thirty thousand uniformed officers in the New York Police Department (NYPD). With its civil-ian employees, the NYPD is larger than the entire Federal Bureau of Investigation. Per capita, the city's police force is nearly twice the size of that of Los Angeles. The NYPD has made over 5 million "stop and frisk" street interrogations since 2002. Under this policy, curtailed in 2014, the police targeted Black and Brown New Yorkers, mostly male and usually young, for walking down the street, hanging out with friends, getting on the subway, buying a soda—nearly nine out of ten stops were routinely of innocent people going about their lives. Despite robust efforts to curtail their power, police violence against citizens and protesters remains too commonplace, with numerous instances of excessive force during the Black Lives Matter protests of 2020 just some of the latest examples.

New York is thus a city of surveillance and control as much as it is a city of freedom. Since the terrorist attacks of September 11, 2001, Muslim communities have been extensively and illegally surveilled by the NYPD, as have student and other activist groups. Even before 9/11, the NYPD developed some of the most constraining methods of crowd control, restricting the freedom of movement of protesters, kenneling them behind steel barricades and, later, "kettling," moving masses with plastic fencing. Weapons of repression of yesteryear like batons and horses continue to be used with the pepper spray, tasers, and sonic cannons of today. Many city landmarks, plazas, and buildings are behind barricades and under constant security surveillance. These public or semi-public spaces are often filled with "defensive architecture," such as spiked ledges or metal bars on benches, which signal to the public low tolerance for loiterers and none for the unhoused.

With a social organization that is both centripetal and centrifugal, global and insular, public and private, and free while policed and constrained, the city of New York invents and reinvents itself along these faultlines. As you read this book, we hope you will note their interplay and contradictions, and read the city's streetscapes with us as the conflicted results of their dynamic interactions.

The Sites We Chose

To extend the closing line of the classic television show *Naked City*, there are *many more* than 8 million stories in New York. Just looking at downtown Manhattan, one could ask, why include entries for the home of abolitionist David Ruggles (36 Lispenard Street), and not the home of Sojourner Truth (74 Canal Street), or the New York Anti-Slavery offices (143 Nassau Street) which served as an underground railroad location for Harriet Tubman, among others? Why anarchist Emma Goldman's house on East 13th Street and not communist and journalist John Reed's house at 1 Patchin Place? Why Occupy Wall Street's occupation of Zuccotti Park but not Bloombergville, an encampment at City Hall named for the mayor that immediately preceded Occupy? Among the country's oldest and, for centuries, its most populous city, there are many thousands of individuals and events that should fit into *A People's Guide to New York City*.

Why did we select the ones we did? To an extent, we used hindsight to limit our historical choices: we selected places whose stories could be seen as emblematic of the social forces they put in motion or continue to propel. From there, as much as possible, we sought to avoid repetition with regard to such larger stories and themes. We also sought, as often as possible, to choose places and people whose experiences resonate deeply in this city in particular—more than, or as much as, the broader world. Our main story tells how the ordinary and, at times, extraordinary people of New York supply the weft to the warp of the place, establishing and making significant the sites of the built environment we send you to. Often bright threads were woven through as well, or new patterns emerge from the multiplicity of actions: new art or invention, dominant historical trends and events. When we chose people or events we kept an eye on these broader stories and sought to include as many different ones in different places as we could, while we bring it back to this specific city and its particular landscape.

A number of themes are nevertheless touched on repeatedly throughout the book. We have dedicated parts of the index to list these themes and the sites related to them (most site entries touch on more than one theme and so appear repeatedly across these lists). Our thematic organization is not all-encompassing, of course, and we encourage the reader to see the sites through the prism of other broad and interactive urban processes, beyond those we've named as themes. Gentrification, for example, is named, but discrimination is not; immigration is named, xenophobia is not—but each certainly links dozens of our sites. And please note that "class" does not appear as a thematic category—neither working class, nor rich, nor poor, nor middle, because it is precisely the assertions of each, and the struggles within and among these groups, that shoot through nearly all of the entries in the book.

A final note regarding the division of the book. We considered a number of alternate topographies for our organization, but ultimately our book follows the conventional divisions of New York City's geography into boroughs. We considered highlighting the wealthiest parts of the central city and its gentrifying outer-borough outposts, moving south in Brooklyn, and east in Brooklyn and Queens from the waterfront; or pulling out the business centers of downtown, midtown, downtown Brooklyn, and Long Island City, Queens, to better examine their interaction with immediately adjacent residential communities. We thought about expanding the boundaries of the book to the metropolitan region, so as to emphasize the close ties between the city and its suburban workers, "back offices," and ports in the neighboring state of New Jersey, New York's Westchester and Nassau Counties, and the monied suburbs of Connecticut. Had we moved beyond the political boundaries of the city, a different mapping of the urban region might have made more sense. Here, Manhattan and the close urban parts of all the boroughs and

waterfront New Jersey could be cut off from the more suburban areas of the outer boroughs and the surrounding suburbs of New Jersey and Orange, Westchester, and Nassau counties.

We decided against these paths, however. First, we try to capture such spatial dynamics in our tours and in many of our entries, which often make explicit the forces and policies that link and interlink parts of the city, as well as the metropolitan region in which it sits. We have also inserted, between the boroughs, essays on water, islands, mass transit and transportation infrastructure that together underscore regional and interborough interconnections. But most important, we see that each of the boroughs, like the city as a whole, is home to multiple, layered dynamics that help to shape it in similar ways. Immigration, gentrification, displacement, police abuse—these characterize Washington Heights in Manhattan, Morrisania in the Bronx, Flatbush in Brooklyn, and Manhattan's Chinatown. The push and pull of real estate development and community resistance explains what is happening at the Fulton Mall in Brooklyn, Mott Haven in the Bronx, Hunters Point in Queens, and on the North Shore of Staten Island. As we dove into the whole of the city, we realized that our geography would *less* cut up the map in new ways and *more* scratch the surface of the layers of the city, going deeper and deeper as we see these patterns in borough after borough. In this way, our book mirrors the development of the city itself—a small area built, rebuilt, purposed, and repurposed. For over one hundred years, the city has not spread. It has creatively destroyed itself in place, time and again.

We are also aware that a geographically innovative book may not be a book you'd want to read, at least as a guidebook. While we are writing this guide as a text that can be read far from New York, in classrooms and for study, we still want this book to be useful as you explore the city by foot, transit, bicycle, or taxi. If you are visiting the city, you will likely approach it as boroughs, purchase a Metrocard (or whatever future pass we will use to take the subways and buses), and divide your time by neighborhoods. We have therefore also made every effort to create clusters of sites for those who are setting out to neighborhoods; and to limit our tours to areas you can travel via foot, bike, or public transportation. We hope this book will be brought to all of the five boroughs of this greater New York, and even up to the top of the Empire State Building, where on a clear day you can see nearly all of the people's city, in all its majesty.

1

Bronx

Bronx

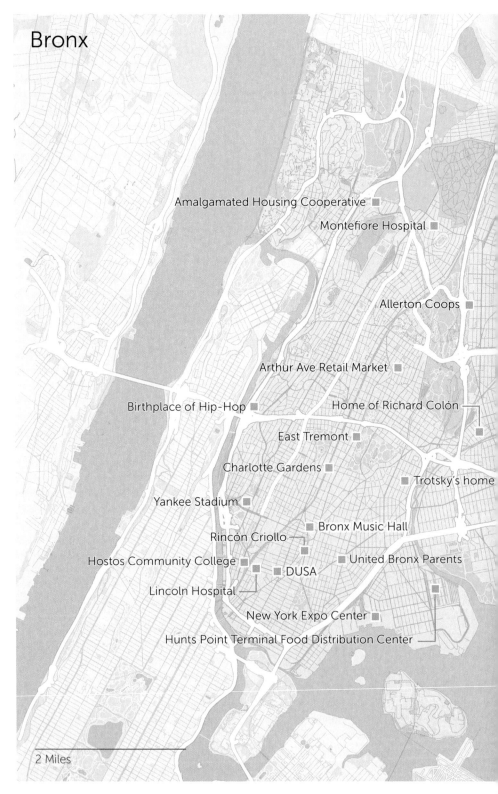

Amalgamated Housing Cooperative ■

Montefiore Hospital ■

Allerton Coops ■

Arthur Ave Retail Market ■

Birthplace of Hip-Hop ■   Home of Richard Colón —

East Tremont ■

Charlotte Gardens ■

                                            ■ Trotsky's home

Yankee Stadium ■

                    ■ Bronx Music Hall
Rincón Criollo —

Hostos Community College ■   ■ United Bronx Parents

                    ■ DUSA
Lincoln Hospital —

New York Expo Center ■

Hunts Point Terminal Food Distribution Center —

2 Miles

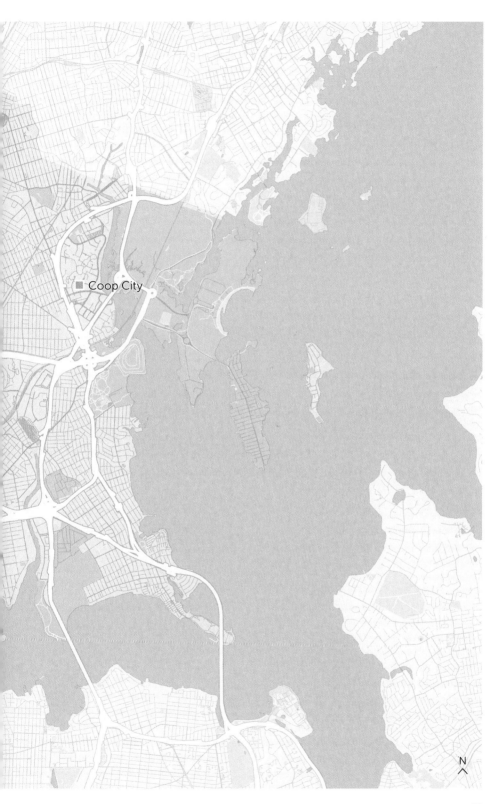

Coop City

N

Introduction

IN OCTOBER OF 1977, PRESIDENT JIMMY
Carter visited a stretch of Charlotte Street
near Boston Road in the heart of the South
Bronx. He stood amid rubble on a vacant
lot, flanked by eight-foot-high piles of bulldozed brick. Behind him were the remnants
of a block of five-story walkup apartment
buildings, charred and missing windows,
some boarded, others spookily exposed.
Carter brought the world's eyes to the South
Bronx in the late 1970s, which came to stand
as the national symbol of urban blight and
decay, a stark reminder of the "failure" of
the nation's cities in the wake of the civil
rights movement.

Carter also headed about ten blocks
down the road to visit 1186 Washington Avenue. There, Bronx resident Ramon Rueda
led the nascent People's Development Corporation (PDC) to renovate a six-story tenement with forty volunteer homestead-
ers. Rueda believed that if the people of
the Bronx were given adequate resources,
they could reclaim abandoned buildings
and revitalize them, fueled as well by their
sweat equity and deep commitment to the
borough. The PDC was one of dozens of
community groups working to improve
and rebuild their beloved Bronx in the late
1970s—a place of mass devastation but also
of unparalleled fertility, where the people's
culture thrived, where jazz and doo-wop
music had flourished, where salsa grew and
hip-hop culture was born. Disinvestment,

resilience, organizing, innovation: all frameworks for understanding today's Bronx.

Bronx is the city's northernmost borough—
across the Harlem River from uptown Manhattan and across the East River from northern Queens—and the only part of New York
City on the US mainland. It borders affluent
Westchester County, and, in keeping with
its neighbors, the northern part of the borough is home to some of New York City's
most affluent communities. Riverdale and
Fieldston, just west of Van Cortlandt Park,
have some of the highest median incomes in
New York City, as do Pelham Bay / Gardens
and the surrounding communities along the
borough's eastern coast. Fieldston is one of
a handful of privately owned neighborhoods
within New York City limits, with maintenance provided by the property owners'
association rather than the city (another is
Forest Hills Gardens, in Queens).

Much of the rest of the Bronx is poor
or working class. Poverty and unemployment rates in the borough are consistently
the city's highest, and its residents the least
educated of all the boroughs. But since the
height of deindustrialization and unemployment in the 1970s, the Bronx has seen a
steady increase in employment opportunities, particularly in health care, retail, social
services, and food service. The health-care
industry—including Bronx Lebanon Hospital Center, Calvary Hospital, James J. Peters
VA Medical Center, and Montefiore Medical Center—constitutes the largest source of

jobs in the borough. But poverty and unemployment rates remain stubbornly high.

The Bronx is the only borough in New York City with a Latina/o/x majority, made up primarily of Puerto Ricans and Dominicans, with sizable Mexican and Honduran populations as well. It has the smallest concentration of non-Hispanic whites in the city, and a relatively large Black population (43 percent). Nearly 60 percent of residents of the Bronx speak a language other than English at home; almost half of residents speak Spanish at home. The borough is also home to Jamaican, Irish, Ghanaian, Senegalese, and Albanian enclaves, among others.

Remarkably, even though the Bronx is the nation's third most densely populated borough after Manhattan and Brooklyn, fully one-quarter of the borough is open space, including Pelham Bay Park, the city's largest public park, and Van Cortlandt Park, which includes the nation's first public golf course. Despite the vast open space, the Bronx is among the most polluted areas of the city. Traffic pours in and out of Hunts Point, a major food distribution hub that also houses a third of the city's waste transfer facilities, and along the borough's major highways. Air pollution is a significant problem in the dense neighborhoods that border the seven highways that crisscross the borough. Asthma rates in the South Bronx are among the nation's highest.

Today's Bronx was once known as the Lenapehoking territory, inhabited by the native Siwanoy of the Algonquian-speaking Wappinger Confederacy, until the Dutch colonized it for farmland beginning in 1639.

It remained thus until the mid-1800s, when German and Irish immigrants created small suburban communities near new railroad stations in Mott Haven, Melrose, and Morrisania—all part of today's South Bronx. Rapid transit extended into the Bronx with the elevated Third Avenue line in the final decades of the nineteenth century, along with the city's streetcar system. After the subway linked Melrose to Manhattan in 1904 and what are now the 1, 2, 4, and 6 train routes began snaking through the Bronx, immigrant workers from crowded East Harlem and the Lower East Side flocked to the Bronx for more space and better housing conditions.

By 1930, the Bronx held nearly 1.3 million people and would have been the fifth largest city in the country had it not already been part of New York—its density was rivaled only by Manhattan. Boosters for Queens, Brooklyn, and Staten Island built small single-family homes, but, by and large, in the Bronx it was large apartment houses that beckoned new residents. By 1940 the Bronx was second only to Manhattan in rental housing and large apartment buildings. Hundreds of thousands of the city's immigrants aspired to live in the Bronx's large, modern units, particularly in the West Bronx along the Grand Concourse, with their vast marble lobbies and shiny parquet floors, eat-in kitchens, and tiled bathrooms and kitchens. As Constance Rosenblum (2011) notes, "from the early 1920s through the late 1950s, the Grand Concourse represented the ultimate in upward mobility and was the crucible that helped transform hundreds of thousands of first- and second-generation Americans—mostly Jewish but also Irish and Italian, along with smatterings of other nationalities—from greenhorns into solid middle-class Americans." The newcomers shopped at the nearby department stores along Fordham Road, went to movies at the luxurious Loew's Paradise just south of it, and watched their beloved Yankees play in the country's most famous ballpark. Their children played stickball in the streets and drank egg creams and malteds at the corner candy stores.

While Irish and Italians settled in the Bronx in great numbers between 1920 and 1960, it would come to be known as the "Jewish borough," with Jews comprising nearly 40 percent of residents by 1940. Hundreds of synagogues and other Jewish cultural institutions dotted the borough. Left-wing Jewish workers founded some of the most important cooperative housing projects in the nation there (see **The "Allerton Coops, Amalgamated Housing Cooperative, Co-op City**, p. 29).

Those with means followed the new subway lines north and into the neighboring West Bronx, including Morris Heights, University Heights, Kingsbridge, and Highbridge—places that were largely closed to Black and Latina/o/x New Yorkers at that time. White flight from the South Bronx pushed landlords in the Mott Haven, Morrisania, Melrose, and Hunts Point-Crotona Park East communities to begin renting to upwardly mobile Black residents from Harlem, new Black migrants from the Jim Crow South and the Caribbean, and Puerto Ricans escaping economic depression on the island.

These neighborhoods were the oldest, most dilapidated, and poorest parts of the borough. But they also facilitated the melding and mixing of these groups, particularly in the 1940s and 1950s with the white ethnics who stayed. Morris High School in Morrisania, historian Mark Naison (2016) notes, "was perhaps the most integrated secondary school in the United States" during this time.

Still, over a ten-year period, the South Bronx went from being two-thirds white in 1950 to two-thirds Black and Latina/o/x in 1960, as white flight from the entire borough began to take hold. This, coupled with the loss of industry from the city, utterly transformed the borough in the 1960s and 1970s. Racism and federal policies that supported homeownership in white suburbs pulled the white ethnics, who had once strongly supported the city's strong network of public services, out of most points south of Fordham Road and pushed them to newly constructed Co-op City, suburban Westchester County, and New Jersey. Unlike in other boroughs, notably Queens, new residents did not make up the difference: between 1970 and 1980, the Bronx lost 20 percent of its population; the South Bronx lost at least 40 percent—and, by some estimates, more than half its residents. Those who stayed contended with rising poverty in the places left behind, the vast majority of them Black and Latina/o/x.

At the same time, the industrial elements of the mixed economy that had supported the Bronx were disappearing by the 1970s. Manufacturers moved from the city to the

South or abroad. Shipping moved to the deep water ports at Newark and Elizabeth, New Jersey. And as the city slipped into a fiscal crisis, the Bronx was the borough hardest hit. Between the mid-1960s and 1970s at least half a million New Yorkers lost their jobs. By 1972, around one in eight New Yorkers received public assistance.

As a result of these shifts, dwindling public coffers were under dramatically more stress. The city's tax revenue dried up, and public infrastructure and institutions were crumbling. (The West Side Highway in Manhattan, for example, had quite literally collapsed in various places.) The city's response to this crisis was to adopt a version of what presidential advisor Patrick Moynihan had been suggesting to then-President Nixon as a national urban policy—"benign neglect." As NYC Housing Commissioner Roger Starr described it, the city would engage in "planned shrinkage," or eliminating city services from the neighborhoods that were experiencing the most abandonment and disinvestment to further encourage population decline so that services could be eliminated entirely in those places and directed toward "healthier" communities. Subways slowed. Hospitals and clinics closed, including Fordham and Morrisania Hospitals in the Bronx. Libraries limited their hours. Garbage littered the city's streets, as a near–record low number of employees staffed the city's street sweepers. Quality of life in the city seemed to be at rock bottom.

And the Bronx was burning, as arsonists torched swaths of the borough for insurance payments, and accidental fires blazed through poorly maintained buildings (see **Charlotte Gardens / Mid-Bronx Desperadoes**, p. 39). In line with its planned shrinkage policy, the city responded by eliminating 10 percent of its fire companies—in the communities in which most of the fires were raging—and cut fire inspections by 70 percent. By the end of the 1970s, parts of the Bronx lay in ruins. The borough's poverty rate had risen nearly 10 percent—from 19.5 percent to 27.6 percent. Landlords neglected the grand apartment buildings that did not burn, where elevators stopped working and broken glass and trash littered the marble lobbies. Meanwhile, the most that non–New Yorkers ever heard about the Bronx they learned from panicked, racist mass culture representations, in movies like 1981's *Fort Apache, The Bronx.*

But even after the widespread fires and abandonment, as researchers Deborah Wallace and Rodrick Wallace point out, more people lived in the South Bronx than twice the population of Buffalo, and the melding of cultures nurtured extraordinary creativity. Even as the fires burned, in one two-week period in August of 1973, the Bronx was home to foundational moments in the growth of both hip-hop and salsa music. On August 11, 1973, DJ Kool Herc spun at his sister Cindy Campbell's party to lay the foundation of a new musical tradition—hip-hop (see **Birthplace of Hip-Hop**, p. 34). Just fifteen days later, on August 23, more than forty thousand people sold out Yankee Stadium to hear the Fania All-Stars in one of the most important live music events in Latin music history (see **Fania All-Stars at Yankee Stadium**, p. 42).

The people of the Bronx also began to rebuild nearly as soon as the devastation began. Squatters reclaimed abandoned and city-owned properties. Groups of Nuyoricans began to clear abandoned lots for *casitas* (see **Casita Rincón Criollo**, p. 48). By the time Ramon Rueda's People's Development Corporation began work rehabilitating 1186 Washington Avenue, Genevieve Brooks had established the Mid-Bronx Desperadoes and Dr. Evelina López Antonetty founded United Bronx Parents (see **United Bronx Parents**, p. 51; and **Charlotte Gardens / Mid-Bronx Desperadoes**, p. 39). Other community groups also worked to rebuild the Bronx in the 1970s and 1980s, including the Banana Kelly Community Improvement Association, the Longwood Community Association, and the Southeast Bronx Community Organization, led by Father Louis Gigante, among others. Indeed, the Bronx spearheaded community-led development that would go on to be imitated around the United States, particularly the formation of community development corporations that leveraged public and private funding while retaining community control.

The 1980s and 1990s continued this slow process of resurgence, fueled by community groups, public and private investment, and the dynamic culture of the borough—and new immigrants. Dominicans and West Indians came to the Bronx in huge numbers, along with Haitians, Chinese, Greeks, Koreans, Vietnamese, Mexicans, and Russians. Albanians settled in Little Italy and Cambo-dians near Fordham. The Bronx is home to the largest number of Garinagu (Garifuna), the Afro-Indigenous group, outside of the Central American coast.

Today's Bronx represents "the nation's largest urban rebuilding effort," the product of both officially sanctioned and guerilla-style revitalization, having seen steady population growth since the 1980s. It is still a place of simultaneous destruction and renewal, where investment pales in comparison to the rest of the city, but where innovative cultures flourish. Its Latina/o/x majority—primarily Puerto Rican and Dominican—have made it "El Condado de la Salsa." Bachata, with origins in the Dominican Republic, adds to the soundscape, as does the traditional music and dance of the Garinagu.

Big retail has also begun to dominate the Bronx, bringing jobs—albeit low-paid. So far, the borough has been spared the kind of gentrification that has come to Manhattan, Brooklyn, and to some extent Queens, but it is on the horizon. Since 2015 the Bronx's population has grown at a faster rate than any of the other boroughs, although this is certainly partly due to a continuous settlement of immigrants. But real estate developers have been increasingly converging on the Bronx. For example, an attempt to rebrand the Mott Haven neighborhood as the "Piano District," a nod to a time when pianos were manufactured in the area, includes seven high-rise luxury residential towers filled with two-bedroom apartments that could command more than three thousand dollars a month in rent, swimming pools, gyms, and a new waterfront park. Small coffee shops, fashion boutiques, and art galleries also dot the area—many of which are, for now, owned and run by local residents. (*Quote from Matthew Purdy, "Left to Die, the South Bronx Rises from Decades of Decay," New York Times, 1994.*)

TO LEARN MORE

Gonzalez, Evelyn Diaz. *The Bronx.* Columbia History of Urban Life. New York: Columbia University Press, 2004.

Jonnes, Jill. *South Bronx Rising: The Rise, Fall, and Resurrection of an American City.* New York: Fordham University Press, 2002.

Naison, Mark, and Bob Gumbs. *Before the Fires: An Oral History of African American Life in the Bronx from the 1930s to the 1960s.* New York: Fordham University Press, 2016.

Rosenblum, Constance. *Boulevard of Dreams: Heady Times, Heartbreak, and Hope along the Grand Concourse in the Bronx.* New York: NYU Press, 2011.

■ ■ ■

North Bronx/ Norwood

1.1 Montefiore Hospital/ Local 1199 Health and Hospital Workers Union

111 E. 210th Street, Bronx, NY

An organizing drive at Montefiore Hospital in 1958 marked the first successful recognition campaign for hospital workers in the United States and the beginning of the transformation of a small independent union of pharmacists into the gigantic national local that today has 400,000 workers in four states

and Washington, DC. Today, what became the Service Employees International Union 1199 is one of the country's largest and most influential health-care unions. Among other things, 1199 is famous for its organizing model, which was developed in its earliest organizing days.

The postwar era saw a great expansion in the health-care industry in New York and around the nation. Yet the Tydings Amendment to the union-restricting Taft Hartley legislation of 1947 specifically denied organizing rights to workers at nonprofit hospitals. Like agricultural workers and domestic workers, hospital workers were also excluded from social security, minimum wage, and fair labor standards.

The majority of workers in health care were not professional workers with higher degrees, and they were often erroneously characterized as "non-skilled." Dieticians, cooks, aides and servers, laundry workers, housekeeping, building service workers and engineers, nurse's aides, orderlies, security—the diverse workforce that served in health care was both highly stratified and segmented, separated into autonomous departments with their own skill and promotion ladders. Montefiore's workforce reflected its immigrant working-class neighborhood, with Puerto Rican, Afro Caribbean, and white ethnic workers. Black and Puerto Rican workers as a whole made up 80 percent of the hospital service and maintenance force.

Many of these workers earned subminimum wages and were frequently forced to seek public relief despite working full time. Some workers received "free" food but

Montefiore workers on strike in 1959. CREDIT: COURTESY OF SEIU1199 HEALTH AND HOSPITAL WORKERS UNION

less pay; others who were paid below subsistence had arrangements for "living in" at the hospital. At Montefiore, food workers worked six days a week, in twelve-hour shifts. Not surprisingly, given these conditions, the hospital had extremely high rates of staff turnover.

By the 1950s, Montefiore was transforming from chronic care into an acute care facility. As short-term patients replaced long-term, the "bed turnover" rate also skyrocketed. Work was both intensified and restructured, with new efficiencies introduced everywhere.

At the time of the Montefiore campaign, the core of 1199 members were pharmacists. Many of the original members, like many organizers in hospitals, had at some point been members of the Communist Party or traveled in CP circles, and their political orientations tended to reflect that history even

after they'd left the party. The 1199 organizers explicitly foregrounded racial and social justice frameworks in their organizing, and sought to build organizations that went beyond bread and butter concerns to develop broad leadership, political education, and connections to the community.

The Montefiore campaign was in part successful because the organizers found and supported leaders in the different work areas who brought their semi-autonomous units together. Further, it was the multiracial service workers who led the way, not the professionals who had typically been the leftists leading much of the organizing in the previous two decades.

In addition to broad and deep shop-floor organization, the union waged a public campaign in the press that highlighted the low wages and poor working conditions at the hospital, garnering support from, among others, Eleanor Roosevelt, the city's Central Labor Council, and even the *New York Times* editorial board. A credible strike deadline led to an emergency intervention by the mayor's office. In December, the union won an overwhelming vote in the hospital, and a first contract was signed in March 1959.

This victory in the Bronx was the first domino to fall. Later that year, seven voluntary hospitals struck for a bruising forty-six days until they essentially won union recognition. As health services became an increasingly central part of New York's economy, 1199 followed, organizing across the systems. For many years, its strong shop steward system, internal political education, and cultural program (known as "Bread and Roses," from the famous women-led 1912 strike in Lawrence, Massachusetts) were the envy of the city's unions. And 1199 continues to exercise considerable political clout in New York State, with a robust electoral program, lobbying, and impressive street presence, turning out its members for union, civil rights, antiwar, and other demonstrations. In 1998, 1199 merged with the Service Employees International Union, becoming 1199SEIU United Healthcare Workers East.

TO LEARN MORE

1199SEIU United Healthcare Workers East, https://www.1199seiu.org/

Fink, Leon, and Brian Greenberg. *Upheaval in the Quiet Zone: 1199/SEIU and the Politics of Healthcare Unionism*, 2/e. Urbana: University of Illinois Press, 2009.

1.2 The "Allerton Coops," or United Workers' Cooperative Colony

2700–2774 and 2846–2870 Bronx Park East, Bronx, NY

Amalgamated Housing Cooperative

Between Van Cortlandt, Van Cortlandt Park South, Dickson, and Sedgwick Avenues, Kingsbridge, NY

Co-op City

Between I-95 and the Hutchinson River, Baychester, NY

Three of the most important nonprofit cooperative housing projects in the United States, the United Workers' Cooperative Colony, the Amalgamated Houses, and Co-op City, were built within three miles of one another in the Bronx. The projects are milestones in the ambitious effort to create an alternative to privately owned housing for working-class families. At the height of the cooperative housing movement, well over one hundred thousand New Yorkers lived in nonprofit projects they collectively owned, which helped the city sustain its vibrancy during the post–World War II years when most other large American cities suffered critical population loss.

The United Workers' Cooperative Colony (commonly called the Coops or Allerton Coops), constructed between 1927 and 1929, was the first large-scale, nonprofit, cooperative housing project in New York City, sponsored by an organization of left-wing Jewish workers, which had earlier created smaller cooperative projects and a workers summer camp, Nitge-daiget ("No Worries" in Yiddish), in Beacon, New York. Seeking to escape overcrowded conditions on the Lower East Side, the group bought land adjourning Bronx Park, still a largely rural area but with a subway connection allowing easy access to Manhattan's garment district, where many of the "Coopniks" worked. In addition to nearly seven hundred apartments—some designed for families, others for single men or women with shared kitchens—the

A library for residents in the Amalgamated Housing, 1929.
CREDIT: WURTS BROS. (NEW YORK, NY). MUSEUM OF THE CITY OF NEW YORK. X2010.7.1.6793

complex had substantial spaces for communal activities, including a library, assembly hall, and gymnasium. With many of the residents in or close to the Communist Party, the Coops were a beehive of left-wing activity. But financially, the project proved unsustainable, as the Great Depression cost many dwellers their jobs. Eventually, in 1943, ownership of the Coops reverted to a mortgage holder and it became a rental complex. Evidence of its origins can still be seen in such touches as carvings of a hammer and sickle over one entranceway and of smoking factories over another.

Other cooperative housing projects near the Coops followed, founded by different groups of left-wing Jewish workers. The largest, the Amalgamated Houses, sponsored by the Amalgamated Clothing Workers union, took advantage of a newly passed state law which gave tax abatements to housing projects that limited their profits and targeted low-income residents. Like the

Coops, the Amalgamated Houses adopted a "garden apartment" design, with internal courtyards and extensive plantings providing privacy and views of greenery from every apartment. Beginning with 303 apartments, the complex, still a nonprofit cooperative, now houses 1,482 families in eleven buildings.

After World War II, other unions took up the nonprofit housing model. To promote such developments, existing cooperative complexes and unions created the United Housing Foundation (UHF), headed by Abraham Kazan, who had been the driving force behind the Amalgamated Houses. Working with state officials, the UHF sponsored a series of ever-larger projects, including Rochdale Village in Queens (**Rochdale Village**, p. 207). In 1965, it unveiled plans for its largest effort, Co-op City, a massive housing development first suggested by Governor Nelson Rockefeller and Robert Moses as a way to keep middle-class families in the city. With 15,372 apartments, five schools,

Residents of Co-op City rally to save their local post office, 2020. CREDIT: COURTESY OF THE *CO-OP CITY TIMES*

three shopping centers, a library, three community centers, extensive recreational facilities, and indoor parking for ten thousand cars, Co-op City was the largest housing development ever undertaken in the United States. Designed by Herman J. Jessor, who as a young architect had worked on both the Coops and the Amalgamated Houses, the sprawling complex lacks the charm and modest scale of its predecessors, with thirty-five twenty-four to thirty-three-story "tower in the park" buildings. But the apartments are large, with parquet floors, central air-conditioning, walk-in closets, and, in many cases, spectacular views.

From the start, Co-op City was plagued by financial and construction problems. Rapid inflation and the challenges of building on marshy ground drove up costs and led the project management to raise the monthly carrying charges for residents to far above what they had been led to expect. A prolonged battle ensued, including a rent strike that lasted over a year. Ultimately, the state, which had supplied the bulk of funding through a mortgage, took over the project (which remained a co-op). Even as its finances were slowly put in order, shoddy construction led to ongoing problems with settling buildings and water leaks. An extensive renovation program in the 2000s replaced or improved many of the defective elements.

The first generation of Co-op City residents was overwhelmingly white, working-class, and predominantly Jewish, not that different from the founders of the first Bronx housing cooperatives. But over time, the population diversified and became majority nonwhite. For all of its difficulties, Co-op City, with over forty thousand residents, succeeded in providing an affordable, attractive housing option for New Yorkers with modest incomes as the demography of the city changed and the housing market became increasingly difficult for all but the very wealthy.

—*Josh Freeman*

TO LEARN MORE

Frazier, Ian. 2006. "Utopia, The Bronx." *New Yorker,* June 6, 2006.

Freeman, Joshua B. *Working-Class New York: Life and Labor Since World War II.* New York: New Press, 2001.

[N.Y.C.] Landmarks Preservation Commission, "United Workers' Cooperative Colony, June 2, 1992, Designation List 245.

NEARBY SITE OF INTEREST

New York Botanical Garden
2900 Southern Boulevard, Bronx, NY
Established in 1891, this 250-acre garden is the country's largest urban botanical garden, and contains the only old growth forest in New York City's borders. City residents can get a reduced, grounds-only entrance fee.

Belmont

1.3 Arthur Avenue Retail Market

2344 Arthur Avenue, Bronx, NY

Opening the doors of the Arthur Avenue Retail Market, you immediately smell coffee and cannoli. More than a dozen stalls sell Italian sweets and pastries, cured meats, cheeses, pastas, fresh fruit and vegetables, sandwiches, and coffee. The market caters to locals and tourists alike and is the most prominent institution to anchor Arthur Avenue, long known as the Little Italy of the Bronx. The market is one of only a handful of the original multi-vendor covered or indoor markets left in the United States, though many cities have recently opened up related "food hall" types of establishments. Arthur Avenue, like the original Thirteenth Avenue Retail Market in Borough Park, Brooklyn (now the "Gourmet Glatt"), or the now relocated Essex Street Market in Manhattan, came out of reformers' efforts to abolish pushcarts, once a ubiquitous feature of city life.

Starting in the 1880s, immigrant neighborhoods in New York City were home to thousands of pushcarts, the street vendors of yesteryear. Peddling their wares from pickles and cured fish to tinctures and housewares, pushcart vendors provided cheap and accessible goods and food for thousands of New Yorkers. By 1940, there were over forty-five thousand pushcart vendors in New York City. From the perspective of the working class, pushcarts were cheap and accessible. From the perspective of progressive reformers, pushcarts were dirty, unsanitary, and made poverty conspicuous. And as Daniel Bluestone points out, "Various reform efforts to curb the pushcart markets went hand in hand with xenophobic Americanization and immigration restriction campaigns directed at working class immigrants." While the attempted elimination of pushcart vendors had a lengthy history dating back to the nineteenth century, it was not until the 1930s that Mayor Fiorello La Guardia was finally able to largely eradicate them. In 1938, La Guardia used Works Project Administration (WPA) funds to build indoor markets where former pushcart vendors could rent stalls, forever changing the landscape of New York City. One of the primary catalysts for La Guardia's war against the pushcarts was to "clean up" the

The bounty at Arthur Avenue Indoor Market, 2017. CREDIT: SCOTT DEXTER

city in preparation for the 1939 World's Fair. La Guardia and the reformers who supported him wanted to present an image of New York as a "modern" metropolis, and pushcarts represented the "old world."

Pushcart vendors hailed from many different backgrounds, but it was an especially important industry for Jewish and Italian immigrants, providing much needed jobs for those who had limited English and were otherwise excluded from the economy's formal sectors. At the beginning of the twentieth century, Italian immigrants lived throughout New York City, but were concentrated in East Harlem and the Lower East Side. Of the millions of Italians who immigrated to the United States in the first decades of the twentieth century, many thousands made their way to the Bronx, following better housing and job opportunities. Migration to the Bronx boomed after World War I with the extension of the subway system, and push-

cart vending remained an important occupation for Italians there throughout the 1930s.

Mayor La Guardia's push for indoor markets was deeply unpopular with both pushcart vendors and their working class, immigrant customers who were used to the convenience of shopping on the street. Many vendors were forced out of business because they could not afford the markets' four dollars daily rent, a substantial increase from the one dollar a day pushcart permits. Despite significant resistance, including from pushcart vendors who simply would not move from their locations, La Guardia prevailed, and ten indoor markets were built across New York City. The Arthur Avenue Retail Market opened in 1940 with seventeen stalls.

Some pushcart vendors eventually recognized the advantages of having an indoor space where they wouldn't have to worry about weather and could hold regular hours, offering them more time with their families.

However, keeping the Arthur Avenue Retail Market open has been a struggle. After repeated near closures in the 1960s and '70s, in the 1980s a group of vendors managed to create a cooperative to keep it open.

City government has always sought to protect established businesses and merchants over street vendors, and La Guardia's call to build indoor markets was not that different from previous wars against pushcart vendors or the periodic crackdowns on street vendors that currently arise in the city. Today, the relationship between street vendors, city regulations, and small businesses remains vexed. The debates are essentially identical to those of eras past: small and large businesses complain about the competition street vendors represent, city regulators are concerned about health, sanitation, and taxes. Today there are approximately twenty thousand street vendors all over New York City, many of them immigrants from Africa, Latin America, and Asia. As with past immigrants, they often do not have access to credit allowing them to establish themselves as small businesses, so they turn to the informal economy of street vending. Those with some financial stability manage to secure street vending licenses. And street vendors continue to organize around their rights, today through organizations like the Street Vendors Project. As of this writing, only four original markets remain open: Arthur Avenue, Bronx Terminal Market, La Marqueta (E. Harlem), and Moore Street Market (Brooklyn). (Quote is from Daniel Bluestone, "The Pushcart Evil: Peddlers, Merchants, and New York City Streets," p. 79.)

TO LEARN MORE

Bluestone, Daniel M. "'The Pushcart Evil': Peddlers, Merchants, and New York City's Streets, 1890–1940." *Journal of Urban History* 18, no. 1 (1991): 68–92. https://doi.org/10.1177/009614429101800104.
Wasserman, Suzanne. "Hawkers and Gawkers: Peddling and Markets in NYC." In *Gastropolis: Food and New York City*, edited by Annie Hauck-Lawson and Jonathan Deutsch. Arts and Traditions of the Table. New York: Columbia University Press, 2010.

NEARBY SITE OF INTEREST

Borgatti's Ravioli and Egg Noodles
632 E. 187th Street, Bronx, NY
Opened in 1935, this family-run homemade pasta shop is a neighborhood institution.

West Bronx

1.4 Birthplace of Hip-Hop
1520 Sedgwick Avenue, Bronx, NY
On August 11, 1973, Cindy Campbell threw a party in the rec room of this apartment building. Her brother Clive (better known as DJ Kool Herc) hooked up the PA system he had been experimenting with to spin dancehall, soul, and funk for their one hundred guests, and what would come to be hip-hop culture was born.

DJ Kool Herc was born and grew up in Kingston, Jamaica, where he snuck out to watch the comings and goings at the local dances, too young to go in. He came to the Bronx at the age of twelve in 1967. Once the family settled in the Bronx, Herc's father

DJ Kool Herc at Cedar
Playground, 2005.
CREDIT: JOSEPH CONZO

was an avid record collector, and his mother Nettie took him to house parties. When his father bought a PA system to serve as a soundman for a local R&B group, Herc tinkered with it until he made it operate at its peak. After throwing their first party with the newly optimized equipment, Cindy and Herc continued to throw monthly parties in the rec room with Herc spinning records, interspersing little rhymes and shout-outs in his echoing mic, Jamaican yard dance style.

Eventually Herc moved the parties to nearby Cedar Park, where he, like the other DJs popping up all over the South Bronx, hooked his equipment up to the lampposts for power. Journalist Jeff Chang writes, "The moment when the dancers really got wild was in a song's short instrumental break, when the band would drop out and the rhythm section would get elemental. Forget melody, chorus, songs—it was all about the groove, building it, keeping it going. Like a string theorist, Herc zeroed in on the fundamental vibrating loop at the heart of

the record, the break." People came out to the park to hear Herc hone his Merry-Go-Round technique, where by playing two copies of the same record he could keep the break going (see **Former Home of Richard Colón ["Crazy Legs"]**, p. 38).

While Herc continued to spin in the West Bronx parks, Afrika Bambaataa was founding the Universal Zulu Nation, the "first hip-hop institution," out of the Bronx River Houses; Grandmaster Flash was deejaying with the Furious Five; and Grand Wizzard Theodore was inventing scratching not far from Charlotte Street. Bronx youth, starved for the opportunity to learn to play instruments in their schools, listened to the radio and their parents records and invented a musical style using what they had—PA systems, microphones, records, and their speaking voices. Along with their fellow artists scribbling graffiti on the subway and dancing in the cypher, they birthed what continues to be one of the most significant cultural movements in the world. (*Quote is from Jeff*

Chang, Can't Stop Won't Stop: A History of the Hip-Hop Generation, *p. 79.*)

TO LEARN MORE

Chang, Jeff. *Can't Stop, Won't Stop: A History of the Hip-Hop Generation.* New York: Picador, 2005.

NEARBY SITES OF INTEREST

Cedar Playground
1890 Cedar Avenue, Bronx, NY
DJ Kool Herc and others spun in this park in 1974.

High Bridge
University Avenue and 170th Street, Bronx, NY
The High Bridge is the oldest bridge in New York City, and it once carried water by gravity from Westchester County, north of the city, to (now defunct) Manhattan reservoirs. Today it is a pedestrian bridge that connects Highbridge Park in Manhattan to the Highbridge neighborhood of the Bronx.

East Tremont

1.5 East Tremont

Crotona Park North and Fulton Avenue, Bronx, NY

Standing at the corner of Crotona Park North and Fulton Avenue, you can see the current Cross-Bronx Expressway, recently rated the most congested urban roadway in the United States. When erected, this highway paved over what used to be a community of about fifteen thousand people. But the stretch of Crotona Park North from this corner to Crotona Park East could have been the site of an *alternative* Cross-Bronx Expressway, one proposed by the residents who were

eventually displaced from the surrounding East Tremont neighborhood for the project. This alternative route was cheaper and would have displaced far fewer people.

In a story made famous by city planner Robert Moses's biographer Robert Caro, Moses saw East Tremont as the ideal location to connect traffic from the George Washington Bridge (linking Manhattan to New Jersey) to the Triborough and Bronx-Whitestone bridges leading to Queens and Long Island. The only problem was that thousands of people lived along the route. A community built largely by Jewish refugees and the children of refugees from Eastern Europe, East Tremont boasted excellent mass transit—particularly to Manhattan's garment district where many of its residents worked—as well as neighborhood jobs, shopping, parks, and excellent schools. It was also home to a rich set of community institutions, including bookstores, cultural clubs, seven synagogues, and social anchors like the Young Men's Hebrew Association,

Cross-Bronx Expressway under construction in East Tremont, 1957. CREDIT: LEHMAN COLLEGE, CUNY, LEONARD LIEF LIBRARY, BRONX CHAMBER OF COMMERCE COLLECTION

which ran the largest day and sleepaway camps of any New York City institution at very affordable prices. The neighborhood was a hotbed of political activism, with many residents active in the Socialist, Communist, American Labor, and Progressive parties. And while East Tremont was predominantly Jewish, it was also significantly diverse, with many Black and Puerto Rican residents.

Moses declared this unusually integrated, vital, and affordable neighborhood a "slum," and proposed demolishing fifty-four apartment buildings that together housed around five thousand people to clear space for his expressway. A group of determined East Tremont residents and business owners resisted the plans, including a particularly resolute group of housewives. They pointed to a report issued by the Bronx County Chapter of the New York State Society of Professional Engineers, which suggested an alternative route for the Cross-Bronx Expressway through East Tremont—one that required moving the route two blocks to the south, saving 1,530 apartments at no cost. Moses refused to even consider it; it is unclear why. One prominent explanation is that while the alternative route would have condemned only 6 buildings, as opposed to the 159 required by Moses's plan, one of them was the Third Avenue Transit depot at the corner of 175th and Southern Boulevard. The Third Avenue Transit Company— in which a set of Bronx politicians held interest—had tremendous political power during this period, and they actively lobbied Moses to keep the building intact.

With the threat of demolition looming, East Tremont residents began to leave, taking poorer quality apartments at higher prices in the neighborhoods from which they had already come earlier in life. The expressway directly displaced five thousand people, 8 percent of the neighborhood's population. But when construction started, ten thousand others who lived adjacent to the construction also began to move out. The violent explosions that were necessary for building the highway damaged remaining buildings and polluted the area, requiring further evacuations of residents. Vandalism and crime increased at construction sites, and insurance premiums predictably increased.

By the time the portion of the Cross-Bronx Expressway through East Tremont was completed in 1960, the most expensive road constructed in all of history at that time at $250 million, landlords stopped maintaining the surrounding buildings and rented only to the lowest-income New Yorkers. Sidewalks were unwalkable, littered with garbage and debris, and streets were rendered one-way by the expressways.

TO LEARN MORE

Ballon, Hilary, and Kenneth T. Jackson. *Robert Moses and the Modern City: The Transformation of New York*. New York: W. W. Norton, 2007.
Caro, Robert A. *The Power Broker: Robert Moses and the Fall of New York*. New York: Vintage, 1974.

Pelham Parkway

1.6 Former Home of Richard Colón ("Crazy Legs")

1669 Garfield Street, Bronx, NY

Richard "Crazy Legs" Colon lived here as he helped to birth the b-boy (breaking) movement in dance in the late 1970s. He led the preeminent Rock Steady Crew to bring their signature, NYC–bred style of dance all over the world. What would eventually become known as hip-hop culture, consisting of deejaying, MCing, breaking, and graffiti, grew out of the Bronx and then other parts of the city in the late 1970s. Bronx youth invented some of the most influential cultural forms of the late twentieth century in the borough's parks, schoolyards, and abandoned buildings (see **Birthplace of Hip-Hop**, p. 34).

Crazy Legs got his start dancing when his brother took him to an outdoor party at the corner of Crotona Avenue and East 180th Street in the summer of 1977, watching b-boys bounce, turn, twist, freeze, and drop to the floor, with lightning-fast footwork that was equal parts James Brown and street fight. B-boy crews of Black and Puerto Rican youth formed all over the Bronx between 1975 and 1979, including the Zulu Kings, the Bronx Boys, and the Crazy Commanders. Competition between individual dancers and crews at the P.S. 129 schoolyard, St. Martin of Tours Roman Catholic Church, and countless other places quickly bred new moves as b-boys looked to one-up each other at battles.

Crazy Legs left the Bronx for Inwood in Manhattan in 1979, where he continued to dance. He recruited his battle opponents into the new Rock Steady Crew, which became a collection of more than five hundred dancers that eventually spurred other crews like the New York City Breakers and the Dynamic Rockers. They frequently prac-

Richard "Crazy Legs" Colón, breaking at a Soulsonic Force show at The Ritz, 1982.
CREDIT: EBET ROBERTS/ GETTY IMAGES

ticed at the "Happy Warrior" playground at 98th and Amsterdam in Manhattan, which is now often referred to as the "Rock Steady." The Rock Steady Crew would go on to tour in the early 1980s, spreading their distinctive wing of hip-hop culture all over the world. "We were just innocently having fun," Crazy Legs says, "not realizing we were setting a foundation for what is a multibillion dollar a year industry" (*Quote is from Jeff Chang,* Can't Stop Won't Stop: A History of the Hip Hop Generation, *p. 176.*)

—*With Lucy Pugh*

In forceful contrast to architecture more typical of the neighborhood, the suburban style of rebuilt "Charlotte Gardens" was seemingly designed to erase the history of neglect and arson that these homes replace, 2017.
CREDIT: SCOTT DEXTER

TO LEARN MORE

Chang, Jeff. *Can't Stop, Won't Stop: A History of the Hip-Hop Generation.* New York: Picador, 2005.

Charlotte Gardens, South Bronx

1.7 Charlotte Gardens/ Mid-Bronx Desperadoes

Charlotte Street and E. 170th Street, Bronx, NY

Rounding the corner from Boston Road to walk along Charlotte Street in the Bronx today, you could be on any suburban block. A man walks his dog; two children in uniforms from the school across the street wait at the corner. Scattered pear trees, planted in the past couple of decades, provide some summer shade. Over the vinyl-sided ranch houses, a few five-story apartment buildings line parallel streets.

From the time those buildings went up in the first decades of the twentieth century, through to the early 1970s, Charlotte Street looked just like its neighboring blocks. Its big, walk-up apartment buildings had housed Irish, Italian, and Jewish immigrants pursuing the American Dream; by the 1970s, they housed Black and Puerto Rican families doing the same. But Charlotte Street was a casualty of the severe fiscal crisis of the 1970s, when New York City came close to declaring bankruptcy. Landlords torched hundreds of multifamily buildings for profitable insurance payments, and hundreds of other nearby buildings decayed and burned from general neglect and the city's "planned shrinkage" policy—removing essential services from neighborhoods deemed failing.

South Bronx empty lots during the fiscal crisis, 1977.
CREDIT: SUSAN LORKID KATZ (1947–). MUSEUM OF THE CITY OF NEW YORK. 84.203.25

Landlords abandoned the city en masse. Maintenance costs had soared, but the people and families who remained in New York's poorest neighborhoods could not afford rents—even with rent control. Many of these neighborhoods, including in the South Bronx, had been redlined for decades, ineligible for mortgage investment because of their mix of racial groups and social classes. So landlords withheld maintenance and collected rents for as long as they could, and then abandoned or in many cases burned their buildings for insurance money. The number of fires in New York's poorest neighborhoods increased dramatically during the 1960s, and fire became a routine part of city life in the 1970s. Seven census tracts in the Bronx lost more than 97 percent of their buildings to fire and abandonment during the 1970s, and forty-four tracts lost more than half. More than a quarter of a million people were displaced from the South Bronx in the 1970s due to fire and abandonment.

Charlotte Street was the backdrop to visits from United States presidents during its crisis years and beyond. When President Jimmy Carter visited in October of 1977, part of Charlotte Street had been quite literally erased, removed from the city map in 1974. With Carter's visit, it came to stand as the national symbol of urban decay. When President Ronald Reagan came in 1980, it was to score political points against Carter's "failed" urban strategies. Yet by the time President Clinton visited in 1995, Charlotte Street had become the picture of neighborhood renewal—and not because of federal largesse or support.

Beginning in the early 1970s, Bronx clergy and residents had formed countless organizations to improve life in the Bronx. One Bronx woman, Genevieve Brooks, went door-to-door in her neighborhood, organizing a block association to clean up the streets and establishing the Seabury Day Care Center under community control to help local families with childcare. She then organized and established the Mid-Bronx Desperadoes (MBD), a coalition of neighborhood groups that fought for investment and services in the Bronx and eventually built or rehabilitated thousands of units of affordable housing in the South Bronx.

The MBD transformed this stretch of Charlotte Street that America came to associate with urban catastrophe into a new neighborhood of prefabricated modest single-family homes by leveraging public and private funding. In the mid-1980s more than five hundred people applied to purchase the eighty-nine subsidized homes for sale between fifty thousand and sixty thousand dollars. And by the turn of the century, MBD managed thirty-eight buildings throughout the South Bronx in its own right. Brooks would later become the first woman to be Deputy Bronx Borough President in 1990.

Leon Trotsky's 1918 home in the Bronx, 2017. CREDIT: SCOTT DEXTER

TO LEARN MORE

Gonzalez, Evelyn. *The Bronx*. New York: Columbia University Press, 2004.

Jonnes, Jill. *South Bronx Rising: The Rise, Fall, and Resurrection of an American City*, 2/e. New York: Fordham University Press, 2002.

1.8 Former Home of Leon Trotsky

1522 Vyse Avenue, near 172nd Street, Bronx, NY

"In New York, where I stayed for two months, the newspapers had me engaged in any number of occupations, each more fantastic than the one before. If all the ad-ventures that the newspapers ascribed to me were banded together in a book, they would make a far more entertaining biography than the one I am writing here." So begins Russian revolutionary and leading Bolshevik Leon Trotsky's autobiographical description of his time in New York City, beginning in January 1917. Though his time in the city was brief—a longer exile was cut short by news of the February Revolution in Russia in 1917—and perhaps not as eventful as the local press would have it, during his time in New York Trotsky nevertheless influenced the direction of the groupings that were to become the US Communist Party.

The three-room apartment he shared here with his wife and two sons had appliances they had not lived with before: electric lights, a bath, a garbage chute and an elevator for the building—and importantly, a telephone, which became vital when their nine-year-old son got lost on a walk the night before their departure, but was able to remember the phone number and call from a police station. During the months Trotsky spent in New York, he split his time between the New York Public Library on 42nd Street, where he immersed himself in analyzing the economic history and recent performance of the United States; the offices of *Novy Mir*, a Russian Socialist daily published out of a cellar at 77 St. Marks Place in Manhattan; and meetings, lectures, and more meetings: "I plunged into the affairs of American Socialism too quickly, and I was straightway up to my neck in work for it."

New York City was home to a distinctly international socialism. Homegrown American radicals like journalists John Reed and Louise Bryant, the writer Upton Sinclair, Crystal Eastman and her brother Max, and others created an extensive left political culture, most notably in Manhattan's Greenwich Village. New York had many German Social Democrats in residence who were close to the leaders of the Second International, which had decided to back their national governments at the outbreak of hostilities in 1914. New York was also home to Dutch, Latvian, Italian, and Russian socialists who were familiar with the incipient calls for a Third International, founded against the Second's capitulation to the Great War. The United States had not yet entered the World War, and the same divisions that had split the international movement—whether to support their national governments in times of war, or reject militarism and maintain opposition to their national bourgeoisie—were straining the country's left as well. During Trotsky's time in New York, he agitated alongside those socialists who would form the Communist Party, arguing that should the United States enter the war, socialists should reject this imperialist adventure and call for strikes and protests seeking to disrupt war mobilization. By 1920, and for decades afterwards, the US Communist Party that formed out of these debates had no greater base than the city Trotsky briefly called home. He left New York "with the feeling of a man who has had only a peep into the foundry in which the fate of man is to be forged."

TO LEARN MORE

Ackerman, Kenneth D. *Trotsky in New York, 1917: A Radical on the Eve of Revolution.* Berkeley, CA: Counterpoint, 2016.

Trotsky, Leon. *My Life: An Attempt at an Autobiography.* New York: Charles Scribner's Sons, 1930.

Highbridge

1.9 Fania All-Stars at Yankee Stadium

Yankee Stadium, 1 E. 161st Street, Bronx, NY

On the night of August 23, 1973, more than forty-four thousand people sold out Yankee Stadium to hear the Fania All-Stars play their burgeoning, signature brand of salsa

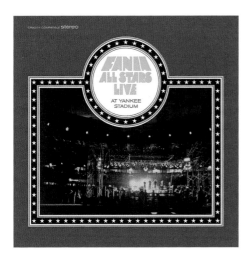

Fania All-Stars Live at Yankee Stadium album cover, 1973. CREDIT: COURTESY OF FANIA RECORDS AND CRAFT RECORDINGS

in one of the most legendary historical moments in Latin music, at one of the most iconic sites in New York City. The concert is one of only 525 recordings enshrined in the US National Recording Registry. The Fania All-Stars concert represented a culmination of the salsa movement and the beginning of its spread worldwide. What eventually became salsa music developed little by little over the decades, as different musical styles morphed and melded with each other, with the Bronx—also known as "El Condado de la Salsa"—central to its evolution.

Fania, a small, NYC–based music label, was created by Jerry Masucci, a former NYC police officer and divorce lawyer from Brooklyn, and Johnny Pacheco, a Dominican bandleader and flautist from the Bronx's Mott Haven. Formed in 1964, the Fania label produced revolutionary sounds—music with Afro-Cuban rhythms played by Latinos in New York City, the majority of whom were

Nuyoricans (New Yorkers of Puerto Rican descent). The term "salsa" had been bandied about before and used in songs since Septeto Nacional recorded "Echalé Salsita" in Cuba in the 1930s. But the descriptor only gained currency after Masucci and Pacheco adopted it to describe the music their label produced. Fania literally spread the "salsa" word by delivering their first records to New York's record stores from the trunk of their car, assembling the Fania All-Stars to play the 1973 Yankee Stadium concert (and similar shows in Puerto Rico, Chicago, and Panama), and releasing the movies *Our Latin Thing* (1972) and *Salsa* (1975), both directed by Leon Gast.

The soundtrack to New York's Latina/o/x youth coming of age in the 1960s was not their parents' big band mambo (see **Bronx Music Hall**, p. 49). Their increasing political empowerment and resentment of the social and physical conditions of their neighborhoods (see **Lincoln Hospital**, p. 45; and **Garbage Offensive**, p. 84) were better accompanied by salsa's dynamic arrangements and electrifying horns. The Afro-Cuban rhythms remained in the forefront, but the musical arrangements leaned toward either the old guard Cuban *conjunto* sound or the more updated New York City power trombone style with trumpets.

Musicians from the Bronx played a significant role in Fania and were members of the Fania All-Stars (the label's super group). In addition to Johnny Pacheco, Pete "El Conde" Rodriguez, Willie Colón, Eddie Montalvo, Nicky Marrero, and Ray Barretto all grew up in the Bronx, and Yomo Toro,

Hector Lavoe, La Lupe, and Mongo Santa-maria all lived in the Bronx at one time or another.

After the Fania All-Stars' famed concert in 1973, not a single Latin music concert would be held at Yankee Stadium again until 2014, when the Bronx's own king of *bachata* music, Romeo Santos, would sell out two back-to-back shows. Though now the Bronx's soundscape includes new Latin music sounds like the Dominican *bachata*, salsa still remains a part of the borough's legacy and identity, with the SalsaFest being held every August promoted by the Bronx Tourism Office.

—*Elena Martínez*

South Bronx

1.10 Hostos Community College

500 Grand Concourse, Bronx, NY

When Hostos Community College began offering classes in the fall of 1970, it brought unprecedented educational opportunity to the people of the predominantly Black and Puerto Rican South Bronx. The first college on the US mainland to be named after a Puerto Rican person, Eugenio María de Hostos Community College was the only bilingual college in the New York City area. Founded to meet the education and social needs of the South Bronx, it remains a bastion of Spanish/English bilingual education and maintains the *Las Casitas* archive that documents the social and cultural life of distinctive Puerto Rican–style houses with gar-

Students occupy Hostos Community College building as part of the Save Hostos Campaign, 1978. CREDIT: HOSTOS COMMUNITY COLLEGE ARCHIVES

dens that dot the Bronx (see **Casita Rincón Criollo**, p. 48).

Hostos is one of seven community colleges that, together with eleven "senior" colleges, one undergraduate honors college, and seven additional schools make up the City University of New York (CUNY), the largest urban public university in the world. What became CUNY was created piecemeal over time, with Hostos, York, and Medgar Evers Colleges created in 1968 to remedy the lack of representation of Black and Latina/o/x New Yorkers in the city's public colleges in the postwar period. At that point, Black and Puerto Rican youth made up 40 percent of the city's high schools, but only 13 percent of CUNY senior colleges and 32 percent of community colleges.

Between 1973 and 1979, students, faculty, CUNY's faculty and staff union, and community members in the Save Hostos Movement engaged in all manner of protest to keep the school in operation. One group blocked traffic on the Grand Concourse—a major Bronx traffic artery—with classroom chairs, holding classes in the middle of the street. Another group eventually took over the entire Hostos campus by locking all but the main entrance that was guarded by students and setting up a day-care center in the president's office. The Save Hostos Movement and its allies ultimately succeeded in keeping Hostos open. Hostos remains in the South Bronx today, after fifty years, a community anchor, symbol, and engine of social mobility.

"Atención Compañeros, el edificio "500" ha sido Tomado" flyer by Organización De Estudiantes Puertorriqueños at Hostos Community College, 1978.
CREDIT: HOSTOS COMMUNITY COLLEGE ARCHIVES

TO LEARN MORE

Hostos Community College – www.hostos .cuny.edu

Phillips-Fein, Kim. *Fear City: New York's Fiscal Crisis and the Rise of Austerity Politics.* New York: Metropolitan Books, 2017.

A new "open admissions" policy that guaranteed a seat to every high school graduate in 1969—partially the result of student protests across CUNY to better serve Black and Latina/o/x New Yorkers—created great demand for classes at Hostos (see **City College**, p. 70). In September of 1970, 623 students attended their first Hostos classes in an old tire factory on the Grand Concourse in the South Bronx. But facing unfathomable budget cuts during the city's fiscal crisis, CUNY moved to shutter the school only five years into its existence. By closing Hostos, along with John Jay, Medgar Evers, and York Colleges, all of which served a disproportionately Black and Latina/o/x student body, the system reasoned that it could save the remaining campuses.

1.11 Lincoln Hospital

234 E. 149th Street, Bronx, NY

Lincoln Medical Center, formerly known as Lincoln Hospital, is part of New York City's public hospital system, the largest such public system in the country. Lincoln and its ten sister hospitals admit patients regardless of their immigration status or ability to pay, making them crucial parts of the city's health-care safety net. Lincoln has the busiest emergency room in the city and frequently

A barricaded hallway in Lincoln Hospital during the "Lincoln Offensive," the Young Lords and community occupation, 1970. CREDIT: JACK MANNING/*NEW YORK TIMES*/REDUX

the country. The care provided here would likely not exist today had it not been for the efforts of the radical Puerto Rican Young Lords Party and other revolutionary medical activists from the community.

The South Bronx was, and to some extent remains, a medically underserved neighborhood with few local physicians and a community that experiences high levels of poverty-related chronic diseases such as diabetes and asthma. In the 1960s, decrepit and crowded housing that often lacked heat additionally meant that neighborhood residents had high rates of pneumonia, tuberculosis, and lead poisoning, or "diseases of oppression," as a Young Lords member

called them. By 1970, Lincoln Hospital was in a state of profound disrepair and dysfunction, referred to by some as "the butcher shop." Children contracted lead poisoning while getting care there, and rats were often seen inside the emergency room. It was housed in a condemned building, and funds the city had earmarked for its renovation had been budgeted annually for twenty-five years without being spent.

On the morning of July 14, 1970, the Young Lords (YL) were helped inside the hospital by sympathetic staff. Doctors continued to see patients while the YL seized the administrative office and barricaded themselves inside. During their twenty-four-hour takeover, the YL also opened unused spaces in the hospital to expand tuberculosis and lead poisoning screening, and set up a day-care center (that the hospital later continued). The occupation represented the coalescence of various social justice organizations into a revolutionary health movement in the early 1970s, represented in the Bronx by the Health Revolutionary Unity Movement (HRUM) and the South Bronx organization Think Lincoln Committee, comprised of hospital workers and patients. During the occupation, the YL and the HRUM drafted a list of ten demands that included community and staff governance, door-to-door preventative and educational services, an end to all fees, jobs for people from the neighborhood, and a new building for Lincoln Hospital. Representatives from the mayor's office noted that it was difficult to be angry with the Young Lords, who simply demanded the same treatment that patients received in hospitals downtown.

The Young Lords decided to stand down in exchange for a quiet and safe exit from the hospital; the mayor's office agreed to a new facility. Six years later, the new $2-million Lincoln Medical Center was reopened four-teen blocks away from the old hospital. Most importantly, the "Lincoln Offensive" marked a new chapter in community health efforts throughout the NYC health system, and over time many of the demands placed by the YL and their allies have become com-mon practice in NYC clinics and hospitals (see **Garbage Offensive**, p. 84).

In addition to its community connec-tions, Lincoln Hospital has a long history of engagement with artists. During the Great Depression, the Works Progress Administra-tion artists painted murals that stood in the entrance of the old building; Abram Cham-panier's "Alice in Wonderland in New York City" from 1938 can still be seen in the lobby of the women and infant care area. Romare Bearden also contributed a mural to the hos-pital in 1974, and the hospital still houses one of his collages. In 2012, the hospital began a program titled the Lincoln Arts Exchange, in which uninsured artists or art workers can barter their artwork, performances, and the like, in exchange for medical treatment.

—*With Carly-Jo Rosselli*

TO LEARN MORE

Fernández, Johanna. *The Young Lords: A Radical History*. Chapel Hill: University of North Carolina Press, 2020.

1.12 Dominicanos USA

369 E. 149th Street, 11th Fl., Bronx, NY

Located on a busy street of pawnbrokers, banks, and fast food restaurants in one of the hubs of the Dominican community in the Bronx, Dominicanos USA (DUSA) is making change, block by block. Since 2013 the organization has been working to increase the civic participation and the economic and social integration of Domini-canos in New York City. The Bronx is home to 355,000 Dominicanos, the largest con-centration of Dominicanos outside of the Dominican Republic, outpacing Washington Heights as the heart of the Dominican com-munity in New York City. Yet, political repre-sentation is greatly lacking for a community so deeply rooted in the city. There is a long history of Dominican migration to New York City, with the most recent and largest wave coming in the 1960s after the fall of General Rafael Trujillo, the US-supported dic-tator of the Dominican Republic (1930–1938, 1942–1952). Dominicans are the second larg-est Latina/o/x group in New York City, fol-lowing Puerto Ricans, who, unlike Domini-cans, have US citizenship status. Like Puerto Ricans, Dominicans have historically been relegated to low paying jobs and underserved neighborhoods with limited access to qual-ity education. Despite their numbers (over 600,000 in NYC) they have historically had little political power, with only a few elected officials. DUSA plays an important role in trying to change these dynamics. In its few short years, the organization has registered over 150,000 Latina/o/x voters, the majority of whom are Dominican. DUSA also works with naturalized immigrants to help them obtain citizenship status and has recently launched a workforce development project. The organization continues to play a key role in voter registration and voter turnout.

TO LEARN MORE

Dominicanos USA—www.dominicanosusa.org/.

Grasmuck, Sherri, and Patricia R. Pessar. *Between Two Islands: Dominican International Migration.* Berkeley: University of California Press, 1991.

Hernández, Ramona. *The Mobility of Workers under Advanced Capitalism: Dominican Migration to the United States.* New York: Columbia University Press, 2002.

1.13 Casita Rincón Criollo

749 Brook Avenue, 157th Street, Bronx, NY

Taking inspiration from houses in the Puerto Rican countryside, casitas are small houses with gardens surrounding them. They were initially constructed in the 1920s and 1930s in rural regions of Puerto Rico, in response to the large sugar companies that moved onto many locals' land following the 1898 takeover of the island by the United States. Although it was illegal to build these houses, they were protected by a law that stated that if the homes were completed, they could not be demolished.

These little houses from the countryside influenced the design of the small houses that were built on abandoned lots in Puerto Rican neighborhoods throughout the city. The oldest and largest site in New York City is the Casita Rincón Criollo. Rincón Criollo was built in the late 1970s, when José Manuel "Chema" Soto and his neighbors reclaimed an abandoned lot after a nearby club they spent time in had been razed. Soto began clearing the area of debris and rubbish, inspiring around fifty other local residents to join him and leading them to establish a home of their own, calling it Rincón Criollo ("Downhome Corner"). Casita members used this corner to socialize, engage in gardening, and pass down musical and cultural traditions. Plena music and dance that originated in Puerto Rico at the beginning of the

The characteristically colorful and vibrant facade of Casita Rincón Criollo, n.d.
CREDIT: WILLIAM CASARI

twentieth century was Chema Soto's great passion, and he helped teach hundreds or more from around the Bronx and the world from this "little bit of PR in the South Bronx."

In 2006, Rincón Criollo's land was reclaimed for low-income housing. However, after local support to keep local casitas in the neighborhood resulted in a court case, the grassroots cultural center was reestablished on another city-owned property down the block at East 157th Street and Brook Avenue. The site was saved through local activism, but countless other gardens and casitas, from the Bronx to East Harlem to the Lower East Side to Brooklyn, have closed as a result of housing development on their land.

Unlike the old site, where the home was built from recycled scrap lumber and other objects, the new casita is constructed entirely of wood with a large front room for community activities and a small back room that is used as an office. The distinctive teal color of the casita replicates the old design, but also replicates color schemes of Caribbean environments. The site continues to play a pivotal role in the Puerto Rican community within New York, serving as a space for community celebrations, art, and performance. Rincón Criollo is where the renaissance of Puerto Rican traditional music took hold in New York City in the 1980s, led by NEA National Heritage Award winner Juan Gutiérrez and Los Pleneros de la 21.

—*Sarah Fuller with Elena Martínez*

TO LEARN MORE

Las Casitas Collection, Hostos Community College, Bronx, NY

1.14 Bronx Music Hall

Intersection of Washington Avenue and E. 163rd Street, Bronx, NY

The Bronx Music Hall (BMH) celebrates and promotes the unique musical, cultural, and artistic heritage of the Bronx. With a mission to disseminate the beauty of the borough's soundscape, the BMH seeks to present an alternative vision of the Bronx that counters the stereotype of "urban blight" too often linked to its streets.

While the neighborhood surrounding the BMH was ground zero of the Bronx's devastation story, it has also been home to some of the Bronx's most important and prolific musicians. Although historians often locate the birthplace of hip-hop on Sedgwick Avenue in the West Bronx where DJ Kool Herc performed, one of hip-hop's founding DJs, Grandmaster Flash, and the originator of scratching, Grand Wizzard Theodore, innovated close by (see **Birthplace of Hip-Hop**, p. 34). A jazz scene that rivaled Harlem's thrived along nearby Boston Road, with famous musicians Maxine Sullivan, Thelonious Monk, Elmo Hope, and others living in the neighborhood. Music programs in the Bronx's public schools in the area nurtured famed jazz trumpeter Jimmy Owens, pianist Eddie Palmieri, and percussionist Ray Barretto, who would become National Endowment for the Arts Jazz Masters. Morrisania, the neighborhood where the BMH is located, was also one of the homes to "doo wop" music, where The Chiffons ("He's So Fine"), The Chords ("Sh-Boom"), and The Chantels ("Maybe") all formed in the 1950s and 1960s.

Mambo ruled in Longwood/Hunts Point, where Bronx newcomers from Puerto Rico and Cuba by way of East Harlem sang and played percussion and horns in apartments, in the streets, and in the neighborhoods' clubs—Hunts Point Palace, Club Tropicoro, Tropicana, and Teatro Puerto Rico, where Tito Rodriguez,

Members of Libana Maraza, Alex Colón and James Lovell, perform a traditional Garifuna Warangua dance for a Bronx Rising! Parranda con Paranda program at the Bronx Music Heritage Center, now the Bronx Music Hall. CREDIT: ELENA MARTINEZ

Tito Puente, Machito, Arsenio Rodriguez, and many others played. This music would come to be called salsa (see **Fania All-Stars at Yankee Stadium**, p. 42).

Today the surrounding neighborhoods host many West African musicians from the Gambia and Mali, and some of the most famous Dominican *bachata* musicians attended the local high schools. The Bronx is home to the largest Garifuna community outside of Central America, who perform their distinctive musical style in various venues around the borough ranging from schools to catering halls. The Bronx Music Hall is a home for these and other sounds from the borough, past and present.

In late 2019, the Women's Housing and Economic Development Corporation (WHEDco), the creator of the BMH, completed construction on Bronx Commons, a mixed-use affordable housing development that is also home to the new world-class BMH venue. Featuring a 250-seat theater, plazas with amphitheater seating for outdoor performances, classrooms for music and dance instruction and rehearsal, and exhibit space, the BMH is a dynamic center that amplifies and reflects the Bronx's musical and artistic legacy and talent.

—*Elena Martínez*

TO LEARN MORE

Flores, Juan. *Salsa Rising: New York Latin Music of the Sixties Generation*. Tempo: A Rowman & Littlefield Music Series on Rock, Pop, and Culture. New York: Oxford University Press, 2016.

Singer, Roberta, and Elena Martínez. "A South Bronx Music Tale." Centro XVI, no. 1 (2004): 177–201.

1.15 United Bronx Parents

791 Prospect Avenue, Bronx, NY

This building was slated for demolition in 1965 when Dr. Evelina López Antonetty and a group of parents took it over for the headquarters of the newly established United Bronx Parents (UBP), a grassroots group dedicated to improving schools in the Bronx. UBP moved on, but the building still stands today. Many of the most significant efforts to improve housing, education, health care, and basic social services in some of the Bronx's most underserved communities have been organized by Black and Latina/o/x women.

In the mid-1960s, Dr. Evelina López Antonetty, known as the "Hell Lady of the Bronx," and her daughter, Lorraine Montenegro, founded United Bronx Parents to fight for bilingual education, training local parents to advocate for better schools. It also established a bilingual day-care center, youth

programs, and AIDS outreach programs. In 1990 it opened La Casita, a residential drug treatment center for homeless women that allowed them to keep their children with them in treatment. United Bronx Parents continues to provide a wide range of social services for residents of the South Bronx.

Building on the crucial work of women like López Antonetty and Genevieve Brooks (see **Charlotte Gardens / Mid-Bronx Desperadoes**, p. 39), women continue to organize and lead strong, dynamic grassroots movements and organizations to improve educational opportunity and quality of life all over the Bronx. Mothers on the Move, for example, was founded in 1992 out of an adult literacy class and began as an educational justice group advocating for fair educational leadership and resources for the schools in the neighborhood. Compared to the whiter and wealthier schools in the north Bronx, Hunts Point students had less experienced teachers and fewer textbooks and other crucial resources. The group successfully elected members to the local school board, and eventually their agitation and advocacy won area schools more support and recognition from the city's Department of Education.

United Bronx Parents headquarters with its founder, Evelina López Antonetty, leaning out the window, n.d. CREDIT: UNITED BRONX PARENTS ARCHIVES, EL CENTRO DE ESTUDIOS PUERTORIQUEÑOS, HUNTER COLLEGE–CUNY

Early in their organizing, responding to the record level of asthma rates among students at P.S. 48, Mothers on the Move turned their attention to the issue of environmental justice as well, an issue around which they have been a neighborhood force for the past two decades. They are joined by Nos Quedamos, founded by Yolanda García, which works to resist development that would displace Melrose residents and fights for environmental justice in the Bronx, and countless other organizations and grassroots groups.

TO LEARN MORE

Jonnes, Jill. *South Bronx Rising: The Rise, Fall, and Resurrection of an American City*, 2/e. New York: Fordham University Press, 2002.

Su, Celina. *Streetwise for Book Smarts: Grassroots Organizing and Education Reform in the Bronx*. Ithaca, NY: Cornell University Press, 2009.

Hunts Point

1.16 Hunts Point Terminal Food Distribution Center

Between Halleck Street and Food Center Drive, Bronx, NY

Relocated in the 1960s from a series of markets in lower Manhattan at the former Washington Market (cleared to build the World Trade Center), the firms that comprise the Hunts Point Food Distribution Center make it the city's largest food hub. The center's 329 acres constitute nearly half of the peninsula, and the site contains over 160 public and private firms specializing in produce, meat, and fish, employing over eight thousand workers. The fish market is second only to Tokyo's in size and supplies nearly half of the city's fresh fish; the produce firms move 25 percent of all fresh fruit and vegetables in the five boroughs. The Distribution Center as a whole receives over 130,000 truck deliveries a year, and, in turn, delivers goods to tens of thousands of sites around the city—restaurants, supermarkets, bodegas, and other markets. Fully 12 percent of the food consumed in the five boroughs passes through this corner of the Bronx.

Food, in particular fresh produce, demands rapid delivery. When the city acquired this land in 1962, it appeared an ideal answer to the logistical challenge of large scale distribution, given its proximity to the new highways and existing rail-to-port connections. Yet while the location proved efficient from a transportation standpoint, it was highly detrimental to the peninsula's twenty-seven thousand residents who have faced the profound health impacts of clustered industry. The barrage of trucks that pass through the Hunts Point Food Distribution Center contribute to a host of other sources of air and ground pollution, including particulate pollution from thousands of additional trucks trips to and from the Point's waste transfer stations, vehicles on the area's many highways, and air pollution from the Hunts Point Wastewater Treatment Plant, adjacent to the market's southwest corner. This contemporary stew is reinforced by the legacy of the gasworks and asbestos plants; other industries, such as paint and varnish manufacturing, also contribute. In addition, for

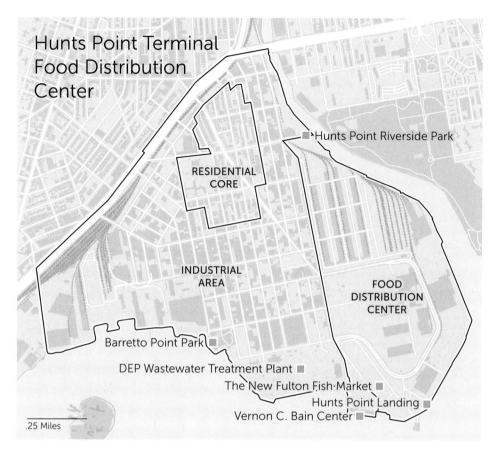

Hunts Point Terminal
Food Distribution
Center

Hunts Point Riverside Park

RESIDENTIAL
CORE

INDUSTRIAL
AREA

FOOD
DISTRIBUTION
CENTER

Barretto Point Park

DEP Wastewater Treatment Plant

The New Fulton Fish Market

Hunts Point Landing

Vernon C. Bain Center

.25 Miles

decades the waterfront was home to illegal and in some cases unremediated dumping. According to health studies, local exposure to fine particulates has been as much as eighteen times higher than the compliance rate set by the Environmental Protection Agency (EPA). The environmental impact of industry and poor housing can be most closely observed in the area's children, whose asthma hospitalization rates exceed two to three times those in other boroughs and continue to rank among the nation's highest.

Ironically, Hunts Point and the adjacent Longwood are also some of the neighborhoods least served by supermarkets, with a third less food market square footage than the city's average. For residents who live on the peninsula, access to fresh food is particularly hard, as the area's bigger markets are found in Longwood, across the long, poorly lit, and traffic-treacherous underbelly of the Bruckner Expressway. The community organizing described in other entries addresses many of these ongoing concerns (see **New York Expo Center / Former site of the New York Organic Fertilizer Company**, p. 54; and **United Bronx Parents**, p. 51).

Small, weekly farmers markets throughout the city suggest the possibility for interaction and exchange that food markets offer, and they have been at the forefront of community efforts aimed at food justice. Meanwhile, New York City's foremost food market, with its industrial scale and geographic isolation, offers none of the vibrant public space that urban markets have sustained across the city's history.

—*With Xhoana Ahmeti*

TO LEARN MORE

"Five Borough Food Flow, New York City Food Distribution & Resiliency Study Results." New York: NYC Economic Development Corporation, the Mayor's Office of Recovery and Resiliency, 2016. https://www1.nyc.gov/assets/foodpolicy/downloads/pdf/2016_food_supply_resiliency_study_results.pdf.

King, L., K. Hinterland, K. L. Dragan, C. R. Driver, T. G. Harris, R. C. Gwynn, N. Linos, O. Barbot, and M. T. Bassett. "Community Health Profiles 2015, Bronx Community District 2: Hunts Point and Longwood." 14, no. 59 (2015): 1–16. https://www1.nyc.gov/assets/doh/downloads/pdf/data/2015chp-bx2.pdf.

NEARBY SITES OF INTEREST

Rocking the Boat
812 Edgewater Road, Hunts Point Riverside Park, Bronx, NY
Adjacent to the market is a community-won slice of green called Riverside Park, the first green development victory of Sustainable South Bronx, a local environmental justice and workforce development organization. Next to the park is Rocking the Boat (RTB), which began as a volunteer project in 1996 and has been a community nonprofit since 2001. Hundreds of Bronx high school students work with RTB each year and commit to years of study and apprenticeship in boat building, environmental science, or sailing.

Concrete Plant Park
Bronx River between Westchester Avenue and Bruckner Boulevard, Bronx, NY
Another green space located a mile north of Hunts Point Riverside, also converted from its industrial use through efforts led by the Youth Ministries for Peace and Justice.

1.17 New York Expo Center/ Former Site of the New York Organic Fertilizer Company

1108 Oak Point Avenue, Bronx, NY

This ten-acre venue space that brings trendy music to "SoBro" (real estate developers' new name for the South Bronx) occupies the site of a former scourge of the neighborhood, the National Organic Fertilizer Company. For much of the twentieth century into the twenty-first, the Hunts Point peninsula, where the Bronx and East Rivers meet, has been associated with dirty industrial development and deep poverty. Yet in recent years the sustained organizing of residents has paid off in some small and large improvements to their quality of life. A prime victory was the closing of this fertilizer plant in 2010.

Environmental contempt and negligence marked some of the earliest large scale development in the area. "Although it is true that the odors which arose from the land last Summer were not altogether delightful, yet, so far as they have been able to learn, no harm has resulted to anybody from them." So reported the *New York Times* in 1893, when the East Bay Land and Improvement Corporation was found to be filling in the salt marshes along the west side of the peninsula

Mothers on the Move protesting the New York Organic Fertilizer Corporation, 2008. CREDIT: PHOTO BY SUSAN WATTS/NY DAILY NEWS ARCHIVE VIA GETTY IMAGES

for industry, with a residential corridor extending west-east along Hunts Avenue and Lafayette Avenue on its northern side. The poorly maintained, low foot-traffic industrial landscape and constant truck traffic helped make it a hub for illegal drugs and sex work for many decades. The brutal Spofford Juvenile Detention Center was in operation on the Point until 1998 (though the site was used as a detention center through 2011), and the Vernon Bain "floating" jail is still moored to the south of the Fulton Fish Market.

with "garbage, gas house refuse, cellar earth, and the accumulation of filth with which the city streets are apt to be replete." The wealthy, whose estates had dotted the rich farmland of the Bronx River estuary for hundreds of years, rapidly abandoned the Point in the first decades of the twentieth century as their former estates holdings and undeveloped marshland were parceled out for residential and industrial development. Most notable among the area's many firms were the American Banknote Company, at 1231 Lafayette Avenue, whose hulking 1911 plant is now one of the two designated landmarks on the Point. In 1926 Consolidated Edison opened a coal gasification plant on the peninsula's east side, which for the next three and a half decades converted coal to gas, leaving thousands of tons of toxic coal tar in the land and water. National Gypsum Company, producer of asbestos wall boards (1940–1979), further contaminated the waterfront. Much of the Point was zoned

It is this concentration of social ills and inequality that inspired local residents to launch multiple justice organizations and campaigns over the years that have helped to make the Point a safer, healthier and still affordable neighborhood. In 1997, residents of the nearby Port Morris neighborhood joined with other South Bronx citizens in the South Bronx Clean Air Coalition to close a medical waste incinerator, whose opening in 1993 heralded a doubling of local asthma hospitalizations. But environmentally racist city policy did not end with this victory. In 1992 the healthy-sounding New York Organic Fertilizer Company (NYOFC) won a multiyear, multimillion dollar contract with the city to process half the city's sludge into fertilizer pellets in the neighborhood.

The smell from the fertilizer plant was a fetid mix of sulfur, "filthy toilet," and "rotting meat." Residents closed their windows and abandoned their gardens; schools canceled recess on the days when the smell was unbearable. Multiple community organizations, such as the Hunts Point Awareness Committee and the South Bronx Clean Air Coalition, organized against the plant in its early years, and with some success, as their early advocacy spurred the plant to briefly adapt some better practices to control the stink. But the smells inevitably returned. In 2004, Sustainable South Bronx purchased sufficient shares from the NYOFC's parent company, Synagro, to put forward shareholder resolutions calling for emission and health impact studies from the plant. School teachers raised awareness among families by asking them to calendar the "Smelly Days." Mothers on the Move held a candlelight vigil at the plant where they symbolically buried the Bronx, explaining, "The South Bronx is dying from the odor." Finally, in 2009, the National Resources Defense Council sued the company on behalf of Mothers on the Move and a group of residents, claiming it was a public nuisance. The state Attorney General followed with another lawsuit, the combined effects of which finally led to the plant's closing. When the plant was closed in 2010, one resident told the *New York Times*, "This will be the first summer we'll be able to breathe."

TO LEARN MORE

Sze, Julie. *Noxious New York: The Racial Politics of Urban Health and Environmental Justice.* Cambridge, MA: MIT Press, 2007.

NEARBY SITE OF INTEREST

Barretto Point Park
Viele Avenue between Tiffany and Barretto Streets, Bronx, NY

On the outskirts of this still industrial zone sits this landscaped twelve-acre park on the East River waterfront, won through community struggle. With views of the Brother Islands and the Manhattan skyline to the south, Barretto Point Park includes broad, grassy expanses, a playground, an outdoor amphitheater, picnic tables, and, in the summer, a twenty-five meter floating pool.

FAVORITE NEIGHBORHOOD RESTAURANT

La Morada
308 Willis Avenue, at 140th Street, Bronx, NY

Next to the Point, in Mott Haven, is one of the city's best Oaxacan restaurants that is also an educational and organizing hub for South Bronx residents organizing for immigrant rights and against the encroaching gentrification of the neighborhood. Owned by an undocumented family, the restaurant served free food during the early days of the COVID-19 pandemic and has since established a mutual aid kitchen with the support of the neighborhood, as the immigration status of the owners disqualified them for federal loans.

Water

By Lize Mogel and Sara Evans

New York City provides more than 1 billion gallons of drinking water every day to 9.5 million people in the city and four other counties. Water comes from a 2000-square-mile area that spans both sides of the Hudson River, and stretches as far as 125 miles north of the city. This gravity-fed water system includes nineteen reservoirs and three controlled lakes, two major aqueducts, three water tunnels underneath city streets, water mains, and other infrastructure. About 10 percent of the city's water comes from the Croton System in Westchester, and 90 percent of it from the mountainous Catskills region. Together, this system produces what some have called "the champagne of drinking water," but not without consequence for the Catskill communities from which it flows.

In the 1700s, New York City's water mostly came from Collect Pond (see **Collect Pond Park**, p. 161), which was soon polluted by overuse. When the expanding city brought cholera and fires into the mix of urban life, city leaders began to seek other sources for fresh water. The city first tapped the Croton River in Westchester, acquiring farms and other land in the process. Water came down through wooden pipes and the brick aqueduct at High Bridge in East Harlem to reservoirs in what are now Central Park's Great Lawn and Bryant Park. But as the city grew, so did its need for more water. City leaders explored potential water sources as far north as the Adirondacks and determined that Esopus Creek in the Catskills had the rapid flow, good water quality, and surrounding forests that were ideal.

In 1905 New York State passed legislation that would pave the way for rapid development of water infrastructure in the Catskills. Colloquially known as the McClellan Act (after the mayor at the time), it gave the city the power of eminent domain for this purpose. In 1907 the city began constructing the Catskills System, which includes the Ashokan Reservoir, the Catskills Aqueduct, and the Schoharie Reservoir.

In order to clear the land for these marvels of engineering, the city employed the McClellan Act to seize property with as little as thirty days' notice (although longer

Department of Environmental Protection (DEP) signs dot the landscape, 2019.
CREDIT: HATUEY RAMOS FERMÍN

in practice). The city paid an initial fee to the owner, and then negotiated the rest of the settlement, often through a number of local commissions set up for this purpose. The commissions operated from 1935 to 1993, and some cases took years to settle.

The city displaced twenty-two communities and 5,807 people in the Catskills over the sixty years of reservoir and aqueduct construction there. People lost their land, homes, businesses, jobs, livelihoods, and most importantly, their communities. Some had been on the land for generations and had a deep attachment to it. The former towns are memorialized by ubiquitous brown signs placed around all city reservoirs, and residual bitterness toward the city persists.

In the 1920s the city planned another expansion of the system, hoping to capture water from the Delaware River. This was a more complicated endeavor since the Delaware supplies four states with drinking water. When interstate negotiations stalled, the city successfully appealed to the Supreme Court. The city constructed the Rondout, Neversink, and Pepacton Reservoirs, as well as the Delaware Aqueduct that travels ninety miles deep underground to New York City. Drought and subsequent water shortages in 1950 led the city to put the final piece of the plan in place and construct the Cannonsville Reservoir. However, the most successful strategy for water conservation, residential water metering, was not put into place until 1986 because of pressure from the real estate lobby.

Labor practices changed between the construction of the Catskills and Delaware systems. Seventeen thousand people worked on the Catskills system alone, and many of them were European immigrants or Black people migrating from the South. Workers lived in large labor camps—effectively small towns—that were segregated by race and nationality. This was dangerous work, much of it done by hand, and there were hundreds of deaths and thousands of injuries. By the time the Delaware system was constructed, unionization and resulting workplace safety policies resulted in far fewer fatalities and injuries. Changes in transportation (i.e., personal cars) meant that labor camps were no longer needed, and nearby towns swelled at the seams as workers and their families moved in for the duration, and some stayed.

In the 1970s, the Clean Water Act and related laws changed the way municipalities managed their drinking water sources. Cities would need to filter their water, unless they could control pollution at the source and get a waiver from the EPA. Building a filtration plant would cost New York City billions of dollars in construction and annual operations; it was more cost effective to prevent pollution upstream.

Discussions between the city's Department of Environmental Protection (DEP) and Catskills leaders soon became acrimonious. For the first time, towns in the Catskills organized, forming the Coalition of Watershed Towns (CWT). The new DEP Commissioner, Marilyn Gelber, was the first woman and the first urban planner to hold the position. She took a very different approach than her predecessors. She recalls, "We had to start from some personal rela-

A sign that commemorates the town of Neversink before it was flooded to build the reservoir, 2014. CREDIT: PAUL LLOYD SARGENT

land acquisition now relies on voluntary sellers, not eminent domain. Much of the 174,000+ acres of land and water the city owns is open to the public for boating, fishing, hiking, and hunting. New York City will have plentiful and clean drinking water into the future because of this collaboration.

You can see traces of this storied and massive water system around the city today. Look for "Catskills" manhole covers and silver-painted water testing stations. These mark the presence of three subterranean tunnels that carry drinking water to homes and businesses across the boroughs. *(Quote is from Marilyn Gelber, as it appears in Burnett, Nancy, and Scheer, Virginia, "Behind the Scenes: The Inside Story of the Watershed Negotiations.")*

tionship; we had to be able to trust each other. It was only then that we could begin to negotiate a settlement." In 1995 Governor George Pataki brokered a yearlong negotiation between the DEP, the CWT, and environmental groups like Riverkeeper. This exceptionally difficult and lengthy process was democracy in action, as stakeholders with opposing perspectives were able to work through their differences and biases, and come to a detailed agreement. This was finalized in a Memorandum of Understanding (MOU), signed on January 17, 1997.

The MOU lays out a relationship based on "payment for ecosystem services." The Catskills adheres to the city's water quality policies, restrictions that affect economic development, farming and other land use, and keep the local economy small and reliant on tourism. The city provides financial and other support including grants for economic development, residential septic systems, and watershed education; building and maintaining wastewater treatment plants; and helping with flood control planning. The city's

TO LEARN MORE

Budrock, Helen. 1997. *Summary Guide to the Terms of the Watershed Agreement*. Arkville, NY: The Catskill Center for Conservation and Development, Inc. https://cwconline. org/wp-content/uploads/2017/03/ SummaryGuideToMOA-1.pdf.

Burnett, Nancy, and Virginia Scheer, n.d. "Behind the Scenes: The Inside Story of the Watershed Negotiations." https:// cwconline.org/wp-content/uploads/2017/03/ BehindTheScenesBgdTOC.pdf.

Galusha, Diane. *Liquid Asset: A History of New York City's Water System*. Fleischmanns, NY: Purple Mountain Press, 2016.

Soll, David. *Empire of Water—An Environmental and Political History of the New York City Water Supply*. New York: Cornell University Press, 2013.

2

Man-
hat-
tan

Manhattan Uptown

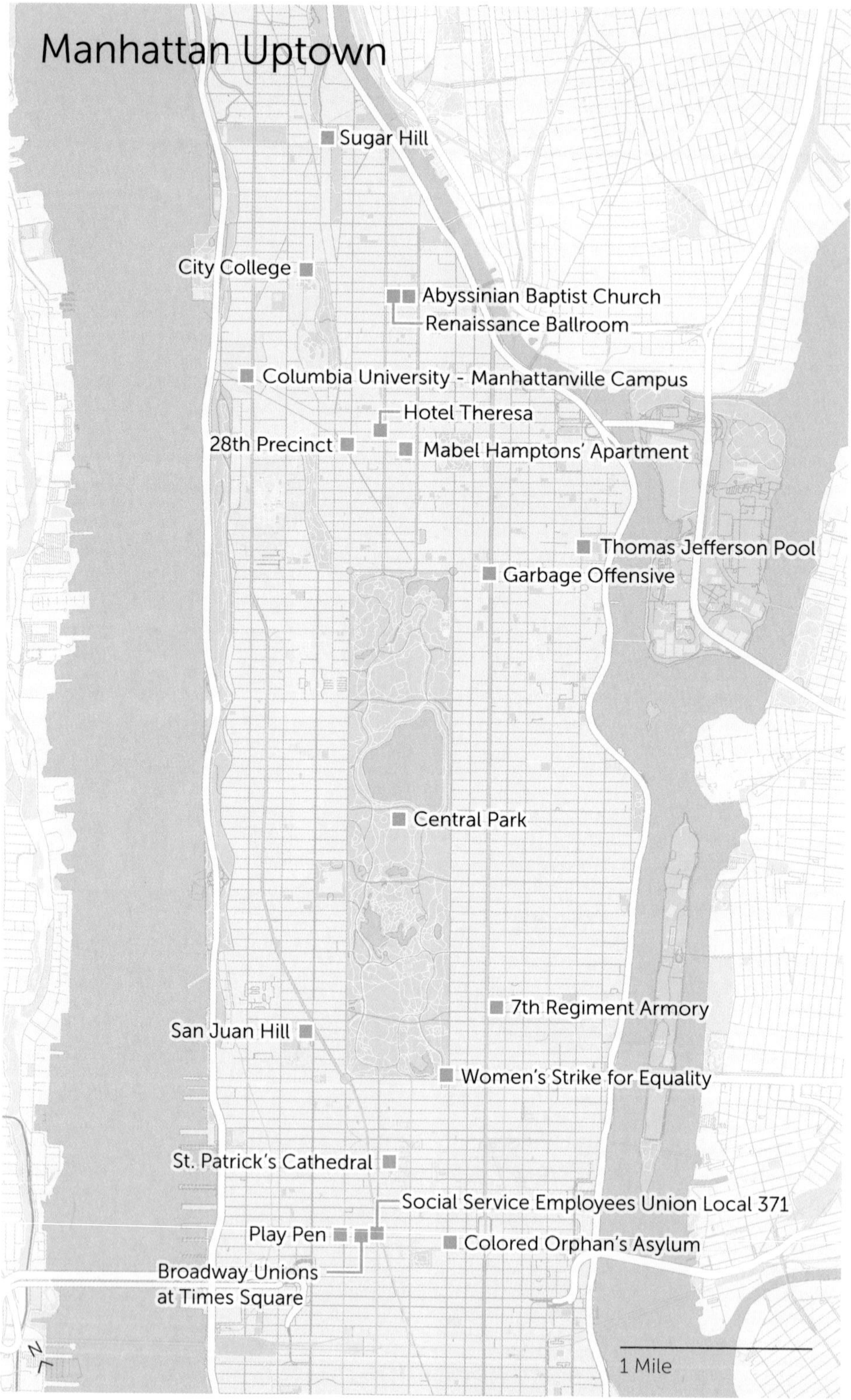

Sugar Hill

City College

Abyssinian Baptist Church
Renaissance Ballroom

Columbia University - Manhattanville Campus

Hotel Theresa

28th Precinct

Mabel Hamptons' Apartment

Thomas Jefferson Pool

Garbage Offensive

Central Park

7th Regiment Armory

San Juan Hill

Women's Strike for Equality

St. Patrick's Cathedral

Social Service Employees Union Local 371

Play Pen

Colored Orphan's Asylum

Broadway Unions
at Times Square

N

1 Mile

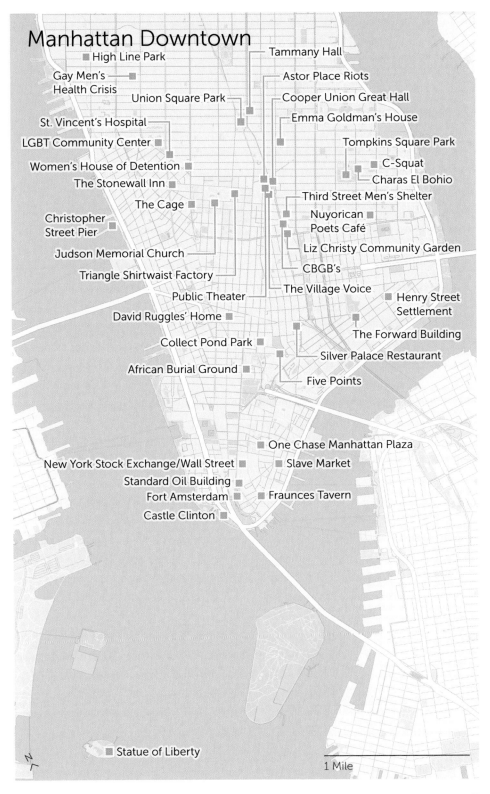

Manhattan Downtown

High Line Park

Tammany Hall

Gay Men's Health Crisis

Astor Place Riots

Union Square Park

Cooper Union Great Hall

St. Vincent's Hospital

Emma Goldman's House

LGBT Community Center

Tompkins Square Park

C-Squat

Women's House of Detention

Charas El Bohio

The Stonewall Inn

Third Street Men's Shelter

The Cage

Nuyorican Poets Café

Christopher Street Pier

Liz Christy Community Garden

Judson Memorial Church

CBGB's

Triangle Shirtwaist Factory

Public Theater

The Village Voice

David Ruggles' Home

Henry Street Settlement

Collect Pond Park

The Forward Building

African Burial Ground

Silver Palace Restaurant

Five Points

One Chase Manhattan Plaza

New York Stock Exchange/Wall Street

Slave Market

Standard Oil Building

Fort Amsterdam

Fraunces Tavern

Castle Clinton

Statue of Liberty

1 Mile

Introduction

GANSEVOORT STREET WAS ONCE THE CENTER of the city's meatpacking district. From the 1880s until at least the 1990s you could find sides of beef and more hanging from hooks under the eaves of the wholesale storefronts, blood pooling between cobblestones, occasionally hosed down by the butchers and cutters over the course of the day. Beginning in the 1970s New York's gay scene moved up and over from the Village and downtown piers into clubs that opened in the slaughterhouses and shops that the meat sellers had begun to abandon. By the 1990s, high-priced condominiums had gone up along the edges of the district, and high-end retail followed thereafter. A smattering of meat wholesalers hold on in the neighborhood, but their businesses don't open to the streets. With the High Line (see **High Line Park**, p. 108) and now the Whitney Museum sitting at its western edge, Gansevoort Street has become "glamorous," "trendsetting," and one of the "hottest" tourist areas of the city.

This is a typical Manhattan evolution: working-class neighborhoods, or rough and dirty industry, recolonized by marginalized groups, then recolonized by wealthy entrepreneurs. With the island's space limitations and high capacity for reinvention, the action has moved the other way as well. The early mansions of the well-to-do that lined the streets of far downtown were demolished for warehouses (and eventually corporate headquarters); the single-family townhouses of the Village became boarding houses and studio rentals; the fancy hotels of midtown turned into single-room-occupancy flats for impoverished men.

But today the action of Manhattan is mostly like Gansevoort: a one-way street pointed toward the interests of the wealthy elite. One in twenty-five New Yorkers today is a millionaire, *excluding* the value of their primary residences. While the state, region, and city also rank high in inequality indexes, New York county (Manhattan), when measured alone, easily outpaces all other populous counties in the United States. Nearly a million dollars separates the average income of the top 5 percent of Manhattanites from the bottom 20 percent; the average income of the top 1 percent of earners in Manhattan is 113 times the average income of the remaining 99 percent. These gaps in income are racial as well. Before the Great Financial Crisis of 2008, the census found increasing numbers of Manhattan families with preschool age children—a "baby boom," chirped the local media. The median incomes of these new families were $87,838 for Asian families, $41,351 for Black families, and $33,961 for Hispanic families. Meanwhile, white families with kids under the age of five, the plurality of such families in the borough, had median incomes of $377,030 in 2020 dollars.

Costs of living are correspondingly high. As a whole, the city is about 80 percent more costly than the nation's average, and 50 percent more costly than the rest of

No. 53 Gansevoort Street in the meatpacking district in the 1930s. CREDIT: GANSEVOORT, BERENICE ABBOTT, COURTESY OF THE NYPL DIGITAL COLLECTIONS

No. 99 Gansevoort Street, also known as the Whitney Museum, and the start of the High Line in 2016. CREDIT: BY BEYOND MY KEN - OWN WORK, CC BY-SA 4.0, WIKIMEDIA COMMONS

New York State. The average monthly rent for a two-bedroom apartment in Manhattan is roughly the same as the entire monthly income of the median worker in the United States, forty-two hundred a month in 2020 dollars. Averages in Manhattan hide disparities between the top and the bottom in housing, income, and most other measures. It is a borough of exceptional tales and long statistical tails, of very poor and very rich, and fewer and fewer people in between.

These divergent households often live just blocks from one another—in some neighborhoods, directly across the street. Hyper-gentrifying Chelsea, whose housing prices have doubled and tripled since the High Line Park was developed, is also home to great expanses of affordable housing for the poor in the Elliot-Chelsea Houses and

the Fulton Houses; as well as the middle class, in the sprawling cooperative houses of Penn South, developed by the International Ladies Garment Workers Union for the garment workers who worked in the nearby garment district of the West 20s and 30s. Carnegie Hill, named after steel baron Andrew Carnegie (whose mansion is now the Cooper Hewitt Museum on 91st Street), is blocks from East Harlem, one of the poorest districts in the country. On the east side, the median income of most blocks south of 96th street is over ten and twenty times higher than any of those north. Similar disparities can be found in TriBeCa, Chinatown, and the Financial District, and even within central Harlem, where ever-expanding pockets of multiracial affluence exist within the broader Black working-class neighborhood.

In recent years, great tensions flowed up and down 125th Street as the local Pathmark Supermarket, the best grocery store in the neighborhood, was closed with nothing to replace it, as developers vied with one another proposing different, but similarly outlandish plans for new, more luxury developments. (As of 2020, development plans call for luxury condominiums, with some affordable housing included.)

What does it do for the social fabric of a city to have the power elite pressed up against its proletariat? Shocking as the numbers are today, this is not a new story for Manhattan. The rich of New York City have always lived there, and so have its poor. More than any of the other boroughs, Manhattan can be characterized by extreme variation along multiple vectors. Class and economic disparity have been a constant, but so have differences among its inhabitants in race and ethnicity, politics, sexuality, and cultural and lifestyle expression, causing a *frisson* that is both highly creative and combustible. As much as it has been the city's artistic and intellectual mecca, with innovations and popularizations of multiple and important forms of music, art, dance, theater, thought, and ideology, Manhattan has also been the center of New York City's organized protest and visible social unrest for all of its history. It has been home to dozens of uprisings and riots, hundreds of mass demonstrations, and thousands of protests over the centuries. Slavery and racism, interethnic violence, sexism and homophobia, working conditions and labor rights, poverty and housing, free speech and policing—these are just some of

the local issues that New Yorkers have taken to the streets to fight over, not infrequently with violence. If official ideology contends that New York is a melting pot, Manhattan is where the pot boils over.

Some of its combustible nature can no doubt be traced to its crowds. At the time of the American Revolution, Manhattan had fewer than thirty thousand people living in it. Beginning in 1810, and for the next century, the borough's population roughly doubled every twenty years. By the nation's centennial, the small town had become a dense metropolis of 1 million people, most still living below today's 14th Street. (As locals will tell you, when the Dakota apartment building on West 72nd Street opened in 1884, it was thus named for being a lonely stakeholder in lightly developed farmland, so far north and west of the action of the city that it could take the name of the Dakota territories.) Manhattan reached its peak population of 2.3 million in 1910, 700,000 more people than it holds today, in fewer housing units, with a fraction of today's vertical density. We are more accustomed in today's global metropolises to great crowds and congestion. But Manhattan's growth, diversity, and inequalities made it a unique experiment in social density over much of its history, one that has both succeeded and failed, in turns and at once.

Europeans first established New Amsterdam on the island of Manhattan as an outpost of the Dutch West India Company. The Lenape and Wappinger people who lived on the island had a seasonal relationship to its different parts, setting up regular camps along the island's length corresponding to the health and abundance of food crops and hunting. The island was traversed by a trading route, the Wickquasgeck trail, that later became Broadway. In its upper reaches, this trail brought you to the caves of today's Inwood Park, one of the seasonal homes of the island's people. Lower "Mannahatta," as the island was referred to by the Lenape, was home to regular gathering sites such as the Council Elm near present-day Bowling Green, and another meeting site at today's Astor Place.

The sustainable farming, hunting, gathering, trade, and light settlement that characterized Manhattan life for centuries was destroyed, with most of the people who had created it, over the course of the seventeenth century with European conquest. When the British took over the Dutch colony of New Netherland in 1664, they renamed its main trading center and fortified town New York, and its role in global mercantile exchange increased dramatically. By the mid-nineteenth century, New Yorkers had made fortunes, in banks that financed the ships that moved enslaved Africans and the products of their labor; in transportation itself; in the trading and manufacture of dry goods; and then, and seemingly forever, in real estate. Following the Civil War, Manhattan was the country's preeminent Gilded Age city, with robber baron residents who made their fortunes in railroads (Vanderbilt, Harriman, and Gould), oil (Rockefeller), steel (Carnegie, Frick, and Schwab), and finance (Morgan and Fisk), living amid the country's worst urban poverty. The fortunes of today

are mostly financial—hedge funds, investments, private equity—with media, fashion, and real estate moguls populating the city as well: Michael Bloomberg, Stephen Ross, Ralph Lauren, Ron Perelman, Rupert Murdoch, Carl Icahn, Donald Newhouse, and the late David Koch, to name just some of the recent billionaires who call Manhattan at least one of their homes. They are also international: Manhattan apartments have become a preferred currency among the global elite who spend millions on homes that sit empty much of the year, darkening the skyline and turning their neighborhoods into ghost towns. Viewed from a distance, today's visual signs of inequality, with its mostly empty, barely lit 57th Street pied-a-terre "Billionaire Row" towers just yards away from what had once been 5th Avenue's Millionaires Row, could be seen as Manhattan returning to form: a neoliberal and sanitized version of its Gilded Age past.

But migrants and immigrants, artists and bohemians have given this borough its character at least as much as its Wall Street barons and bankers. This includes the great waves of European immigration; the founding of Chinatown; the Great Migration that brought African Americans from the South to Harlem, alongside their Afro-Caribbean neighbors; artists, radicals, misfits, and visionaries who wanted the freedoms of the big city; Puerto Ricans settling in East Harlem and the Lower East Side; and today's largest immigrant group in the city, Dominicans, who moved to Washington Heights (before heading to the Bronx)—migrations of people who settled on blocks or in buildings near people from their hometowns or provinces, but also amid teeming strangers. Manhattan's historic vitality is the product of these peoples, and its neighborhoods continue to reflect their imprint despite the pressures of displacement and gentrification.

These diverse New Yorkers have not affected these changes just by their presence, but more usually, through willful disruption of the status quo. The first to rebel were enslaved Black people, whose first revolt of 1712 marked a first social movement in the city's history (see **Wall Street: Capitalism and Protest Tour**, p. 342). Abolitionism and its opposite—a fervent support for slavery endemic to this city, so enmeshed in the profits, products, and ideologies of the murderous practice—generated a number of eighteenth and nineteenth century riots. Beginning in the 1830s, Manhattan's artisans and mechanics, at first usually "native" whites, formed some of the country's first unions and labor parties and enacted some of its first strikes. The "mob" was the city's ultimate arbiter of unruly justice for decades following independence, with regular rioting downtown over jobs, food prices, taxes, and laws—even theatrical casting decisions (see **Astor Place Riots**, p. 135). The end of the nineteenth century and the early twentieth century were marked by such unrest that the modern police force was supplemented by an extensive militia and armory system to control street protest (see **7th Regiment Armory**, p. 96).

After the city's unification in 1898, Manhattan became the center of citywide protests, and the preferred location for all groups seeking local redress. Disrupting Manhattan had greater consequences for elites and gave greater notice to media than such protests would carry in the other boroughs: you could directly "take it to the Man" there; it was indeed more often true that the "whole world is watching." Eventually, New York even attracted mass protests of national character, including some of the largest antiwar demonstrations of the Vietnam and Iraq war eras, the country's largest-ever anti-nuclear rally, and hundreds of thousands participating in the Women's Marches of the Trump era and the March for Climate Justice.

Manhattan was the first of the boroughs to house successive generations of artists and political communities, across the borough, and to birth numerous distinct artistic and intellectual movements. From the anarchism, socialism, and communism that grew in downtown taverns and meeting halls, to the many musical, literary, and dance innovations of the Harlem Renaissance, from the Beats to Abstract Expressionism, pop art, and the New York punk scene, from Malcolm X through ACT-UP, Manhattan long encouraged revolutionary and radical expression and action, as many of our sites detail.

The Manhattan described in the following sites is a product of the contributions that people's movements, political and cultural, have made to its social landscape. It is also the product of the ongoing tensions between its haves and have nots, a struggle that accounts for the very shape and size of its apartments buildings, the location of its parks and city services, and its alternating spaces of neglect and renewal.

■ ■ ■

Harlem

2.1 Sugar Hill

555 Edgecombe Avenue and
409 Edgecombe Avenue, New York, NY

If you are white and are reading this vignette, don't take it for granted that all Harlem is a slum. It isn't. There are big apartment houses up on the hill, Sugar Hill, and up by City College—nice high-rent houses with elevators and doormen, where Canada Lee lives, and W.C. Handy, and the George S. Schuylers, and the Walter Whites, where colored families send their babies to private kindergartens and their youngsters to Ethical Culture School.

—Langston Hughes (1944)

Reflective of the "sweet life" on the hill, Sugar Hill became especially prominent during the Harlem Renaissance. Wealthy Black professionals, artists, and musicians seeking decent housing moved to Sugar Hill, a neighborhood of row houses, sweeping views of the Harlem river, and middle-class apartments such as these two buildings. The first, 555 Edgecombe, was home to renowned jazz musicians, singers, and actors such as Count Basie, Duke Ellington, Coleman Hawkins, Paul Robeson, and Lena Horne. Also in residence was Kenneth Clark, the psychologist known for his work on the effects of segregation on children, and the first African American full professor at City College.

Just down the street at 409 Edgecombe lived Julius Bledsoe, a classical concert singer and composer; Aaron Douglas, a painter who is often referred to as the "father of Black American art"; William Stanley Braithwaite, a poet; and Clarence Cameron White, a violinist and composer. It was also the home to leaders in the NAACP, such as Walter Francis White and Roy Wilkins, who both headed the organization at different times. W. E. B. Dubois moved into the building in the early 1940s when he returned to work for the NAACP as a research director. Perhaps most famously, Thurgood Marshall, lawyer for the NAACP and then justice of the Supreme Court, also moved into the building in the 1940s. Sugar Hill has been a historic district since 2002.

TO LEARN MORE

Hughes, Langston. 1944. "Down Under in Harlem." *New Republic*, March 27, 1944. https://newrepublic.com/article/90505/down-under-in-harlem.

NEARBY SITES OF INTEREST

Home of Abolitionist Minister Dennis Harris
857 Riverside Drive, New York, NY
The house, which as of January 2021 is the site of a Landmarks Commission fight, was possibly used as part of the underground railroad network. Minister Harris was known for his unwavering activism against slavery.

St. Nicholas Park
St. Nicholas Avenue and St. Nicholas Terrace between 128th and 141st Streets, New York, NY
In popular imagination, the Black Panther Party started in Oakland, but there were actually a number of Black Panther branches across the

United States before the Oakland branch opened and the party formalized. In June of 1966, local activists David White, Al Patella, Ted Wilson, and Max Stamford (now Ahmad Muhammad), among others, met here at St. Nicholas Park to launch the branch.

**FAVORITE NEIGHBORHOOD
RESTAURANT**

El Malecon (in Washington Heights)
4141 Broadway, New York, NY
A popular restaurant for Dominican classics like mofongo.

2.2 City College–City University of New York

160 Convent Avenue, New York, NY
The first college of what was to become the City University of New York (CUNY) system, City College (CCNY) was initially founded as the Free Academy of the City of New York in 1847. From that time to today, City College, and the CUNY system of which it is a part, has embodied various and at times divergent definitions of what it means to be a "public" university in the United States, especially in the context of New York City and its diverse public. To begin with, as its original name makes clear, it is the only public university that was free to students for the bulk of its history.

The Free Academy was a radical exercise in democratic institution building. In the mid-nineteenth century higher education was reserved only for the wealthiest families. But as its first president, Horace Webster, described upon its opening in January 1849, "the experiment is to be tried, whether the

children of the people, the children of the whole people, can be educated; and whether an institution of the highest grade, can be successfully controlled by the popular will, not by the privileged few."

The experiment was tried in earnest, and for decades proved a great success for the men, overwhelmingly white working and middle class, who enrolled. CCNY was soon followed by Hunter College, founded as the Normal College in 1870, which admitted women, training them to become teachers in New York City's public school system. Immigration and the city's dramatic increase in population pushed the legislature to establish additional free campuses, including Brooklyn College (1930) and Queens College (1937). Admission was based on high school rankings and grades. As such, the system as a whole became increasingly competitive: admission to City College in 1965, for example, required a 92 average in high school. Still, CUNY remained free for full-time day students, and evening and part-time students paid modest tuition. CCNY and other CUNY campuses admitted Jewish students when many private universities did not, but the system remained predominantly white. In 1961, the independent public municipal colleges of New York City were united in a centralized university system, known today as the City University of New York.

Tensions over the meaning and mission of CUNY erupted in 1969, when Black and Puerto Rican students at City College demanded that the college administration create programs to meet the needs of Black and Puerto Rican students. Their five-point

Student Strikers
Calling for Support
for the five demands
at City College 1969.
CREDIT: ARCHIVES,
THE CITY COLLEGE OF
NEW YORK

demands included establishing a school of Black and Puerto Rican studies; establishing a separate orientation program for Black and Puerto Rican students; giving students a voice in the administration of the Search for Education, Elevation, and Knowledge (SEEK) program; ensuring that the number of minorities in the freshman class reflect the 40–45 percent ratio of Blacks and Puerto Ricans in the total school system; and, finally, making Black and Puerto Rican history courses and Spanish language courses compulsory for education majors. The struggle for access, diversity, and curricular change at CCNY soon spread to other campuses in the CUNY system, encouraged and empowered by the social movements of the era. Administration buildings at CCNY and across CUNY were occupied for much of that spring semester.

The student strikes across CUNY put enormous pressure on administrators, the Board of Higher Education (BHE), and Mayor John Lindsay. As a result, the BHE voted to accelerate the timeline for its plan to implement open admissions, which it had already approved, but had planned to phase in through 1975. Open admissions guaranteed a placement in CUNY for every New York City high school graduate (senior colleges or community colleges). Importantly, the board did not agree to the demand for proportional representation at the senior colleges—its policy guaranteed students admission to a senior college, so long as they graduated with an 80 percent average or in the top 50 percent of their graduating class. Rather, all students were guaranteed entrance to a community college. Students with higher rankings were given preference as to which school they would like to attend. As it turned out, this policy most benefited working-class white students, many of Irish and Italian descent, who also had a difficult time entering CUNY under its highly restrictive admissions policy. Nonetheless, the open admissions policy gave greater numbers of Black and Puerto Rican students access to a college education than ever before. In the first year of the new policy, the overall population of Black and Puerto Rican students across the system rose to 24 percent.

CUNY's policy of free tuition was anathema to the ascendent neoliberal policy makers in Washington, who singled it out when justifying their refusal to "bail out" New York during its fiscal crisis. This, coupled with the increased demands on the dramatically expanded system (250,000 by 1975), forced CUNY to institute a tuition policy—doing so, significantly, in 1976, the first year a majority of its students were Black and Brown. The opportunity of a free public higher education offered to white students for most of the university's history was effectively denied students of color.

Open admissions ended for the senior colleges in 1999 with the elimination of remedial programs, but it had a profound effect on CUNY. Today, City College is 37 percent Latina/o/x, 24.7 percent Asian, 16.1 percent Black, and 14.5 percent white. This remarkable diversity is a direct result of student organizing in the 1960s, culminating in the student strike of 1969. Unfortunately, tuition is now nearly seven thousand dollars a year, and the system continues to be chronically underfunded. The budget short-fall at City College alone is in the double-digit millions of dollars. And CUNY as a whole suffers from neglect of much needed maintenance to its infrastructure. Despite all these challenges, working-class students, mostly students of color, continue to receive a top-notch education at CUNY, making it one of the most effective institutions of higher education to serve as an engine of economic mobility.

TO LEARN MORE

Brier, Stephen. "Why the History of CUNY Matters: Using the CUNY Digital History Archive to Teach CUNY's Past." *Radical Teacher* 108 (May 2017): 28–35.

CUNY Digital History Archive, https://cdha.cuny.edu/.

Gunderson, Christopher. "The Struggle for CUNY: A History of the CUNY Student Movement." Thesis. New York: Hunter College-City University of New York, 2001.

2.3 Renaissance Ballroom and Casino

Adam Clayton Powell Boulevard between 137th and 138th Streets, New York, NY

"College Formal: Renaissance Casino"

by Langston Hughes, *Montage of a Dream Deferred*, 1951

Golden girl
in a golden gown
in a melody night
in Harlem town
lad tall and brown
tall and wise

The long-abandoned Renaissance in 2014. The site is now home to "The Rennie," luxury condominiums.
CREDIT: BY BEYOND MY KEN - OWN WORK, CC BY-SA 4.0

college boy smart

eyes in eyes

the music wraps

them both around

in mellow magic

of dancing sound

till they're the heart

of the whole big town

gold and brown

West of the main building of the Abyssinian Baptist Church is the site of the former Renaissance Ballroom and Casino, which from 1921 through the 1960s served as a center of Harlem arts, sports, and culture. Its grand opening announced, "This Theatre is the first and only Theatre in the City of New York that has been built by Colored capital and is owned and managed by Colored People . . . This Theatre should appeal to your sense of racial pride." Cab Calloway, Duke Ellington, and Count Basie led bands on its stages, where Paul Robeson also performed and Joe Louis fought. As the most prominent Black-owned establishment of the Harlem Renaissance, it helped define the culture of that period and beyond.

The Renaissance also gave its name to the first Black-owned, all-Black professional basketball team, the New York Renaissance, also known as the "Harlem Rens." Until the National Basketball League recruited its first African American players in 1946, basketball leagues in the United States were segregated, and many gymnasiums and clubs were whites-only. Ballrooms like the Renaissance, with their large dance floors and balcony seating, opened their doors to the players and game, and the Renaissance became home base to the Rens for twenty-five years. The Rens were the most successful of the "black five" teams and arguably one of the best teams of the century. They won an outstanding 83 percent of their games, including one streak in 1933 of eighty-eight straight wins in eighty-six days. They won the Colored Basketball World's championship a number of times and, in 1939, won the first World Professional Basketball Championship, defeating the all-white Oshkosh All Stars, the (then-segregated) National Basketball Association champions.

After the Renaissance closed in 1979, the property stayed vacant on this corner for decades. Since 1989 its neighbor, the Abyssinian Baptist Church, has operated a nonprofit entity called the Abyssinian Baptist Development Corporation (ABD). After passing through other failed owners, the property was acquired by the ABD in 1991. The church promised to restore and reopen the Renaissance and held the property for another two decades. Anticipating investments, in 2007 the ABD fought against landmark designation for the dilapidated building, assuring preservationist supporters that its redevelopment of the site would preserve the ballroom and the building's historic façade. The building was not designated a landmark, however, and the investments fell through. A different development company bought the Renaissance from the ABD in 2014, and the un-landmarked theater was demolished in 2015 despite community protests, weekly demonstrations, and arrests of preservationists and neighborhood historians, who demanded "Save Harlem Now!" Today a luxury condominium development, "The Rennie," stands at 2351 Adam Clayton Powell Boulevard, with 20 percent of its units being sold as "affordable," as part of a state program that provides long-term tax abatements for housing developments that set aside that minimum of units.

TO LEARN MORE

Gray, Christopher. 2007. "A Harlem Landmark in All but Name." *New York Times*, February 18, 2007, sec. Real Estate.

McGruder, Kevin, and Claude Johnson. n.d. "Requiem for a Demolished Harlem Shrine."

Black Fives Foundation. Accessed July 29, 2020. https://www.blackfives.org/requiem-for-a-demolished-shrine

NEARBY SITE OF INTEREST

Former Site of the Savoy Ballroom

596 Lenox Avenue, New York, NY

The Savoy ballroom, one of Harlem's iconic dance halls, opened in 1926 and was racially integrated from its inception. It was home to numerous drag balls throughout the 1920s and '30s, with awards for best costumes. Closed permanently in 1958, the Savoy is commemorated by a plaque on Lenox Avenue between 140th and 141st Streets.

2.4 Abyssinian Baptist Church

132 W. 138th Street, New York, NY

In the middle years of the twentieth century, the Abyssinian Baptist Church (ABC) was the city's leading Black church and unsurpassed in Harlem as a center for African American self-help and political organization, embodied in the "social gospel" preached by its two most prominent leaders, Adam Clayton Powell Sr. and his son, Powell Jr. The ABC was founded by a group of African American and Ethiopian merchants in 1808, when twelve women and four men refused to accept the segregated seating arrangement in the First Baptist Church in New York and instead established their own. The ABC had followed its congregation further and further uptown from Worth Street in lower Manhattan to Waverly Place in the Village, to West 40th Street in what was then known as the Tenderloin district. It finally became established at its Harlem location in 1923 by Reverend Dr. Adam Clayton Powell

The Abyssinian Baptist Church moved here to 138th Street in 1923, over a century after its founding downtown. CREDIT: DENNISINAMSTERDAM - FLICKR, CC BY-SA 2.0

oriented, and assisted rural Black migrants and emigres arriving in urban areas, connecting them with spiritual brethren and providing direct material assistance, including connecting people with social services such as housing, health care, and recreation. The ABC rose to prominence as it tithed its better-off congregants to expand its geographic footprint, creating housing for the aged and community centers, and using funds to support impoverished migrants, including most notably directly providing childcare for many of the thousands of Black women working long hours as domestics. During the Depression, the ABC, along with other Black churches, fed thousands of the unemployed every month.

Sr., four years after the first of the "Royal King" houses of "Strivers Row" further west along 138th street were permitted to be sold to affluent Black people who had begun to move to Harlem. In Harlem, middle-class Black Americans leaving the rougher areas of the Tenderloin and San Juan Hill were joined by tens of thousands of Black Americans migrating from the South who set new roots in New York during the early years of the Great Migration, as well as thousands of Blacks emigrating from the West Indies. Across upper Manhattan, white congregations sold their churches to Black congregations, and new churches were built to meet the growing demand for seats and services.

In 1925, in an essay titled "The Church and the Negro Spirit," George Hynes described the peculiar functions and challenges facing the Black church in the northern city at the time. The churches were the central social institution that welcomed,

Powell Sr.'s "social gospel" combined invectives against social vices with preaching and organizing for social justice. Powell Sr. helped to organize for the Silent Protest Parade of 1917, the largest civil rights demonstration of its kind to date to speak out against race riots, lynching, and Jim Crow segregation; he helped found the National Urban League; and he repeatedly organized the Harlem community for jobs and fair political representation. Powell Jr. succeeded his father as ABC's pastor in 1937, rising to greater prominence in both civil rights activism and political power. In 1941, he became the first African American elected as a council member to the newly formed City Council; three years later, he was elected to the US House of Representatives, where he served fourteen consecutive terms from 1944 to 1969. Before going to Washington, Powell had organized boycotts, pickets, and civil disobedience in New York City for Black employment and workers' rights; in Congress he served on the House Education and Labor Committee implementing and expanding multiple social and civil rights programs. The avenue west of the ABC is now named Adam Clayton Powell Jr. in his memory.

Today the ABC continues to be supported by nearly four thousand congregants, hosts dozens of ministries that range from economic and political empowerment to youth spirituality to historical preservation and culture, and it is home to the renowned Cathedral Choir.

TO LEARN MORE

Abyssinian Baptist Church, http://www.abyssinian.org.

NEARBY SITES OF INTEREST

Dark Tower
108–110 W. 136th Street, New York, NY
(no longer standing)
Millionaire A'Lelia Walker, Madame CJ Walker's daughter, turned the top floor of her townhouse into a salon that hosted Harlem writers, visiting European and African royalty, and mostly white writers from the Greenwich Village literary scene. Langston Hughes's "The Big Sea" and Countee Cullen's "From the Dark Tower" both reference the salon.

Harlem YMCA
180 W. 135th Street, New York, NY
Claude McKay, Richard Wright, Jesse Owens, and Malcolm X all lived at the Harlem YMCA at some point.

Schomburg Center for Research in Black Culture
515 Lenox Avenue, New York, NY
With over 10 million items, the Schomburg is "generally recognized as the world's leading research library devoted exclusively to documenting the history and cultural development of peoples of African descent worldwide." It is a public library, and guided tours are also available by appointment. (For more information, see https://www.nypl.org/events/tours/schomburg.)

2.5 Manhattanville Campus, Columbia University

3227 Broadway, New York, NY

Columbia University is the second largest private landowner in New York City, followed by New York University (Riverbay Corporation, owner of the Bronx's Co-op City, is the first). These elite institutions of higher education have amassed extraordinary amounts of land, increasing their holdings by 150 percent in the last fifteen years, sometimes through the use of eminent domain. Columbia University's most recent expansion into Manhattanville, redeveloping seventeen acres that will eventually be home to four new buildings, has been particularly controversial. Its displacement of residents in the mostly Black and Latina/o/x community of West Harlem has exacerbated a longstanding localized "town-gown" relationship between community and institution.

This dynamic is neither new nor unique to Columbia. Major battles against the University ensued during its first phase of expansion in the 1960s when it sought to open a gymnasium in Morningside Park, destroying valuable green space for Black

Columbia University's expanded campus, after acquiring land in the Manhattanville neighborhood through eminent domain, 2019.
CREDIT: STEPHANIE LUCE

residents in Morningside Heights and limiting campus access to community members. In 1968 Columbia students launched an unprecedented series of student strikes and occupations, while the surrounding community engaged in mass protests. As a result of these mobilizations, fostered by the civil rights, labor, feminist, and antiwar movements of the time, Columbia was forced to abandon plans for the gymnasium.

Having learned important lessons from the past, Columbia articulated a new vision for Manhattanville: to revitalize an industrial zone and create a campus "with none of the gates and walls that define traditional campuses," intending to frame the development as a public good. The Columbia Master Plan, accepted by the city's Economic Development Corporation in 2008, pressed for the University's exclusive control over the seventeen-acre Manhattanville industrial area.

Ultimately, this Master Plan won over a competing plan developed by West Harlem's Community Board 9 as early as 1991 that pushed for economic development, local business opportunities, and improvement of public transportation. In contrast to the Morningside community protests of the 1960s, which occurred in the midst of an era of strong social movements and were therefore able to halt expansion altogether, Manhattanville residents did not bring the same energy or leverage to their opposition. Ultimately, Black leaders, the NAACP, the governor, mayor, and borough president supported Columbia's Master Plan that yields little for its Black and Latina/o/x working-class neighbors.

Columbia's uptown exploits are mirrored in the real-estate ventures of its downtown competitor, New York University (NYU). The NYU 2031 expansion plan will be adding 6 million square feet to the campus, concentrated in Greenwich Village, 1st Avenue, downtown Brooklyn, and Governors Island. The plan has been criticized by Greenwich Village residents, community boards, and some NYU faculty. The real-estate ventures of these technically nonprofit institutions radically transform the streetscape of their chosen homes, turning great swaths of the city into what sometimes feel like privatized college towns, and straining relations with the neighbors who remain.

—*With Katy Coto-Batres*

TO LEARN MORE

Gregory, Steven. "The Radiant University: Space, Urban Redevelopment, and the Public Good." *City & Society* 25, no. 1 (2013): 47–69. https://doi.org/10.1111/ciso.12011.

Bradley, Stefan M. *Harlem vs. Columbia University: Black Student Power in the Late 1960s.* Champaign: University of Illinois Press, 2009.

FAVORITE NEIGHBORHOOD RESTAURANT

Hungarian Pastry Shop
1030 Amsterdam Avenue, New York, NY
The pastry shop has been serving coffee and scrumptious desserts since 1961. Countless writers, academics, and students have congregated here discussing the politics of the day.

NEARBY SITE OF INTEREST

The Studio Museum of Harlem
429 W. 127th Street, New York, NY
Art museum dedicated to promoting the art of artists of African descent.

2.6 28th Precinct

2271–89 Frederick Douglass Boulevard, New York, NY

After being beaten for protesting the beating of another Black man, Johnson X. Hinton was taken to this police precinct on April 26, 1957. Upon hearing of the attacks, Malcolm X and fifty members of the Fruit of Islam (FOI) went here to the 28th Precinct to demand medical attention for Hinton, and Hinton was eventually released. While common interpretations of the Nation of Islam focus on Malcolm X's call for Black people to arm themselves and fight back against physical assaults by white racists and the police, he also used nonviolent strategies, including attempts to negotiate with police officials, seek legal redress, and employ public pressure through the media—facts that go largely unnoticed and unwritten. The action at the 28th Precinct represents one such instance of how Malcolm X and the Nation of Islam used nonviolent approaches in the fight against police brutality.

On April 26, 1957, Johnson X. Hinton, age thirty-one, left a nearby mosque and met a friend, twenty-three-year-old Frankie Lee Pots, at the corner of 125th Street and Lenox Avenue. At 10:15 P.M., as Hinton and Pots were walking, they came upon patrolmen Ralph Plaisance and Michael Dolan beating Reese V. Poe, who had been in a confrontation with an acquaintance by the name of Martha Andrews. Hinton, clearly disturbed by the beating, asked the officers, "Why don't you carry the man to jail?"

Hinton said he did not interfere with the arrest but moved back into the crowd. Additional police officials came on the scene and began asking people to move away. Police officer Michael Dolan decided that Hinton was not moving fast enough and began beating him over the head with his nightstick, knocking him to the ground. Hinton screamed and shouted, "Allah au Akbar" (Allah is great). He stated that other cops rushed over and also began striking him. Eventually, he was handcuffed and put into a police car, where, he claimed, "blood was running all down my head," and he kept repeating, "Allah au Akbar." Hinton said that one cop threatened to break his neck if he did not "shut up with that damn praying."

Hinton said that he thought that given his condition, the police would take him to the hospital. Instead he was taken to the 28th Precinct, placed in a back room, and handcuffed to a chair. Hinton noted in his affidavit that when he started to pray once again, one cop punched him in the mouth, kicked him in the stomach, and then stomped on him while another cop began hitting him across the knees.

As soon as he heard about the attack, Malcolm went to the 28th Precinct, accompanied by fifty members of the FOI, Nation of Islam men trained in martial arts whose job was to protect the Nation of Islam leadership and its temples. According to *The Autobiography of Malcolm X* (1965), Malcolm said that the police could not believe what they were seeing. The FOI members stood in "rank formation" outside the police station. Residents of Harlem who had gathered at the precinct stood behind the FOI. "I said that until he [Hinton] was seen and we were sure he received proper medical attention, the Muslims would remain where they were." Malcolm noted that the police were "nervous and scared of the gathering crowd outside." Eventually Malcolm was allowed to see Hinton, and, after seeing his inju-

ries, the Minister insisted—and the police agreed—to take him to the hospital. Hinton was released from police custody, but his injuries were so severe he had to have a mental plate placed in his skull.

Many subsequent retellings of this case have romanticized the gallant warrior image of Malcolm and the FOI, thus juxtaposing their militancy with the nonviolent, peaceful protests and negotiation of the civil rights movement just getting underway in the South. A closer look at the Hinton incident, however, reveals that Malcolm X was more pragmatic and more willing to make concessions than the Malcolm of the popular narrative.

Jim Hicks of the *Amsterdam News* who arranged a meeting between Malcolm and a number of police officials noted that there was a give and take between the police and Malcolm. Malcolm was accompanied to the 28th Precinct not only by members of the FOI but also by attorney Charles J. Beavers, who attempted to get Hinton released. In what he called "excellent public relations work on the part of police," Hicks wrote that the police "persuaded the Moslem [sic] leader that every effort was being made to correct any wrong on the part of police and the meeting ended with implied, though not expressed, promise that the Moslems would not cause any trouble Monday night." In an effort not to inflame police–Nation of Islam tensions, Malcolm ordered members of his temple not to appear at Hinton's arraignment in felony court.

Another important element to the Hinton story is the legal strategy. Malcolm retained the services of two NAACP Legal Defense Fund attorneys on behalf of Hinton, and in May 1960, an all-white jury, after deliberating for almost four hours, voted unanimously to award Johnson X. Hinton seventy-five thousand dollars, the largest settlement awarded to date to a victim of police brutality in New York City.

The Nation of Islam was an important force in the challenge to police assaults on Black people in postwar America. It was not, as the common narrative suggests, a group of Black racists bent on confrontation with law enforcement or a disciplined paramilitary force ready to use self-defense when confronting police brutality. Rather, it adopted nonphysical but forceful de-escalation strategies, such as meetings, negotiations, and lawsuits to address law enforcement's intimidation and physical assaults against Black people.

—*Clarence Taylor*

TO LEARN MORE

Taylor, Clarence. *Fight the Power: African Americans and the Long History of Police Brutality in New York City*. New York: NYU Press, 2018.

X, Malcolm, and Alex Haley. *The Autobiography of Malcolm X*. New York: Grove Press, 1965.

2.7 Hotel Theresa

2082–96 Adam Clayton Powell Jr. Boulevard, New York, NY

Established in 1913 as a whites-only hotel, the Hotel Theresa was bought in 1937 by Love B. Woods, a successful African American entrepreneur, ending its exclusionary policies. Black entertainers, artists, entrepreneurs, politicians, and athletes who were turned away from most other hotels in Manhattan helped establish the Theresa as "the Waldorf of Harlem." In addition to being a hotel, the Theresa also housed organizations such as A. Philip Randolph's March on Washington Movement (1940s), which sought to desegregate the armed forces, and the Organization of Afro-American Unity (1960s), created by Malcolm X. The hotel is perhaps most famous for Fidel Castro's visit in 1960, when he came to New York for a meeting of the United Nations. Initially holding reservations at the Hotel Shelburne in Manhattan, Castro and his entourage moved to Hotel Theresa after a dispute with the Shelbourne's management. During his ten-day stay, Castro met with Soviet Premier Nikita Khrushchev, Malcolm X, poets Langston Hughes and Allen Ginsberg, and sociologist C. Wright Mills, among others. The Theresa flew the Cuban flag, and the hotel became the site of raucous street protests, with pro- and anti-Castro groups jostling, egging, and occasionally fighting each other. When Eisenhower excluded Castro from a luncheon of Latin American leaders at the United Nations, he organized his own banquet at the hotel, to which he invited "the poor and humble people of Harlem."

TO LEARN MORE

Hall, Simon. *Ten Days in Harlem: Fidel Castro and the Making of the 1960s*. London: Faber and Faber, 2020.

Smith, David. "Fidel Castro in the US: Cars, Cigars, and a Meeting with Malcolm X."

Fidel Castro talking to reporters outside the Hotel Theresa in 1960.
CREDIT: BETTMAN/GETTY IMAGES

Guardian, November 27, 2016. http://www.theguardian.com/world/2016/nov/27/fidel-castro-new-york-malcolm-x.

FAVORITE NEIGHBORHOOD RESTAURANT

Sylvia's

328 Malcolm X Boulevard, New York, NY

Sylvia's is perhaps Harlem's most famous soul food restaurant, serving delicious meals since 1962 when Sylvia Woods opened it.

NEARBY SITE OF INTEREST

Apollo Theater

253 W. 125th Street, New York, NY

A legendary theater that opened in 1914, the Apollo moved to this location in 1934. The theater was crucial to the development of jazz, swing, bebop, and other genres, and remains a vibrant cultural institution today.

2.8 Mabel Hampton's Former Apartment

120 W. 122nd Street, New York NY
(demolished)

In the early-twentieth century, Harlem and Greenwich Village emerged as the two primary New York districts filled with gathering spaces for queer people, a group becoming more visible than ever before. Harlem emerged as the epicenter of Black queer culture, epitomized not only by the more well-known literary figures of the Harlem Renaissance but also "everyday" people who helped connect the community and lived boldly long before the modern gay rights movement. Mabel Hampton is such an "everyday" figure, whose apartment here during the 1920s and '30s was home to parties hosted by Hampton and her neighbors for their female friends who also loved women—commonly known as "lady lovers" at the time.

Mabel Hampton and Lillian Foster. CREDIT: PHOTO COURTESY OF LESBIAN HERSTORY ARCHIVES, MABEL HAMPTON COLLECTION

In 1923, at the age of twenty, North Carolina–native Hampton moved into an apartment at this address after a friend who lived next door recommended it to her. Hampton was performing as a chorus girl at the Lafayette Theatre and the Garden of Joy in Harlem at the time, and many well-known performers attended the parties that she and her neighbors began to throw regularly. Hampton rubbed shoulders with many stars of her day, such as Broadway singer and actor Ethel Waters, blues recording artist Alberta Hunter, and Gladys Bentley, whose piano skills, sharp tuxedo, and dirty ditties kept crowds up all night in Harlem speakeasies during the Prohibition era. Sometimes Hampton and her friends would hold "pay parties" in her neighbors' basement apartment where they would serve food, such as chicken and potato salad, and guests would pay to take part. This was somewhat akin to the "rent parties" Hampton and others attended in Harlem during Prohibition and the Great Depression, where apartment dwellers sought to ease the burden of their high rents through charging guests money for drinks, which would go toward their monthly rent bill. At these parties, many women arrived in skirts, worn for safety on the street, but took them off to reveal pants, which were still rarely worn in public by women. During a time in which Harlem was "in vogue" with white "slumming" elites who sought to loosen their regimented lives and embrace the "primitive" and "exotic" amid the local Black community, house parties like Mabel Hampton's served as significant spaces for Black women who did not want to be objects of the white gaze. This site memorializes the important role women like Hampton played in creating and sustaining emerging Black queer networks in the early twentieth century that today serve as a legacy to the rich culture and community of "Gay Harlem."

—*Cookie Woolner*

TO LEARN MORE

Duberman, Martin B., ed. *Queer Representations: Reading Lives, Reading Cultures: A Center for Lesbian and Gay Studies Book.* Gay and Lesbian Studies. New York: NYU Press, 1997.

"Mabel Hampton Residence." https://www.nyclgbtsites.org/site/mabel-hampton-residence/.

Nestle, Joan. *A Fragile Union: New & Selected Writings.* San Francisco: Cleis Press, 1998.

East Harlem

2.9 Thomas Jefferson Pool

2180 1st Avenue, New York, NY

Eleven magnificent pools were created across New York City during the depths of the Great Depression—four each in Manhattan and Brooklyn, and one for every other borough. Financed by the Works Progress Administration (WPA), each to the tune of $1 million, the city created jobs by developing parks, beaches, and pools, including the Astoria Pool in Queens, Crotona Pool in the Bronx, Lions Pool in Staten Island, Betsy Head, McCarren, Red Hook, and Sunset Pools in Brooklyn, and the Hamilton Fish, Highbridge, Colonial Park (now Jackie Robinson), and Thomas Jefferson Pools in Manhattan. These became sites of leisure across New York that continue to attract millions of visitors each year.

Situated within the lush grounds of Thomas Jefferson Park, Thomas Jefferson Pool opened in June of 1936, with over ten thousand people in attendance and a performance by the Jones Beach water troupe. In addition to the main pool, the size of several Olympic-size pools put together, there was a bathhouse, a wading pool, and a diving pool. These pools were not just architecturally beautiful; they represented state of the art engineering and advances in sanitation, including chlorination. Hidden underneath the pools were large and complex filtration systems, heating units, and lighting systems. While on the one hand this level of investment in the health and quality of life of New York City residents was an experiment in urban liberalism, the pools also reproduced structural racism and the tensions underlying an increasingly diverse city.

With the exception of the Betsy Head, McCarren, and Highbridge Pools, the WPA

The grandeur of Thomas Jefferson Pool, 1936. CREDIT: NYC PARKS PHOTO ARCHIVE

pools in the city were largely segregated. In 1936, East Harlem was a predominantly Italian neighborhood, though Puerto Ricans were increasingly moving to its outskirts. Central Harlem was predominantly Black. Despite the proximity of these neighborhoods, the Thomas Jefferson pool was almost exclusively used by the neighborhood's Italian American community, many of whom often physically blocked people of color from accessing the pool. Even though many Puerto Ricans lived only three blocks from Thomas Jefferson pool, they were essentially forced to use Colonial Park Pool three miles away in Black Harlem. This dynamic later changed as more Puerto Ricans moved to East Harlem. Power in numbers allowed the Puerto Rican community to stake a claim to the neighborhood and the pool. Even with segregation, New York City pools differed from WPA pools across the country. In many places, African Americans and other groups of color were excluded from using public pools altogether. Today, thousands of adults and kids continue to utilize the city's fifty-four public pools.

TO LEARN MORE

Gutman, Marta. "Race, Place, and Play: Robert Moses and the WPA Swimming Pools in New York City." *Journal of the Society of Architectural Historians* 67, no. 4 (2008): 532–561. https://doi.org/10.1525/jsah.2008.67.4.532.

Martinez, Elena, and Marci Reaven, "Thomas Jefferson Pool." In *Hidden New York: A Guide to Places That Matter*, edited by Marci Reaven and Steve Zeitlin. New York: Rivergate Books, 2006.

2.10 Young Lords' Garbage Offensive

Tito Puente Way (110th Street), 3rd Avenue to Park Avenue, New York, NY

This strip marks one section of the "Garbage Offensive," the first public campaign of the New York City chapter of the Young Lords (YL) in July 1969. East Harlem is one of New York City's largest Puerto Rican communities—hundreds of thousands emigrated from the island after World War II and tens of thousands settled in what was known locally as "El Barrio" uptown. In the decades of Puerto Rican migration, El Barrio underwent dramatic material transformations that eroded community cohesion and power. From World War II to the 1970s, El Barrio was home to the city's most intensive urban renewal initiative, with 178 acres of housing and businesses razed and over a dozen large scale housing projects erected; within blocks in each direction of this intersection are "superblocks" and towers typical of such projects. Scattered between these rising developments were distressed, condemned, and abandoned buildings, and dozens of empty lots. The rapid decline in manufacturing jobs in New York City (a 26 percent decline from 1962–1971) also hit the Puerto Rican community hard, as it experienced high levels of unemployment and left the largely unskilled and low-educated workers with few options replacing the blue collar jobs lost.

As they reached out to the community in the weeks following their 1969 founding, the young, mostly second-generation Puerto Rican activists of the YL were sur-

Trash blocking 3rd Avenue during the Young Lords' Garbage Offensive in 1969. CREDIT: BEV GRANT/GETTY IMAGES

prised to discover that the greatest community problem identified by El Barrio's residents was the filth on the streets—a tangible, sensory sign of public disinvestment and private demoralization. As described in the YL paper, *Pa'lante*, between the projects "there is glass sprinkled everywhere, vacant lots filled with rubble, burned out buildings on nearly every block, and people packed together in the polluted summer heat. . . . [and] the smell of garbage, coming in an incredible variety of flavors and strengths." Respecting the community's priority, they set out to clean the streets, convening that July with their house brooms to bag the garbage. Realizing their domestic equipment was not up to the task, the group went to the neighborhood sanitation depot to borrow higher-quality brooms and were

refused. Felipe Luciano, chairman of the YL in New York City, recalls this moment as pivotal in escalating the struggle and engagement of the YL, as he decided to get the equipment himself. "All I did was push him to the side and went inside and got the broom myself," said Mr. Luciano, "It sounds almost cute. It sounds benign. But it was the most revolutionary thing that I could do at that point." Mr. Luciano said it changed the group's attitude as they were "not willing to confront in those days."

The struggle continued to escalate as the YL's demands for street cleanups from the NYC Sanitation Department were ignored. After several weekends of cleaning the streets themselves, the YL began confronting the New York City Department of Sanitation by blocking Lexington, Madison, and 3rd Avenues several times. The YL took bags of garbage and piled them along East 110th Street close to Park Avenue and then built five-foot-tall barricades along 3rd Avenue, halting traffic. The group and community members then set the garbage on fire and burned several abandoned cars at 111th and Lexington Avenue, which brought out police and firefighters (though not sanitation workers). Later, the YL participated in a one-thousand-person march to the 126th police station, and on other occasions confronted the NYPD for their heavy-handed policing of the neighborhood. Their guerilla tactics proved ineffective in decreasing police harassment, but the garbage service improved, though it was never what it was in wealthier neighborhoods.

—*With Laura Peñaranda and Jack Suria Linares*

TO LEARN MORE

Enck-Wanzer, Darrel. *The Young Lords: A Reader.* New York: NYU Press, 2010.

Gandy, Matthew. *Concrete and Clay: Reworking Nature in New York City.* Cambridge, MA: MIT Press, 2002.

NEARBY SITES OF INTEREST

The People's Church
163 E. 111th Street, New York, NY
This church was the site of repeated occupations by the Young Lords in 1969–1970, during which thousands of community residents participated in social, cultural, and health programs similar to those initiated by the Black Panther Party in Oakland, including free breakfast. Although the occupation ended in mass arrests, a result of their actions was that the national council of the Meth-

odist Church began to provide space available for public programs like those launched by the YL.

Museum of the City of New York
1220 5th Avenue, New York, NY
Outstanding museum founded in 1923 to preserve the history of New York City and its people. For information on programming, permanent and current exhibits, see https://www.mcny.org/.

Site of 1914 Anarchist Bombing
1626 Lexington Avenue, near 103rd Street, New York, NY
The facade of this building still bears the scars from where it was rebuilt, following the explosion of a bomb being built there by anarchists who intended to bomb the estate of John D. Rockefeller in Tarrytown, NY (see **Standard Oil Building**, p. 169).

Upper West Side

2.11 Central Park

From 59th Street to 110th Street between Central Park West and 5th Avenue, New York, NY

Not the city's largest park but certainly its preeminent public space, Central Park epitomizes the pressing, divergent interests and aspirations of the city's people. A visit to the park can reveal its fractious history, its contradictory elite and democratic ideals, and its public and private obligations.

Construction of Central Park began in 1857, with the park officially opening in 1859. In creating such a vast park, the city ventured beyond the smaller public spaces it had helped to create and maintain to that point. Investment in the design, construction, upkeep, and security of the park represented

Central Park rules change frequently, including even keeping off the grass. CREDIT: NYC PARKS PHOTO ARCHIVE

a leap in public planning and provision. The creation of Central Park also marked the city's first extensive use of eminent domain to claim privately held land for public purpose.

Central Park was initially conceived by, and largely for, elites. City boosters, reformers, and social engineers who advocated for its creation imagined it as both the regal park a leading city like New York deserved, and the "lungs" the city needed for reasons of public health. And it was designed with contradictory social functions in mind. It was to be a place where the rich could promenade before one another and greet their neighbors, a favorite urban pastime; and conceived as a possible boon to land and housing values along its edges. But in the often paternalistic vision of the park's promoters, it was also imagined as a place where workers might come both to find relief from urban life and to better themselves. As social reformer Charles Loring Brace wrote in 1855, "One of the elevating influences most needed in our City, is a park for the working classes; grounds where statuary, and flowers, and objects of beauty, should call away some, at

least, of the crowd from rum-shop, and gambling halls, and prize-fights." The park's initial advocates, however, would prove to have only so much influence on the eventual uses to which the park would be put.

PARK RULES SIGN—
GRAND ARMY PLAZA ENTRANCE

Rules governing park attendance have been excessive since its earliest days. Specially trained police known as "sparrows" were hired by the park to police visitor behaviors and the park itself. When the park first opened, commercial wagons were not allowed entry. This meant that the primary private vehicles of the working class and shopkeepers of the city could not, say, enter the park on a Sunday for a family picnic in the same manner that a carriage belonging to the city's elite might. There was neither bathing nor fishing in the various lakes and reservoirs. Initially, baseball and cricket were barred from the park, only schoolchildren had limited access to playgrounds (many working-class children did not attend school beyond elementary), and, most famously, park goers were told everywhere to "Keep Off the Grass." A century later, in the 1960s, liberal parks commissioners intent on opening the park to the people of the city replaced some of the rules signs with ones that simply said, "Enjoy." One can measure the extent to which the park has been "for the people" in no small part by the evolution of the park's own rules, how often and how vigorously the public has challenged them, and how often and vigorously its police have enforced them.

CENTRAL PARK ZOO

This area was once christened "Pigtown" by the *Journal of Commerce*. When most of the residents of the city still lived below 14th street, uptown was home to farms, varied manufactures, country estates, and numerous asylums and institutions. Park engineer Egbert Viele was embellishing in more than one way when he described the future park land: "The entire ground was the refuge of about five thousand squatters, dwelling in rude huts of their own construction, and living off the refuse of the city, which they daily conveyed in small carts, chiefly drawn by dogs, from the lower part of the city." Likely there were approximately sixteen hundred residents in the park lands at the time of the first evictions in 1856. The southern stretch of the park was home to altogether a few hundred Irish and German immigrants who rented or squatted on land owned by others, using some of the land as a commons to raise livestock and small gardens, and use trees as lumber. They worked in neighboring soap and candle making factories, and at least two bone boiling plants at 66th Street and 75th Street (bones were frequently collected and scavenged across the city from its many livestock and horses; bone char was used for refining sugar). Ironically, some of the Irish residents evicted from Pigtown found work helping to create the park, after a mass rally demanding such employ was held during the Panic of 1857 outside the Arsenal, the building that stands on the east side of the Zoo, which then and today served as headquarters for the Parks Department.

Vietnam antiwar protest in Naumburg Bandshell.
CREDIT: NYC PARKS PHOTO ARCHIVE

MALL AND BANDSHELL

Initially built as the central promenade of the park, the Mall is the only intentionally straight-lined path in the park, and an element of formal landscaping uncommon to the park as a whole (the Conservatory Garden at E. 104th Street is its only formal garden, for example). Here, on the Mall, on Sunday, July 6, 1884, over sixty thousand people assembled to hear the first mass concert in the park. The park had been home to concerts from its opening, but the concerts were held during work hours for most New Yorkers: Sunday was the only day most workers had free from work, and the park's initial restrictions against music being played on the Christian Sabbath were felt acutely by the laboring public. After a long campaign waged by Democratic Party politicians, labor unions, and various immigrant organizations, Central Park finally relaxed its rules governing concerts on Sunday. Following this first concert, the *New York Times* reported, "it is within bounds to say that Central Park never so thoroughly fulfilled the object of its existence, as a pleasure ground for the people, as it did last Sunday." The Beethoven statue marks the site of the park's original cast-iron bandstand; the Naumburg Bandshell, across from the statue, was built in 1923. The musical traditions that started then continue to this day, with concerts at the bandshell and nearby Rumsey Playfield, where one can find the annual SummerStage festival running from May to September. Most performances are free.

BETHESDA FOUNTAIN AND TERRACE

In 1969 *Newsweek* magazine dubbed it "Freak Fountain," as this was a favorite gathering space of counterculture youth in 1960s and '70s multiracial New York. Musicians also created an explosive music scene near and at the fountain, described in part as the "Central Park Rumba"—the area hosted regular drum circles with bongos and congas, and other trios, singers, saxophonists, and guitarists, sometimes with transistor radios playing accompaniment.

Bethesda Fountain itself, "Angel of the Waters," was sculpted by Emma Stebbins, the sole female artist commissioned for statuary in the park's early years; part of the funds for its casting were raised by Stebbins's life-partner, Charlotte Cushman, one of nineteenth-century–New York's most famous actresses, and one of the few prominent openly gay women of the period. Tony Kushner chose it for the closing scene of his play *Angels In America*, about AIDS in New York City in the 1980s, explaining, "the plaza,

"It feels like the center of New York City, and the center of the universe, in a way." —Tony Kushner
CREDIT: PENNY LEWIS, 2019

the setting and the angel herself—it feels like the center of New York City, and the center of the universe, in a way." The angel in this statue is one of only a handful of female statues in the park, nearly all of which are allegorical (Mother Goose; Alice in Wonderland; Mary from the book *The Secret Garden*; dancing maidens; and Romeo's Juliet); by contrast, there are twenty-three statues of male historical figures. In 2020, the first female historical figures to be honored in the park joined the men at the Literary Walk on the Mall: Sojourner Truth, Elizabeth Cady Stanton, and Susan B. Anthony, early leaders of the fight for women's rights and suffrage in the United States.

SHEEP MEADOW

The 1960s marked a period in which the park leadership, in keeping with the spirit of the times, directly encouraged the park's more egalitarian possibilities, even embracing the counterculture. Sheep Meadow held various "happenings," like annual Avant Garde celebrations, 1967's Love-In, annual "be-ins," and the 1970's Gay-In. The Spring Mobilization against the War in Vietnam was given access to the Meadow in 1967 for its rally. The increased use of the park as a kind of political and cultural commons came with costs, however, with public budgets straining as upkeep costs soared. Like other expansive municipal agencies, the parks department was targeted as poorly managed and in need of private oversight.

Following New York's fiscal crisis of the mid-1970s, the park's budget was dramatically reduced, losing at times as much as 60 percent of its real funding—cuts that included layoffs of hundreds of parks work-

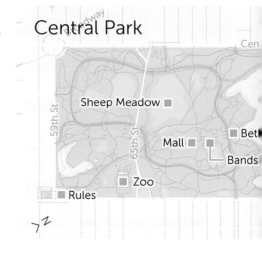

ers. The era of neoliberal governance that followed profoundly changed Central Park's financing and oversight and, ultimately, its workforce. Since the 1970s, the Parks Department's maintenance worker staffing has been reduced by half, and in Central Park almost eliminated. The city has made up for the cuts to staffing through private contracts and various forms of free or inexpensive labor. The Central Park Conservancy was launched in 1980 as a private board of trustees to oversee park financial support, whose primary responsibility was fundraising for its upkeep. It has evolved into the entity that raises three-quarters of the park's budget and is under contract with the city to manage the park. Nearly all park staff are now employed by the non-

Part of a "cartoon performance happening" in Sheep Meadow in 1966.
CREDIT: NYC PARKS PHOTO ARCHIVE

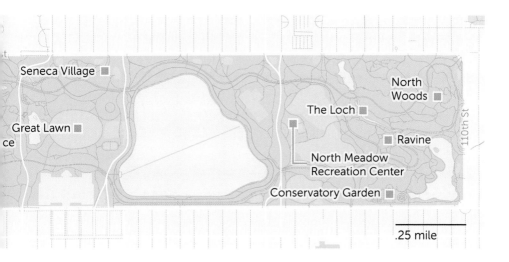

Seneca Village

Great Lawn

ce

The Loch

North Woods

Ravine

North Meadow Recreation Center

Conservatory Garden

110th St

.25 mile

profit Conservancy, without the union, job security, or pay and benefit packages enjoyed by city park workers.

A new, reseeded Sheep Meadow was one of the first successful projects of the Conservancy. But the green oasis came with new restrictions, including no organized sports, limited points of entry and hours, and winter closures. Political gatherings, on the rare occasion they are granted park access, have moved uptown to the Great Lawn.

SENECA VILLAGE

(82nd to 89th Street, West Side of Park)
In these blocks stretching along the West 80s once lived the largest community of free Black people in New York City. In 1825, a year before slavery was abolished in the state, a free bootblack named Andrew Williams purchased the first plots of land that established the area as a homeowning space for Black New Yorkers. By 1855, over two hundred people, mostly African Americans, as well as a good number of Irish immi-

grants who had recently fled Ireland, had settled there. The community, which was home to three churches, including African Methodist Episcopal, was marked by remarkable stability in the ever-changing city, with 75 percent of the residents canvassed in the 1840's census still living there in 1855. Given the strict landholding requirements for Black suffrage, Seneca Village residents were distinctly politically engaged: of nearly twelve thousand African American residents of the city, less than one hundred could vote, and ten of these voters lived in Seneca. In the years that the creation of the park was being debated, park supporters frequently disparaged the people of Seneca Village, and impugned the stability of the community as part of their efforts to justify the seizure of Black-owned property. The city evicted the people of Seneca Village in 1857 after their two-year fight to stay, and the village was razed for the park shortly thereafter. Memory of Seneca Village largely if not entirely receded, and it was only with renewed historical attention to the park and its founding in recent decades that the village has been acknowledged. A plaque commemorating the village stands at 85th Street.

GREAT LAWN

When the park was first created, the Great Lawn was the site of a large, perfectly rectangular "Lower Reservoir," adjacent to the current reservoir at its north edge. In the early part of the twentieth century, debates raged about what to do with the no-longer-used water reservoir: the city, the park, and its supporting associations agreed that it should be drained, but were at odds over what should replace it. "Preservationists," themselves often wealthy neighbors to the park or allies with them, desired more natural, open space, in line with park designer Frederick Law Olmsted's initial vision for the park, and their own desire to maintain the park as a province for the elite. Progressive reformers and working-class park users wanted more space for recreation, including ball fields and playgrounds.

For a few years at the beginning of the Great Depression, neither side got their way, as the then-drained reservoir became home to Central Park's "Hooverville," a shanty town erected in the reservoir's crater named after the president of the United States, Herbert Hoover (like many other such settlements of the period). After making use of the shacks that the reservoir workers had used while draining the water, the unemployed craftsmen and laborers of the shantytown built more shelters on the site from 1931 to 1933. One was christened "The

Manor": a twenty-foot-high brick building (constructed by unemployed bricklayers), complete with a fireplace, carpets, curtains, three beds, and armchairs. Tightrope walkers and musicians performed shows, and Central Park's Hooverville became an attraction for park visitors, many of them likely also unemployed and just scraping by. For over two years the city government allowed it to stand and expand, rarely arresting anyone for any kind of vagrancy. When Robert Moses became parks commissioner in 1933, the former reservoir was filled in, transformed into the oval meadow we see today, with playgrounds to the north and, eventually, ball fields. On June 12, 1982, nearly 1 million people assembled here as part of the Nuclear Freeze movement for what was at that time considered the largest single demonstration in the country's history.

NORTH MEADOW RECREATION CENTER

Though the park initially forbade organized sports, concessions to the needs and desires of regular city dwellers were eventually made. The recreation center here contains basketball and handball courts, and is adjacent to twelve fields in North Meadow, for baseball, softball, and soccer. The twelve handball courts here are a fraction of the approximately two thousand across the five boroughs. Brought by Irish immigrants to New York in the mid-nineteenth century, handball is arguably New York City's most popular sport—"all you need is a ball and a wall."

To the north and west of the recreation center lies the North Woods, including the

Ravine and the Loch, which were designed to resemble the Adirondacks, reflecting the goal of park planners that New Yorkers, who rarely left their neighborhoods, let alone their city, might enjoy natural surroundings. Ninety acres of woodlands and a winding stream create one of the only parts of the park to evoke the landscape of a Manhattan pre-European settlement (though, like all of the park, it too is completely landscaped: there are no "natural" areas of Central Park). To explore a park that more fully realized a vision of natural landscapes with minimal formal landscaping, a visit to Brooklyn's Prospect Park is in order, which designers Olmsted and Calvert Vaux saw as their crowning achievement.

TO LEARN MORE

Central Park, https://www.nycgovparks.org/parks/central-park.

Central Park Conservancy, https://www.centralparknyc.org/.

Jottar, Berta. "Central Park Rumba: Nuyorican Identity and The Return to African Roots." *Centro Journal* 23, no. 1 (2011): 4–29.

Krinsky, John, and Maud Simonet. *Who Cleans the Park? Public Work and Urban Governance in New York City.* Chicago: The University of Chicago Press, 2017.

Rosenzweig, Roy, and Elizabeth Blackmar. *The Park and the People: A History of Central Park.* Ithaca, NY: Cornell University Press, 1992.

NEARBY SITES OF INTEREST

79th Street Boat Basin
79th Street and Riverside Park, New York, NY
Sole year-round houseboat community in New York City.

New York Historical Society
170 Central Park West, New York, NY
New York's first museum, it continues to serve in that capacity, and as a library.

2.12 San Juan Hill/Lincoln Center for the Performing Arts

10 Lincoln Center Plaza, New York, NY

From 57th Street to 64th Street, stretching from Amsterdam Avenue to the Hudson River in the heart of the Upper West Side, San Juan Hill was a center of Black cultural life in New York City and a multiethnic working-class community. It was demolished to make way for construction of the "Lincoln Square Renewal Project," which included construction of the Lincoln Center for the Performing Arts, an expansion of Fordham University, and eight high-rise luxury apartment buildings under the city's slum clearance / urban renewal program of the 1950s and 1960s. The project included space for the Philharmonic Hall, the Metropolitan Opera, the New York State Theater, the Vivian Beaumont Theater, the New York Public Library for the Performing Arts, and the Juilliard School. The Lincoln Center development displaced between thirteen thousand and fifteen thousand people while helping to reaffirm New York's status as a world class cultural capital in the mid-twentieth century.

Led by planner Robert Moses, New York carried out the largest urban renewal program in the United States, accounting for more than a third of all slum clearance and urban renewal construction activity in the entire country. The Lincoln Square Renewal

Project was the city's biggest at forty-five acres (the average size of urban renewal projects in Manhattan during this period was sixteen acres), and perhaps the most influential of such projects across the national stage. At Lincoln Square, Moses sought to expand the city's cultural and educational institutions, as well as its middle-class

San Juan Hill neighborhood before demolition. CREDIT: NYC PARKS PHOTO ARCHIVE

housing, all as a counterweight to mass suburbanization (which, ironically, many of his other infrastructure projects facilitated [see **Bridges, Tunnels, and Expressways**, p. 291]).

Moses's goals required razing communities like San Juan Hill. By 1950, white ethnics (primarily Italian, Irish, German, Russian, and Greek) shared the neighborhood with Puerto Rican and Black residents, who made up about a quarter of San Juan Hill's population. Indeed, San Juan Hill was the setting for the 1957 musical *West Side Story*, whose gang rivalry between the white Jets and the Puerto Rican Sharks depicts the tensions that could arise in such a diverse community during this time.

But in general it was a stable neighborhood, home to a diverse economy and a cultural center in its own right. For example, the Lincoln Arcade building on Broadway between 65th and 66th Streets held a bowl-

ing alley, a theater, various shops, lawyers, dentists, fortune-tellers, detective agencies, dance studios, artists' studios, and residents. It had also been a home to some of the Ashcan School of realist painters—an art movement that depicted everyday life of New Yorkers, particularly the city's poor.

Yet the city's Committee on Slum Clearance declared the area a "slum" by the 1950s, citing dilapidated housing stock and the fact that many apartments did not have complete bathrooms, central heat, or hot water. Building owners had very little incentive to repair or upgrade the dwellings—the federal government and private banks refused to lend for mortgages or repairs in the entire area given its diverse, polyglot, congested mix of New Yorkers.

The federal urban renewal program, which provided funds for slum clearance and new construction, stemmed from the belief that "slums" were cancers on the city, costing the city excessive tax dollars, fostering deplorable living conditions and, perhaps most importantly, blocking new private development of prime central-city land. Meanwhile, venerable institutions of the arts and high culture, like the Metropolitan Opera and the Philharmonic-Symphony Orchestra, badly needed updated facilities in New York's competitive real estate market.

Moses partnered with well-connected wealthy elites, including John D. Rockefeller III, to envision the Lincoln Square Renewal Project. The coalition married $45 million in public funds with more than $140 million raised from private sources for the project. Federal slum clearance / urban renewal programs in the postwar era, including the Lincoln Square Project, thus laid the foundation for some of the first experiments with public-private partnerships—the dominant mode of urban redevelopment and investment today. Under Moses's leadership, the city selected renewal sites like San Juan Hill, bought or seized the land, relocated residents if they were lucky, demolished whatever stood on the land, and then sold it to private developers. The land that would eventually hold Lincoln Center was sold by the city to private developers well below market value because the project was believed to serve a "public" purpose—to drive up neighboring property values and spur nearby economic development.

The Lincoln Square project did not proceed without resistance. Two groups organized collective opposition to the renewal project: the Lincoln Square Residents' Com-

mittee, organized and led by neighborhood women; and the Lincoln Square Businessmen's Committee. Neither group was opposed to slum clearance in principle, but they did assert that it should be accompanied by sufficient relocation opportunities and compensation. Their efforts were a particularly high-profile component of a larger, loosely organized opposition to Moses's heavy-handed approach to urban renewal across the city, most notably spearheaded by journalist and activist Jane Jacobs.

But there was simply not enough housing in the city to provide for the displaced, and not enough money devoted to relocation services. In 1960 alone, the city was short nearly half a million units for relocation of tenants from renewal sites. Sites were also being cleared for highways and public housing, displacing thousands of other individuals and families. Public housing construction did not meet demand. And while all New Yorkers were affected by the shortage and corresponding prices, Black New Yorkers were hurt most, as discrimination in the housing market further limited the supply and drove prices even higher for them. While there is no known reliable record of what happened to everyone displaced by the Lincoln Square project, one survey of the first five hundred evicted families showed that 70 percent moved out of the Upper West Side, their rent increased by an average of 25 percent, and only one in ten moved into public housing.

Ultimately, Moses oversaw seventeen urban renewal projects citywide: thirteen in Manhattan, two in Brooklyn, and two in

Queens, including the New York Coliseum, the United Nations headquarters, Shea Stadium, and the Fordham, Pratt, and Long Island University campuses, among others. An unknown number of New Yorkers were displaced for these projects; our best estimates suggest around half a million in addition to the quarter of a million people displaced for Moses's highway projects (see **East Tremont**, p. 36).

TO LEARN MORE

Ballon, Hilary, and Kenneth T. Jackson. *Robert Moses and the Modern City: The Transformation of New York*. New York: W. W. Norton & Co., 2007.

Zipp, Samuel. *Manhattan Projects: The Rise and Fall of Urban Renewal in Cold War New York*. New York: Oxford University Press, 2010.

Upper East Side

2.13 7th Regiment Armory

643 Park Avenue, New York, NY

"In the last dire extremity behind the policeman's club glistens your bayonet." So intoned the editor of *Harper's Weekly* to the Seventh Regiment at the opening of its new headquarters in 1881. Before the development of the modern police force and the standing army, state militias were the basic military unit of the United States. Directly following the Great Railroad Strikes of 1877, the war department created an armory system throughout the country's major cities to house militias for the express purpose of suppressing civil disorder—putting down

and preventing further uprisings among the industrial working classes while protecting property and the resident rich. Middle-class militia members, screened for their class loyalty, were more reliable and effective at popular repression and strike breaking than their police counterparts. By 1877, the city's many militias had already helped put down nearly a dozen popular riots (see **Astor Place Riot**, p. 135). The Seventh Regiment was the most celebrated of them all, nicknamed the "Silk Stocking" regiment for its well-to-do members and wealthy patrons, including many of New York's most prominent families. By the mid-1890s there were nearly thirteen thousand National Guardsmen in New York City who specialized in controlling street riots; over the next two and a half decades, over two dozen armories were built in New York City alone and militias like the Seventh were called out on over three hundred occasions to put down strikes across the United States (see **Knights of Labor, District Assembly 75**, p. 235).

A new home for the Seventh had already been planned when the 1877 strikes broke out, but state funding was scarce and the militia had not raised the capital necessary to build. But donations skyrocketed following the Tompkins Square police riot (see **Tompkins Square Park**, p. 148), including substantial funds from families like the Astors, Vanderbilts, and Morgans, and companies like Singer Manufacturing and Equitable Life. The result was the country's largest and grandest armory, occupying the full city block from Lexington to 4th (later Park) Avenue on 66th to 67th Streets.

When originally constructed, gatling guns were mounted on the corner towers of the 7th Regiment for possible use against New Yorkers massing below, 2010. CREDIT: GRYF-FINDORDERIVATIVE WORK: CC BY-SA 3.0, WIKIMEDIA COMMONS

Like the castles it resembles, the armory was built to withstand sieges. Its outward opening oak door is half a foot thick, and its iron portcullis (gate) can secure the fort while allowing for an opening sizable enough for men to pour out of the building when on the attack. The Seventh even has a crenellated parapet, which in the medieval era would have allowed for protection for archers as they fired below. Gatling guns were mounted at the corner towers, ready to fire upon any crowds massing below.

The armory's large and imposing form was an effect of its function as an indoor drill shed for the companies of guardsmen, but it also communicated the might of the state and the presence of armed support for the surrounding wealthy neighborhood. Other Manhattan armories near Gramercy Park and in Carnegie Hill were similarly defensively located. These armories reflected their adjacent affluence in other ways as well. The Seventh includes administrative offices and meeting rooms designed by Gilded Age luminaries Louis Comfort Tif-

fany and Stanford White. Like other armories, it served as a recreation site for guardsmen and their families, with a gymnasium, bowling alley, and mess hall for the men to use and gather, and the regiment sponsored numerous festivals, picnics, and community events in the vast drill hall.

The 1898 Spanish American war marked the beginning of a period of military expansion and imperialism in the United States, and the decentralized state militias of the National Guard were replaced with a regular standing army. Together with the professionalization of the police forces in the first decades of the twentieth century, and a subsiding of labor unrest (itself due to a combination of political and economic concessions to labor and successful repression), the need for additional standing armies in the cities faded. Citywide, armories today serve as recreation centers, homeless shelters, schools, apartments and, on occasion, homes to National Guard units. Today the Park Avenue Armory is one of the city's foremost centers for performing and visual arts.

TO LEARN MORE

Bellesiles, Michael A. *1877: America's Year of Living Violently*. New York: New Press, 2010.

Park Avenue Armory, http://www.armoryon park.org/index.php.

Todd, Nancy L. *New York's Historic Armories: An Illustrated History*. Albany: State University of New York Press, 2006.

NEARBY SITES OF INTEREST

Schaller and Weber

1654 2nd Avenue, New York, NY

Opened as a butcher shop in 1937 in what was then still the predominantly German neighborhood of Yorkville, today Schaller and Weber still specializes in German sausages and other specialties.

740 Park Avenue, New York, NY

From John D. Rockefeller Jr. to Jacqueline Kennedy Onassis to Steven Schwartzman of the Blackstone Group, this building houses the largest concentration of billionaires in the United States.

Midtown

2.14 Women's Strike for Equality

5th Avenue from Central Park to Bryant Park, New York, NY

"Don't Iron While the Strike is Hot" was the slogan of the Women's Strike for Equality on August 26, 1970. With over fifty thousand estimated participants in New York City alone, the strike/march was credited with bringing the second wave feminist movement center stage. Betty Friedan, known for her book *The Feminine Mystique*, and the National Organization for Women (NOW), then only three years old, organized the event in commemoration of the fiftieth an-

niversary of the Nineteenth Amendment that gave women the right to vote. Strikers gathered on 5th Avenue and 59th Street at Central Park at 5:30 P.M. and marched to Bryant Park where many more were gathered for the rally that evening.

The goal of the nationwide action was to expose the continued oppression of women in US society. At the time, there were limits on how many hours women could work (as maximum work laws existed in some states), on their ability to own property without a husband, and on access to credit. Women were dying because they didn't have access to safe abortions. And in 1970, only 8.2 percent of US women had a college degree, compared with nearly 36.6 percent in 2019. While there were tensions between organizers of the event, particularly between more radical feminists, women of color, and reformists, they eventually settled on three key goals: free abortion on demand, access and equality in employment and education, and the establishment of 24/7 childcare centers. (New York had just legalized abortion earlier that year, the second state to do so, and the first with no residency requirements; New York's bill informed the passage of the 1973 *Roe v. Wade* decision that legalized abortion nationally.)

A defining feature of the day was its mobilization as a "strike" for equality. Friedan called on women to stop both paid and unpaid work for the day. As she urged,

> I propose that the women who are doing menial chores in the offices as secretaries put the covers on their typewriters and close

(Left) Suffrage Parade moving along 5th Avenue at Madison Square Park in 1915. CREDIT: MUSEUM OF THE CITY OF NEW YORK. PHOTO ARCHIVES. X2010.11.10836

(Below) Women's Strike for Equality, 5th Avenue, 1970. CREDIT: PHOTO © FREDA LEINWALD, SCHLESINGER LIBRARY, RADCLIFFE INSTITUTE, HARVARD UNIVERSITY

their notebooks and the telephone operators unplug their switchboards, the waitresses stop waiting, cleaning women stop cleaning and everyone who is doing a job for which a man would be paid more stop. . . . And when it begins to get dark, instead of cooking dinner or making love, we will assemble and we will carry candles alight in every city to converge the visible power of women at City Hall.

It is unclear how many women participated in the actual strike, but it was certainly in the many thousands, and the event brought great attention to the feminist movement: NOW reported a 50 percent increase in its membership after the event.

The march self-consciously reprised the great suffrage parades of the 1910s along the same route—a route frequented by other movement marches over the years. In the suffrage parades, women of all ages walked or rode horses carrying multicolored banners, repeatedly bringing out tens of thousands of marchers and hundreds of thousands of supporters. Similar to abortion rights, women won the vote in New York in 1917, three years before the passage of the Nineteenth Amendment.

TO LEARN MORE

Dow, Bonnie J. *Watching Women's Liberation, 1970: Feminism's Pivotal Year on the Network News*. Champaign: University of Illinois Press, 2014.

NEARBY SITE OF INTEREST

Art Students League

215 W. 57th Street, New York, NY

The League was started in 1875 by art students who felt American art schools were teaching outdated "classic art" rather than the (then) revolutionary arts sweeping through Europe. They hired an instructor to teach them what they wanted to know. The students still control the school: no entrance requirements; no grades; and, occasionally, no instructors; and tuition is less than 20 percent of other schools ranked about the same internationally. Its degree "for art education" (the only one it gives) is highly regarded around the world.

2.15 ACT UP Protest at St. Patrick's Cathedral

5th Avenue between 50th and 51st Streets, New York, NY

On December 10, 1989, St. Patrick's Cathedral became the site of one of the most controversial AIDS activist protests of the era. By 1989, AIDS was the leading cause of death for men ages twenty-five to forty-four in New York City, and 87 percent of the 26,336 cases of AIDS reported in the

Thousands protest against John Cardinal O'Connor's comments on abortion, homosexuality, and AIDS, disrupting a mass at St. Patrick's Cathedral in 1989. CREDIT: DITH PRAN/*NEW YORK TIMES*/REDUX

state of New York that year were located in the five boroughs. Targeting the Catholic Church's policies on homosexuality, abortion, and abstinence-only sex education, the New York chapter of the AIDS Coalition To Unleash Power (ACT UP) worked with Women's Health Action and Mobilization (WHAM!) to organize a mass protest during Cardinal John O'Connor's Sunday morning mass. Cardinal O'Connor was known for his rigid views on homosexuality and abortion and also explicitly condemned education about condom use as a means to prevent the spread of HIV/AIDS.

In the largest demonstration against the Catholic Church to date, an estimated four thousand to seven thousand protesters gathered outside St. Patrick's on Sunday morning. The "Stop the Church" action was part of ACT UP's larger strategy of employing theatrical, militant tactics as a way to garner public attention. Activists held up mock tombstones and carried signs such as "Curb Your Dogma," along with a giant torpedo-size condom labeled "CARDINAL O'CONDOM." Dressed as Jesus Christ, complete with a crown of thorns, activist Ray Navarro gave interviews to the press, condemning O'Connor's positions and stating, "We want to go to heaven too." Members of "Operation Ridiculous" parodied the anti-abortion group Operation Rescue by dressing up in clown costumes and distributing safer sex information and free condoms while chanting slogans such as "Safer sex is good morality! Cardinal O'Connor, face reality!" The protest culminated with a mass "die-in" in the street. Meanwhile, several dozen activists entered the cathedral unnoticed and staged their own "die-in" by lying down in the aisles of the church during the service. While many of the protesters remained silent during the action, some chose to use other forms of disruption, from throwing condoms to standing on pews and shouting "Stop killing us!" and "We will not be silent!" According to a New York Times article, 111 protesters were arrested in connection to the demonstration, including 43 inside the church.

The action drew heavy criticism from the public. Mayor-elect David Dinkins described the protest tactics as "clearly improper behavior," while the New York Times editorial board castigated the demonstrators for turning "honorable dissent into dishonorable disruption." For his part, Cardinal O'Connor asserted that mass would be interrupted "over [his] dead body," stating, "no demonstration is going to bring about a change in church teachings and it's certainly not going to bring about any kind of yielding on my part." Responses to the action on the part of activists were mixed, as some felt that the disruptive actions inside the church had an alienating and therefore potentially counterproductive effect. Others involved, however, saw it differently. ACT UP member Ann Northrup explained: "We said for years in ACT UP that our job was not to be liked. . . . And we weren't liked, but we forced people to pay attention, and forced change." In the words of one protester as she was carried out of the church on a stretcher, "We're fighting for your lives too."

—*Karisa Butler-Wall*

TO LEARN MORE

Bordowitz, Gregg, and James Sampson Meyer. *The AIDS Crisis Is Ridiculous and Other Writings: 1986–2003*. Cambridge, MA: MIT Press, 2004.

Crimp, Douglas. *AIDS Demo Graphics*. Seattle: Bay Press, 1990.

Gould, Deborah B. *Moving Politics: Emotion and ACT UP's Fight against AIDS*. Chicago: University of Chicago Press, 2009.

Hubbard, Jim. *United in Anger: A History of ACT UP*. Documentary. New York State Council on the Arts, Ford Foundation, 2012.

2.16 Broadway Unions at Times Square

229 W. 43rd Street, New York, NY (former site of *New York Times*)

Named in 1904 for its prominent tenant, the *New York Times*, whose headquarters remain in the area (242 W. 41st Street), Times Square is currently known for theater, Disney, and family tourism; previously it was known for theater, adult entertainment, and a uniquely New York brand of seediness. But it should be just as well-known as a labor stronghold. The Broadway industry is one of the most densely organized in the country, with union membership rates remarkable even for a union town like New York City.

For a century, New York's premier theater district has been home to dozens of large-scale and frequently elaborate theaters, today numbering around forty, but in the past as many as seventy-eight. Having a show "on Broadway" is not about location per se, but reflects the size of the theater and the rates negotiated in the labor contracts that the actors, stagehands, musicians, and other Broadway artists are working under. Tony Awards (named for an early leader of the American Theater Wing) can only be awarded to shows produced in official Broadway theaters. The labels "Off Broadway" and "Off-Off Broadway" correspond to theaters with fewer seats, and therefore fewer ticket sales and, usually, lower contractual rates for their entertainment workers and artists.

Most Broadway theaters are commercial, which means that they are rented by shows seeking to turn a profit. Producers would like to keep costs low; entertainment workers want to receive a fair share of the profits they create. The work is risky for investors and workers alike: shows run while they're in the black, and close when the producers are losing money (or foresee losses in the future). The struggle between producers and the theater artists over pay rates and job stability has yielded some of New York's most colorful strikes; the subsequent contracts have made theater an industry with career ladders and living wages for tens of thousands of New Yorkers.

The most well-known of the entertainment unions in the area is Actors Equity (165 W. 46th Street). Around forty-five thousand stage actors and stage managers belong to Equity, and Equity determines minimum rates for Broadway, Off-Broadway, and Off-Off Broadway. Equity began a century ago with a strike that closed down production in New York and Chicago. Striking actors were seeking recognition of their union, which they had organized as a response to the shoddy work conditions in the field. Actors often had to supply their own costumes and pay for their own travel, rehearse for free, and absorb last minute closures or cancellations with no pay. Contracts even had clauses that allowed managers to fire actors whose performances they did not like. Their 1919 strike included famous local actors parading down Broadway and across Wall Street, picketing outside of theaters, raising money for strikers, and encouraging solidarity walkouts by Teamsters and stagehands. The public and the broader labor movement supported the

The 1919 Actors Equity Strike. CREDIT: COURTESY OF ACTORS EQUITY ASSOCIATION

actors, and the producers caved after a few weeks, recognizing the union and signing the first contract.

SAG-AFTRA, or the merged Screen Actors Guild–American Federation of TV and Radio Artists, is also located in the area (1900 Broadway), and it represents over one hundred thousand members nationwide. The industry's first union, IATSE, the International Alliance of Theatrical Stage Employees (320 W. 46th Street), began in 1893 and today has nearly 130,000 members nationwide, working in theater, film, and television. They represent everyone "behind the scenes" in Broadway productions, including makeup, set design, painters, costume design, sound design, lighting design, and all technical stagecraft. Many are

members of Local 829 of the United Scenic Artists that is now part of IATSE, but had been an independent union for most of its history. Broadway musicians are represented by Local 802 of the American Federation of Musicians (322 W. 48th Street). The musicians struck in 2003 to protest a proposal to reduce the orchestra size in Broadway productions, which despite a decent settlement has nevertheless shrunk by half over the last fifty years. Numerous other unions and professional associations have buildings and offices in the area. The Broadway unions have fought for professional working standards in theater for over one hundred years, demonstrating the close relationship between power in the workplace and excellence in craft.

2.17 Play Pen

Former site of the Cameo Theater

687 8th Avenue, New York, NY

The Play Pen is one of the last vestiges of the once thriving adult entertainment industry that blanketed this neighborhood. For decades the Cameo Theater was located here, marking the first of a number of adult theaters that ran up the avenue to the Adonis at 51st Street. Most of the great burlesque and movie houses along West 42nd Street had become "grindhouse" theaters by the middle of the twentieth century, playing continuously running double (and triple) features for cheaper prices. These included second-run Hollywood films, lower budget "B" movies, sexploitation, and, eventually, hard-core films. The sex-oriented adult theaters, particularly along 8th Avenue, would sometimes run all night, and were frequently sites of semi-anonymous sexual encounters, both paid and unpaid.

These theaters characterized the streetscape of this unique neighborhood, along with the adult bookstores and peep shows for straight and gay alike, massage parlors, dive bars, indoor and outdoor drug marts: from the years after World War II through the 1990s, Times Square was NYC's premier red light district and center for easy vice. A transit hub, with most of the city's subways and suburban transit systems passing through or near the neighborhood, and with the Lincoln Tunnel to New Jersey on its western edge, the Times Square area is uniquely situated for commuter commerce: a perfect place for a brief visit, or to stop after work. Hundreds of thousands of people come through Times Square each week—and, for decades, one of the area's primary draws was the sex, drugs, and other forms of adult entertainment available there.

The sex trade in the theaters and the drugs exchanged in marts were mirrored by robust street trade. Sex workers and hustlers rented rooms by the hour in small hotels lining the side streets. By the 1970s, child sexual exploitation joined the adult trade, with young male "chickens" preyed upon by "hawks," as the police described it. Alcoholic and drug addicted men (and some women) occupied many of the sidewalks. By the 1980s, one had to avoid crunching the crack vials that littered many of the entrances to and gaps between the area's buildings. The crime, visible addiction, and tawdriness generated by the sex and drug trades in the area catalyzed multiple calls over many years to "clean up Times Square," with uninterested or fearful locals and tourists avoiding the area at night and "legitimate" businesses complaining that their profits suffered (the profits of the illegal businesses were doing just fine, though, which is one of the reasons that organized crime invested there).

Today Times Square is emblematic of the sheer power of urban planning and capital investment to rebrand an urban space. The city's director of Midtown Planning and Development was off by over a decade, but otherwise accurate in his 1972 prediction that "over the next 10 years the whole area's going to be redeveloped and, as it's redeveloped, the sleazier activities—the massage parlors, the porno shops, the prostitution hotels are going to be driven

One of the last sex emporiums of Times Square, 2020. CREDIT: STEPHANIE LUCE

ubiquitous description of today's Times Square as "safe" for families now, and "Disneyfied."

But the Disney label goes beyond the provenance of the cleanup. The Times Square that emerged had thrown off the crime, exploitation, and desperation that marked so much of its red light past. But it traded them in for an urban landscape whose sterility and aggressive embrace of capitalist consumption erased the history and meaning, tawdry and deadly though it often was, from the space. Times Square today has an ersatz feel to it, like a place that is running according to script and under surveillance. It may be literally and figuratively perverse to have nostalgia for the old Times Square, but it is not an atypical feeling among old-time New Yorkers, who remember a period when thousands operated outside the boundaries of taste, the law, and safety, often out of choice (though too often not), establishing their own corner of the city. (Quote from McCandlish Phillips, "Chorus Getting Louder: Clean Up Times Square." *New York Times*, July 17, 1972.)

out by economic forces." In the mid-1990s it was the Disney Corporation's commitment to rebuilding the New Amsterdam Theater that initiated the successful redevelopment that followed, including the construction of numerous new office towers and corporate headquarters. Mayor Rudolph Giuliani made the cleaning up of the vice industries a cornerstone of his law-and-order, "broken windows"–oriented policing, and in 1995, the City Council successfully changed zoning laws that effectively kicked most of the sex trade out of the neighborhood. Hence, the near

TO LEARN MORE

Delany, Samuel R. *Times Square Red, Times Square Blue*. New York: NYU Press, 2001.

Sorkin, Michael. *Variations on a Theme Park: The New American City and the End of Public Space*. New York: Macmillan, 1992.

2.18 Social Service Employees Union Local 371

1501 Broadway, New York, NY

During the 1960s, public service workers in New York City won the capacity to collectively bargain largely due to the courageous actions of the members of this union. In the bitter cold of January 1965 the Social Service Employees Union (SSEU) and Local 371 of District Council 37, American Federation of State, Council, and Municipal Employees led a month-long joint strike at over two dozen welfare offices across the city. SSEU was a new union of welfare caseworkers, home economists, and counselors who worked directly with welfare recipients. Unsatisfied with the union representation provided by Local 371, young militant civil servants, many of whom had experience organizing in the civil rights movement, including in the Student Non-Violent Coordinating Committee and the Congress of Racial Equality, won representation rights to their own union, SSEU, in 1964. SSEU brought social justice advocacy to their demands, what today we might call "bargaining for the common good," calling for lower caseloads, better offices, and better and bigger welfare grants for their clients, in addition to salary demands. The new city unions did not yet bargain collectively, though they technically had the right to; in general, they acted collectively and made demands of the city and struck deals short of contracts. When a city panel rejected the union's demands, SSEU voted to go out on strike and Local 371 joined them. Together they successfully closed ten of the twenty-five welfare offices in the city and crippled the ones that remained open.

Striking was illegal, and the city took extreme action, firing the eight thousand strikers and eventually jailing nineteen of their leaders. But the striking workers were joined by welfare recipients on their picket lines and had the support of the community. Their unifying slogan was "Rehabilitation not Humiliation," speaking for their clients as well as themselves. Eventually the city settled, meeting nearly all the demands of the strikers. More importantly, as a result of their strike, the city formed the Office of Collective Bargaining, normalizing a public sector bargaining framework.

The caseworkers returned the solidarity shown them by their clients the following year when they shared the government's complete lists of "minimum standards" for households directly with welfare recipient organizers. Until that time, women seeking welfare assistance were only selectively informed of particular minimum standards for which they were entitled to gain public assistance, including adequate levels of food and clothing for themselves and their children. As a result, their payments were much lower than what they were rightfully owed. Armed with the complete lists, mothers on welfare flooded the agencies demanding significantly higher monthly payments to reach the whole gamut of minimum standards. It was out of this direct action campaign that the National Welfare Rights Organization was formed in 1967.

TO LEARN MORE

Kornbluh, Felicia Ann. *The Battle for Welfare Rights: Politics and Poverty in Modern America.* Philadelphia: University of Pennsylvania Press, 2007.

Maier, Mark H. *City Unions: Managing Discontent in New York City.* New Brunswick, NJ: Rutgers University Press, 1987.

2.19 Colored Orphan's Asylum/Draft Riots

509 5th Avenue, New York, NY

In 1834 three Quaker women, Mary Murray, and Anna and Hanna Shotwell, learned that Black children did not have access to any of the orphan asylums (orphanages for children who did not have a legal guardian) in New York City. They either had to use local poorhouses, which often refused children of color, or be left to the street. Outraged by this injustice, the three women started the city's first Colored Orphan's Asylum. By 1845, the location on 5th Avenue housed 145 children all under 12. The orphanage was considered a model institution, not only providing clothing, food, and shelter, but also education to its wards. In 1846, Dr. James McCune Smith, the country's first Black medical doctor and prominent abolitionist, became the orphanage's medi-

cal director. The orphanage was a haven for hundreds of children during decades of economic crisis, racial tension, and unprecedented immigration.

These tensions came to a head during the Civil War in 1863, when Congress passed draft legislation requiring men to serve in the army or navy, except those who could pay a three hundred dollar fee (about nine thousand in 2017 dollars) to the government or hire a substitute. (It also excluded men who had a physical ailment, were not US citizens, or were the sole supporters of an elderly mother or motherless children.) The legislation disproportionately affected the white immigrant working class, the poorest of whom were the Irish. Years of pent up anger over low wages, bad working conditions and poor housing among these communities were unleashed in what came to be known as the "Draft Riots." Instead of taking out their frustrations on the elite and wealthy classes or on Congress, the white rioters brutally attacked African Americans, equating them with the cause of the War and thereby blaming them for their woes. During the riots, rioters targeted the homes of abolitionists, prominent African Americans, Black people they found on the streets, as well as men and women in interracial relationships. By the third day, the riots had also spread to Brooklyn and Staten Island.

After burning down the marshal's office where the draft was taking place, they headed to the Colored Orphan's Asylum, a symbol of white charity to Black children. An estimated five hundred Irish rioters, including women and children, axed down the front door. While the rioters ransacked the orphanage, the matron Jane McClellan led 233 children to safety at a nearby police precinct. They burned the orphanage to the ground despite the heroic efforts of two fire-fighters, and the children were later transported to Blackwell's (now Roosevelt) Island where they remained until that fall.

The riots changed the demographics of Manhattan. Historians estimate that 119 or 120 people were killed during the riots, most of them Black, making the Draft Riots the bloodiest in US history. As a result, many African Americans no longer felt safe in their integrated neighborhoods and fled to Brooklyn and elsewhere. In 1867 the orphanage moved to 143rd Street and Amsterdam Avenue, as mansions on 5th Avenue sprang up and the city was no longer willing to subsidize the charity to rebuild the orphanage in the same location. In 1907 the orphanage moved to Riverdale in the Bronx.

TO LEARN MORE

Anbinder, Tyler. *Five Points: The 19th-Century New York City Neighborhood That Invented Tap Dance, Stole Elections, and Became the World's Most Notorious Slum.* New York: Plume, 2002.

Bernstein, Iver. *The New York City Draft Riots: Their Significance for American Society and Politics in the Age of the Civil War.* New York: Oxford University Press, 1991.

Schecter, Barnet. *The Devil's Own Work: The Civil War Draft Riots and the Fight to Reconstruct America.* New York: Walker Books, 2007.

NEARBY SITES OF INTEREST

Koreatown

32nd Street between Madison and 6th Avenue / Broadway, New York, NY

New York City is home to the second largest population of ethnic Koreans outside of Korea. K-town has over 150 businesses in Manhattan's garment industry. This small geographical area is home to Korean restaurants, karaoke clubs, cafes, bookstores, and beauty supply stores.

"The Little Church Around the Corner," Church of the Transfiguration

1 E. 29th Street, New York, NY

This church, a former stop on the underground railroad that also protected Black New Yorkers during the Draft Riots, has had close ties to the theater community since the late nineteenth century. Its nickname can be traced to the refusal by a neighboring church to hold a funeral for an actor, as actors were then commonly held to be disreputable "rogues and vagabonds." The rector instead sent the actor's friends to "the little church around the corner," whose doors were always open. The first same-sex marriage in the Episcopal Diocese of New York was held at this church in 2012.

Chelsea

2.20 High Line Park

From W. 34th Street to Gansevoort Street, between 10th and 11th Avenues (multiple entrances), New York, NY

The High Line is a city park built atop an abandoned elevated railway that winds through the southwestern side of Manhattan, thirty feet above street level. At the turn of the twenty-first century, the crumbling tracks were slated for demolition. Saved by community residents, the rail has since been redeveloped and radically transformed into an aesthetically innovative and internationally renowned 1.5 mile-long linear park. Celebrated as a win for participatory planning and community engagement, it has also been the focus of criticism for helping to facilitate the hyper-gentrification of Chelsea and Manhattan's far west side, and for the inequitable funding it has received from both public and private sources.

The original railway was built in 1934 to carry freight above Manhattan's west side streetscape, replacing the 10th Avenue train track that had previously run down the middle of the avenue, where pedestrians were so frequently killed by the train and other traffic it was nicknamed "Death Avenue." It runs through three neighborhoods that were former centers for transportation and industry: the Hudson Yards area, far west Chelsea, and the Gansevoort Meatpacking District. It wended between a building inventory that included many garages, factories, and warehouses. The last train ran on the High Line in 1980.

For nearly three decades, the rail was left to rust; atop its tracks, weeds and grasses grew wild. Despite initial opposition from nearly all the powerful stakeholders who debated the rail line's fate (the railroad, the city, real estate developers), a neighborhood group called Friends of the High Line (FHL) pursued their quixotic vision of remediating the industrial (and increasingly natural) landscape for public use.

The High Line Park was developed through a process of participatory plan-

High Line park has contributed to the hypergentrification of Chelsea, 2018. CREDIT: SCOTT DEXTER

ning and design that included community and local designers. A design competition yielded massive international interest, and the final design was chosen in 2005 by the FHL together with the city government. The execution of these design ideas was eventually made possible by the city: in 2005 the City Council rezoned West Chelsea to allow for mixed commercial and residential development where it had previously been zoned for light industry, and the Council further included $85 million toward the conversion of the High Line into a park. Since then, the city has contributed another $40 million, the federal government another $20 million, and FHL has raised $45 million from private sources.

Subsequent years have seen an explosion in luxury development in the area, soaring values for local real estate, and greater public service delivery. Star architects have designed dozens of new buildings along the new park, and the Whitney Museum has moved to its southern base. At

The elevated tracks along Manhattan's west side before the High Line was created.
CREDIT: J HEWITT - OWN WORK, CC BY-SA 4.0, WIKIMEDIA COMMONS

its northern end, the gigantic Hudson Yards has received billions of dollars of public subsidies for its towering residential, office, and shopping mega-development.

These years have also witnessed the broad displacement of lower-income Chelsea residents and businesses unable to pay the newly exorbitant area rents. Gentrification was not new to the area; since the 1980s it had become a center for New York's art galleries and, further east, a vibrant gay neighborhood, as gay men moved north from the increasingly expensive West Village. The high-end development that followed the area's rezoning and the creation of the High Line, however, has been displacing the earlier wave of gentrifying businesses and residents, along with those whose tenure in the neighborhood extended to its working-class past.

In the first seven years since the park opened, the median price for home sales

in the immediate vicinity doubled, and on some blocks even tripled, the comparative prices nearby, wildly outpacing rates in the rest of the city. The elderly and fixed-income tenants of the neighborhood are particularly affected by the rising prices of the local stores; one of the few affordable supermarkets at the south end of the neighborhood closed in 2016 when their rent was increased by 500 percent. When a neighborhood restaurant, La Luncheonette, closed its doors after thirty years, its owner explained that the restaurant's "hot" corner at 18th and 10th Avenues had become an irresistibly expensive sell; "My landlord's not a bad guy, but how you can you say no to offers of $30 million?"

Friends of the High Line has become a nonprofit conservancy that oversees the maintenance and operations for the park, along with its public programming. As such, it has become an example of the inequitable funding and support received by city parks, and the erosion of full public access to the city's public spaces. The original founders of FHL rue their unintentional role in the hyper-gentrification of their neighborhood. One explained, "We were from the community. We wanted to do it for the neighborhood. Ultimately, we failed." They have since created the High Line Network, an association for park equity advocates and activists across the globe who are concerned with ensuring that their park planning proceeds with equity goals and protections for housing affordability from the outset of their plans. (Quote from *Jeremiah's Vanishing New York*, "La Luncheonette," October 6, 2014.)

—*With Liat Halpern*

TO LEARN MORE

The High Line, https://www.thehighline.org/about/.
Lindner, Christoph, and Brian Rosa. *Deconstructing the High Line: Postindustrial Urbanism and the Rise of the Elevated Park*. New Brunswick, NJ: Rutgers University Press, 2017.
Jeremiah's Vanishing New York (blog), http://vanishingnewyork.blogspot.com/.

2.21 Gay Men's Health Crisis

318 W. 22nd Street, New York NY (now the Colonial House Inn)

In 1981, new reports of alarming rates of a rare cancer among gay men galvanized 80 men from the community to gather at New York writer Larry Kramer's apartment to discuss how to respond. The following year, six of these men worked together to estab-

lish the Gay Men's Health Crisis (GMHC) as one of the earliest AIDS service organizations. During the early years of the epidemic, when there were no support services and very little information available about AIDS, GMHC pioneered a range of programs to respond to the crisis. In addition to establishing the first AIDS crisis counseling hotline, GMHC created a "Buddy" volunteer program to assist people with AIDS in their day to day lives with tasks from grocery shopping to providing basic medical care. GMHC sought to raise awareness by holding public forums, distributing a newsletter, and later producing a cable television show, "Living With AIDS." The organization also supported the Lambda Legal Defense Fund in the first AIDS discrimination case in 1983, going on to provide legal services and client advocacy to people with AIDS. In the absence of government-funded research, prevention, or treatment programs, GMHC's response to the epidemic was formative in shaping public health policy for years to come. In 1984, GMHC was asked by the Centers for Disease Control to help plan public conferences on AIDS and the organization participated in the planning of the first International AIDS Conference in Atlanta the following year.

By the mid 1980s, GMHC had also emerged as a leader in the development of educational materials as a means of HIV/AIDS prevention. In a climate of fear and sex negativity, GMHC helped to popularize safer sex as a way to help gay men reduce risk of HIV transmission without giving up sex altogether. GMHC distributed posters with slogans like "Affection is our best protection" and "Safe sex is hot sex," and offered workshops on "eroticizing safer sex."

From its beginnings as a grassroots volunteer-based organization, GMHC grew quickly to keep pace with the spreading epidemic. In 1988 it moved from its original location in a hotel on West 22nd Street into a six-story building on West 20th Street. In 1997 GMHC expanded to the nine-story Tisch Building at 119 West 24th Street and began providing onsite HIV testing and counseling services. While its early focus was on serving predominantly cisgender white gay men in Chelsea, the organization has expanded its client base significantly, aiming to reach all people affected by HIV/AIDS, including men, women, and gender nonconforming people of various sexual orientations throughout the five boroughs. In the late 1980s GMHC began to actively establish programs and services geared toward people of color, and in the 1990s GMHC sponsored programs such as the Lesbian AIDS Project and the Deaf AIDS Project. GMHC also supports IV drug users through its Free Syringe Access Program. Today, the organization is located at 446 West 33rd Street and provides a wide range of services from mental health counseling and recreational programs to legal representation and client advocacy.

—*Karisa Butler-Wall*

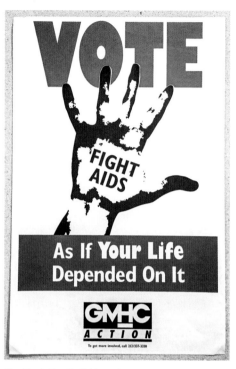

Gay Men's Health Crisis poster. CREDIT: GAY MEN'S HEALTH CRISIS ARCHIVES, THE LGBT COMMUNITY CENTER NATIONAL HISTORY ARCHIVE

Kayal, Philip M. *Bearing Witness: Gay Men's Health Crisis and the Politics of AIDS*. Boulder, CO: Westview Press, 1993.

Lune, Howard. *Urban Action Networks: HIV/AIDS and Community Organizing in New York City*. Lanham, MD: Rowman & Littlefield, 2007.

Shilts, Randy. *And the Band Played On: Politics, People, and the AIDS Epidemic*. 20th-Anniversary Edition. New York: St. Martin's Griffin, 2007.

NEARBY SITES OF INTEREST

Asian American Writer's Workshop
110–112 W. 27th Street, Suite 600, New York, NY
The Asian American Writer's Workshop (AAWW) was founded in 1991 as an "organization devoted to the creating, publishing, developing, and disseminating of creative writing by Asian

TO LEARN MORE

Chambré, Susan Maizel. *Fighting for Our Lives: New York's AIDS Community and the Politics of Disease*. New Brunswick, NJ: Rutgers University Press, 2006.

Americans." It hosts conversations, readings, fellowships, and online publications focused on Asian American creative culture, journalism, and writing on the stories of metropolitan Asian America (including those of Middle Eastern, South Asian, Southeast Asian, as well as East Asian diasporas) often overlooked by mainstream media, and cultural and political immigration movements.

Communist Party Headquarters
235 W. 23rd Street, New York, NY
Building owned by the Communist Party USA.

Chelsea Hotel
222 W. 23rd Street, New York, NY
Opened in 1884 as one of the city's first private apartment cooperatives, and at the time its tallest building, the Chelsea is the famed home and crash pad for generations of writers, artists, actors, and musicians, including Mark Twain, Thomas Wolfe, Larry Rivers, Robert Mapplethorpe, Lillie Langtry, Dennis Hopper, Ethan Hawke, Edith Piaf, Janis Joplin, Leonard Cohen, and Madonna. Such history was largely obliterated in the 2010s, as its owners have renovated most rooms for luxury service. As of this writing, the hotel remains closed, and a few dozen tenants from its period as a rent-stabilized single room occupancy hotel remain.

Union Square

2.22 Union Square Park
Union Square East to Union Square West, E. 17th to E. 14th Streets, New York, NY
As many observers note, Union Square was named for being the "union" of many roads in one place, but a casual observer of its history would be forgiven for believing that Union Square was named for its importance to New York City's labor and radical left

movements. In particular, Union Square is inseparable from New York City's celebration of International Worker's Day, or May Day, a tradition that began over a century ago and has maintained itself with few interruptions to the present day.

Like other parks created in the period before the Civil War, Union Square was originally planned as part of the economic development aspirations of the city government forecasting the city's uptown expansion. Such parks were not embraced for the inherent benefits of public green space, but for the maintenance of elite residents in the city, the improvement of property values, and the ongoing growth of the tax base. To prevent the wrong kind of people from settling nearby, a private park a few blocks to the north and east, Gramercy Park, had comprehensively restricted its adjacent land use to prohibit "any livery stable, slaughter house, smith shop, forge, furnace, steam engine, brass foundry, nail or other iron factory, or any manufactory of gunpowder, glue, varnish, vitriol, ink, or turpentine, or for the tanning, dressing or preparing skins, hides or leather, or any brewery, distillery, public museum, theater, circus, place for the exhibition of animals, or any other trade or business dangerous or offensive to the neighboring inhabitants."

By the late nineteenth century the elite residential neighborhood surrounding Union Square had become commercial, and the park was at the center of New York's theater district, known as the "Rialto." It had also become the place where many of the city's parades and demonstrations began or ended. In 1882, it hosted the country's first Labor Day Parade, which included thirty thousand marchers demanding the eight-hour workday, with signs urging people to "Agitate, Educate, Organize."

In the first decades of the twentieth century, anarchists, socialists, and labor leaders used the park for rallies, dispatched soap box speakers to attract the shopping crowds, and made the place a meeting point for impromptu marches responding to sudden crises. Multilingual signs and speakers asserting their rights to free speech exhorted crowds that "in unity there is strength." Union Square became known as the city's "Speaker's Corner."

But it was the Communist Party that cemented Union Square's place in radical history. During the years of the Party's greatest influence and membership, from the early 1930s through the early 1950s, its headquarters was at 35 East 12th Street. Annual May Day demonstrations— the biggest of which, in 1946, involved over one hundred thousand participants—marched to or from the square. Dorothy Day brought the first copy of *Catholic Worker* newspaper to the 1933 May Day march, describing the scene as "a hot undulant sea of hats and sun-baked heads, over which floated a disordered array of banners, placards and pennants."

Union Square's association with radicalism attracted the notice of the local government, which expended substantial resources policing the gatherings held there, including the CP's International Unemployment Day rally, which brought out tens of thousands to the square on March 6, 1930. The police attacked the rally, resulting in over one hundred injured protesters. A 1939 New York state investigation reported, "The names and addresses of some of [the radical organizations] are as follows and it is important to note that their offices are located around the Union Square district at 14th Street, New York City. American League for Peace and Democracy, 268 Fourth Avenue. Amalgamated Clothing Workers (C.I.O.), 15 Union Square. American Association for Social Secu-

The first Labor Day Parade to march in Union Square in 1887. CREDIT: L. G. STRAND. MUSEUM OF THE CITY OF NEW YORK. X2010.11.3444

rity, 41 Union Square. American Civil Liberties Union, 31 Union Square. American Federation of Teachers, Local No. 5, 114 East 16th Street . . ." And the list continues.

The radical schools of the city were all within a few blocks of the Square. The CP ran the New York Workers School from 1923 to 1944, first at 48–50 East 13th Street and then at 35 East 12th. The Workers School was aimed at training the party's cadre, but more in keeping with the Popular Front period was their Jefferson School of Social Science at 575 6th Avenue, which replaced the Workers School in 1944, and provided continuing education and Marxist studies to a broader community. The Socialist Party had its Rand School in a townhouse at 140 East 19th Street. The New School for Social Research moved to the neighborhood in 1931, to its (still existing) modernist home at 66 W. 12th Street.

In the twenty-first century, the two largest May Day demonstrations thus far were both centered at the Square as well. In 2006, "A Day Without Immigrants," the largest general strike of US history, saw thousands of immigrants and their supporters rallying at Union Square. And in 2012, six months after Occupy Wall Street had been evicted from their encampments downtown, Union Square was the center of the broadest union-endorsed May Day demonstration the city had seen since the McCarthy era.

NEARBY SITES OF INTEREST

The Strand Bookstore
828 Broadway, New York, NY
"Home to 18 miles of books," the Strand opened in 1927 and is the last remaining store of what had once been "booksellers row" on nearby 4th Avenue. It is arguably the city's greatest independent bookstore, with the widest selection of books, from bestsellers to antiquarian, and a highly knowledgeable and unionized staff.

Cedar Tavern
24 University Place, New York, NY
Closed and replaced in 2006, this popular bar for New York writers and artists was known as an important site for the development of the Abstract Expressionist movement. Jackson Pollock, Mark Rothko, Mercedes Matter, Allen Ginsberg, and Jack Kerouac, among others, were known to frequent the establishment.

2.23 Tammany Hall

100 E. 17th Street, New York, NY

Tammany Hall, also known as the Sons of St. Tammany, was the most important Democratic Party political machine to have existed in New York, and perhaps the United States as a whole. As a political organization, it controlled the nominations for Democratic Party positions and, through patronage, many of the local government jobs. For decades, things would move in New York if Tammany said so; if it objected, nothing moved. And while its reputation is largely of corruption and graft, prominently featuring William "Boss" Tweed, there was much more to the organization. Perhaps most importantly, Tammany served the urgent needs of immigrants in exchange for votes for Tammany politicians. It was successful because its members were on the ground, meeting the needs of the community, year round.

The Society of St. Tammany formed in 1788, but did not become a powerful political organization until nearly a century later. It was at first exclusively comprised of "pure" or native-born Americans (that is, mostly the descendants of English and Dutch), but after a protest by Irish immigrants in 1817, and its growing appreciation of the pragmatic advantages of organizing New York's immigrant population, Tammany changed its policies. By the 1850s the organization had significant Irish membership, whose numbers in New York had swelled due to the ravages of the potato famine, and who were by then over a quarter of the city's population. Still, throughout the 1850s, the Irish accurately complained that they were not given access to leadership positions in the organization.

In this pre–New Deal era, Tammany essentially functioned as a public welfare system. Impoverished immigrants would go to Tammany representatives for jobs, housing, loans, medical assistance, legal assistance, and emergencies. Tammany was quick to push people through the citizenship process, and under Boss Tweed developed "naturalization committees" that ensured greater numbers of faithful voters. While this strategy would make Tammany the city's leading political machine until the election of Republican Fiorello LaGuardia in 1934, its power occasionally unraveled due to its own corruption. It was sporadically challenged by reform candidates, who usually ran with the support of the city's more elite media entities, such as the *New York Times* and *Harper's Weekly*. The push/pull of the "reform-machine" dynamic typified New York politics for nearly a century.

Tammany Hall's power was severely constrained by the Lexow Committee investigation in 1894 that uncovered widespread police corruption, including extortion, voter intimidation, election fraud, and brutality. Perhaps the most visible remaining sign of how corruption worked in the city is the Tweed Courthouse (52 Chambers Street). The Italianate style courthouse was built over a twenty-year period to the tune of $11–$12 million (1914 dollars), and only a fraction of the total was used in the actual construction of the building. Boss Tweed used the construction of the courthouse to embezzle enormous sums of money from the state for personal gain and Tammany operations. Eventually, the corruption scandals caught up with him and Tweed was tried and convicted in the then unfinished courthouse in 1873.

Despite the fall of Tweed, Tammany once again rose to prominence at the turn of the twentieth century and reached its peak membership in 1928 with the presidential campaign of New York's Tammany-backed governor of Al Smith, who was wildly popular in the state, with a reputation for supporting the working class. Tammany's good fortunes were short-lived, and a corruption scandal rocked Tammany once again in 1932, permanently ending its hold on the city's politics. The following year, Fiorello LaGuardia, a man synonymous with the most progressive reformism of the New Deal era, won the NYC mayoralty on the Republican ticket.

Unable to make mortgage payments at its final location on Union Square, which it had occupied since 1927, Tammany sold the building to the International Ladies Garment Workers Union in 1943; it has passed through other owners since, and renovations on the landmarked building were completed in 2020. Other locations for Tammany were Nassau and Frankfort Street (1812–1867) and the building at 141 East 14th St (1867–1927). Corruption scandals, the New Deal, and the assimilation of its key constituents, the Irish and other white ethnic immigrants, meant that Tammany ceased to exist by the late 1950s.

TO LEARN MORE

Anbinder, Tyler. *Five Points: The 19th-Century New York City Neighborhood That Invented Tap Dance, Stole Elections, and Became the World's Most Notorious Slum.* Reprint edition. New York: Plume, 2002.

Golway, Terry. *Machine Made: Tammany Hall and the Creation of Modern American Politics.* New York: Liveright, 2014.

Moody, Kim. 2007. *From Welfare State to Real Estate: Regime Change in New York City, 1974 to the Present.* New York: The New Press.

NEARBY SITES OF INTEREST

Andy Warhol's Factory
33 Union Square, New York, NY (1967–1973)
860 Broadway, New York, NY (1973–1984)
These buildings housed the second and third locations for Andy Warhol's Factory, where artists, musicians, actors and other "art workers" and "superstars" starred in and helped to make his films and other artworks. Warhol and his entourage helped to establish the popularity of nearby Max's Kansas City.

Max's Kansas City
213 Park Avenue South, New York, NY
This bar, restaurant, and nightclub was frequented by Andy Warhol and members of his Factory en-

tourage, among numerous other artists, sculptors, art dealers, writers, and of course, the musicians who played in its two-floor performance space, most notably the Velvet Underground and New York Dolls. Today the space is a deli.

West Village

2.24 The Lesbian, Gay, Bisexual, and Transgender Community Center of NYC

208 W. 13th Street, New York, NY

The Lesbian, Gay, Bisexual, and Transgender Community Center of New York City (a.k.a. LGBT Center or the Center) opened its doors in 1983 at 208 West 13th Street. The building was purchased from the City of New York by a private coalition of (then

The Center in the 1980s. CREDIT: THE LGBT COMMUNITY CENTER NATIONAL HISTORY ARCHIVE

identified) lesbians and gays. The Center included transgender people in their title in 2001 and bisexuals a few years before that.

As of 2017, the Center's website recorded more than 300,000 visitors per year and over 400 community groups using the site, ranging from issues of racism to veganism, aging to addiction, youth groups to health insurance. Founded during the early days of the AIDS crisis, the initial aim of the Center was to serve as a "health, counseling and social facility." More so, the founders of the Center believed it would "consolidate the community and give us a point of focus" in the center of Greenwich Village, the heart of LGBTQ life in New York City since the nineteenth century. The founders proved correct.

Perhaps the Center's greatest accomplishment is that its impacts in arenas of activism, art, health, and community building are ongoing rather than merely historic. In a 1987 event at the Center, activist Larry Kramer delivered his speech denouncing the climbing deaths from HIV / AIDS and the US government's lack of response as a "plague," which would lead to the founding of ACT UP, the AIDS Coalition to Unleash Power (see **ACT UP Protest at St. Patrick's Cathedral**, p. 100). ACT UP met weekly at the Center for years, and its guerilla activism would inspire people in cities and towns around the world to form their own chapters. In the ensuing years, other radical and equally international groups such as Gay & Lesbian Alliance Against Defamation (GLAAD), Queer Nation, and the Lesbian Avengers would also be founded at the Center in 1985, 1990, and 1992, respec-

Keith Haring at twentieth anniversary of Stonewall exhibit at the Center, 1989. CREDIT: THE LGBT COMMUNITY CENTER NATIONAL HISTORY ARCHIVE

tively (see **Lesbian Avengers**, p. 204). Activist groups continue to organize from the Center. In 1989, unable to afford a significant and much-needed full remodel, (now)-famous queer artists produced murals on the Center's walls, some of which can still be seen. Most well-known and a must-see is Keith Haring's "Once Upon a Time" in what was once a bathroom on the second floor. The painting fills the entire room and its sex-filled and sexy response to attitudes toward gay men's sex during the HIV / AIDS epidemic pushes the viewer to think of their own relationship to the body, desire, and health.

History is also kept alive on site at the Center. Since 1985, the well-known Second

Tuesdays program has brought prominent artists, writers, performers, academics, and politicians to speak with the LGBT community. These speakers have included authors Audre Lorde, Leslie Feinberg, Gayatri Spivak, Quentin Crisp, Jonathan Ned Katz, Sarah Schulman, and Allen Ginsberg; authors and founders of ACT UP and Lesbian Avengers, Larry Kramer and Joan Nestle; artists Bill T. Jones, Catherine Opie; and politicians David Dinkins and Reverend Al Sharpton; among many others. The Center also hosts the easily accessible LGBT Archives, which includes LGBTQ artifacts, papers, and ephemera dating back to the 1920s. Highlights include the multi-decade photo collection of LGBTQ beaches and cruising areas by archivist Rich Wendel, and the records of all NYC-based people with squares in the AIDS Memorial Quilt: The Names Project. The Pat Parker/Vito Russo Center Library offers hundreds of books and materials of LGBTQ literature. At the time of publication, the Center hosted the only LGBTQ bookstore in the city, the Bureau of General Services, Queer Division Bookstore.

—*Jen Jack Gieseking*

NEARBY SITE OF INTEREST

James Baldwin's Home
81 Horatio Street, New York, NY
Reading books like *Another Country*, one can see the Village as experienced by James Baldwin during his time living at this location. Baldwin was born and raised in Harlem and lived much of his adult life in France, but he made the Village his home from 1958–1961.

2.25 St. Vincent's Hospital

Former Site of Spellman and Cronin Buildings, St. Vincent's Hospital
155 W. 11th Street, New York, NY

"There's a sense we're here for the mission, and it truly permeates," explained the chair of Emergency Medicine, shortly before its closing. That mission, including "respect, integrity, compassion and excellence," had steered St. Vincent's for over 150 years and established it as the city's foremost people's hospital. But its people-before-profits orientation, rising competition in the health industry, and fiscal mismanagement all led to the hospital's closure in 2010.

The last Catholic general hospital in New York City, St. Vincent's was formed by the Sisters of Charity at a time when city services for the poor were nearly nonexistent. Regardless of religious affiliation, the poor, the working class, and the anonymous in need of urgent care were welcomed throughout its history, and the hospital was famous, through its final years, for not charging those who could not afford it. With one of the city's first ambulance systems (originally horse-drawn carriages), St. Vincent's treated the victims of the cholera epidemic of 1849, took in the survivors of the Triangle Shirtwaist Factory Fire and the sinking of the Titanic, as well as those bloodied during the Stonewall uprising and the Fraunces Tavern bombing (see **Triangle Shirtwaist Factory**, p. 129; **The Stonewall Inn**, p. 123; and **Wall Street: Capitalism and Protest Tour**, p. 342). Until its closing, its multilingual community outreach, wellness programs, senior support, and warm accessibility made it the preferred hospital for pre-gentri-fied downtown.

Of all of its model moments in public health, the AIDS crisis stands out. One of the first cases of AIDS, then called Gay Related Immunodeficiency (GRID), was diagnosed at St. Vincent's in 1981. The hospital was at the center of the city's largest gay commu-nity, and it was overwhelmed with emer-gency visits in the first years of the epidemic. By 1984 St. Vincent's had opened the second dedicated AIDS ward in the country (after San Francisco). The unit was in the Spell-man Building at 143–47 West 11th Street, an older building that soon proved too small, so it was expanded to the "new" building, Cro-nin, at 133–41 West 11th Street. The seventh floor wards were connected by a hallway, and together they became known as "the sevens." Life and death on the sevens were unlike that of any other ward. Many describe it as much as a hospice ward as a hospital unit, espe-cially in the early years when there were no drugs, and patients came in sick with multiple life threatening dis-eases; in the early years of the epi-demic, St. Vincent's was a place of fear and death for most of its AIDS patients. In some critical ways, St. Vincent's changed to meet the needs of its com-

munity. Patients sometimes lived there for weeks or months on end and were eventu-ally permitted to decorate their rooms with items from home. Partners were allowed to spend the night; patients were allowed to smoke. Nurses snuck patients out on days like the Pride parade, pretending they had tests in other buildings. Locals would come to the hospital regularly to volunteer—help-ing change bed linens, holding the hands of the sick and dying. ACT-UP hosted yearly Christmas shows for the patients in the ward, many of whom had no families visiting, which included a transgender Santa and Mrs. Claus. Years later, when eight hundred survivors of the terrorist attacks of 9/11 were sent to St. Vincent's, the hospital asked the nurses who had worked on the seventh floor to attend to them, for their "war zone" experience.

As a Catholic hospital, these changes were not made without resistance and contention, especially given the official

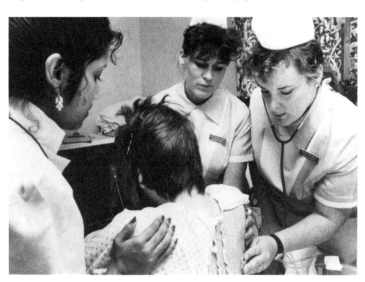

St. Vincent's Hospital School of Nursing students caring for an AIDS/HIV patient, ca. 1982–1985. CREDIT: SISTERS OF CHARITY OF NEW YORK ARCHIVES

homophobia of the church. The administration was opposed to distributing condoms, for example, and hospital staff often did so behind the backs of the Catholic nurses in the early years. When a security guard evicted a man who had kissed his lover in the Emergency Room (ER), ACT-UP activists marched to the hospital to demand a change in policy. During negotiations with the hospital administrators, the protesters held a forty-five minute "kiss-in," blocking the doors of the 7th Avenue entrance. ACT-UP won sensitivity training for hospital staff. But memoirs and media consistently describe the compassion and care provided by the sisters in the sevens.

At its closing, the ER walls were covered with letters from grateful patients, pictures of babies who had been born in the hospital, and protest posters from the many neighbors who'd fought to keep the hospital open. Corporate health-care centers of New York City are unlikely to approximate the care that developed, through struggle, in the sevens, or to once again see the mission of compassion trumping finances as consistently as it did at St. Vincent's. (Quote from Anemona Hartocollis, "The Decline of St. Vincent's Hospital," *New York Times*, February 2, 2010.)

TO LEARN MORE

Eubanks, Tom. *Ghosts of St. Vincent's*. New York: Tomus, 2017.
MacLeod, Sinead. 2015. "Life & Death at Saint Vincent's Hospital." Researching Greenwich Village History (blog). January 12, 2015.
"St. Vincent's Remembered." *Out* magazine, August 17, 2010.

FAVORITE NEIGHBORHOOD BARS

Cubbyhole
281 W. 12th Street, New York, NY
Famed lesbian bar.

White Horse Tavern
567 Hudson Street, at W. 11th Street, New York, NY
The original bar that opened in 1880. It was a center of New York's literary scene in the 1950s and 1960s, counting Bob Dylan, Jane Jacobs, James Baldwin, Anaïs Nin, Dylan Thomas, and others as notable guests. Norman Mailer supposedly thought of the *Village Voice* there; Jack Kerouac lived upstairs for a time.

2.26 Christopher Street Pier
Christopher Street and Hudson River Park, New York, NY

"It's a place where I can be myself." This refrain, describing the "queer pier," is repeated across the decades, from drag queens in the 1960s to LGBTQ youth of color decades into the twenty-first century. Cut off from the rest of the island by the then-elevated West Side Highway, the working waterfront had long been an area where various "vices" were tolerated, including sex work and drug use, and had been a cruising spot for gay men since World War I. By the dawn of the movements for gay and sexual liberation, the abandoned piers had become gathering spots for gay men and drag queens to cruise openly and proudly. They were places for sunning, partying, and relaxing; and artists painted vast murals on the decaying containers and pier buildings that littered Piers 45, 46, 48, and 51 along the Hudson. These structures gave shelter to those seeking

Sunbathing on the piers during the 1970s, photographed by Leonard Fink. CREDIT:
LEONARD FINK ARCHIVE/THE LGBT COMMUNITY CENTER NATIONAL HISTORY ARCHIVE

that then thrived on the street and along the piers, and they were increasingly not welcome in the largely white and now gentrified West Village. New fissures opened up between the increasingly wealthier gay and straight Village residents and the "bridge and tunnel" working-class queer youth who were attracted to the pier and the street for its relative tolerance and acceptance.

anonymous sex or a place where they could bring or find lovers, free from the eyes of the largely homophobic straight world where many lived closeted existences. "Free" took on many meanings: free to be out, free to dress in drag, free to not dress at all (on sunny days, hundreds of naked men could be found on the piers). And the piers were also literally free: you didn't need to pay an entrance fee or buy a drink, you didn't need to know someone or have an invitation. Homeless gay youth gravitated toward the piers, living there or spending their days there. Pier 45, known as the Christopher Street pier, was the epicenter of this physically secluded yet open and embracing gay community.

The AIDS epidemic drastically curtailed sexual activity along the piers during the 1980s. But by the mid-1990s, with crime falling, the epidemic stabilizing, and more surviving, the area rebounded. Black and Latino/a/x youth dominated the queer scene

While the Christopher Street pier remained a community space for queer and trans youth of color into the 2010s, it did so under the extreme stress of privatization and gentrification. In 2001 the piers were shut down and renovated as part of the establishment of the Hudson River Park. When Christopher Street Pier reopened in 2003 it remained a mecca for gay and trans youth, particularly youth of color. But the sanitized and landscaped piers now had a curfew, and their affluent neighbors complained about the loud crowds that gathered, especially when the park closed at 1 A.M.

In 2000, LGBT youth founded FIERCE (Fabulous Independent Educated Radicals for Community Empowerment) to ensure that the youth of color and homeless youth who used the piers would continue to be represented in the planning process for the park's renovations and the plans for the

Pier 45 in 2020. CREDIT: PENNY LEWIS

community. FIERCE maintained its agitation for twenty-four-hour homeless services and youth services in the neighborhood, and fought for later hours for the piers so that the young people who gathered there could leave and return across the night.

While the West Village has lost many of its gay tenants as housing prices continue to rise and wealth is the common factor among residents, the gay community that remains in lower Manhattan is also typically affluent, and out of the closet, and has less need for a place like the piers than do the working-class youth from around the city who more often cannot express their sexual or gender identities in their everyday lives. Unsurprisingly, the extreme gentrification of the Hudson River Park, the Village, and neighboring Chelsea has made it impossible for FIERCE and similar groups to maintain physical presence in the neighborhood: after fifteen years, high rents forced FIERCE to leave the borough; the renovated pier is now largely an unremarkable stretch of park.

TO LEARN MORE

"Greenwich Village Waterfront." n.d. NYC LGBT Historic Sites Project. Accessed August 19, 2020. https://www.nyclgbtsites.org/site/greenwich-village-waterfront-and-the-christopher-street-pier/.

NEARBY SITES OF INTEREST

Former Sites of STAR House(s)
640 W. 12th Street, New York, NY
(also 211 Eldridge Street; 213 E. 2nd Street)
STAR (Street Transgender Action Revolutionaries) was founded by Sylvia Rivera and Marsha P. Johnson in 1970 as a way to house LGBTQ youth who were and continue to be a vulnerable population in New York City. Sylvia and Marsha started STAR house out of their own living quarters: they would rent hotel rooms and try to house as many homeless LGBTQ young people as possible.

Westbeth Artist Housing
55 Bethune Street, New York, NY
This former headquarters of Bell Telephone Laboratories was converted in 1968 into affordable housing for artists.

2.27 The Stonewall Inn
53 Christopher Street New York, NY
"Do you think homosexuals are revolting? You bet your sweet ass we are." In the summer of 1969, these provocative flyers could be found in the neighborhood surrounding the Stonewall Inn, where conventional wisdom teaches that the modern gay rights movement was born.

On June 28, 1969, police raided the Stonewall Inn for the second time that week, a common practice in American cities at that time. Although homosexuality was already

First Christopher Street Liberation Day, commemorating the anniversary of Stonewall in 1970. The annual marches that followed became known as Pride. CREDIT: LEONARD FINK ARCHIVE/THE LGBT COMMUNITY CENTER NATIONAL HISTORY ARCHIVE

themselves in the bar where protestors cut the phone lines, preventing them from calling for backup (among those trapped inside was a *Village Voice* reporter, who would later recount these details). The crowd outside grew to hundreds, and one group tore a parking meter out of the ground and used it as a battering ram against the bar's door where officers were trapped.

This was not the first time LGBTQ people rebelled against police or the first place people organized for "gay rights." But it was the first time a rebellion was commemorated and celebrated by the larger, growing movement for gay liberation. As sociologists Elizabeth Armstrong and Suzanna Crage argue, "While Stonewall was not the first riot, Stonewall activists were the first to claim to be first," and it was the right time and place to claim this honor. Activists in New York, Chicago, San Francisco, and Los Angeles coalesced to organize the first gay pride parades the following year, in 1970, to mark the anniversary of the Stonewall riot. The idea that Stonewall sparked the modern LGBTQ rights movement was a kind of origin story created by Stonewall activists and embraced by the larger liberation movement, with a collective goal of growth.

The sculpture "Gay Liberation" by George Segal, featuring four bronze fig-

legal in New York State by the 1960s, the NYPD enforced both formal and informal laws that targeted the LGBTQ community, such as the 3 Piece Rule, which required that people wear at least three articles of "gender appropriate" clothing while in public, or risk going to jail. Police frequently raided LGBTQ bars to enforce the 3 Piece Rule, and in the case of Stonewall, to cripple the Mafia-owned business despite their regular bribes to police.

When the NYPD raided the Stonewall just after 1 A.M. on June 28th, patrons fought back. They threw coins at the police, yelling "Here's your pay off." Sylvia Rivera, a transgender "street queen" leaving the bar, joined the crowd gathering outside and threw the first bottle. A police car was turned over, and people began to un-arrest each other. The police, vastly outnumbered, barricaded

ures painted in white lacquer, was erected across the street from Stonewall in Christopher Park in 1992 as part of the Stonewall National Monument, designated as such by President Barack Obama in 2016. The statues have been critiqued for sanitizing and whitening a struggle that was largely led by queer and trans people of color. To redress this erasure the city is erecting statues of Marsha P. Johnson and Silvia Rivera at nearby Ruth Wittenberg Triangle.

—*With Julieta Salgado*

TO LEARN MORE

Carter, David. *Stonewall: The Riots That Sparked the Gay Revolution.* New York: St. Martin's Griffin, 2010.

Duberman, Martin. *Stonewall: The Definitive Story of the LGBTQ Rights Uprising That Changed America.* Revised edition. New York: Plume, 2019.

Baumann, Jason, Edmund White, and New York Public Library, eds. *The Stonewall Reader.* New York: Penguin Books, 2019.

FAVORITE NEIGHBORHOOD BARS

Julius'
159 W. 10th Street, New York, NY

One of the oldest gay bars in New York City, it is famous for the pre-Stonewall 1966 "sip in" organized by the Mattachine Society that protested the New York's liquor authority's policy of revoking the licenses of bars that served gay men and lesbians.

Marie's Crisis Cafe
59 Grove Street, New York, NY

An 1850's brothel turned gay piano bar, Marie's Crisis was named for its first owner, Austrian singer Marie DuMont, and for Thomas Paine's

series of articles, *The American Crisis*, which gives the bar its slogan: "The world is my country, to do good is my religion, and all mankind are my brethren."

Greenwich Village

2.28 Women's House of Detention/Jefferson Market Library and Garden

425 6th Avenue, New York, NY

For over a century, the triangular corners of 6th Avenue, West 10th Street, and Greenwich Avenue have been the site of numerous emblematic city institutions: a market, a courthouse, a jail, and today, a library and garden. Beginning in the 1830s, the sheds of Jefferson Market sold poultry, fish, and other goods alongside a fire lookout tower and jailhouse on the edge of two neighborhoods: the up and coming Washington Square, and the more impoverished area to the west. In an early instance of urban renewal, the structures on the block were replaced in the 1870s by a district courthouse (the current library), a larger jail, and an enclosed market. The courthouse, designed in part by Calvert Vaux, one of the architects of Central Park, was considered among the most beautiful buildings in the city, and a visit to the library today confirms that impression. Fifty years later, the market and jail were replaced by the Women's House of Detention, an imposing structure of eleven stories sitting atop today's garden that dominated the street until 1974.

The Women's House of Detention was infamous. During its Depression era

When the library was a courthouse, photographed by Berenice Abbott in the 1930s. CREDIT: BERENICE ABBOTT, COURTESY OF THE NEW YORK PUBLIC LIBRARY DIGITAL COLLECTIONS

inaugural years, it was described as a "luxury" model jail, where, unusually for the time, its "prisoners" were to be described as "inmates." Artwork for the jail included a Works Progress Administration fresco titled "Cycle of a Woman's Life" by Lucienne Bloch, who had apprenticed to Diego Rivera. Bloch depicted a working class, interracial community where mothers watched their children at play; in later years, the "House of D" was also known ironically as "the playground" by the women imprisoned in its halls. In the decades of its operation, the densely settled neighborhood heard the cries of the women inside, in particular from the fourth floor psychiatric ward. The families, friends, pushers, pimps, and lawyers of the jailed gathered outside at all hours to visit or to communicate by yell-

ing back and forth with the women inside; when writer Grace Paley was jailed there for an antiwar protest, she watched her children go to school from the windows. Numerous political prisoners were held here, including Ethel Rosenberg, wrongly accused of (and eventually executed for) atomic espionage; other Vietnam antiwar protesters including feminist Andrea Dworkin; and Afeni Shakur, a member of the Black Panthers and mother of Tupac Shakur. Shakur was indicted along with twenty-one other members of the Party for plotting to bomb the New York Botanical Garden, department stores, and police stations. After successfully defending her own case, she was let out on bail. Angela Davis was also held there for two months in 1970. By that time, the local jails of New York were overflowing, typically holding twice the number of inmates they had been designed to imprison. With increasing numbers of political prisoners and radicalized inmates, those years saw a dramatic uptick in jailhouse organizing, including hunger strikes and hostage-taking. Neighborhood jails were easy targets for street protests, and the imprisonment of women like Shakur and Davis catalyzed thousands to march and rally outside their doors. The city's objective became to remove the prisoners from the heart of the city, effectively isolating them from their external supports and removing their treatment from the public eye.

During this period stories of rampant abuse within the jail were making their way out to the public. Dworkin and a friend testified to violent body cavity searches by the jail's doctors, treatment that had been the norm for years among the jail's mostly poor, Black, and Brown prisoners; in 1967 sociologist Sara Harris published *Hellhole: The Shocking Story of the Inmates and Life in the New York City House of Detention for Women*, whose interviews confirmed stories like Dworkin's and told many more. Following a grand jury investigation, the women at the House of Detention were

Basketball at The Cage in the West Village, 2017. CREDIT: SCOTT DEXTER

transferred to a new facility on the growing Rikers Island in 1971, and the building was eventually razed, replaced by the community-run city garden that local residents had successfully agitated for (see **Islands**, p. 189; and **Liz Christy Bowery Houston Community Garden**, p. 146).

TO LEARN MORE

Harris, Sara. *Hellhole: The Shocking Story of the Inmates and Life in the New York City House of Detention for Women*. New York: Dutton, 1967.

Oral History of Jay London Toole, *Digital Transgender Archive*, New York Public Library, https://www.digitaltransgenderarchive.net/.

2.29 The Cage

320 6th Avenue, New York, NY

This basketball court is legendary to New Yorkers and basketball fans all over the world for featuring some of the best and most competitive street basketball in New York City and beyond. It hosts the West 4th Summer Pro-Classic League, the oldest summer basketball program in the city. Over the years, hundreds of thousands of spectators have lined the chain-linked fences that surround the nearly half-regulation-size-court (hence, "The Cage") to watch its signature brand of street basketball, which is more physical and less structured than traditional basketball.

The first game was played at The Cage in 1950, but it gained real notoriety after limousine driver Kenny Graham founded the West 4th Summer Pro-Classic League in the 1970s and began hosting it here. Dozens of professional basketball players earned their stripes on the West 4th courts, including Anthony Mason, Mario Elie, Stephon Marbury, Rod Strickland, Jayson Williams, and Smush Parker, and the court has hosted celebrity pickups. But its real significance comes from the hundreds of thousands of street basketball players throughout New York City that have carved out a globally influential signature style of play inside its walls. Games are year-round, but the court is more crowded in the warmer months. To enter the game, sign your name to the list, and claim your spot.

TO LEARN MORE

Martindale, Wight, Jr. *Inside the Cage: A Season at W. 4th Street's Legendary Tournament*. New York: Simon Spotlight Entertainment, 2005.

FAVORITE NEIGHBORHOOD BARS/RESTAURANTS

Henrietta Hudson's
438 Hudson Street, New York, NY
Oldest lesbian bar in the city.

2.30 Judson Memorial Church

55 Washington Square South, New York, NY

The stately Judson Memorial Church was built in 1890, a period of significant transition in New York City. Washington Square Park, the Church's front yard, served as a dividing line between the elites who were increasingly moving north of the park, and the working-class immigrant populations who lived south of the park. Edward Judson, the founder of the Church, envisioned it as a space to serve the growing Italian immigrant population through health, nutrition, education, and religious training. At the same time, the Church was designed to appeal to the aesthetics of the wealthy, and was backed by John D. Rockefeller. Edward's dream was to bring the wealthy and the poor together through a common religious bond. It soon became apparent, however, that while the wealthy were happy to finance the Church, they were not interested in attending the same church as poor immigrants. Judson nonetheless continued his dream to serve immigrant populations. Ahead of its time, the Church ran a health center, dental clinic, and settlement house, and became known for its interest in social justice. In the 1950s and '60s, Judson Memorial had become active in the civil rights movement, created a counseling program

Black Lives Matter Protest at Washington Square Park with Judson Memorial Church in the background.
CREDIT: EDENPICTURES, CC BY 2.0, FLICKR

for drug addicts, provided abortion counseling and referrals before abortions were legal, and played a pivotal role in the free speech movements of the time.

Perhaps most famously, Judson was at the center of the Beatnik Riot of 1961. On March 27, then City Parks Commissioner Newbold Morris issued a ban on musicians' permits for Washington Square Park. Since the 1940s, folk musicians like Pete Seeger and Woody Guthrie had played in the park, but Morris wanted the park to mirror high culture, rather than what was perceived as low-brow, riffraff music. On April 9, 1961, thousands flooded Washington Square Park to protest the ban. Among them was Judson's senior pastor, Reverend Howard Moody, who helped organize the protest and subsequently created the "Right to Sing" committee after dozens of people were arrested. After six weeks of protests the ban was reversed—a huge victory for free speech in New York City.

Judson Memorial has continued its activist legacy to this day. In the 1980s it was one of a few churches to acknowledge the AIDS crisis and provided funerals for those who had died of AIDS and whose families had been turned away from other churches. It was also one of the first churches to provide relief to the families of the restaurant workers who died on 9/11. Most recently, the church has taken a leadership role in the sanctuary movement for immigrants.

TO LEARN MORE

"Judson Memorial Church." n.d. Judson Memorial Church. Accessed August 19, 2020. https://www.judson.org.

Petrus, Stephen, and Ronald D. Cohen. *Folk City: New York and the American Folk Music Revival.* New York: Oxford University Press, 2015.

NEARBY SITES OF INTEREST

The Tamiment Library and Robert F. Wagner Archives
Bobst Library, NYU
70 Washington Square South, New York, NY
A treasure for researchers, one of the country's leading archives of the US left and labor movement.

2.31 Triangle Shirtwaist Factory

23–29 Washington Place, New York, NY (now Brown Building at New York University)

On the afternoon of March 25, 1911, a fire erupted on the eighth floor of the Triangle Shirtwaist Factory. One hundred and forty-six workers, the vast majority of whom were young Italian and Jewish immigrant women, lost their lives. To this day, it continues to be one of the worst industrial disasters in US history, yet one that galvanized a generation of workplace activists and helped push through unprecedented labor and health and safety legislation.

In the early twentieth century, garment was New York City's leading industry. The work was sex-segregated, with men typically employed in higher skilled jobs, such as cutting or pressing, while women sewed. By the early twentieth century, the home-based "sweating" system, which consisted largely of small family-based shops doing piece-work, had largely given way to larger shops, with many girls on many machines. In the

The Triangle Shirtwaist Factory on fire, March 25, 1911. Today the Asch building is part of the NYU campus.
CREDIT: NEW YORK WORLD 3/26/1911

before the fire, on November 22, 1909, a meeting was called at Cooper Union to discuss the possibility of a general strike in the garment industry (see **Cooper Union Great Hall**, p. 138). After several hours of listening to male labor leaders, including Samuel Gompers of the American Federation of Labor (AFL), as they decried working conditions in the industry, debated a strike, and pronounced vague declarations of solidarity, a twenty-one-year-old garment worker named Clara Lemlich demanded the stage. In Yiddish, she roused the crowd: "I am a working girl, one of those who are on strike against intolerable conditions. I am tired of listening to speakers who talk in general terms. What we are here for is to decide whether we shall strike or shall not strike. I offer a resolution that a general strike be declared now."

Cooper Union erupted and thousands of women workers flooded the streets. Known as the "Uprising of the 20,000," women demanded union recognition, better wages, and improved working conditions. The strike paralyzed the industry as a whole, and many of the smaller employers quickly settled with the union, dramatically improving wages and working conditions. This was a remarkable breakthrough for women in the garment unions as well as the industry. For instance, the International Ladies Garment Workers Union hired young but veteran organizer Pauline Newman to extend its organizing of working women; female-led shops were organized across the city. Two of the largest employers, however, Triangle and Leiserson, held out. In addition to refusing

years before the fire, women had been organizing strikes across the garment industry. They protested low wages, unsanitary conditions, long hours, and the regular humiliation they had to endure at the hands of management in the new factories. Workers at New York City's largest manufacturers of shirtwaists (women's tailored shirts with details copied from men's shirts; these eventually became known as blouses), the Triangle Company, Rosen Brothers, and Leiserson Company, went on spontaneous strikes.

As the strikes gained momentum, the male-dominated unions in the sector struggled with their response. Until that point they had been reluctant to organize women, viewing them as weak or too docile to participate in trade unions. Less than two years

to meet workers' demands, they blacklisted many women who participated in the uprising, usually replacing them with younger Italian immigrants whom they paid even lower wages. The Triangle was a nonunion shop in an increasingly organized sector.

The Triangle Company occupied the eighth, ninth, and tenth floors of the Asch building on the corner of Greene Street and Washington Place. Immigrants Max Blanck and Isaac Harris owned the factory, and Triangle was the largest of their operations, often employing up to 600 workers at a time, and it exclusively produced shirtwaists. With no union agreement in place, women at the Triangle factory worked ten to twelve hours a day without breaks and had to also work on Saturdays. Wages continued to be low, a mere fifteen dollars per week, but higher than the ten dollars they were paid in 1909. Health and safety laws did not exist, and ventilation in the factory was particularly poor. As was common practice in the industry, Blanck and Harris locked the doors of the factory so that they could check women's purses on their way out to ensure they were not stealing factory property.

On the afternoon of March 25th, a fire started in a bin of scraps and quickly spread. A telephone line permitted contact between the eighth and tenth floors, giving workers on the tenth floor the opportunity to escape to the roof and cross to a neighboring building, where they were able to take stairs and elevators to safety. Some workers on the eighth floor were able to escape by going down the elevators (maximum capacity of twelve), going up to the roof, or going down the one non-blocked entrance before it became engulfed in flames. Workers on the ninth floor, however, were almost entirely trapped. A few made it down the elevators before they stopped working, but many more were stuck. In an act of desperation many girls threw themselves out of windows or down elevator shafts, at points crashing through the sidewalk. Others simply burned alive. When firefighters arrived, they quickly faced the reality that their ladders did not reach above the seventh floor.

In the days after the fire, thousands of workers marched in the streets. Blanck and Harris were charged with first and second-degree manslaughter, but were found not guilty of all charges. In 1913 some families who sued the owners settled for seventy-five dollars each, but the vast majority of the women's families received nothing at all.

Shortly after the fire, the New York State Legislature created a commission to investigate factories. The report led to landmark changes in the state's labor code and health and safety provisions. Between 1911 and 1913 over sixty new laws were put into place. Meanwhile, the International Ladies Garment Workers Union, with new women members and leading staff, became a powerful force in the city's labor movement.

TO LEARN MORE

Greenwald, Richard. *The Triangle Fire, Protocols of Peace: And Industrial Democracy in Progressive Era New York.* Philadelphia: Temple University Press, 2005.

Orleck, Annelise. *Common Sense and a Little Fire: Women and Working-Class Politics in the United*

States, 1900–1965. Chapel Hill: University of North Carolina Press, 1995.

NEARBY SITE OF INTEREST

Housing Works Bookstore and Café
126 Crosby Street, New York, NY
A large and comfortable community institution that features some of the city's best readings, Housing Works proceeds provide housing, health care, and services to New Yorkers living with HIV/AIDS.

East Village / Astor Place / Loisaida

2.32 Emma Goldman's House
208 E. 13th Street, New York, NY

Feisty, iconoclastic, and brilliant, Emma Goldman defined what it meant to be a feminist in the twenty-first century—only she did it in the nineteenth. Born in Kovno, Russia, in 1869, Goldman's early life was organized around the strict order imposed by her father at home and the violent anti-Semitism that plagued public life for Jews in imperial Russia. She found freedom in intellectual and political pursuits, which helped fuel a desire to emigrate to the United States in 1885 at the age of sixteen. Her first American home was Rochester, New York, where she worked in a sweatshop and was forced into a mercifully brief, but loveless marriage to a fellow immigrant. By 1889, however, she made her way to New York City. There, she was embraced by the active anarchist community developing at Sachs's cafe on Suffolk Street on the Lower East Side. She met other

women like herself, thirsty for independence and revolution, as well as leaders in the movement, such as Johann Most and Alexander Berkman (who soon would become her lifelong romantic and intellectual partner.) Through her new friends, she developed a personal map of the city, which included not only Sachs's and her various Lower East Side apartments, but the William Street offices of the German anarchist newspaper *Freiheit*; Prospect Park in Brooklyn; the Great Hall of Cooper Union where she marked the anniversary of the Chicago Haymarket demonstration; the shops of Hester Street; the Murray Hill Lyceum where British anarchist John Turner was arrested under the Anti-Anarchist law of 1903; and Terrace Garden concert hall on 3rd Avenue and 59th Street where Johann Most romanced her.

Goldman's reputation as a courageous and inspirational orator, writer, and organizer for anarchism, labor rights, feminism, and free love grew rapidly in these years, not least because her ideas found a welcome audience in a decade characterized by labor unrest and disastrous economic depression. Goldman truly earned her bona fides along these lines when she was implicated, along with Berkman, in the attempted murder of Henry Clay Frick, chairman of the board of Andrew Carnegie's Homestead mills in Pittsburgh and a reviled, brutal strikebreaker. (Goldman escaped prosecution, but Berkman was imprisoned for fourteen years.) Goldman spent the next decades joining strikes and speaking around the country on topics as varied as free speech, prostitution, anti-militarism, and birth control. From 1906 to 1917, she

Emma Goldman in 1917. CREDIT: COURTESY OF LIBRARY OF CONGRESS, LC-DIG-GGBAIN-24437

also published *Mother Earth* from her apartment at 210 East 13th Street, a journal covering all of these topics and more, particularly ones that challenged sorely outdated Victorian moralism. (Some sources suggest the actual address was 208 East 13th Street.)

By 1917, however, Goldman's radicalism was no longer tolerable to a government set on national unity and conformity in the context of a world war. She was imprisoned that year for conspiring against the draft and was deported back to Russia in 1919—a country she had left more than thirty years before. For the next two decades, Goldman continued her activism, eventually leaving Russia to settle in England and finally Canada. She died in 1940, leaving a trove of revolutionary and visionary thought upon which new generations continue to build.

—*Becky Amato*

TO LEARN MORE

Goldman, Emma. *Living My Life*. New York: Penguin Books, 2006.

FAVORITE NEIGHBORHOOD RESTAURANT

Veniero's Pasticceria

342 E. 11th Street, New York, NY

Antonio Veniero opened up his pastry shop in 1894, and it has been continuously run by his family ever since. Veniero's first started out as a pool hall and cafe, where he sold strong Italian coffee and homemade candies. Eventually, he brought in Italian *mastro pasticcieres* to work for him, got rid of the pool tables, and expanded the cafe. Enjoy the delicious coffee and traditional Italian pastries.

FAVORITE NEIGHBORHOOD BAR

The International

102 1st Avenue, New York, NY

Its third home in its fourth decade, the International has a roster of East Village regulars who still love a good dive bar.

2.33 Village East Cinema/ Yiddish Rialto

181–89 2nd Avenue, New York, NY

Four majestic Yiddish theaters once lined this stretch of 2nd Avenue, an area that was known as the "Yiddish Rialto" from the 1910s through the 1940s. This movie theater, once the Yiddish Art Theater and also known as the Yiddish Folks Theater, was built in 1925, landmarked in 1993, and today it is the last one standing. Its main theater seats over four hundred audience members, who watch their films in an elaborately decorated space, under a shallow dome at whose center glows

The landmarked theater, built in 1925-26, hosted Yiddish theater for decades, and retains much of its original interiors. The musicals "Grease" and "Joseph and the Amazing Technicolor Dreamcoat" opened here in its years as an off-Broadway theater. CREDIT: EDENPICTURES, CC BY 2.0, FLICKR

a chandelier within a large, turquoise-and-gold leaf Star of David.

Over the decades of its popularity, from the late nineteenth century through the early postwar years, Jewish theaters and Jewish theatrical productions could be found from Grand Street to the Bowery, east to Avenue B and farther north, including Broadway. The move to 2nd Avenue after the turn of the twentieth century marked a step up, reflecting the confidence that theater owners and investors had in the ongoing interest and breadth of their audience. Unlike all other immigrant groups at the time, Eastern European Jews tended to stay within the city upon arrival in the "New World." By the early twentieth century over

half of all Jewish Americans lived in the city; by 1910 a quarter of New York City was Jewish. While most were following new bridges and better housing to Brooklyn and the Bronx, the Lower East Side remained the cultural center for the community, where stores, restaurants, cafes, and even the Hebrew Actors Union (at 31 E. 7th Street) supported the lively stage life and promoted the general *Yiddishkeit* of the neighborhood.

Performances ranged from melodrama to realist dramas, musicals, and vaudeville, variety shows which started in New York and attracted vast working-class Jewish audiences. Jewish vaudeville in particular had long-term impacts on the country's entertainment industry, through the televised variety shows of midcentury to late-night shows of today. Regardless of the medium, with humor or pathos all Yiddish theater engaged thematically with questions about preserving one's culture, and the perils and promises of Americanization. Political themes, including labor struggles, anti-Semitism, and women's rights frequently surfaced as well, though the theater companies who took up the most political topics of the era, such as the Group Theater and the Yiddish communist Arbeter Teater Farband / Workers Theater Alliance, known as the Artef, mostly worked uptown.

Stella Adler, daughter of Yiddish theater's most beloved actor Jacob Adler, was a leading member of the Group Theater, and her Acting Studio became one of the country's leading theater schools. Irving Berlin, as well as George and Ira Gershwin all grew up in the neighborhood. Many Yiddish theater luminaries are commemorated on the "Yiddish

Walk of Fame," a series of sidewalk plaques along the southeast corner of 2nd Avenue and 10th Street. This landmarked sidewalk was once directly outside of the 2nd Avenue Deli, which some old-time New Yorkers would argue had the best pastrami on rye in the city (not to mention the pickles). Fans can still sample them at one of the deli's two current locations, both opened after the closing of its historic site (162 E. 33rd Street and 1442 1st Avenue, at 75th Street).

One hundred years after its founding, a theater company known today as the National Yiddish Theater Folksbiene continues to produce Yiddish theater in the city, such as a Yiddish version of *Fiddler on the Roof* (Fidler Afn Dakh) off-Broadway in 2019–2020.

TO LEARN MORE

Nahshon, Edna, ed. *New York's Yiddish Theater: From the Bowery to Broadway.* New York: Columbia University Press, 2016.

NEARBY SITE OF INTEREST

Poetry Project
St. Mark's Church-in-the-Bowery,
131 E. 10th Street, New York, NY
New York's premier site for poetry readings, it was founded in 1966 to continue the work of various Lower East Side café reading series that had been held in the 1950s–60s. The New Year's Day Marathon Reading is now an annual event.

FAVORITE NEIGHBORHOOD RESTAURANTS

Veselka
144 Second Avenue, New York, NY
Opened in 1954 by a Ukrainian immigrant, Veselka (rainbow in Ukrainian) almost immediately became a neighborhood institution, and hearkens to the recent past when the neighborhood was heavily Ukrainian. The restaurant produces over three thousand handmade pierogies a day.

Sake Bar Decibel
240 East 9th Street, New York, NY
The area around East 9th Street is often referred to as "Little Tokyo," for the decades-long commercial presence of Japanese food and drink concentrated in the area. Along 9th and neighboring streets one can find Japanese street food; numerous sushi, ramen (including Momofuko Noodle Bar, at 171 1st Avenue), soba and udon restaurants; and even a supermarket, Sunrise Mart (4 Stuyvesant Square). More than most, the atmospheric, dark, and somewhat grungy Decibel is said to transport the visitor to Tokyo and boasts what might be the city's best sake list.

2.34 Astor Place Riot
Astor Place (Astor Place and Lafayette),
New York, NY

In 1849 at least twenty-two people died and dozens more were injured in what became known as the Astor Place Riot or "Shakespeare Riot." Thousands of demonstrators had massed to protest a British actor's performance of *Macbeth*, ending in a militia-led massacre and over one hundred arrests. The standoff confirmed that social class divided New York's people in both space and culture, challenged the arbitrative authority of the urban crowd, and emboldened the elite to create an increasingly militarized police force ready to defend its property and priorities.

In the middle of the nineteenth century, the New York theater scene was concentrated downtown along the Bowery and lower Broadway. For New York's working people, theater was interactive, with audi-

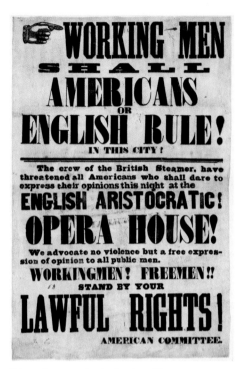

☞ WORKING·MEN
SHALL
AMERICANS
OR
ENGLISH RULE!
IN THIS CITY?

The crew of the British Steamer, have
threatened all Americans who shall dare to
express their opinions this night at the
ENGLISH ARISTOCRATIC!
OPERA HOUSE!
We advocate no violence but a free expres-
sion of opinion to all public men.
WORKINGMEN! FREEMEN!!
STAND BY YOUR
LAWFUL RIGHTS!
AMERICAN COMMITTEE.

This poster, appearing in streets and taverns across
downtown, helped agitate the thousands who turned
out on May 10, 1849. CREDIT: COURTESY OF THE FOLGER
DIGITAL IMAGE COLLECTION

ences shouting their approval and hissing their displeasure, often reciting lines with the actors onstage and pelting them with treats if they loved them and with refuse if they didn't. It was also a point of republican pride: New York theater goers associated their democratic theater norms with the freedoms and equality of their relatively new nation, and passionately rejected the norms of the English theater they left behind.

Upper-class Knickerbockers also enjoyed the theater, unlike their fellows among the Protestant "Yankees," but together these elites shared a desire for class segregation in the increasingly raucous and crowded city. Lafayette Place had been created in the 1820s by the Astor family patriarch as an enclave for the wealthy as they moved "uptown" to escape downtown's congestion and working classes. The Astor Opera House, whose imposing colonnade stretched along Astor Place from Broadway to what is now 4th Avenue, filling the block back to Eighth Street, represented a double exclusion. First, opera itself was associated with European aristocracy, and it was far from the popular theater playing for downtown audiences, which included minstrelsy, Shakespeare, and burlesque. Second, the theater itself attempted to impose a decidedly upper-class European behavioral code on American theatergoers. Attendees were expected, for example, to wear kid gloves and sport a freshly shaven face.

The immediate catalyst for the bloody riot was a long-simmering, press-inspired rivalry between an American-born actor named Edwin Forrest, who embodied a more physical and dramatic style, and the British stage star William Macready, whose studied and subtle style was revered among British elites. In spring of 1849, both men were slated to perform *Macbeth*, Forrest at the Broadway theater downtown. Even among the growing "upperten" of New York society there proved insufficient audience for opera, and by 1849, the managers of the Opera House had taken to programming the more popular Shakespearean dramas. When Macready was announced in the title role of *Macbeth* at the Astor Opera House, fans of the American favorite Forrest were livid and organized a protest. Eggs and insults rained down during Macready's first performance—and he wanted to quit, but prominent New Yorkers, including Herman Melville and Washington Irving, signed a public letter urging that he stay the course, assuring him of the city's protection.

On the night of May 10, 1849, Macready performed in Macbeth once more. This time, thousands of native-born white artisans and workers joined by a large number of Irish immigrants, massed outside, having been agitated by posters that appeared throughout downtown, asking, "Shall Americans or English Rule in this City?" The crowd pressed for entrance to the theater and began throwing paving stones at the windows. Meanwhile, the city had mobilized its new police force, and, as backing, the well-trained Seventh Regiment who had helped put down other disturbances over the previous decade (see **7th Regiment Armory**, p. 96).

Much more than casting decisions hung in the balance. The year before, Europe had erupted in hundreds of revolts, many of them revolutions, of an increasingly class-conscious character. Irish immigrants to the United States had barely survived the famine that was killing millions of their countrymen, and they blamed Britain for their fate. The nativists and newly arrived Irish made strange but logical bedfellows in their joint hatred of the British and everything that the mannered acting style and opera house represented in the nascent class conflicts of midcentury New York City. As part of a long tradition of democratic massing in the streets of New York, the rally at Astor Place represented an assertion of power among the lower orders against what they

began to see as an aristocracy emerging in their midst.

The violent suppression of the riot, the first time in the city's history that the militia were ordered to use force in an overtly political demonstration, was hailed by much of New York's ascendent bourgeoisie. As one paper editorialized, "The promptness of authorities in calling out the armed forces, and the unwavering steadiness with which the citizens obeyed the order to fire upon the assembled mob, was an excellent advertisement to the Capitalists of the old world, that they might send their property to New York and rely upon the certainty that it would be safe from the clutches of red republicanism, or chartists, or communionists [sic] of any description." The class fault lines exposed in this conflict continued to shape the city for decades to come.

—*With Dana Steer*

TO LEARN MORE

Burrows, Edwin G., and Mike Wallace. *Gotham: A History of New York City to 1898.* Illustrated edition. Oxford University Press, 1998.

Levine, Lawrence W. "William Shakespeare and the American People: A Study in Cultural Transformation." *The American Historical Review* 89, no. 1 (1984): 34–66.

Smith, Neil, and Don Mitchell, eds. *Revolting New York: How 100 Years of Riot, Rebellion, Uprising, and Revolution Shaped a City.* Athens: University of Georgia Press, 2018.

NEARBY SITE OF INTEREST

Astor Place Hair
2 Astor Place, New York, NY
NYC's largest walk-in barbershop, which Andy Warhol helped popularize, opened in 1947. It

helped bring mohawks, asymmetrical cuts, and buzzed Batman logos to the Village in the '80s, and reliable and inexpensive fades, blowouts and good cuts, with little to no wait.

2.35 Cooper Union Great Hall

7 E. 7th Street, New York, NY

Cooper Union, and its Great Hall, are the legacy of Peter Cooper (1791–1883), an inventor and industrialist whose ideas about wealth and civic responsibility distinguished him from the rich and robber barons of his age. Unlike most of his peers, he acknowledged that the "cooperation of multitudes" and the "will of society" underwrote his and others fortunes. As such, he believed the rich should administer their wealth "for the benefit of society." In keeping with these beliefs, he founded a school to which "all young people of the working classes, who desired to be good citizens, and to rise in life, could resort, without money and without price"—and Cooper Union's School of Arts and Engineering remained tuition free from its establishment in 1859 through 2012.

In keeping with its founder's ideals, the Great Hall opened with the mandate that it host speakers holding all views. Seating nine hundred people, it remained the largest secular meeting hall in Manhattan until the opening of Town Hall in 1921. In 1860, the then largely unknown Abraham Lincoln delivered his famous "right makes might"

speech to an assembled Republican crowd; his arguments that evening are frequently credited with his winning the presidential nomination of that party. Three years later, Frederick Douglass welcomed the Emancipation Proclamation from its stage, proclaiming, "We are all liberated by this Proclamation. Everybody is liberated."

In the decades to come, the Great Hall hosted other leaders in struggles for social justice, including suffragists Susan B. Anthony and Victoria Woodhull and reformer Jacob Riis; it hosted the overflowing New York memorial to Karl Marx in 1883. In 1909, the "Uprising of the 20,000" women shirtwaist workers began in the Hall, with Clara Lemlich's passionate speech (see **Triangle Shirtwaist Factory**, p. 129). Speakers in those years, such as Emma Goldman and Norman Thomas, railed against the inequities of the class system. The nearby ballroom Webster Hall (125 E. 11th Street) was another site of overflow crowds of labor and radical activists during these years.

The grand Cooper Union where Lincoln addressed slavery and where the Uprising of 20,000 was launched, 2017. CREDIT: SCOTT DEXTER

In 1921, the Town Hall (123 W. 43rd Street), funded by suffragists, opened in midtown and offered another, even larger meeting space for democratic debate (and performance). The scale of the movements of the 1930s made bigger venues—parks like Union Square and arenas like Madison Square Garden—the sites of the city's most famous oratory of that era; and this was true for the 1960s as well, with Tompkins Square, Washington Square, 5th Avenue, and Central Park the great gathering spaces. But over the course of the twentieth century and into the twenty-first, the Great Hall has continued to host, in the words of *The New York Times*, "Presidents, social reformers, leaders in the arts and sciences, literary lions and assorted troublemakers and dreamers."

The Great Hall remains, but Cooper's tuition-free policy for graduate students ended in 2012 when the school faced fiscal insolvency, due to what most observers agree were poor management decisions by the school's trustees, including over-investment of the endowment in hedge funds and excessive expenses for a new building, which, in the tradition of nearby NYU, expands the geographic footprint of the school and its real estate holdings in the expensive East Village. Student protests rocked the school for years, including a student takeover of the tower room of the Campus in 2012. When students and alumni sued the school to stop the plan to charge undergraduate tuition in 2015, a New York State judge observed that some of the trustees "may have lost sight of Peter Cooper's ideals, including that of free education." She found that the school could

charge tuition, but that an independent monitor would be appointed to support the school moving back to its tuition-free status. In 2018, the Board of the school developed a ten-year plan that would reintroduce free undergraduate education to its students by 2028.

TO LEARN MORE

The Cooper Union, https://cooper.edu/welcome.

Many of Peter Cooper's writings are assembled by the University of Pennsylvania's Online Book Page, https://onlinebooks.library.upenn.edu/webbin/book/lookupname?key=Cooper,%20Peter,%201791–1883.

2.36 Public Theater

425 Lafayette Street, New York, NY

One of New York's great people's institutions since its founding in 1954, the Public Theater has committed itself to accessibility and relevance. Such accessibility does not only pertain to the public, for whom there remains free "Shakespeare in the Park" performances at the Delacorte Theater in Central Park, as well as "Mobile Unit" productions of Shakespeare throughout the five boroughs. It also pertains to the artists themselves, as the Public's commitment to bringing new and diverse voices into theater has helped launch the careers of dozens of the country's leading playwrights, actors, and musicians. Its founding artistic director was Joseph Papp, born Papirofsky, who had been raised in Williamsburg and later Brownsville, Brooklyn (see **Brownsville Labor**

The Public Theater, 2017. CREDIT: SCOTT DEXTER

the first play by an African American to win the Pulitzer Prize; and Larry Kramer's *The Normal Heart*, which brought the first sympathetic look at the AIDS crisis to the American stage. More recently, the Public has been first home to Alison Bechdel's *Fun Home*, a "tragicomic" lesbian coming of age story; John Leguizamo's *Latin History for Morons*; and Lin Manuel Miranda's *Hamilton*.

TO LEARN MORE

Epstein, Helen. *Joe Papp: An American Life*. Boston: De Capo Press, 1996.

2.37 **The Village Voice**

36 Cooper Square, New York, NY (former office headquarters)

Lyceum, p. 253). He joined the Young Communist League as a teenager during the 1930s, and for many years before founding the Public was involved in various left-wing theater initiatives in and out of New York. The Public began with summertime performances of Shakespeare in the Park, and it wasn't until 1967 that a year-round theater was established here, at the former Astor Library.

Under Papp's leadership, the Public produced works such as *Hair*, the musical of the 1960s' antiwar movement and counterculture; Ntozake Shange's play, *For Colored Girls Who Have Considered Suicide / When the Rainbow Is Enuf*, which it picked up from Off-Off Broadway productions; the original production of *A Chorus Line*, which went on to serve as one of Broadway's longest and most beloved musicals (and to help bankroll the Public, which had some control over its production rights); Charles Gordone's play, *No Place to Be Somebody*, which was the first Off-Broadway play and

When writer Dan Wolf, psychologist Ed Fancher, and novelist Norman Mailer founded the *Village Voice* with ten thousand dollars, publishing their first edition on October 26, 1955, the three World War II veterans who had studied philosophy on the GI Bill hoped to fill a void they saw in Eisenhower's America, complacent in its consumerism. Little could they have foreseen that the *Voice*, first at 22 Greenwich Avenue, then Sheridan Square, then University Place, Broadway, and finally here at Cooper Square from 1991 to 2003, would burst forth as an enduring literary phenomenon. Over the coming decades the *Voice* fueled the ferment of New York culture and politics, alternately celebrating and berating (and often making the careers of) rising artists and activists, in dynamic, at times druggy, prose.

Early free-associative essays on the habits of cafe beatniks and editorials advocating for neighborhood causes—notably ending car traffic through Washington Square Park and challenging the local reign of Democratic Party boss Carmine DeSapio—soon gave way to more ambitious engagement with the swirl of movements rippling out to the nation from lower Manhattan. Young writers jostled to speak out through the *Voice* as champions, chroniclers, and critics, with a freedom unknown in conventional journalism. From early on, readers lined up each week outside the *Voice* offices and, later, the newsstand at Astor Place to be first to get their hands on the paper (and locate coveted apartments through the classified ads.) By 1967, the *Village Voice* would become the best-selling weekly newspaper in the United States and inspired a legion of "alt-weekly" imitators.

The paper's leadership found itself pressed more and more insistently by social forces outside their experience—from the radical left, feminists, and the queer revolution that found its strength at the Stonewall Inn (see **The Stonewall Inn**, p. 123). Changes in ownership accelerated the *Voice*'s transition from gawking commentator on social and creative trends to a paper written by participant-observers in the ferment of movements remaking the culture. Its force as an agent of social change persisted even when

New York Post owner Rupert Murdoch added the *Voice* to his portfolio in the 1970s.

Feminists, among them music critic Ellen Willis and dance writer Jill Johnston, challenged through argument and cultural critique the authority of the men who ran the *Voice* and held disproportionate power in personal and public life. Jack Newfield and Wayne Barrett investigated local politics with moral fervor, focused on betrayals of public trust including those of Mayor Ed Koch, whose rise as the giant of Village political reformers the *Voice* had helped secure. Nat Hentoff wrote on jazz and later on civil liberties, with his firm stance against abortion as a violation of fetal rights a testament to *Voice* editors' enduring tolerance for iconoclastic views.

Founding arts critic Jerry Tallmer invented the Obies, prizes for the best of Off-Broadway theater productions still awarded today. Michael Musto covered nightlife and gossip. Willis, Richard Goldstein, Lester Bangs, and Robert Christgau largely invented rock 'n' roll criticism, finding the words to do justice to the music that entranced and energized their generation. Lucian Truscott IV, a veteran from a distinguished military family, chronicled the debacle in Vietnam. Jonas Mekas, a driving force in the avant-garde cinema scene, and later Andrew Sarris, reviewed film. Dissonantly, the rise of African American and Puerto Rican power from New York streets was largely a story told from the outside in, by white, middle-class writers making sense of forces roiling their city and nation. *Voice* photographers like Fred McDarrah and

An issue of the iconic *Village Voice*.
CREDIT: SYLVIA PLACHY

Sylvia Plachy chronicled the city's streets, characters, and frequent protests.

The *Voice* found renewed relevance in the 1980s, when it broke ground with ahead-of-the-curve coverage of the politics, culture, and science of AIDS (culminating in a Pulitzer Prize, the paper's third) and broadened the Voice's voices to include regular contributors engaged in Latino/a/x-, Caribbean- and Asian American grassroots activism. For a period in the 2000s, the *Voice* lost much of its local identity in an acquisition by the Miami-based *New Times* chain. The *Voice* was purchased in 2015 by a Pennsylvania-based publisher who assured the public that the paper would "survive and prosper." That proved to be untrue: the weekly newsprint edition ceased publication in 2017, and the paper's website closed to new mate-

rial in 2018, though as of this writing a new, quarterly print edition of the *Voice* has been launched.

—*Alyssa Katz*

2.38 Third Street Men's Shelter

8 E. 3rd Street, New York, NY

Homelessness has been a defining feature of New York City, which has also served as a laboratory for ways of managing street homelessness. This seven-story building was once among the city's only shelters for homeless men, operating just off the Bowery, New York's skid row, stretching from the Brooklyn Bridge to Cooper Square in lower Manhattan. Since 1979, New York City has operated under a unique, court-ordered and, thereby, legally enforceable policy that it must provide shelter to anyone who requests it. When the city adopted this right to shelter, the Men's Shelter at 3rd Street became the intake point for all people seeking shelter citywide.

But before this, it was the Bowery branch of the YMCA. For more than thirty years the Bowery Y provided short- and long-term housing, meals, and employment services to men struggling in the city's economy. In 1931 alone, it housed more than one hundred thousand men. Almshouses and private charities like the YMCA had aided the city's poorest residents since its beginning, but the burgeoning population of homeless and alcoholic men that populated the Bowery's flophouses and hotels during and after the Great Depression overwhelmed the small network of services in the area. In 1947, the

YMCA sold the building to the city, which began to operate it as a shelter of last resort for homeless men on the Bowery. Deindustrialization in the post–World War II period created a permanent group of chronically homeless men, largely divorced from economic opportunities and social networks. The Men's Shelter and the single-room occupancy hotels along the Bowery were the only housing options for the city's homeless at that time.

While the Bowery was home to thousands of homeless men, homeless families were relatively rare in New York until the late 1960s. By then a never-resolved housing shortage, worsened by the city's urban renewal program that had bulldozed urban neighborhoods without sufficiently replacing affordable homes, led to a critical mass of homeless families (see **San Juan Hill/Lincoln Center for the Performing Arts**, p. 93). The Lindsay administration began housing them in so-called welfare hotels—decrepit hotels found all over the city and New Jersey. The city provided shelter for a fraction of those who needed it, and the conditions at the welfare hotels and the men's shelter were so dangerous that by the late 1970s, many of the city's homeless preferred to sleep in the streets and subway stations.

To improve and expand shelter for the city's homeless, the Coalition for the Homeless filed a lawsuit against the city with the goal of guaranteeing a right to shelter for anyone who sought it. *Callahan v. Carey* went before the New York State Supreme Court in 1979. Plaintiffs, supported with accounts of those who worked with homeless men,

argued that the men's shelter at East 3rd Street was so crowded that men were routinely turned away during the winter months, only to suffer from hypothermia, frostbite, and death.

In response to the suit, New York City recognized "with the force of law a right to shelter." A 1982 lawsuit resulted in the extension of the right to homeless women, and a court order followed in 1983 that assured that emergency shelter for homeless families must meet "minimal standards of health, safety, and decency suitable for young children."

Over the following years, the city scrambled to provide shelter to a ballooning homeless population, opening new shelters on Ward's Island and new makeshift shelters at area armories, including two for women at the Flushing and Lexington Avenue Armories. After nearly thirty years of experimental homelessness policies, the city still relies on a vast network of shelters to house the largest homeless population New York has ever seen. As of 2017, more than sixty thousand homeless people, including more than fifteen thousand homeless families and twenty-three thousand homeless children, slept in the municipal shelter system each night. Families make up more than 75 percent of the shelter population. (*Quote from* Nunez, Ralph da Costa, and Ethan G. Sribnick, *The Poor Among Us: A History of Family Poverty and Homelessness in New York City*, p. 248.)

TO LEARN MORE

Main, Thomas J. *Homelessness in New York City: Policymaking from Koch to de Blasio.* New York: NYU Press, 2016.

Nunez, Ralph da Costa, and Ethan G. Sribnick. *The Poor Among Us: A History of Family Poverty and Homelessness in New York City.* New York: White Tiger Press, 2013.

2.39 Former Site of CBGB & OMFUG

315 Bowery, New York, NY

Punk and new wave, "underground rock"—the music, the scenes, and the attitudes—gestated across New York City for years before the 1973 arrival of CBGB & OMFUG (Country, Bluegrass, and Blues & Other Music For Uplifting Gourmandizers). Yet this club housed the core bands that defined those musical eras, as well as many of the alternative sounds that would set the directions of rock and roll for years to come. That CBGB, usually referred to as CB's, would become the birthplace of punk was itself a bit of a cosmic accident: owner Hilly Kristal had intended to profile the country and blues music he'd highlighted in the club's title. But when early bands like Television brought their proto-punk sound and drew some interesting crowds, Kristal was open to the change in direction. In time, the Ramones played their first gig here and were regulars. Originally onstage as members of the Stilettos, Debbie Harry and Chris Stein formed Blondie, whose first base was this Bowery dive. After many years at the center of the poetry and art scenes downtown, Patti Smith formed her Patti Smith Group and debuted with Television on CB's stage in 1975. CB's propelled the Talking Heads, the Dictators, the Dead Boys, Joan Jett and the Blackhearts,

the Fleshtones, the Voidoids; introduced acts like the B-52s, Elvis Costello, and the Police to New York—all bands that moved in different directions but shared always iconoclastic and at times defiant sensibilities that stood in contrast to nearly all musical genres popular at the time.

CBGB also helped to define punk style. The club was covered in graffiti inside and out (its epically filthy bathroom perhaps most so); the simple space consisted of a long bar with a fairly small open floor in back with a platform stage that jutted out, a room in back for the bands, and "it had the best PA [sound system] in the city." It was at CB's that designer, artist, and (at the time) New York Dolls manager Malcolm McClaren first saw Television's Richard Hell with his spiky (unwashed) hair, wearing a torn shirt (from a fight with his girlfriend), perhaps held together with safety pins. McClaren imported this look to London, where his next band, the Sex Pistols, would make it synonymous with the new punk movement at the international scale.

But New York was the first to see a punk subculture develop, and in fact it was from the writers and critics watching CB's shows that "punk" got its name. Rejecting optimistic hippies and folk rock, as well as the corporate musicality of progressive rock, and growing up in the rougher terrain of a city teetering on the edge of its fiscal crisis, punk rockers created stripped down rock and roll, often nihilistic and combative. In New York at the time they were mostly white and often male, though there has always been some racial and gender diversity in the scene, as Bad Brains (popular at CB's) from Washington, DC, or Debbie Harry and Patti Smith would attest to, and the more recent Afropunk scene highlighted in an annual Brooklyn festival draws from a national platform with many bands and musicians of color. Most musicians were from working class, middle-class, or more struggling backgrounds. Band members frequently hailed from Queens, the Bronx, and the New York suburbs, where white families

After CBGB closed in 2006, the grate memorialized owner Hilly Kristal, the bands, and lyrics—"Hey, Ho, Let's Go!" CREDIT: NOETICSAGE AT ENGLISH WIKIPEDIA, CC BY 2.5, WIKIMEDIA COMMONS

had moved to flee the urban environment their children would go on to define and—ambivalently, sardonically—embrace. Alienation, anger, and rejection coursed through much of the New York punk scene. Musical virtuosity was usually not the point. Lyrics about drugs, sex and politics tended to be stark, grim, and unromantic, but they were not necessarily the point, either. Live performance, especially in spaces like the cramped, rank CB's, was perhaps the most powerful element of punk's first years, a trend that only intensified as the proto-punk bands of the '70s gave way to the New York hardcore (NYHC) scene of the '80s and beyond. Bands like the Agnostic Front, the Cro-Mags, and many others, brought the edginess, speed and volume of the '70s bands to new levels. Throughout the 1980s, CB's hosted all-age matinee punk shows on Sundays, where energetic mosh pits and stage diving defined many of the raw, physical performances of the NYHC scene.

The Bowery of the 1970s was a fitting corner of the city for this music to take off. It was marginal to Manhattan's nightlife, gritty, known for its men's shelters ("Bowery bums"), and a light-industry streetscape, with its shoddy loft buildings, wholesale kitchen supply shops, gas stations, and many empty storefronts (see **Third Street Men's Shelter**, p. 142). Underground theater, film, music—there was experimentation and innovation happening in old theaters and new and often temporary performance spaces. Rents were cheap all around the neighborhood, and by the time CB's opened, La MaMa Experimental Theatre Club had settled in a few spaces around the neighborhood; Jean Cocteau Repertory was nearby; the Anthology Film Archive, initially envisioned by director Jonas Mekas, was still in SoHo but eventually moved to its current home at 32 2nd Avenue, a couple of blocks from CB's.

Uptown, hip-hop was evolving at the exact same time, among similarly disenchanted youth (see **Birthplace of Hip-Hop**, p. 34; and **Former Home of Richard Colón ["Crazy Legs"]**, p. 38). The two scenes were to meet and inspire each other in these early years, with bridge figures like Fab Five Freddy (highlighted in Blondie's song "Rapture") in other venues like the after-hours Mudd Club on the west side. Like hip-hop, New York punk and new wave were a testament to the resilience and creativity of young music makers, who brought a whole way of life to the art and the spaces they created. The CB's scene did not survive the gentrification of downtown, culturally or economically—rent at CB's was twenty-three thousand dollars a month in its final period. It closed in 2006, long after the scene it had created had moved on.

TO LEARN MORE

Blush, Steven. *New York Rock: From the Rise of The Velvet Underground to the Fall of CBGB.* New York: St. Martin's Griffin, 2016.

McNeil, Legs, and Gillian McCain. *Please Kill Me: The Uncensored Oral History of Punk.* 20th Anniversary edition. New York: Grove Press, 2016.

NEARBY SITES OF INTEREST

Former Site of Basquiat Studio

57 Great Jones Street, New York, NY

A plaque at this site commemorates the legendary artist Jean-Michel Basquiat, who lived and worked in this building between 1983–1988.

Former Site of Justus Schwab Saloon

50 E. 1st Street, New York, NY

The plaque on this building commemorates Justus Schwab, a radical labor organizer who lived and operated an anarchist saloon at this building. The saloon played a critical role in the political

life of the city and was frequented by well-known anarchists such as Emma Goldman (see **Emma Goldman's House**, p. 132).

KGB Bar

85 E. 4th Street, New York, NY

Kitschy, Soviet Union–themed bar, with a great reading series.

2.40 Liz Christy Bowery Houston Community Garden

East Houston Street between 2nd Avenue and Bowery, New York, NY

Founded in 1973, the Liz Christy community garden is known as the first community garden in New York City. Many kinds of informal gardens existed before throughout the city, but the Liz Christy Garden could be considered the first of the contemporary community gardening movement. The garden's namesake, Liz Christy, was a founding member of the Green Guerrillas, activists who used window boxes and "seed bombs" (water balloons with wildflower seeds that were thrown over fences) to green abandoned vacant lots. Against a backdrop of scarce green space in most working-class neighborhoods, vacant lots proliferated in the 1960s and 1970s as a result of disinvestment and cutbacks in services caused by the city's fiscal crisis, which led to building collapses and arson. Community gardening meant more than beautification. It became a way for people to preserve and strengthen the bonds of community in neighborhoods reeling from neglect and an array of social problems. In 1974, the Guerrillas persuaded the city to lease the lot to their group for one dollar a month. Starting with sixty

Liz Christy in the Community Garden, 1975. CREDIT: DONALD LOGGINS

gardeners mobilized to demonstrate and litigate against these plans, and they successfully forced the reluctant administration to negotiate a permanent preservation plan for the city's gardens. Today, most gardens in New York are preserved through land trusts. The Liz Christy Garden was finally permanently protected by an agreement with New York City in 2002. The work done by community gardeners over the decades since the first seed bombs were thrown debunked the idea that gardens were only temporary uses for land, and it transformed our collective understanding of what neighborhoods needed in order to be just and livable. More than an amenity, gardens have innumerable environmental benefits and promote improved nutrition, sociality, and creativity.

raised beds, the Liz Christy Garden became a resource provider and training site for people across the city who were interested in starting gardens on lots in their communities. By the time Mayor Ed Koch created Operation GreenThumb to recognize and normalize gardens, almost six hundred gardens across the city were already organized and prepared to request recognition. Although the city was prepared to benefit from the volunteer labor that transformed lots into beautiful, vibrant green space, and maintained them for decades, the Green Thumb program deliberately defined gardens as a "temporary use," assuming that they would eventually be turned over to private developers when the market improved. The garden movement surged into visibility again in 1997, when Mayor Rudolph Giuliani moved to terminate the leases of hundreds of gardens around the city and auction them to real estate developers. From 1997 to 1999,

To the north and east of the Liz Christy Garden in the East Village, one will find dozens of community gardens that share a similar history. Each garden has its own origin story, and the design and plantings reflect the labor and love of decades of gardeners. Many East Village gardens were started by Puerto Rican gardeners who created spaces to invoke and celebrate the beauty of Puerto Rico and Puerto Rican culture. Lower East Side gardens are usually rather small, but in the Bronx and Brooklyn, gardens are large enough to be working farms, or multi use cultural centers (see **Casita Rincón Criollo**, p. 48; and **East New York Farms!**, p. 256).

—*Miranda Martinez*

TO LEARN MORE

Martinez, Miranda. *Power at the Roots: Gentrification, Community Gardens, and the Puerto Ricans of the Lower East Side.* Lanham, MD: Lexington Books, 2010.

FAVORITE NEIGHBORHOOD RESTAURANTS

Russ and Daughters

179 E. Houston Street, New York, NY

Joel Russ immigrated from Poland in 1907 and first worked selling schmaltz herring out of a barrel before moving up into the pushcart business and finally opening his appetizing store in 1914. In the 1930s Russ partnered with his daughters (he had no sons) and renamed the store Russ and Daughters, the first store to use "and daughters" in the United States. The store is known for its exquisite Jewish food, much of which is produced on-site. In 2014, on its one hundredth anniversary, the fourth generation owners opened Russ and Daughters Cafe on nearby Orchard Street; the Jewish Museum also has a Russ and Daughters Café; another outpost opened in the Brooklyn Navy Yard in 2020.

Katz's Delicatessen

205 E. Houston Street, New York, NY

Katz's is one of the few old-school delis left in New York City. Founded by the Iceland Brothers in 1888, the store has been curing meats and pickles ever since. Come for a giant deli sandwich made with house cured pastrami or corned beef.

Yonah Schimmel

137 E. Houston Street, New York, NY

The last remaining knish bakery in Manhattan. Yonah Schimmel, a Romanian rabbi, first started selling his knishes out of a pushcart on Coney Island in 1890. He soon became famous and opened this store on the Lower East Side in 1910.

2.41 Tompkins Square Park

7th to 10th Streets between Avenues A and B, New York, NY

More than any other public park in New York City, Tompkins Square Park has been the site of conflict over who has access to, and control over, the public spaces of the city. Daily actions and interactions within the park have served as a barometer of unrest among the working class and poor, private and public civic development and control, and class power in Manhattan.

One of the original planned "squares" to dot the downtown landscape during the robust period of city planning of the early nineteenth century, Tompkins Square served as a commons for working-class communities until very recently. From the 1830s to the 1990s, Irish shipbuilders, skilled German workers, southern and eastern European immigrants, Puerto Ricans, and African Americans, overlapping and in turn, settled the streets around Tompkins Square and helped to shape and reshape the park and its uses.

Socialists and unions held mass rallies in the park during the riotous 1870s. In 1874, over one thousand police charged a peaceful crowd of thousands of workers and their families who had gathered at the park to demand public works programs to employ those unemployed due to the Panic of 1873, the largest demonstration of its kind to date in New York. Labor leader Samuel Gompers, standing on 8th Street, described the police riot as an "orgy of brutality."

As new immigrants arrived and the neighborhood surrounding the park became

Arbor Day at Tompkins Square, 1904. CREDIT: BYRON COMPANY (NEW YORK, NY). MUSEUM OF THE CITY OF NEW YORK. 93.1.1.17807

more impoverished at the turn of the twentieth century, philanthropists, progressives, and social workers chose the park as a prime site for social uplift for local families. One of the city's first playgrounds was built there in 1894, a Boys Club and the Children's Aid Society were established on its perimeter, and a Young Women's Settlement House was eventually redeveloped to become the sixteen-story Christadora House (143 Avenue B). This 1927 "skyscraper settlement" included a theater, music school, library, gymnasium, and swimming pool for its tenants and neighborhood residents. In the aftermath of World War II, large public housing projects were built to the east of the park along Avenues C and D. Along with the inexpensive tenement rentals in the rest

of "Alphabet City," such affordable housing guaranteed that Tompkins Square remained the recreational center for a large, diverse, poor and working-class "Loisaida" (a Spanish pronunciation of Lower East Side; now the name of the stretch on Avenue C from Houston to 14th Street (see **Nuyorican Poets Café**, p. 155).

Throughout this time, the park retained connections to its more radical past, acting

Resisting the park curfew during the 1988 "Tompkins Square Riot." CREDIT: ANGEL FRANCO/*NEW YORK TIMES*

as a staging ground for labor's marches to Union Square during the turbulent 1930s, and as a flashpoint of Vietnam antiwar protest in the 1960s. Working-class roots, radical activism, and the developing crisis of affordable housing combined in the 1980s to propel Tompkins Square as the national focal point for conflicts

Bucolic Tompkins Square Park, 2017. CREDIT: SCOTT DEXTER

over urban gentrification. In the mid-1980s, a sizable homeless population began living among the musicians, anarchists, teenagers, heroin addicts, chess players, and elderly immigrants who also called the park home. At the same time, affluent young urban professionals began to move to the neighborhood in earnest, following the artists and entrepreneurs who had transformed the "East Village" into one of the hippest spots in the city. Yuppies and business owners bordering the park wanted the homeless out; long-term local renters feared their own displacement in the face of rising property values.

Under pressure from Mayor Koch's office, a divided community board approved a park curfew during the summer of 1988, confining the homeless encampment that had been created in the park to the southeast corner. Protests erupted, and on August 7th protesters carrying the banner "Gentrification is Class War" were brutally swept

from the park by the police in what became known as the Tompkins Square Riot, in which dozens of homeless people, other activists, and passersby were injured and arrested in the police-provoked melee, highly reminiscent of the riot from a century past.

The following three years saw an uneasy alliance between housing activists, local squatters, many local residents opposing gentrification, houseless park residents, and anti-police brutality organizers. But while the protesters won some battles, they eventually lost the war. In June 1991, days after the police shut down a "Housing Is A Human Right" concert in the park, Tompkins Square Park was evacuated, surrounded by wire fencing, and shut for a year while it was completely refurbished.

Tompkins Square's history of class contention and multicultural creativity and clashes ended (for now) with a combination of a bang and a whimper in the 1990s. By the time the fencing around the park came down, the

Christadora's conversion to condominiums in 1986 had become old news, as rent deregulations, squatter evictions, and other conversions continued to steer the neighborhood in its current affluent direction. Wider paths opened the park to police cars, and the park was substantially remodeled to make it more user-friendly for its wealthier neighbors.

The park has not entirely shed its exuberant, community-oriented, and gritty past, however. A needle exchange outreach team runs a field site once a week, and overdose prevention kits are periodically stashed in the public bathrooms. The benches are informally divided into spaces for tourists, homeless youth and adults, parents and children, drug users, and periodic waves of HIV outreach workers and/or research field staff. Planning meetings for what became Occupy Wall Street were held in its central field, and the Hare Krishna tree stands as a shrine for followers among the beautiful elms of the park. On the Friday of June's Gay Pride weekend, the semi-annual Drag March gathers on the Avenue A side of the park and then steps out onto 9th street to march across town to Christopher Street, as it has done most years since 1994, and the park remains the end point of the annual Dance Parade that winds its way through Greenwich Village each May.

—*With Naomi Braine*

TO LEARN MORE

Smith, Neil, and Don Mitchell, eds. *Revolting New York: How 400 Years of Riot, Rebellion, Uprising, and Revolution Shaped a City.* Athens: University of Georgia Press, 2018.

Van Horn, Laurel. n.d. "A History of Tompkins Square Park." *LESPI-NYC* (blog). Accessed September 1, 2020. http://lespi-nyc.org/a-history-of-tompkins-square-park/.

NEARBY SITE OF INTEREST

Good Old Lower East Side (GOLES)
171 Avenue B, New York, NY
Good Old Lower East Side has worked to preserve affordable housing in the neighborhood since 1977.

FAVORITE NEIGHBORHOOD RESTAURANT

Ray's Candy Store
113 Avenue A, New York, NY
An immigrant from Iran, Ray Alvarez opened this deli/soda fountain in 1974. During the Tompkins Square riot of 1988, Ray kept the store open, because many of the protestors were his customers. The store has been featured in a number of books and movies and is known for having the best egg creams in New York City.

2.42 CHARAS/El Bohio
350 E. 10th Street, New York, NY

P.S. 64 opened its doors to the Lower East Side's Italian, Russian, and Jewish immigrant students in 1906. Its H-shape maximized windows and light, and its location in the middle of the block shielded it from the noise and traffic at corners, making it an ideal meeting space for children and adults alike, in a neighborhood lacking such spaces. On any given weeknight and most weekends, the auditorium would be packed with community members listening to free lectures or attending performances, assimilating to American values.

By the 1970s, the demographics of the Lower East Side had dramatically changed. Puerto Ricans had made the neighborhood home during the great migration from Puerto Rico to the United States in the 1950s. The colonial relationship between the United States and Puerto Rico (especially through Operation Bootstrap,

Charas, boarded up and in limbo, 2017. CREDIT: SCOTT DEXTER

which transformed the Puerto Rican economy into an export-oriented one), and US labor shortages, pushed Puerto Ricans to New York City. Migration to the Lower East Side dramatically changed its culture and character. Spanish was spoken on the streets, bodegas flourished, and a Puerto Rican music and arts scene developed, culminating in the "Nuyorican moment" and the neighborhood's new colloquial name "Loisaida" (see **Nuyorican Poets Café**, p. 155). At the same time, the neighborhood continued to experience disinvestment, with abandoned tenements dotting the streets.

After P.S. 64 closed in 1977 during a time of significant population loss, the building, which was slated to be torn down, was taken over by CHARAS, a Puerto Rican community organization that had grown out of the Real Great Society, a 1960s-era organization of former gang members that sought to "fight poverty instead of each other" and exert community control. CHARAS represented the names of its founding members,

Chino, Humberto, Angelo, Roy, Anthony, and Salvador.

With a long-time lease from the city, CHARAS / El Bohio cleaned and renovated much of the dilapidated school, turning it into a dynamic community arts and education center. Film-makers, painters, poets, choreographers, and activists used the space. The auditorium hosted performances and the gymnasium served as a rehearsal space. The founders created an art gallery. Among the many artists that were nurtured in El Bohio was Spike Lee, who showed his first student film in the space. The founders also implemented an arts and martial arts programs for neighborhood children. Other community organizations such as Picture the Homeless held their first meetings at CHARAS, and the multiple classrooms hosted groups ranging from Narcotics Anonymous to the Latin Kings gang.

As gentrification began to take hold in the 1990s, however, the city decided to auction the building despite neighborhood opposition and protests. It auctioned CHARAS/ El Bohio for $3.8 million, but not before protesters dressed in suits drove up the bidding and released thousands of live crickets into the auction room. After years of street protest and legal wrangling, the center was evicted from the building on December 27, 2001. The space remains empty to this day, due in good part

C-Squat and the Museum of Reclaimed Urban Space, 2017. CREDIT: ROBERT K. CHIN - STOREFRONTS/ALAMY STOCK PHOTO

to ongoing community resistance. In 2006, the community successfully pushed for it to receive Landmark status; its deed requires it to be used for community affairs. As of this writing, the fate of the building remains in limbo, decades after the city profited from its sale.

TO LEARN MORE

Mottel, Syeus, Ben Estes, and R. Buckminster Fuller. *Charas: The Improbable Dome Builders.* Brooklyn: Pioneer Works Press/The Song Cave, 2018.

Starecheski, Amy. *Ours to Lose: When Squatters Became Homeowners in New York City.* Chicago: University of Chicago Press, 2016.

2.43 C-Squat (See Skwat) and Museum of Reclaimed Urban Space

155 Avenue C, New York, NY

Amid the restaurants, bars, and boutiques in now gentrified Alphabet City lies C-Squat,

a former urban squatter community now turned into a housing cooperative, museum, and art / music space. After the city's fiscal crisis in the 1970s, urban squatters occupied abandoned publicly and privately owned buildings in some of the city's poorest neighborhoods. Squatters ranged from activist punks to undocumented immigrants to people displaced from city and private development projects with the common goal of claiming housing as their right. Squats thrived throughout the 1980s and 1990s.

By the 1980s, New York City had repossessed more than ten thousand tax-delinquent properties, and squatters had claimed many all over the city, but particularly on the Lower East Side. Squatters were inspired by the neighborhood's radical history and by the Young Lords, who had squatted buildings in the area in the 1970s, as well as by hippies, Yippies, and the European squatters' movements. Illegal squatters agitated to take ownership of their homes, laying claim to them with "sweat equity"—the physical labor they used to make the spaces inhabitable.

Remarkably, their actions—particularly Operation Move-In, in which more than two hundred mostly Latina/o/x families occupied vacant Upper West Side apartments in 1970—led to city support for urban homesteading in 1974. This support was primarily channeled into the Urban Homesteading Assistance Board (UHAB) with some federal support in the 1970s. UHAB provided assistance to low- and moderate-income creditworthy homeseekers to rehabilitate abandoned properties as a condition of ownership, and outlawed sales for three to five years (see **Crown Heights Tenant Union**, p. 268). UHAB also trained renters to purchase and manage buildings as cooperatives, providing assistance through the bureaucratic process. But despite the fact that famous squatting actions contributed to the formation of UHAB, the city generally did not support squatters taking ownership. At its peak in the late 1980s, there were over two dozen squatted buildings on the Lower East Side and another two dozen in East Harlem, Washington Heights, and the South Bronx, and they defended themselves in wave after wave of attempted evictions. A concentration of squats emerged along 13th Street, where activists crafted signs to mark squats that read "This land is ours," "Property of the people of the Lower East Side," and "Not for sale." A similar sign still marks C-Squat, founded in 1989 after the city took ownership of the abandoned tenement, and most well-known for its mostly white, male,

punk squatters and its riotous parties and shows.

By 2002, the squatters' strenuous and consistent defense of their homes yielded some official recognition, and the city, through UHAB, offered some the option of becoming limited-equity owners of the buildings they inhabited if they brought them up to code. Eleven squats entered into a deal in which UHAB would rehabilitate the properties to meet city codes and transfer the debt that would fund the project to the residents. Thus, C-Squat remains, although its residents are no longer squatters, but limited-equity cooperative owners who hold the building's debt. C-Squat also houses the independently run Museum of Reclaimed Urban Space on its first two floors, which features photographs, a screening space, and a community board, and it provides literature and low-cost zines that document the history of the Lower East Side.

—*With Julieta Salgado*

TO LEARN MORE

Starecheski, Amy. *Ours to Lose: When Squatters Became Homeowners in New York City*. Chicago: University of Chicago Press, 2016.

NEARBY SITES OF INTEREST

Other Famed LES Squats
- **Glass House (1992–1994)**: former Ideal Glass factory on Avenue D and E. 10th Street
- **13th Street "Home Sweet Home"**: 44 E. 13th Street
- **Umbrella House**: 21–23 Avenue C, between E. 2nd and 3rd Streets
- **Serenity House**: 733 E. 9th Street
- **Bullet Space**: 292 E. 3rd Street (also has tours)

- **Dos Blocos (1992–1999):** 713 E. 9th Street
- **Tenth Door:** 377 E. 10th Street
- **209–209** E. 7th Street
- **ABC No Rio:** 157 Rivington Street

2.44 Nuyorican Poets Café

236 E. 3rd Street, New York, NY

"The poet blazes a path of fire for the self. He juggles with words. He lives risking each moment. Whatever he does, in every way he moves, he is a prince of the inner city jungle. He is the philosopher of the sugar cane that grows between the cracks of concrete side-walks." —Algarín 1975

Dedicated to the living art of poetry, the Nuyorican Poets Café has hosted poetry, music, film, theater, and the visual arts in this space for over thirty years. Supporting artists of color as well as experienced and first-time performance poets, the Café hosts diverse audiences nightly, including working class and Nuyorican neighbors and poetry buffs from around the city and world.

Started by poet and writer Miguel Algarín in his living room, the early founders were addressing the exclusion of Nuyorican and African American traditions and voices from New York's literary scene. More, the late 1960s had seen the growth of the Nuyorican movement, in which Puerto Rican artists, actors, musicians, and organizers were establishing cultural, community, and political footholds in New York to assert the culture and vision of their communities (see **CHARAS/El Bohio**, p. 151; and **Young Lords' Garbage Offensive**, p. 84). In the first anthology of poetry edited by Algarín that helped give the movement its name, Algarín describes the contradictory position of the Nuyorican poet as giving bilingual voice to the fractured experience of a colonized people living at the heart of the empire. The Poets Café was established with the additional help of playwright Miguel Piñero, whose play "Short Eyes" brought Nuyorican culture to Broadway, poet Bimbo Rivas, whose poem "Loisaida" gave the neighborhood its name, and Lucky CienFuegos, whose poetry and plays were performed at the café from its first years, as well as many other writers, such as Richard August and Ntozake Shange.

Decades later Algarín explained that for the poets of the café, "It is at the heart of the matter to move their work from the Café to other communities of the city in order to

The Nuyorican Poets Café, 2017. CREDIT: SCOTT DEXTER

break down racial patterns that tend to isolate these communities into ethnic pockets that are enclosed and without inter-communication." The café is most well-known first for its Open Room, with its open mic nights, which have been its most defining and egalitarian feature since its founding. Anyone can speak or perform at the weekly open mics, and these gatherings have helped form decades of community for some of the regulars. In the 1990s the poetry slam was introduced to the café, a spirited and compassionate competition between poets delivering their work. The Café's slam champions have consistently achieved national and international awards and acclaim.

TO LEARN MORE

Algarín, Miguel, and Bob Holman. *Aloud: Voices from the Nuyorican Poets Cafe.* New York: Macmillan, 1994.

Algarín, Miguel, and Miguel Pinero. *Nuyorican Poetry: An Anthology of Puerto Rican Words and Feelings.* New York: Morrow, 1975.

"Nuyorican Poets Cafe." n.d. Nuyorican Poets Cafe. Accessed August 27, 2020. https://www.nuyorican.org.

NEARBY SITES OF INTEREST

Bluestockings Bookstore, Café, and Activist Center
116 Suffolk, New York, NY
A frequent meeting spot for all kinds of left intellectual debate and discussion, the store specializes in feminist, queer, and activist fiction, poetry, academic texts, and self-published zines.

Tenement Museum
103 Orchard Street, New York, NY
This museum offers tours of a tenement that recreates the lives of a diverse array of Lower East Side residents, allowing you to vividly interact with the history of the people's New York. Its bookstore is the city's best for books about New York City.

FAVORITE NEIGHBORHOOD RESTAURANT

Congee Village
100 Allen Street, New York, NY
A popular Cantonese restaurant serving traditional congee porridge among many other dishes.

Lower East Side

2.45 The Forward Building
173 East Broadway, New York, NY

"The Forward building will be the home of the Jewish Socialist Movement."

—Abraham Cahan
(Editor and Founder)

Founded in 1897 by Abraham Cahan and other Jewish Socialists, the *Forverts*, or *Jewish Daily Forward* was one of the country's premiere Yiddish language newspapers. By 1910 it had a readership of 100,000 and, at its peak in the early 1930s, reached a national audience of 275,000. Affiliated with the Social Democratic Party of America (founded by Eugene V. Debs), Abraham Cahan wanted to bring socialist and trade unionist ideas to Yiddish-speaking immigrants. However, Cahan was not as committed to radical politics as some of his peers and competitors. He also deeply believed in Americanization and saw the *Forward* as an outlet not only to espouse socialist ideas, but also provide

(Left) The carved faces of Marx, Engels, Lassalle, and Liebknecht can be seen above the door, 2019. CREDIT: PENNY LEWIS

(Below) Celebrating 40 years of *Forverts*, 1937. CREDIT: FORVERTS (NEW YORK, NY). MUSEUM OF THE CITY OF NEW YORK. X2011.7.1

practical advice for recent immigrants. This approach put the *Forward* at the center of many fierce debates, none more intense than those between it and the Communist *Di Frayhayt*, edited by Moyshe Olgin. Cahan was profoundly anti-communist, and these two papers waged a forty-year-long war with each other; Communists took to calling Cahan's paper the "Jewish Daily Backward."

Completed in 1912, the *Forward* Building cemented Cahan's reputation as a prominent newspaper entrepreneur. While the building did, at the time, tower over the Lower East Side, it was also an architectural marvel that boldly supported progressive politics. Over the main entrance reside bas-relief representations of four iconic figures of Socialism: reading with Yiddish from the right, Karl Marx, with Friedrich Engels at the far left, and at the center two leaders of the German social democratic workers movement, Ferdinand Lassalle and Wilhelm Liebknecht. Predictably, some of Cahan's contemporary competitors criticized the building. Critic

Henry Margoshes commented, "The socialist movement in New York will be buried under this 10-story capitalist building."

As Cahan had hoped, though, the building came to represent the Jewish socialist movement. In addition to holding a Yiddish theater, the *Forward* building became an instrumental meeting space for the community response to the Triangle Shirtwaist Factory fire, and it later served as a meeting and office space for many labor and progressive organizations such as the Workers Liberty Defense Union, Workmen's Circle, and the Butchers' Union Local 509. It was also the meeting location for anarchist groups organizing for the defense of Sacco and Vanzetti in 1921 (see **Village East Cinema/Yiddish Rialto**, p. 133; and **Triangle Shirtwaist Factory**, p. 129). The diversity of groups working in the building reflected some of the political diversity of the Jewish community, where anarchism, socialism, Zionism, and communism regularly vied for political supremacy in the first half of the twentieth century.

By the 1950s, changing demographics in the neighborhood and the city at large severely reduced the readership of the *Forward*. In the 1970s the paper relocated, and a Chinese American family bought the building and rented the first floor to an evangelical Chinese Church (the images of the socialists were covered for a time). By the 1990s, after failed redevelopment initiatives, the building fell into disrepair until 2004 when it was turned into luxury condos. *The Forward* newspaper closed its print operations in January 2019, laying off 40 percent of its staff. It continues to maintain an online presence in English and Yiddish.

TO LEARN MORE

Glickman, Toby, and Gene Glickman. *The New York Red Pages: A Radical Tourist Guide.* Westport, CT: Praeger, 1984.

Hoffman, Matthew. "The Red Divide: The Conflict between Communists and Their Opponents in the American Yiddish Press." *American Jewish History* 96, no. 1 (2010): 1–31.

2.46 Henry Street Settlement

263–267 Henry Street, New York, NY

The settlement house movement, a transatlantic effort among socially conscious, often well-educated, middle-class women to bring direct aid to the urban poor, took root in New York in the mid-1880s. Its most recognizable and prolific institution, Henry Street Settlement, was established by visiting nurses Lillian Wald and Mary Brewster in 1895 on Manhattan's Lower East Side. Perhaps of equal fame is University Settlement (184 Eldridge Street). which opened in 1886. Of the Lower East Side, Wald wrote, "All the maladjustments of our social and economic relations seemed epitomized." There, she believed, the indignities of poverty, including scant educational opportunity, limited access to health care, and atrocious living and working conditions, found their most glaring expression. The Settlement, then, became an outpost where Lower East Siders, many of them immigrants, found relief in the form of lectures and classes, childcare, medical assistance, social clubs, and job training. More than that, Henry Street Settlement served as an intellectual home for progressive politics, and a social hub, where residents and reformers alike developed nuanced critiques of industrial capitalism and its excesses.

Campaigns against child labor and unsafe workplaces, as well as organizing on behalf of human and civil rights, comprehensive city planning, improved housing, and access to quality public education sprouted from the settlement house. To Wald and her colleagues, all of these reforms were interconnected and necessary elements in constructing a modern and sustainable democracy. Wald led this charge on local, state, and national stages until her retirement in 1933. Her successor, Helen Hall, further advanced Henry Street Settlement's position as an institutional leader in progressive politics by diversifying the settlement's programming to include addiction services, consumer advocacy, and anti-delinquency training, some of which later influenced funding priorities under the 1960s War on Poverty. Today, under the leadership of David Garza, Henry Street Settlement occupies more than fifteen buildings and its programs serve upwards of sixty thousand people per year. As of this writing, Henry Street is part of a larger umbrella organization, United Neighborhood Houses (UNHNY), which represents over forty settlement houses in New York City.

—*Becky Amato*

NEARBY SITE OF INTEREST

Seward Park
Essex Street, New York, NY

Seward Park became the first municipal playground in 1903, after Lillian Wald and Charles Stover had opened it a few years before as a private playground to promote organized play among children who would otherwise have been working or playing in the city's streets.

FAVORITE NEIGHBORHOOD RESTAURANT

Kossar's Bialys
367 Grand Street, New York, NY

Jewish bakers made the bialy (short for bialystoker kuchen) a popular bread in New York City at the turn of the nineteenth century. Kossar's opened in 1936, one bakery of many in Manhattan. At its peak workers even had their own union association, the Bialy Bakers Association.

TriBeCa

2.47 Former Home of David Ruggles
36 Lispenard Street, New York, NY

Slavery was abolished in New York State in 1827. But for Black residents of the city, that did not mean that the terror was over. "Blackbirders," or slave catchers, came to the city to kidnap the men and women who had escaped slavery elsewhere. It was not only the self-emancipated, but free Blacks as well whose lives were at constant risk as long as slavery existed and the laws protected slave catchers. Until it was ended everywhere, slavery was a national crisis.

David Ruggles came to New York from Connecticut in 1827, and soon thereafter joined the abolitionist struggle. His was the first Black-owned bookstore (first located at the corner of Broadway and Lispenard until it was burned by a white mob in 1835); he also owned the first Black press and published as a journalist in various papers in addition to publishing his own pamphlets. He also put out a periodical, *Mirror of Liberty*,

159

The site of Ruggles's former boarding house, part of the Underground Railroad, 2019. CREDIT: STEPHANIE LUCE

"I had been in New York but a few days, when Mr. Ruggles sought me out, and very kindly took me to his boarding-house at the corner of Church and Lispenard Streets." —Frederick Douglass, in his Autobiography. CREDIT: MATTHEW BRADY, COURTESY OF THE METROPOLITAN MUSEUM OF ART DIGITAL COLLECTION

the first African American magazine, only a few years after *Freedom's Journal*, the country's first Black newspaper had briefly been published from various offices on nearby Church Street from 1827 to 1829. Ruggles used his increasingly prominent written voice to tell the stories of captured Black people, fiercely advocate for the rights of fugitives, and to name the names of slave catchers, some of whom traveled among the Black communities of New York "wolf-like . . . in sheep's clothing," pretending to be abolitionists to gain their trust.

In addition to his writings, Ruggles equally made his mark as a creative and effective organizer and leader in "practical abolitionism." Going beyond the moral suasion more typical of the abolitionist movement, he practiced radical direct action that entailed the self-defense of threatened Black individuals and civil disobedience in the face of racist policies. He helped to found the New York Committee of Vigilance, which directly sheltered and protected Black Americans under threat of capture and arranged for their legal support in cases they brought forward in New York courts. He was a critical connector between the city's abolitionist movement and the upstate places of refuge for the Underground Railroad. He wrote, "Whatever necessity requires, let that remedy be applied. Come what may, anything is better than slavery."

Ruggles used civil disobedience in his refusal to abide by the Jim Crow seating rules on regional rail and steamboats. He was frequently ejected from trains, and on at least one occasion beaten for doing so. He filed lawsuits against the companies and the men who threw him out, and while he was initially unsuccessful, the cases he brought and the inspiration he gave to others to break the rules caused an end to segregated seating in Massachusetts.

Frederick Bailey, a fugitive slave, came to Ruggles in 1838. Ruggles took him in at his house here on Lispenard and helped Bailey to reunite with his fiancé; the two were later married in his home. Ruggles mentored Bailey, introducing him to the New York Committee and other anti-slavery activists, and later gave Bailey a letter to find work, including five dollars to help him get started. Bailey changed his name to Douglass, and like his mentor, spent his life as a fiery journalist and activist leader in the fight against slavery. Frederick Douglass lived to see emancipation; Ruggles, who many recognize as having given his whole life to the cause, died at the age of thirty-nine, in 1849. His house here on Lispenard was demolished around 1875, commemorated by a plaque on this building.

TO LEARN MORE

Hodges, Graham Russell Gao. *David Ruggles: A Radical Black Abolitionist and the Underground Railroad in New York City*. Chapel Hill: Univ of North Carolina Press, 2010.

Wells, Jonathan Daniel. *The Kidnapping Club: Wall Street, Slavery, and Resistance on the Eve of the Civil War*. New York: Bold Type Books, 2020.

Civic Center

2.48 Collect Pond Park
130 Leonard Street, New York, NY

In the centuries before the completion of the epic aqueduct projects of the 1800s, which brought fresh drinking water to the city from rivers and reservoirs upstate, the residents of Manhattan Island—originally the Lenape tribes, then the early Dutch settlers—survived amid the salty estuaries by drinking from a small lake near the southern tip of the island, just below modern-day Canal Street. It went by several names: the Dutch called it the Kalck; later it was known as Freshwater Pond. Today it is most commonly referred to as Collect Pond.

Fed by underground springs, the pond emptied out into two streams, one which meandered toward the East River, the other draining out westward into the Hudson. At high tide, the Lenape were said to have been able to cross the entire island by canoe. Paintings from the early eighteenth century suggest that the Collect was a tranquil and scenic spot, an oasis for early Manhattanites who wished an afternoon's escape from the growing trade center to its south. An imposing bluff—sometimes called Bayard's Mount, sometimes Bunker's Hill—loomed over the northeast edge of the pond; climbing the hundred feet of elevation that led to its summit opened up a spectacular vista of the pond and its surrounding wetlands, with the spires and chimneys of the bustling town in the distance. "It was the grand resort in winter of our youth for skating," William Duer recalled in a memoir of early New York written in the nineteenth century, "and nothing can exceed in brilliancy and animation the prospect it

Collect Pond, ca. 1798. CREDIT: ATTRIBUTED TO ARCHIBALD ROBERTSON, COURTESY OF THE METROPOLITAN MUSEUM OF ART DIGITAL COLLECTION

presented on a fine winter day, when the icy surface was alive in skaters darting in every direction with the swiftness of the wind."

By the second half of the eighteenth century, however, commercial development had begun to spoil the Collect's bucolic setting. Tanneries set up shop on the edge of the pond, soaking the hides of animals in tannins (including the poisonous chemicals from the hemlock tree), and then expelling their waste directly into the growing city's main supply of drinking water. The wetlands at the edge of the pond become a common dumping ground for dead animals—and even the occasional murder victim. In 1789, a group of concerned citizens—and a handful of real estate speculators—proposed expelling the tanneries and turning Collect Pond and the hills rising above into a public park. They hired the French architect and civil engineer Pierre Charles L'Enfant, who would design Wash-

ington, DC, several years later. An early forerunner of the public–private partnerships common today, L'Enfant's proposed Collect Pond Park was to be funded by real estate speculators buying property on the borders of the preserved public space. But the plan ultimately fell through, in large part because the project's advocates couldn't persuade the investment community that the city would ultimately expand that far north.

By 1798, the newspapers and pamphleteers were calling Collect Pond a "shocking hole" that attracted "all the leakings, scrapings, scourings, pissings, and shittings for a great distance around." With the pond's water now too polluted to drink, the city decided it was better off filling the pond and the surrounding marshlands, and building a new "luxury" neighborhood on top of it, attracting well-to-do families that wished to live outside the tumult of the city, not unlike the suburban planned communities that would sprout up on Long Island and New Jersey a hundred and fifty years later. In 1802, the Common Council decreed that Bunker's Hill be flattened, and the "good and whole-some earth" from the hill be used to erase Collect Pond from the map of New York. By 1812, the freshwater springs that had slaked the thirst of Manhattan's residents for centuries had been buried below ground. No one has seen or drunk from them since.

For a time in the early 1820s, a respectable neighborhood flourished over the former site of the pond. But before long, the city's attempt to suppress the natural landscape of the Collect fell victim to a kind of return of the repressed. Below those fashionable new homes, in the "good and whole-some earth" plowed in from Bunker's Hill, an invisible kingdom of microorganisms was steadily working its way through the organic material that had remained from Collect Pond's earlier life: all those decaying animal carcasses and biomass from the wetlands.

The work of those subterranean microbes caused two problems at ground level. As the biomass decomposed, the houses began to sink into the earth. And as they sank, putrid smells began to emanate from the ground. The mildest rains would cause basements to flood with dank marsh water. Typhus outbreaks became routine in the neighborhood. Within a matter of years, the well-to-do residents had fled, and the housing stock had plummeted in value. By the 1840s, when Charles Dickens visited it, it had become the most famous slum in the United States, Five Points (see **Five Points/Columbus Park**, p. 164).

—*Steven Johnson*

Memorial drumming at the African Burial Ground Monument. CREDIT: COURTESY OF THE NATIONAL PARKS SERVICE

TO LEARN MORE

Johnson, Steven. *Farsighted*. New York: Riverhead Books, 2018 (excerpted with permission).
Sanderson, Eric. *Mannahatta, A Natural History of New York*. New York: Abrams Books, 2009.

2.49 African Burial Ground

290 Broadway at Duane Street, New York, NY

In the 1690s, the blocks from Chambers to Duane, and Centre to Broadway lay outside the city limits, in the woods, close to the freshwater pond (see **Collect Pond Park**, p. 161) where city residents drew most of their water. It was there that the first burial ground for enslaved and free Black people was established, referred to as the "Negroe's Burying Ground." In operation for most of the eighteenth century, thousands of men, women, and children were buried there. While it was in use, attending and participating in funerals was one of the few group activities permitted enslaved people. Such burials were also where customs that Africans brought from home could continue.

Memoirs and records of contemporary whites reported hearing drumming and singing during the rituals; graves unearthed with the burial grounds rediscovery uncovered beads, shells, and shroud pins among the skeletal remains. Starting in the 1720s, as whites grew increasingly concerned with controlling the actions of the growing enslaved population, the city passed laws to limit the number of attendees at an enslaved person's funeral to twelve and limited the hours of funerals to before sunset, drastically foreshortening their capacity to mourn collectively, as they had to come when work was done. By the 1790s the city had grown around the burial ground and developers pushed to close it. In 1795 the city's first known religious group for Black people, the African Society, petitioned for land for a church and a new cemetery. For nearly two hundred years, the burial ground was forgotten, itself buried beneath waves of city development.

The burial ground was rediscovered in 1991 during excavations for the construction of a new federal building. After extended public debate and organized pressure from the city's Black community, a small portion of the burial ground was set aside for the monument that stands here today. The visitor's center opened in 2010. The city has since recognized two other African burial sites, in Harlem and East New York, Brooklyn. Thousands of graves still lie under the courthouses, banks, and stores of the surrounding blocks.

TO LEARN MORE

The African Burial Ground: An American Discovery. 1994. Four part documentary series produced by David Kutz, written by Christopher Moore, narrated by Ossie Davis and Ruby Dee.

African Burial Ground National Monument (US National Park Service), https://www.nps.gov/afbg/index.htm.

Harris, Leslie M. *In the Shadow of Slavery: African Americans in New York City, 1626–1863.* Chicago: University of Chicago Press, 2004.

Chinatown

2.50 Five Points/Columbus Park

158 Worth Street, New York, NY

A street named Cross once bisected this corner of the park at the intersection of Baxter and Worth. Cross Street ran northeast through today's Columbus Park, and tiny Mosco Street was its final block. It also continued southwest, through today's New York County Courthouse, whose back you can see from here. Cross and Baxter (formerly Orange) met at near right angles, while Worth (formerly Anthony) came to a dead end here, splitting what would have been a regular four corner intersection into five.

For most of the nineteenth century, and arguably through to this day, the neighborhood known as "Five Points" was the most famous slum in the United States, known for its debauchery and crime. It was here that the "Gangs of New York" first roamed. By the 1820s the neighborhood boasted a plurality of the city's brothels, aided by the

Five Points, as pictured in an 1855 guide to New York City. CREDIT: ARTIST UNKNOWN, COURTESY OF THE METROPOLITAN MUSEUM OF ART DIGITAL COLLECTION

Well-to-do New Yorkers "slumming" in Five Points 1885. CREDIT: FRANK LESLIES ILLUSTRATED NEWSPAPER (STAFF ARTIST), COURTESY OF LIBRARY OF CONGRESS; PUBLIC DOMAIN

open space provided by Paradise Square at the joining of the five streets. The Tombs, New York's infamous jail, was at the corner of Franklin and Centre. Nearby alleys and courtyards had nicknames like Murderers Alley and Bandits Roost.

For all its criminal excesses, the reputation of Five Points distorted its true conditions, which were primarily problems of overcrowding and desperate poverty. During the era of the Irish famine, and for years thereafter, it was the most densely popu-

lated square mile in the world, holding numbers that even today are only equaled by a few places worldwide and unequaled anywhere in the contemporary United States. Crammed into subdivided wooden or the newer brick tenant houses—eventually known as tenements—the tens of thousands of people living in Five Points had no running water in their houses, little or no garbage service, and, for the majority of Irish who had recently arrived, little money, few skills, and highly accented English. That the Irish and free Black people of the neighborhood lived side by side and even intermarried was offensive enough to outside observers. But the inevitable and inescapable filth of the neighborhood compounded its infamy, and regardless of the hard work and diligence of its majority law-abiding residents, for much of the nineteenth century its degraded conditions were blamed on the character of its residents rather than the social environment they occupied.

By the late nineteenth century, the moral panics that had typified the previous decades had begun to be replaced by a more sympathetic attitude among reformist elites regarding Five Points' poor as well as the general conditions of the downtown slums, including New York's nearby Lower East Side. Landlords, real estate speculators, a lack of services, and weak or nonexistent building regulations were more often described as the causes of the neighborhood's deplorable state. Jacob Riis wrote and photographed *How the Other Half Lives,* published in 1890, casting a clear light on the conditions of Manhattan's poor. By the turn of the century, Mulberry Bend, the most infamous of the streets in Five Points, had been razed to form Columbus Park. Some of the houses along the park, including 48–50 Mulberry Street and 102 and 104 Bayard Street, date back to the era.

Hotel 50 Bowery, once the site of the Silver Palace Restaurant, 2017. CREDIT: SCOTT DEXTER

TO LEARN MORE

Anbinder, Tyler. *Five Points: The 19th-Century New York City Neighborhood That Invented Tap Dance, Stole Elections, and Became the World's Most Notorious Slum.* Reprint edition. New York: Plume, 2002.

Baker, Kevin. *Paradise Alley.* New York: Harper Perennial, 2006.

Mele, Christopher. *Selling the Lower East Side: Culture, Real Estate, and Resistance in New York City.* Minneapolis: University of Minnesota, 2000.

2.51 Former Site of Silver Palace Restaurant

50–52 Bowery, New York, NY

The two-story building that once stood on this site was home to the Silver Palace, a nine-hundred seat dim sum restaurant that was the first to become unionized in Chinatown. In 1978 Chinese workers at the Silver Palace organized a union, under the Hotel Employees Restaurant Employees Union. Over time, the union failed to meet the needs of its members and the workers re-affiliated with the Chinese Staff and Work-

Strikers in front of the Silver Palace Restaurant in 1993. CREDIT: JOHN SOTOMAYOR/*NEW YORK TIMES*/REDUX

ers Association (CSWA), a hybrid union and worker center in Chinatown.

The workers faced their biggest challenge in 1993 when, in what became one of the longest labor disputes in New York City history, their employer locked them out for over seven months after the union refused to give up paid health insurance, paid time off, and split tips with managers. CSWA built significant support for the Silver Palace workers from other worker centers like the Lower East Side Worker Center, reform caucuses in unions like New Directions inside the Transit Workers Union (TWU Local 100), student activists, and community organizations like Jews for Racial and Economic Justice and the Committee Against Anti-Asian Violence. In 1994, the forty unionized workers were able to return to work and keep their benefits, but only until 1995, when the Silver Palace filed for bankruptcy. The union insisted that the employer filed for bankruptcy to avoid having to pay the workers the back wages they were owed; indeed, the workers were never paid.

In 1997, Richard Chan bought the assets of the Silver Place and reopened the restaurant as the New Silver Palace, where he was forced by the National Labor Relations Board to hire back some of the workers from the original Silver Palace. At the same time, CSWA was in a battle with the nearby Jing Fong restaurant, also for stolen tips. In 2000, Jing Fong workers received over $1 million in back wages. By 2003 the New Silver Palace restaurant had also declared bankruptcy, but after a long legal dispute, seventeen workers were eventually paid $500,000 in tips and back wages.

In 2013, the Chu family, the building's owners, decided to tear it down to embark on a hotel project. Later that year, a historian trespassing on the property found a wealth of post–Civil War archeological remnants, including possibly the remains of Bull's Head Tavern, where George Washington assembled his troops on evacuation day in 1783. While no conclusive evidence of the tavern has been found, over seven hundred artifacts have been recovered. The Chu family has displayed some of these pieces on the second floor of the hotel.

TO LEARN MORE

Chinese Staff and Workers' Association (CSWA). n.d. CSWA.org. Accessed August 27, 2020. https://cswa.org/?page_id=126&lang=en.

Kwong, Peter. *Forbidden Workers: Illegal Chinese Immigrants and American Labor.* New York: New Press, 1998.

Demonstration outside of Chase Manhattan in 1965. CREDIT: BARTON SILVERMAN, *NEW YORK TIMES*/REDUX PHOTOS

NEARBY SITES OF INTEREST

Sunshine Hotel

241–245 Bowery, New York, NY

The Sunshine is the only Bowery "flophouse" that continues to exist (see **Third Street Men's Shelter**, p. 142). It opened in 1922 and charged ten cents a night at its opening.

Museum of Chinese in America

215 Centre Street, New York, NY

A museum dedicated to Chinese American history.

First Shearith Israel Graveyard

55–57 St. James Place, New York, NY

The only seventeenth century structure in Manhattan, this small plot was part of a larger Jewish graveyard from the country's first Jewish congregation.

Financial District

2.52 One Chase Manhattan Plaza

28 Liberty Street, New York, NY

Before merging with J. P. Morgan's empire, Chase can trace its roots to the Bank of Manhattan Company, a commercial bank created by Aaron Burr in 1799 in what was perhaps the country's first banking swindle. Burr, with the support of his erstwhile adversary Alexander Hamilton, won the right to charter the bank for the express purpose of financing clean water for the city, which had suffered terrible yellow fever epidemics that year and was awash in swampy, dirty water. Burr pledged to bring clean water from the Bronx to the city through the private funds he would be able to raise through his bank. But the bank's charter ultimately granted its trustees significant powers to raise and use capital beyond the water plan, and it quickly became clear that the water plan had been a ruse all along. The Manhattan Company sank one well, which drew off of water used elsewhere, and the pipes they laid damaged the streets. The Bank of Manhattan, however, quickly surpassed its only commercial competitor, the Federalist-controlled Bank of New York. New York City's water supply stayed filthy and scarce until 1842 when the Croton Aqueduct system was put in place.

Museum of American Finance

48 Wall Street, New York, NY

This was the original headquarters of the Bank of New York.

2.53 Former Site of New York Slave Market

74 Wall Street, New York, NY

Enslaved Black people represented nearly an eighth of the population of the city when this market was erected in 1711. The first enslaved Africans in New Amsterdam arrived in 1626, brought by the Dutch West India Company. In the city's first decades, enslaved people helped build Fort Amsterdam and clear Broadway; the wall that gave Wall Street its name was fortified by enslaved Africans. Under British dominion since 1664, demand for labor in the burgeoning new city had grown, with need for construction, farming, and all kinds of service. By the beginning of the eighteenth century, hundreds of private households in what had become New York had purchased human beings to perform essential work.

Enslaved people were frequently leased out by their owners to others for specific projects, their labor bought at half the rate of free workers. Operating through 1762, the market was a site through which the leasing and buying of those in bondage could be centrally organized, with the city collecting taxes on these transactions. In addition to making it easier for white people to find, purchase, or rent the men and women supplying them with labor, the market served to control the association of the slaves themselves, whose freedom of movement around the city was drastically curtailed with the establishing of the market: enslaved individuals were compelled to gather at the market when their owners forced them to seek additional work, and their assignments could be tracked from there. The New York City Slave Market was the country's second most profitable, following Charleston, South Carolina, and New York was second to Charleston also in the breadth of those who held people in slavery among its households. By the mid-eighteenth century, enslaved people were nearly a fifth of the city's population, and over 40 percent of white households held other humans in bondage. A plaque commemorating the market was erected in 2015 at Wall and Pearl Streets, following agitation that began among Occupy Wall Street protesters in 2011.

2.54 Standard Oil Building

26 Broadway, New York, NY

For weeks during the spring of 1914, socialists and anarchists led protests outside these doors, seeking to shame the son of John D. Rockefeller, who had inherited leadership of Standard Oil upon the retirement of his father. Anti-union zealotry by John Jr. had just recently led to what became known as the "Ludlow Massacre" of April 1914, in which an estimated two dozen men, women, and children were killed while striking Colorado coal

The Standard Oil Building, standing at the foot of Broadway, with the Customs House in the foreground. n.d. CREDIT: THE MIRIAM AND IRA D. WALLACH DIVISION OF ART, PRINTS AND PHOTOGRAPHS: PHOTOGRAPHY COLLECTION, THE NEW YORK PUBLIC LIBRARY. "STANDARD OIL BUILDING FROM BOWLING GREEN, NEW YORK, NY" NEW YORK PUBLIC LIBRARY DIGITAL COLLECTIONS

police. The newspapers printed his statement in full, but the public does not hear the miners' side. . . . The public does not understand that the only reason the strikers want a contract with the union is that they have learned by bitter experience that no other kind of a promise is any good."

For months following the massacre, groups of protesters, including a large contingent of members of the Industrial Workers of the World (or "Wobblies"), dogged the Rockefellers here, as well as at their midtown residence, churches, and upstate estate, helping to create a public relations crisis for the family, and eventually helping in the push for various progressive-era labor legislation. The animus against Rockefeller took non-peaceful forms as well, including a plan to bomb the Rockefeller estate in Tarrytown, New York. In July 1914, a bomb intended for Tarrytown nearly leveled 1626 Lexington Avenue uptown, killing four, including three of the men responsible for the plot.

mines under his ownership. The author and journalist Upton Sinclair helped to organize the initial silent pickets, whose participants wore the black crepe armbands of mourning as they marched back and forth in front of the marble entrance. The *New York Times* reported Sinclair's explanation of the pickets, "I do this thing because Mr. Rockefeller is here at the very headquarters of the invisible government with all his prestige and his power and his control of the press and the

2.55 National Museum of the American Indian (Fort Amsterdam)

1 Bowling Green, New York, NY

Soon after settling in 1625, the Dutch erected a fort here to protect the fur trade of the Dutch West India Company, whose commercial exploits were the raison d'être of the settlement. The fort's initial purpose was to deter competition from other European colonial powers interested in controlling the strategic Hudson Bay and river trade

Of the four continents depicted outside the former Customs House, a youthful and vigorous "America," 2020. CREDIT: PENNY LEWIS

route. Fort Amsterdam soon served to protect Dutch settlers from attacks by Native groups, attacks which also served as the primary impetus for the construction of wooden ramparts across the island a few thousand feet north, along what is known today as Wall Street. The various tribes that warred with the Dutch did so in retaliation for Dutch offenses in the area. European casualties were low to nonexistent in most fights, as Native groups sought to drive out and burn down the settlements, wreaking havoc rather than killing people.

Today, underscoring history's ironic path, this spot is home to the National Museum of the American Indian. The landmarked building served as the United States Customs House from its opening in 1907 through the early 1970s.

Despite its contemporary status as an institution devoted to the victims of settler colonialism, the four statues that front today's museum serve as a useful reminder of the continuity of colonial attitudes. "The Four Continents" (1903–1907) are highly symbolic representations of Asia, America, Europe, and Africa that communicate typical cultural stereotypes and biases, and are well worth a close examination for a window into the triumphalist imperialism of the turn of the twentieth century. Of the four seated women, America is the youngest and most vigorous; she is associated with the rich cultivation of the land (corn) and industrial progress (a strong young man holding a winged wheel). Such wealth appears to have been made possible by the support of Native groups, depicted through the figure of an Indian warrior at her back, and their vanquishing, signified by the figure of an Aztec deity under her feet. The figure of Africa serves as the greatest contrast to that of America—the woman nude, asleep; the setting ancient, primitive, underdeveloped. The sculptor who carved these figures, Daniel Chester French, described his Africa representation as "the sleeping continent," whose wealth was untapped and promise undiscovered. The figures of Asia and Europe convey faded glory, though Europe's age is communicated through an older woman with regal bearing, surrounded by evidence of cultural accomplishment. Asia's contemplative pose and spiritual symbolism are symbolically linked to material desperation and poverty of her peoples, who are depicted with Orientalist condescension as submissive and enslaved, bent and broken in figures beside the queenly woman who meditates at the sculpture's center.

(Right) Mabel Dwight's "Old Aquarium," today's Castle Clinton, 1936. CREDIT: MABEL DWIGHT (1876–1955) FOR FEDERAL ART PROJECT

(Below) Luis Sanguino's 1973 "The Immigrants," celebrating the diverse peoples who arrived through lower Manhattan, 2019. CREDIT: PENNY LEWIS

2.56 Battery Park/Castle Clinton

West of State Street, South of Battery Place, New York, NY

The Battery was initially a site of defense, but eventually became the place where New York opened itself to the world. In the years after Fort Amsterdam was razed, New York's West Battery was built in 1808 on an artificial island offshore, as part of the city's defense (at the time, there were fears of an invasion from the British). The circular fort was soon repurposed as an entertainment center, with a bridge connecting it to the mainland, and for years held a beer garden and theater known as Castle Garden. But as the neighborhood's elite moved uptown and immigrants swelled the city, the Garden was once again repurposed into an immigration depot, beginning in 1855; landfill connected the island to the mainland soon thereafter.

As such, Castle Garden became America's first immigration station, predating Ellis Island, and 8 million came through its doors between 1855–1890. Lining the nearby streets were people offering these immigrants jobs and housing, frequently fraudulently. In 1890 the federal government took over immigration, and relocated the facility to Ellis Island, a larger space which also allowed for isolation against "immigrant diseases." Twelve million more immigrants were to arrive at Ellis over the coming decades.

The twenty-five-acre park in which Castle Clinton sits is also a center of the city's memorializing, with the highest density of memorials (particularly war memorials) of any spot. Merchant Mariners, Korean War veterans, Norwegian veterans, and wireless operators are among those memorialized; one can also visit Hope Garden (a memorial to AIDS victims), and several others.

NEARBY SITES OF INTEREST

Vietnam Veterans Plaza
55 Water Street, New York, NY
Memorial honoring New Yorkers that served in the Vietnam War.

Battery Urban Farm
State Street and Battery Place, New York, NY
An educational farm that focuses on teaching students, New Yorkers, and visitors sustainable farming techniques and environmental stewardship.

New York Harbor

2.57 Statue of Liberty
Liberty Island, New York, NY

> "Keep, ancient lands, your storied
>   pomp!" cries she
> With silent lips. "Give me your tired,
>   your poor,
> Your huddled masses yearning to
>   breathe free,
> The wretched refuse of your teem-
>   ing shore.
> Send these, the homeless, tempest-
>   tost to me,
> I lift my lamp beside the golden
>   door!"

With these words from poet Emma Lazarus, the symbolic freight of Lady Liberty has been cemented in the hearts and minds of US citizens and, arguably, observers around the globe. Public school students across the United States are taught that the Statue of Liberty, "Lady Liberty," was a gift from France, celebrating its shared ideals with the United States, and in particular New York, its great port of entry to European immigrants. In truth, the statue was to celebrate the abolition of slavery, not immigration.

Frédéric Bartholdi, a well-regarded French sculptor, had the idea to create the world's largest lighthouse. Facing limited enthusiasm in both France and the United States, Bartholdi came up with the ingenious idea of claiming to the United States that the statue was a gift from France. New York was not the only site considered—both Boston and Philadelphia put in bids. In the end, New York won because President Ulysses Grant agreed to donate Bedloe Island, a former fort, for the project. Ultimately supporting Bartholdi's plan, the French government decided to pay

Liberty enlightening the world—Inauguration of the Bartholdi Statue, Harbor of New York, 1886. CREDIT: LIBRARY OF CONGRESS, LC-DIG-DS-04491

for the statue, while the United States was to provide land, the pedestal, and maintenance. Although the donation of land was not controversial, Congress and other states did not want to use public monies to pay for the pedestal. This put the project at risk, requiring private fundraising. Joseph Pulitzer, owner of the New York World, had the brilliant idea of printing the names of *all* people who donated to the statue in his paper, no matter how small their donation—spurring the first paid canvassing operation in the United States. Hundreds of people were employed across Manhattan to go district by district to raise funds for the statue.

The irony of the iconography of a female Statue of Liberty and Lazarus's "The New Colossus" poem written to help fundraise for the statue was not lost on women, who at the time did not have the right to vote and were not invited to the island to participate in the ceremonial unveiling in 1886 (with the exception of twelve, including Bartholdi's wife). The wives of members of the private fundraisers and other distinguished guests were relegated to nearby steamships. The select twenty-five hundred people allowed on the island, included the French delegation, members of the military, dignitaries, and President Grover Cleveland.

The New York Women's Suffrage Association protested that women were not invited, and when their pleas were ignored, they chartered a steamship to take them as close as possible to the statue. As President Cleveland and others spoke, the Suffragettes used bullhorns to blast their protests, but amid all the ambient noise it was impossible to hear them. The Suffragettes' protest was the first in a long history of protests at the island, including a banner drop stating "Women of the World Unite" in August of 1970, two weeks before the strike for women's equality led by Betty Friedan (see **Women's Strike for Equality**, p. 98); a three-day occupation of the island by Vietnam Veterans Against the War in December 1971, and again in 1976 to bring attention to Veterans concerns; and a banner drop by Puerto Rican nationalists in 1977 calling for Puerto Rico's independence. Most recently, immigration activists dropped a banner on the island protesting Trump's Muslim Ban and the treatment of immigrants and asylum seekers at the United States–Mexico Border.

TO LEARN MORE

Mitchell, Elizabeth. *Liberty's Torch: The Great Adventure to Build the Statue of Liberty*. Reprint edition. New York: Grove Press, 2015.

New York City Islands

With the exception of the Bronx, New York City is itself a conjoining of islands—Manhattan, Staten Island, and the westernmost sections of the great Long Island, which stretches out one hundred miles east to end at Block Island Sound. Additional islands of various sizes dot the waterways around the city. Their geographic footprint has shifted with natural and unnatural forces over the years, as some have been erased by tides and storms, while many others have been extended by landfill to grow, and at times even join with others. The waterways of New York, its natural ports and strategic location for inland and oceanic trade, drew European colonizers to the area. City governments have since exploited the city's fractured physical geography to locate marginal and undesired people and social processes on many of these smaller islands, which are both isolated from, but close enough to, the city to serve such a function. The city's smaller islands are home to jails, mental

hospitals, homeless shelters, and cemeteries, and in the past have also included quarantines, workhouses, military posts, and garbage dumps. Much of the operations on these islands remained hidden during their most active years. With some exceptions, it is only in recent decades that a combination of market forces and organized political pressure has yielded broader public scrutiny and say over the direction these islands might take.

Today's Roosevelt Island, formerly Blackwell's Island, also known as Welfare Island, housed numerous state and private institutions over the course of its history including a prison, a smallpox hospital, and the New York City Lunatic Asylum, in operation for

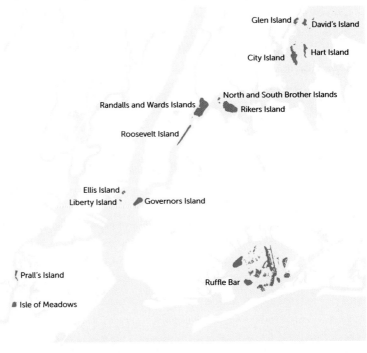

Glen Island　David's Island

City Island　Hart Island

North and South Brother Islands

Randalls and Wards Islands　Rikers Island

Roosevelt Island

Ellis Island
Liberty Island　Governors Island

Prall's Island

Ruffle Bar

Isle of Meadows

much of the nineteenth century. Journalist Nellie Bly went undercover as an inmate at the woman's asylum on the island in 1887, creating one of the first exposés of the terrible abuses that inmates faced in such institutions. Her widely publicized story helped to reform practices at the asylum, including gaining more funding and translators for the immigrant women held there.

Roosevelt Island's close proximity to Manhattan first facilitated these long-time institutional uses, but today supports its gentrification. The Lunatic Asylum's Octagon Tower serves as the lobby entrance to two luxury housing developments at the northern end of the island. While some of the residential housing on the island was initiated under the Mitchell Lama program for middle-class housing and remains affordable today, new developments include luxury rentals and condominiums. The island's upmarket value is mirrored and reinforced by the 2017 opening of Cornell Tech, a Cornell University campus, which was given $100 million and free land to erect its campus near the south end. The 2012 opening of Four Freedoms State Park, a memorial to President Franklin Delano Roosevelt, also served to raise the profile of the workaday island.

Mental health and penal facilities left Blackwells for Ward's Island and Rikers Island farther up the East River. Ward's Island, now joined with the park-filled Randall's Island, continues to hold the Manhattan Psychiatric Center, whose tall and imposing modern façade frequently causes travelers on the Brooklyn–Queens Expressway and the Triborough Bridge to confuse it

Blackwells Island, prisoners breaking stone, photographed by Jacob Riis, ca. 1890. CREDIT: JACOB A. (JACOB AUGUST) RIIS (1849–1914). MUSEUM OF THE CITY OF NEW YORK. 90.13.2.4

with the jails at Rikers. But the multiple correctional facilities at Rikers, including facilities for youth and women, have none of the vertical heft of the hospital. They are spread out over four hundred acres (much of which was created by inmates as landfill), housing as many as ten thousand prisoners a day, the vast majority of whom have not been charged for a crime and are held because they could not afford bail. One such inmate, Kalief Browder, was sixteen years old in 2010 when he was sent to Rikers on suspicion of stealing a backpack. He was held, uncharged, at the facility for three years, two in solitary confinement. He ultimately committed suicide two years after his release. Public outrage over Browder's case and the violent treatment of other incarcerated innocents has led to bail reform, as well as mayoral promises that the jails at Rikers will be closed and replaced by four smaller jails by 2026. As of 2020, incidents of violence from guards to inmates had reached an "all time high," according to the *New York Times*.

Public pressure has also been brought to bear on the evolution of uses for Governors Island, located in New York Harbor just a few thousand feet from Brooklyn. Governors Island was a federally owned military installation for much of its history, holding forts, Army troops and the Coast Guard until the end of the twentieth century. Unusually, the land has been protected for use by the public, and Governors Island has become a popular leisure destination for ferry travelers from Manhattan and, on weekends, Brooklyn, who visit for the kayaking, bike rentals, playground, picnicking, ziplining, and even camping, or for visits to its galleries and numerous museums. The island's New York Harbor School, a public high school, offers students a maritime-themed education, including marine science, transportation and technology, and hosts the Billion Oyster Project, seeking to re-seed New York Harbor with flood-preventing oyster beds.

Another island whose core practices have been recently challenged by the public is Hart Island. Previously used to quarantine the sick during the 1870 yellow fever epidemic, it alternately housed a boys' workhouse and a women's insane asylum. Today, Hart Island is the nation's largest potter's field, or common grave, typically for the unclaimed or indigent, and is the largest tax-funded cemetery in the world. Approximately a million people have been buried on the island since 1869. About fifteen hundred bodies of the poor, homeless, stillborn, and unclaimed are buried every year in caskets

stacked in threes by Riker's Island inmates in seventy-foot-long, ten-foot-deep trenches. A substantial portion of those buried on Hart Island in recent decades ended up there because of neglect or fraud on the part of court guardians and nursing homes. Dozens, if not hundreds, of unclaimed victims of the COVID-19 pandemic were buried here while New York was the epicenter of the disease.

Prior to 2008, relatives and loved ones of those buried on Hart Island had no way of accessing burial records or grave sites. Their agitation and activism led to the city publishing a searchable database of burial records from 1977 to today so that the interred may be identified and spurred the Department of Corrections to run monthly visits to the island for family members.

Somewhat exceptional to the trend, and the most famous of the islands, Liberty Island and Ellis Island sit in New York Harbor and have served as the symbols of the nation's and the city's historical openness, specifically its welcome of European immigrants (see **Statue of Liberty**, p. 173). But in addition to processing nearly 12 million immigrants from 1892 through the first decades of the twentieth century, Ellis Island housed spaces for quarantine and hospitalization for immigrants who were deemed sick upon arrival, and around 1 percent of those seeking admission were sent back from there. Today both islands stand as memorials to that more open past, with Ellis Island's processing center converted to the Ellis Island Immigration Museum, with tours available daily to the statue.

3

Queens

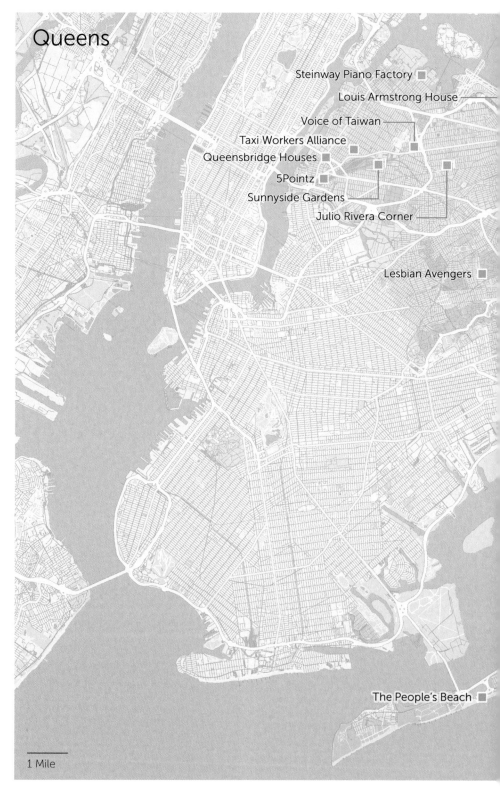

Queens

Steinway Piano Factory ■

Louis Armstrong House ─

Voice of Taiwan ─

Taxi Workers Alliance ■

Queensbridge Houses ■

5Pointz ■

Sunnyside Gardens ─

Julio Rivera Corner ─

Lesbian Avengers ■

The People's Beach ■

1 Mile

Friends Meeting House

Hindu Temple Society of North America

Flushing Meadows Corona Park

Store Front Museum

Rochdale Village

Howard Beach Riots

Jamaica Bay/Wildlife Refuge

N

Introduction

IF ASKED TO PICTURE A NEIGHBORHOOD in Queens, many people will still imagine Archie Bunker's mostly white, blue-collar neighborhood of single family homes from the 1970's television show *All in the Family*. But the borough is, in fact, the most ethnically and linguistically diverse county in the United States, and some consider it the most diverse place *in the world*. This sprawling, largely residential borough sits across the East River from Manhattan, sandwiched between Brooklyn to the west and greater Long Island to the east. Queens is the city's largest borough, geographically speaking, comprising nearly 40 percent of its square mileage, and the second most populous, after Brooklyn. Neighborhoods span highly dense Astoria and Long Island City along the East River to suburban communities like Floral Park and Douglaston in far eastern Queens, nearly indistinguishable from neighboring towns in Long Island; and from the Whitestone and Throgs Neck bridges that provide access to the Bronx in the north to the Rockaways at its coastal southern border, a popular summer beach destination. Large single-family homes on relatively large lots, blocks of townhomes, garden communities, and small and large apartment buildings alike all dot the borough, peppered in its denser communities with discount shops, restaurants, bodegas, and services of all kinds, and in the more sprawling communities with suburban-style shopping centers.

Joining Irish, Italian, Jewish, and other European-descended families with longer roots in the United States, nearly 50 percent of Queens residents are foreign-born, and it is home to large Black middle-class enclaves. In fact, no racial or ethnic group holds a majority here, with white, Black, Asian, and Latina/o/x households each making up about a quarter of the population. The relative affordability of housing and availability of single-family homes have attracted immigrants from all walks of life from all over the world, generation after generation. The majority of immigrants who now call Queens home emigrated from Latin America, and half of the entire city's Asian population lives in the borough. All told, Queens has the city's largest populations of Chinese, Indians, Koreans, Filipinos, Bangladeshis, Pakistanis, Colombians, Ecuadorians, Peruvians, Greeks, and Salvadorans.

Prior to European colonization, the Matinecock, Lekawe (Rockaway), Canarsie, and Lenape populated what we now know as Queens. An intense bout of small pox in 1658 purportedly killed two-thirds of native people in the area, and continued war with Dutch and British colonizers drove them from their settlements. Before the Long Island Rail Road opened in 1836, Queens consisted of farmland dotted with a few small towns, including Flushing, Jamaica, and Newtown, which are now part of New York City, and Hempstead and Oyster Bay, now part of Nassau County, Long Island.

The opening of the Long Island Rail Road jump-started residential development in the borough, and Astoria and Ravenswood were among the earliest suburbs of New York (that is, Manhattan). Large numbers of Irish and German immigrants moved to Queens as industry grew dramatically in the borough in the latter half of the nineteenth century. Distilleries, breweries, oil refineries, chemical plants, and various other manufacturers set up in Long Island City and the surrounding areas. By 1920, Queens was a national leader in industrial production, ranking fifteenth in the country.

When transit options dramatically expanded at the beginning of the twentieth century, Queens grew exponentially. The new East River tunnels and the Williamsburg and Queensboro bridges, built between 1903 and 1909, could carry hundreds of thousands more people between Manhattan and the Queens neighborhoods now served by the 7, E, F, M, and R subway lines. The new neighborhoods were distinctly semi-suburban: while developers and boosters at the time built large apartment buildings in the Bronx and elsewhere in the city, they built low-density townhomes, garden apartments, and detached and semi-detached single-family homes in Queens. In the first three decades of the twentieth century, Queens's population grew by seven times between 1900 and 1930, mirroring the population growth that came with new transit all over the city—but the population of Queens remained smaller than the Bronx, Brooklyn, and Manhattan given the lower density of its new housing. Even still, the industrial

and construction booms of the era attracted new immigrants from southern and eastern Europe, with large numbers of Italians settling in Astoria and Corona and Irish in Woodside and Sunnyside (see **7 Train Tour**, p. 337).

When the United States immigration laws that favored European immigration were changed under the 1952 Immigration and Nationality Act and the 1965 Hart-Celler Immigration Bill, millions of new immigrants from South and East Asia, Latin America, the Caribbean, and Africa settled in New York City. White flight and the city's fiscal crisis of the late 1960s and 1970s left abandoned properties and businesses—spaces of great opportunity for new immigrants all over the city, but particularly in Queens. White flight from Flushing, for example, allowed for Flushing to become "Little India" in the 1970s and 1980s, and South Asians were later joined by Taiwanese and Korean immigrants in what is now the city's largest Chinese enclave. Indians, Pakistanis, and Bangladeshis also formed South Asian enclaves in Jackson Heights and Richmond Hill, which is now also home to large numbers of Guyanese. Greek immigrants settled in Astoria, which now holds the largest Greek population outside of Athens. Once Italian, Irish, German, and Jewish neighborhoods, Cambria Heights and Rosedale are now primarily Afro-Caribbean—particularly Jamaican, Haitian, and Trinidadian.

While ethnic enclaves abound in Queens, many neighborhoods are home to a true diversity of residents. Jackson Heights is primarily known as a South Asian enclave, but it is also home to significant numbers of immigrants from Argentina, Mexico, Ecuador, and Colombia. Elmhurst has no dominant group and hosts its own mix of immigrants from Cuba, China, Korea, the Philippines, Costa Rica, Chile, and Peru.

Relatedly, Queens is exceptional for its religious diversity. Early English settlers fought for and secured religious freedom from the Dutch for Protestant Christian sects, laying the foundation for the remarkable religious pluralism characteristic of the borough today (see **Flushing Friends Meeting House**, p. 201). Flushing alone holds more than two hundred places of worship within a few miles, and greater Queens is home to thousands of places of worship. Flushing has in residence the Free Synagogue of Flushing (the first reform Jewish synagogue to be opened by women), the Hindu Temple Society of North America (the first traditional Hindu temple built in North America; see **Hindu Temple Society of North America**, p. 203), and more than one hundred Korean Christian churches; Elmhurst is home to the Chan Meditation Center of the Dharma Drum Mountain Buddhist Association, the Korean Evangelical Church of New York, and St. Matthews Lutheran Church for the Deaf; Kew Gardens Hills has a thriving Orthodox Jewish population and more than thirty synagogues; Richmond Hill is home to one of the largest Sikh communities in the United States and to the oldest gurdwara in North America.

But while plenty of Queens's neighborhoods are extraordinarily diverse, segregation has a long history and still abounds in the borough. Restrictive housing covenants—deeds or agreements that property owners made not to sell to people of color—laid the foundation for the borough's current racial geography, as did the shape and extent of its transit development.

Restrictive covenants barred African Americans from 85 percent of new housing developments in Queens in the postwar period. But housing in Corona and parts of southeastern Queens was open to Black people, and the affluent and middle-class fleeing urban decline in Harlem and other Black enclaves flocked there. By 1940 the Black homeownership rate in Queens far exceeded that of the other four boroughs, a trend that continues today. During the 1940s and 1950s, St. Albans and Addisleigh Park became bastions of Black affluence and the Black middle class, housing prominent professionals, business people, and entertainers (see **Louis Armstrong House**, p. 197).

While Corona suffered great disinvestment during the era of white flight and fiscal crisis, eventually becoming more heavily Latina/o/x, Addisleigh Park and bordering communities in southeastern Queens remained anchors of the Black middle class. White businesses fled Addisleigh Park during the 1970s and early 1980s, for example, only to be replaced with Black-owned businesses, and the many area churches provided a political and economic foundation for the community. The Black population in the borough earns around the same as whites on average, an anomaly for the city.

Decisions about, and underinvestment in, public transit has also had profound consequences for the racial geography of Queens, as well as its class composition. Competition between the private companies that first developed public transit in New York City meant that the 7 subway line never developed past Flushing in northeastern Queens. This lack of public transit in northeastern Queens resulted in the area remaining white, middle-class, and affluent for much of the twentieth century. These and neighboring communities of Whitestone, College Point, North Flushing, and Douglaston did not experience massive white flight, but they have experienced Asian in-migration. They remain majority white and Asian communities today.

Other large gaps in public rail transit exist, including in western Queens around Maspeth and Middle Village; the broad area between the 7 line to the north and F line to the south, including Kew Gardens Hills, Pomonok, and Fresh Meadows; and much of southeastern Queens, including St. Albans, Addisleigh Park, Queens Village, Rochdale, Laurelton, Springfield Gardens, and Rosedale. These widespread transit holes mean that a large portion of Queens residents must rely on car transit, making it more likely to attract the city's middle class given the relatively high cost of owning a car in the city.

Its middle-class character is further supported by its diverse economy, which is the most varied of all five boroughs, with nearly equal amounts of jobs in health care, retail, manufacturing, construction, transportation, and film and television production. Both of New York City's airports—LaGuardia and JFK—are in Queens and provide a large portion of jobs to Queens residents. Silvercup Studios, the largest film and television production facility in the city, is located in Long Island City, and the historic Kaufman Astoria Studios, home to the city's only back lot, is in Astoria. Education, health services, finance, information, and small businesses employ thousands, and the manufacturing and construction industries are strong. With its long-term stable middle class, homeownership rates in Queens are higher than the city as a whole, unsurprisingly. About 43 percent of Queens residents own their homes versus 31 percent of all New York City residents, with Black homeownership rate the highest in the city at nearly 50 percent.

A note on Queens addresses: Unlike the rest of New York City, Queens has a convention of using neighborhoods in its postal addresses. Rather than separately listing neighborhood names above clusters of sites, as we do in the rest of the book, the neighborhood locations for Queens sites are listed as part of their addresses.

TO LEARN MORE

Gryvatz Copquin, Claudia. *The Neighborhoods of Queens.* New Haven: Yale University Press, 2007.

Hanson, R. Scott. *City of Gods: Religious Freedom, Immigration, and Pluralism in Flushing, Queens.* New York: Empire State Editions, 2016.

■ ■ ■

Steinway Piano Factory workers in Steinway Village, 1908.
CREDIT: THE LA GUARDIA AND WAGNER ARCHIVES, LA GUARDIA COMMUNITY COLLEGE/THE CITY UNIVERSITY OF NEW YORK

3.1 Steinway Piano Factory

18–1 Steinway Place, Astoria, NY

Initially established in 1853 in Manhattan, the Steinway piano factory continues to be one of the largest and most renowned piano factories in the world. Beyond the quality of its instruments, the company is notable for the extreme measures it took to address its labor conflicts: by 1925, Steinway had successfully built the only company town in New York City history for its two-thousand-plus employees.

Steinway's operations had experienced explosive growth during and after the Civil War, and by the 1870s, Steinway's Manhattan factory proved insufficient for the demand. Like many other entrepreneurs of the time, Henrich (Henry) Steinway needed more land, which he would have to purchase outside increasingly dense and already expensive Manhattan. In 1870 Steinway began acquiring land in Astoria, Queens, which

was then predominantly farmland. He built a factory, several foundries, a steam sawmill, and an enclosed dock. Workers began commuting to the Astoria factory by ferry from Manhattan that year.

While Steinway was growing, the workers' movement in New York City was consolidating. The year 1872 marked a pivotal time in the local fight for the eight-hour day—in May over one hundred thousand workers from fifty-two different crafts went on strike across the city. The greatest resistance to the strike was offered by Henry Steinway (as well as another manufacturer who lent his name to his products, Isaac Singer, of sewing machine fame). Steinway offered his workers in Manhattan a 10 percent wage increase if they would continue working a ten-hour day. When word got out that some workers had accepted the offer, a majority of woodworkers in the city marched to the Steinway factory to picket and remove the sellouts. Steinway used his political clout to call the police, who came en masse to protect the factory. Workers were beaten and chased away. Shortly after, on June 18, 1872, the city's industrialists joined forces and formed the Executive Committee of Employers in the City. The goal of the committee was to crush the eight-hour movement. Following Steinway, they used wage increases and police repression, and the strike ended.

By then, William Steinway, Henry Steinway's son, had learned a valuable lesson. It wasn't enough to have an additional factory in Astoria. To maintain control of his workforce he needed to escape the socialists and unionists of New York. In 1873, he extended the area around the Astoria factory and created infrastructure for Steinway Village, the only company town to ever exist within the five boroughs. He installed a sewer system and telegraph lines. He built frame houses for workingmen and established schools. In its heyday, the company town had schools with German language instruction, a post office, a library, and even an amusement park.

Today, Steinway continues to have a visible presence in Astoria. The factory remains in its original location and hosts tours. The company town no longer exists, but it is still possible to see a cluster of the original brick homes constructed for workingmen and their families (for example, 41st Street and 20th Avenue and 20–15 41st Street); the church that Steinway had erected in 1890 (41–01 Ditmars Avenue, Long Island City); and the Steinway mansion (18–33 41st Street, Long Island City).

TO LEARN MORE

Lieberman, Richard K. *Steinway and Sons*. Reprint edition. New Haven: Yale University Press, 1997.

NEARBY SITES OF INTEREST

Museum of the Moving Image
36–01 35th Avenue, Astoria, NY
Located in the historic Astoria Studios, this museum is dedicated to film and media.

Socrates Sculpture Park
32–01 Vernon Boulevard, Long Island City, NY
Site of a former landfill, this park houses large sculptures and multimedia installations.

**FAVORITE NEIGHBORHOOD
RESTAURANT**

Bohemian Hall and Beer Garden
29–19 24th Avenue, Astoria, NY
The oldest beer hall in New York City, opened in 1910 to create a home for the Czech people of Astoria to maintain their customs and traditions. The outside bar and park opened in 1919.

3.2 Queensbridge Houses

Bordered by Vernon Boulevard, 40th Avenue, 21st Street, and Queens Plaza North, Long Island City, NY

Stretching over six superblocks along the formerly industrial waterfront of Queens, across the East River from Manhattan, sits North America's largest public housing development. It is managed by the largest local housing authority in the country, the New York City Housing Authority (NYCHA), which continues to house more than 400,000 tenants citywide and accounts for one in ten public housing units nationwide. While other cities have largely demolished public

Queensbridge Houses. CREDIT: METRO CENTRIC, CC BY 2.0, WIKIMEDIA COMMONS

cies. But while Americans on the whole remained largely indifferent or hostile to the idea of public housing, New Yorkers generally supported public intervention in the housing market.

Over the next three decades, more than three hundred developments were built over all five boroughs. Such projects are recognized by housing advocates as the gold standard in affordability. This permanently affordable housing is available to people of low and moderate incomes, and rents are capped at 30 percent of household income. By the late 1960s, New York City operated one in five public housing units in the country that housed one in every sixteen families in the city. While high-rise public housing in other cities was virtually abandoned and uninhabitable, New York's projects were nearly fully rented and decently maintained, relatively speaking. And as other cities waited for Congress to fight over and ultimately limit the national public housing program, New York created city and state programs to step in. Public housing was consistently maintained by a large operations staff, made possible by political and public support for the growth in government employment in New York in the postwar era.

housing—particularly high-rises—after years of neglect, New York City continues to maintain the most public housing in the nation.

The Queensbridge Houses opened in 1939 and are home to more than sixty-nine hundred people. It was among the first developments constructed by NYCHA. Its twenty-six six-story towers were augmented by two community buildings that included a library, health clinic, nursery and nursery school, and community center.

NYCHA, established in 1934 as the country's first public housing authority, was a model for the nation. The private housing market had failed to provide safe and adequate housing for the city's poor and working classes for decades. The city's old, overcrowded, and dangerous tenements still housed 2 million people on the eve of the Great Depression. Slums were blamed for all manner of social disorder, including crime, health problems, and educational deficien-

Crime, vandalism, drugs, and other social problems increased in public housing in New York City in the 1970s, 1980s, and into the 1990s as the federal government incrementally defunded public housing, and city and state revenue did not fill the gap. Dangerous and decaying conditions at Queensbridge, in particular, were memorialized by significant hip-hop artists of the time, including Nas; Havoc and Prodigy of Mobb Deep; Capone of Capone-N-Noreaga; Blaq Poet; Cormega; Tragedy Khadafi; Screwball; Big Noyd; and MC Shan, Roxanne Shanté, and Craig G of Marly Marl's Juice Crew. Nas's "Illmatic," considered one of the best hip-hop albums of all time, detailed life at Queensbridge in the early 1990s.

Today, the Queensbridge Houses are fully occupied, albeit with a massive security apparatus. Cultural and arts programs abound at the local elementary school, and residents run various social programs. But NYCHA is in crisis, and its future is uncertain. At least $32 billion is needed citywide to repair and renovate its units as complaints about faulty heating, vermin, pests, and lead paint mount. But despite NYCHA's persistent funding and management problems, it remains a significant source of affordable housing in one of the world's costliest cities. Its vacancy rate remains less than 1 percent, and more than twenty-five thousand people sit on the waiting list for a coveted unit.

TO LEARN MORE

Bloom, Nicholas Dagen. *Public Housing That Worked: New York in the Twentieth Century*. Philadelphia: University of Pennsylvania Press, 2009.

Bloom, Nicholas Dagen, and Matthew Gordon Lasner, eds. *Affordable Housing in New York: The People, Places, and Policies That Transformed a City*. Princeton, NJ: Princeton University Press, 2015.

Plunz, Richard. *A History of Housing in New York City*. Revised edition. New York: Columbia University Press, 2016.

3.3 Taxi Workers Alliance

31–10 37th Avenue, Long Island City, NY

On January 28, 2017, thousands of New Yorkers flooded John F. Kennedy Airport protesting then-President Trump's executive order banning Muslims from seven countries (Iran, Iraq, Libya, Somalia, Sudan, Syria, and Yemen) from entering the United States. The protesters had a partial victory that night when Federal Judge Ann Donnelly issued a stay of removal for over a hundred people detained at airports across the country. In solidarity with the JFK protests, the New York Taxi Workers Alliance halted pickups from JFK during the peak of the rally. The majority-Muslim worker center/union, which represents over nineteen thousand taxi drivers, stated, "Today, drivers are joining the protest at JFK Airport in support of all those who are currently being detained at the airport because of Trump's unconstitutional executive order. Drivers stand in solidarity with refugees coming to America in search of peace and safety and with those who are simply trying to return to their homes here in America after traveling abroad. We stand in solidarity with all of our peace-loving neighbors against this inhumane, cruel, and unconstitutional act of pure bigotry."

Taxi workers
protesting Governor
Cuomo's Congestion
Pricing Plan, 2019.
CREDIT: COURTESY OF
THE NEW YORK TAXI
WORKERS ALLIANCE

The Taxi Alliance's work stoppage was a success because they were able to tap into an already mobilized and engaged membership. They began building their base in the mid-1990s and then formalized it when Bhairavi Desai officially founded the Alliance in 1998. Taxi workers went on strike in 1998, and since then the organization has won victories such as obtaining help from FEMA (Federal Emergency Management Agency) in the post 9/11 period, forcing the Taxi and Limousine Commission (TLC) to give drivers a larger percentage of fare hikes, and organizing to extend the cap on for hire vehicles such as Uber and Lyft. The Alliance was the first independent union to become a full member of the New York Central Labor Council, and in 2011, the National Taxi Workers Alliance, also run by Desai, was the first nontraditional workforce to be granted membership into the national AFL-CIO.

TO LEARN MORE

Mathew, Biju. *Taxi! Cabs and Capitalism in New York City.* Ithaca, NY: ILR Press, 2008.
New York Taxiworkers Alliance, https://www.nytwa.org/

3.4 Former Site of 5Pointz: The Institute of Higher Burning

45–46 Davis Street, Long Island City, NY

At its height, 5Pointz was considered the world's premiere "graffiti mecca," featuring close to two hundred artists. Graffiti was born on the streets of Philadelphia, cultivated in Washington Heights, and spread by a teenage Taki 183 in the early 1970s, who wrote his tag in permanent marker wherever he went as a foot messenger—on subway cars, lampposts, and surfaces of all kinds, all over the city. Youth across the boroughs picked up the practice for the attention and recognition it gave them, building a

(Above) 5Pointz Institute of Higher Burnin', 2011. CREDIT: YOUNGKING11 - OWN WORK, CC BY-SA 3.0, WIKIMEDIA COMMONS

(Left) 5Pointz razed and construction on luxury towers begins, 2014. CREDIT: JULIETA SALGADO

burgeoning graffiti movement that, together with hip-hop music and breaking, constituted the emerging hip-hop culture of 1970s and 1980s in New York (see **Birthplace of Hip-Hop**, p. 34; and **Former Home of Richard Colón ["Crazy Legs"]**, p. 38).

Graffiti writers developed innovative signature "wildstyle" letterings, stylized, colorful words and phrases created primarily with permanent markers and aerosol paint. Their work included murals on abandoned buildings and tags and pieces of all sizes that rode with the trains, enabling the artist to go "all city." New York politicians, particularly Mayor Ed Koch, made the elimination of graffiti a high priority during the period, holding up graffiti as the most visible sign of the crime and urban decay that many New

Yorkers feared during and after the 1970s fiscal crisis, and declaring it "public enemy number one." But New York's youth and artists continued to hone the craft all over the city through the 1980s and 1990s.

Built in 1892 as a water meter factory, the building formerly known as 5Pointz was purchased by Jerry Wolkoff in the 1970s. In 1995, Pat Delillo, who started out as an anti-graffiti advocate, convinced Wolkoff to let young people channel their energy into art pieces on his warehouse, which was already a popular spot, given its visibility from the 7 train. Wolkoff agreed to the plan. Pat called the warehouse the Phun Phactory, which eventually became 5Pointz. The name 5Pointz was inspired by the historic Manhattan neighborhood (see **Five Points/ Columbus Park**, p. 164), but it also represented bringing artists together from all five boroughs. In 2003 Jonathan Cohen, the well-known local graffiti artist better known as "Meres One," began to curate 5Pointz.

In 2013 the Wolkoff family decided to demolish the building and build two residential towers on the site. The 5Pointz artists and community members protested and even sought to gain landmark status, but they were denied because they had only existed for thirty years. Before demolishing the warehouse in 2014, the Wolkoff family painted over the graffiti murals overnight and named the new residential project 5Pointz Towers. In 2017, twenty-one artists whose works were whitewashed sued the Wolkoff family, and in 2018 a judge awarded them $6.7 million in damages. The Wolkoff family appealed, but in early 2020 the US Court of Appeals affirmed the award of monetary damages to the artists.

—*With Julieta Salgado*

TO LEARN MORE

Snyder, Gregory J. *Graffiti Lives: Beyond the Tag in New York's Urban Underground.* New York: NYU Press, 2008.

NEARBY SITES OF INTEREST

MOMA at PS1
22–25 Jackson Avenue, Long Island City, NY
Originally founded as the Institute for Art and Urban Resources in 1971, the gallery officially merged with MOMA (Museum of Modern Art) in 2010. Admission at MOMA gets you into both museums.

Top to Bottom Mural Project
43–01 21st Street, Long Island City, NY
Public art space featuring massive murals.

3.5 Sunnyside Gardens

Skillman Avenue to Barnett Avenue, 44th Street to 50th Street, Sunnyside, NY

Once a rural hamlet owned by a French Huguenot family who named it "Sunnyside Hill," Sunnyside developed in earnest after the 1909 opening of the Queensboro Bridge, which provided easy commutes to Manhattan. The most defining feature of the neighborhood is its subsection, Sunnyside Gardens, the first planned garden community in the United States. The goal of the transatlantic garden city movement was to purposefully infuse green spaces into working-class communities.

Built between 1924 and 1928, the complex consists of over seventy-seven acres of apartment buildings, two-family houses, and gar-

(Left) Sunnyside Gardens promotional brochure, 1920s. CREDIT: GREATER ASTORIA HISTORICAL SOCIETY

(Below) Children planting a community garden on the present site of the Wilson Court Apartments at 47th Street north of Queens Boulevard, summer 1926. CREDIT: GREATER ASTORIA HISTORICAL SOCIETY

Leaving tenements and cramped quarters, working-class and white-collar Manhattanites, many of them immigrants, moved into this affordable middle-class housing complex. This migration to Queens was aided further by the fact Sunnyside Gardens had no restrictive covenants against Jews or Catholics.

dens. Over 70 percent of each block is dedicated to green space. When the complex opened, apartment buildings ran like traditional cooperatives, and individuals could purchase single- and two-family homes under affordable and favorable mortgage terms.

According to a survey conducted in 1928, 355 residents were employed in white-collar jobs including teaching, social work, and in the medical and legal professions, and 184 residents had blue collar jobs as chauffeurs, mechanics, and restaurant workers. Sunnyside Gardens was also known as home to radicals, including many communists and socialists. During the Depression these radicals organized mortgage strikes, but, even so, over 60 percent of residents lost their homes during this period.

Through the 1960s, residents were largely Irish, German, Czech, and Dutch, among other white European ethnics. Since the 1980s, Sunnyside Gardens has grown increasingly diverse with many Korean, Colombian, Chinese, Turkish, and Filipino residents. Interestingly, while most of the Irish American community in Queens has migrated to more suburban eastern Queens, recent Irish immigrants, emigrating as a result of economic downturns in Ireland, are once again settling in Sunnyside. But Sunnyside Gardens is no longer the green, affordable alternative to Manhattan it was designed to be, as housing prices continue to rise.

TO LEARN MORE

Buder, Stanley. *Visionaries and Planners: The Garden City Movement and the Modern Community.* New York: Oxford University Press, 1990.

Gryvatz Copquin, Claudia. *The Neighborhoods of Queens.* New Haven: Yale University Press, 2007.

NEARBY SITE OF INTEREST

Sunnyside Gardens Park

48–21 39th Avenue, Sunnyside, NY

One of two private parks in all of New York City, the other being the exclusive Gramercy Park in Manhattan. Membership is open only to those in the designated district, which includes seventeen particular blocks in the community.

3.6 Voice of Taiwan

32–08 60th Street, Woodside, NY

On May 1, 1977, Morgan (Fu-Hsiung) Chang and Eileen (Yi-Yi) Chang, a young Taiwanese couple, started Voice of Taiwan (VOT) out of their rented, third-floor apartment at this address in Woodside. VOT was a call-in service through which one could listen to a taped message produced by the Changs relating the latest political news from Taiwan in Taiwanese, Mandarin, and Hakka. During a pivotal era of Taiwan's thirty-eight-year period of martial law, VOT was often the first and only source of news out of the heavily censored island and covered numerous major events, including the publication of the Presbyterian Church of Taiwan's Human Rights Declaration (1977), the Kaohsiung Incident (1979), the Lin Yi-hsiung family murders (1980), and the death of Carnegie Mellon Professor Chen Wen-chen while in military police custody in Taiwan in 1981. During the Kaohsiung Incident, when the police tear-gassed pro-democracy protesters, VOT captured the moment during a recorded in-

From 1977–1978, Morgan (Fu-Hsiung) Chang and Eileen (Yi-Yi) Chang operated the Voice of Taiwan call-in news service from a third-floor apartment in this building, 2015. CREDIT: WENDY CHENG

terview with someone at the scene: "The explosion of the bombs . . . was loud and clear, and made all of us listeners feel as if we were on location, experiencing it ourselves. This event remains unforgettable in the minds of many to this day," Morgan Chang recalled years later. News of these events galvanized Taiwanese living in diaspora and spurred them to activism, increasing international pressure on the Kuomintang regime to end martial law and democratize.

Inspired by the National Weather Service's then-popular daily weather phone number, Morgan Chang initially proposed the idea as a way to circulate news for the Taiwanese Association of America–New York. The Association footed the costs for the first year, but after the cost of the collect calls became prohibitive, VOT subsequently relied on listener contributions, which poured in from Taiwanese around the world and ranged anywhere from five dollars to one thousand dollars. Over its five years of operation, VOT grew to include forty-one affiliates around the United States and internationally (including Canada, France, Germany, and Brazil). It operated for its first year here in Woodside, and then, after the Changs moved in 1978, from their house in Jamaica, Queens.

New York City is home to the second-largest population of Taiwanese Americans after Los Angeles. Largely middle-class professionals, many came as students due to the specific provisions of the Immigration Act of 1965 and subsequently stayed to pursue business and educational opportunities as well as to escape political oppres-

sion and instability in Taiwan. Since the 1970s, Taiwanese migrants have concentrated in Queens and participated in reshaping the landscapes of Flushing, Elmhurst, and Corona in ways ranging from large-scale development and operating small businesses to high rates of homeownership. Less well-known, and as the story of VOT attests, is New York's significance as a location for Taiwanese diasporic activism: it was the location of Peter Huang's attempted assassination of Chiang Ching-kuo in 1970, a key site of anti-imperial Diaoyutai student protests in 1971, and the headquarters of Taiwan independence organizations including the World United Formosans for Independence and the Taiwan Revolutionary Party. In the mid 1980s, Taiwanese New Yorkers established the first Taiwan Center in the United States in Flushing, which still functions as a lively community center today.

—*Wendy Cheng*

TO LEARN MORE

Chang, Morgan. "Witnessing the Kaohsiung Incident—Selected Tape Recordings of Voice of Taiwan." In *A Borrowed Voice: Taiwan Human Rights through International Networks, 1960–1980*, edited by Linda Gail and Miles Lynn Arrigo, 337–345. Taipei: Social Empowerment Alliance, 2008.

Chen, Hsiang-Shui. *Chinatown No More: Taiwan Immigrants in Contemporary New York*. Ithaca, NY: Cornell University Press, 1992.

NEARBY SITE OF INTEREST

Taiwan Center
137–44 Northern Boulevard, Flushing, NY
http://www.nytaiwancenter.us/

3.7 Julio Rivera Corner

37th Avenue and 78th Street, Jackson
Heights, NY

Julio Rivera was brutally murdered on July
2, 1990, at the age of twenty-nine inside
the P.S. 69 schoolyard by three local young,
white men. Rivera was a gay, Puerto Rican
New Yorker, originally from the Bronx,
who lived in Jackson Heights and worked as
a bartender. Twenty years after his death,
New York City finally commemorated this
history, officially naming 37th Avenue and
78th Street "Julio Rivera Corner."

Rivera's murder resembled the deaths
of at least a dozen other gay men killed in
the neighborhood between 1970 and 1990.
Before his death, none of these hate crimes
had ever been solved or prosecuted. Initially, the NYPD refused to classify Rivera's
death as a bias attack and instead classified it
as a drug-related crime. In response, a local
LGBT group, with help from Manhattan-
centered organizations like Queer Nation,

took action, organizing candlelight vigils
and protests. These actions and the related
media attention pressured the city to reclas-
sify the murder and issue a reward for the
arrest of the killers, who were later found
and convicted.

Jackson Heights has been a kind of haven
for LGBTQ New Yorkers since the 1920s,
when the newly established 7 subway line
made a commute to Manhattan's midtown
possible, attracting actors and vaudevillians
from Times Square. The area has since been
transformed by immigrants, mainly from
Latin America, but remained a relatively
gay-friendly area, but the visibility of the
LGBTQ community increased dramatically
after the murder of Julio Rivera. In a matter
of a few years, multiple organizations were
founded in the neighborhood to provide services to different LGBTQ communities: a
chapter of PFLAG; Generation Q, an after-
school youth drop-in center; SAGE Queens
(now called the Queens Center for Gay

Julio Rivera's family
and members of the
Jackson Heights LGBTQ
community at the
Queens Pride Parade
naming Julio Rivera
Corner, 1998–2000.
CREDIT: LA GUARDIA AND
WAGNER ARCHIVES, LA
GUARDIA COMMUNITY
COLLEGE/THE CITY
UNIVERSITY OF NEW YORK

Seniors); and the community center Queens Pride House.

In 1992, Daniel Dromm and other local gay activists founded the Queens Pride Parade. In 2009, Dromm, a former teacher, became one of the first openly gay City Council members elected from outside Manhattan. Meanwhile, the parade continues to be held in early June of each year and regularly attracts from ten thousand to forty thousand people. It is the second largest Pride in New York City and the second largest parade in Jackson Heights after the Colombian Day Parade.

The neighborhood is the most prominent "gayborhood" in Queens and believed to be the largest concentration of LGBTQ immigrants in New York City. The political organizing and coalition building that emerged in the years after Julio Rivera's death created a new norm of LGBTQ political visibility, coalition building, and action in Jackson Heights that remains to this day. Speaking to a multiethnic, cross-generational crowd festooned with rainbow flags, Dromm explains in Frederick Wiseman's documentary about the neighborhood, *In Jackson Heights*, "Jackson Heights is the most diverse community in the world, literally! We have 167 different languages spoken here. We are very very proud of that diversity. Let's salute that, and let's all be proud of what we have accomplished."

—*Arianna Martinez*

TO LEARN MORE

Wiseman, Frederick, dir. *In Jackson Heights*. 2015. Moulins Films. 190 minutes.

NEARBY SITE OF INTEREST

Desis Rising Up and Moving (DRUM)

72–18 Roosevelt Avenue, Jackson Heights, NY
A community organization founded in 2000 to build the power of low-wage South Asian immigrant workers, youth, and families. After 9/11 the organization was particularly effective at supporting and defending the rights of Muslims and South Asians against attacks and deportations.

FAVORITE NEIGHBORHOOD RESTAURANT

Jackson Diner

37–47 74th Street, Jackson Heights, NY
Famous and well-regarded Indian restaurant operating since 1980.

3.8 Louis Armstrong House

34–56 107 Street, Corona, NY

Tucked into a modest block on 107th Street in Corona, Queens, is the home for more than thirty years of trumpeter, singer, and composer Louis Armstrong. Despite Armstrong's fame and recognition, he and his wife Lucille, known as "Uncle Louis" and "Aunt Lucille" to neighborhood children, made their home in the Black middle- and working-class enclave of Corona in 1943. They were not alone in doing so—many jazz musicians made Queens home during this era. Dizzy Gillespie, Cannonball Adderley, Nat Adderley, Jimmy Heath, and Clark Terry also lived in Corona. Dozens of other jazz musicians lived in nearby St. Albans/Addisleigh Park and in other parts of Queens, including Milt Hinton, Count Basie, Mercer Ellington, Lena Horne, Illinois Jacquet, Russell Jacquet, and Ella Fitzgerald.

Louis Armstrong outside his home. CREDIT: LOUIS ARMSTRONG HOUSE MUSEUM

in the 1940s during the Great Migration, as African Americans continued to move north and west away from the South. In the 1940s, Corona's Black population doubled, and by 1960, Corona's Black residents made up half of the population.

Armstrong, whose grandparents had been enslaved, was born in 1900 in New Orleans. He spoke out against injustice around the world throughout his life, serving as a symbol of the civil rights movement, making a goodwill tour to Western Africa, and boycotting New York clubs that had once excluded him. He was known for serenading neighborhood children from his front stoop. Armstrong was deeply attached to Corona. Part of the house's tour features Armstrong discussing how his song "What a Wonderful World" reminds him of the neighborhood.

Armstrong lived in this home until he died in 1971, and Lucille lived there until her death in 1983. Designated a National Historic Landmark in 1977 and a City of New York Landmark in 1986, Louis and Lucille Armstrong's house opened as a museum in 2003 after a $1.6 million restoration. The rooms and furnishings are exactly as they were when the Armstrongs lived there. The house is filled with the Armstrongs' belongings, including original instruments and recording devices.

—*With Brandon Martinez*

In the early decades of the twentieth century, Corona, like Brooklyn's Bedford-Stuyvesant, offered more affordable, higher quality suburban housing than the established Black belts in Manhattan and Brooklyn for the city's upwardly mobile Black residents. Unlike much of the housing in nearby Elmhurst and Jackson Heights, Corona's housing was not restricted by racial covenants that barred home sales to nonwhite people. In 1940 the Black homeownership rate in Queens dwarfed that of the other four boroughs. A solidly integrated neighborhood between the world wars, Corona's demography drastically changed beginning

TO LEARN MORE

Gregory, Steven. *Black Corona: Race and the Politics of Place in an Urban Community.* Princeton, NJ: Princeton University Press, 1998.

The Langston Hughes Community Library and Cultural Center

A long-standing anchor of Corona-East Elmhurst, the Langston Hughes Community Library and Cultural Center houses the largest circulating Black heritage reference collection in all of New York City. Founded in 1969 by the grassroots Library Action Committee of the local Community Corporation of the Anti-Poverty Program, it is the only American Literary Association–designated literary landmark in New York City outside of Manhattan.

FAVORITE NEIGHBORHOOD RESTAURANTS

Tortilleria Nixtamal

41–11 National Street, Corona, NY

Tortilla factory producing corn tortillas made from corn soaked in an alkaline solution (nixtamal) instead of corn flour. Pick up their rotisserie chicken and a bag of fresh, warm tortillas.

Lemon Ice King of Corona

52–02 108th Street, Corona, NY

The Benfaremo family has been serving Italian Ices at this shop since 1944.

3.9 Flushing Meadows Corona Park

Unisphere, across from the Queens Museum, Flushing, NY

Flushing Meadows Corona Park is the largest park in Queens, bounded by Flushing Bay and three expressways—Union Turnpike, the Van Wyck Expressway, and the Grand Central Parkway. Citi Field (the home field of the New York Mets), the USTA Billie Jean National Tennis Center (current home of the US Open), the Queens Museum of Art, the New York Hall of Science, the Queens Zoo, the Queens Theatre in the Park, the New York State Pavilion, and two large lakes can all be found in its borders. Perhaps most significantly, the city has periodically used this park to project its image as a global economic, cultural, and technological leader, especially as the host of the 1939 and 1964 World's Fair.

This vast park was once a salt marsh, populated by the Algonquian-speaking Matinecock people who lived across much of what is Flushing today. The largely undeveloped marsh became a dumping ground for ash and cinders for Brooklyn Ash Removal Company in 1909. By the 1920s, more than one hundred railroad cars dumped ash and other garbage there daily. The towering, heaping ash pile became known as "Mount Corona," and it grew so massive that police had to direct cars through the fog it generated. In 1925, F. Scott Fitzgerald memorialized it in *The Great Gatsby* as a "valley of ashes"; meanwhile, the nearby Flushing River was an open sewer.

But by the 1930s, city planner Robert Moses saw the heaping ash pile as the perfect site for what he hoped would be the true "Central Park" of the entire city, and boosters hoped the park development would spur gentrification in bordering Queens neighborhoods. At the same time, city business leaders hoped that hosting a World's Fair in New York would help jump-start the struggling Depression economy. Connecting the dots, Moses saw the World's Fair as an opportunity to develop Flushing Meadows wetland into permanent parkland.

Clearing the mountain of ash for the World's Fair, 1934. CREDIT: NYC PARKS PHOTO ARCHIVE

The transformation of Flushing Meadows in preparation for the 1939–1940 World's Fair was, in the words of Ted Steinberg (2015), "the most significant landscape change in this corner of the planet since the retreat of the Wisconsin ice sheet." Before preparation for the World's Fair, working class communities were rooted in the area, which worked almost as a commons, supporting communal fur trapping, with nearby residents and squatters raising vegetables and collecting firewood on the land.

Moses led the charge to raze Mount Corona and redistribute the waste across the sprawling new park site, hollow out Flushing Creek and much of the meadows for man-made lake beds, construct a foundation under the wetlands with imported Pacific Northwest wood, and build two sewers for drainage that were the largest in the world at the time. The city repossessed bordering land for the park and evicted an entire Italian American community; prop-

erty owners were compensated, while renters and squatters received no compensation or aid.

In the end, the World's Fair earned a fraction of the profits the city had anticipated, which Moses had hoped to leverage toward a more grand park at the site. But the city nevertheless used the fair site to open the Hall of Science, the Federal and New York State pavilions, a skating rink, and the Unisphere memorializing the World's Fair.

Decades later, the 1964–1965 World's Fair brought the nation's (and world's) gaze to New York City again to revel in the era's most significant innovations in an effort to strengthen the city's tourism industry. Civil rights activists capitalized on the political moment. In 1964, members of CORE (Congress of Racial Equality) held a press conference at the Hotel Theresa announcing that they had eighteen hundred drivers ready to stall their cars in order to block attendance at the World's Fair, bringing to light joblessness, crime, segregation, and police brutality experienced by the city's Black and Puerto Rican citizens. Mayor Robert Wagner called the tactic "a gun to the heart of the city," sending more than a thousand police officers and dozens of tow trucks to the roads leading into Queens and helicopters that could lift cars into the air if necessary. In the end, the roads were empty—the activists didn't deliver. But the threat and the media storm surrounding it drastically limited fair attendance to about a quarter of what was expected, largely spoiling the city's hypocritical attempt to project itself as an icon of modernization and progress.

Today, new struggles over Flushing Meadows Corona Park have come to pass. The park fell into disrepair for many years after the last World's Fair, but the city approved a 2008 plan to redevelop Willets Point, bordering the park. Various other proposals have included a new Major League Soccer stadium, expansion of the National Tennis Center, a mega shopping mall, and the environmental restoration of the park. Some environmental restoration has begun, while Willets Point redevelopment has moved forward full force. The auto body shops that once populated the area have been demolished, and mixed-income housing, retail space, a hotel, convention center, and some community facilities will replace them in the coming years. (*Quote by Ted Steinberg in "Gotham Unbound: The Ecological History of Greater New York."*)

—*With Ethan Barnett*

TO LEARN MORE

Caro, Robert A. *The Power Broker: Robert Moses and the Fall of New York.* New York: Vintage, 1974.

Steinberg, Ted. *Gotham Unbound: The Ecological History of Greater New York.* Reprint edition. New York: Simon & Schuster, 2015.

3.10 Flushing Friends Meeting House and John Bowne House

137–16 Northern Boulevard, Flushing, NY

Set off of busy Northern Boulevard in Flushing is one of the oldest buildings in New York City: the Flushing Friends Meeting House, built and in continuous operation since 1694. Its preservation reflects the significance of the Flushing Remonstrance and the religious pluralism that still thrives in Flushing, in Queens, and throughout the entire city.

In colonial New Amsterdam, the last of the Dutch West India Company's directors-general, Peter Stuyvesant, did not share the religious tolerance more typically practiced by his forebears and associated with the Netherlands at the time. During his tenure, he persecuted non-Calvinists of all sorts, including Lutherans and Jews. Following their arrival to the colony in 1656, he singled out Quakers in particular, whose worship was targeted by new laws threatening penalties against anyone housing a Quaker. In 1657, a man in Vissingen, as Flushing was then called, held a Quaker meeting in his house against Stuyvesant's new rules and was duly charged.

On December 27, 1657, thirty English (and non-Quaker) settlers of Vissingen stood behind their neighbor and against Stuyvesant, in a petition that became known as the Flushing Remonstrance. It stated that the "freedom of conscience" originally granted to their colonial town by its charter extended to Quakers. More remarkably, it cited a

Friends Meeting House, 2017. CREDIT: SCOTT DEXTER

long list of other religions and peoples in its defense of religious liberty, including those of "Jews, Turks and Egyptians," as well as numerous Protestant sects. Written over a century before the US Constitution, it laid an often-overlooked piece of groundwork for the religious freedom guaranteed under the First Amendment in the US Constitution.

A few years later, settler John Bowne was jailed and eventually banished from New Amsterdam for holding Quaker services in his home. He returned after successfully arguing his case to the Dutch West India Company. In the company's communication with Stuyvesant, defending their decision, they explained their tolerance for sectarians, "we doubt very much whether we can proceed against them rigorously without diminishing the population and stopping immigration, which must be favored at so tender a stage of the country's existence. You may therefore shut your eyes, at least not force people's consciences, but allow everyone to have his own belief, as long as he behaves qui-

etly and legally, gives no offense to his neighbors and does not oppose the government."

Today, Bowne's home serves the Flushing community as a museum and sits blocks away from the Quaker Meeting House for the Society of Friends that he built in 1694. Hundreds of churches, temples, mosques, and other sites of worship seamlessly inhabit the downtown Flushing landscape.

—*With Brandon Martinez*

TO LEARN MORE

Hanson, R. Scott. *City of Gods: Religious Freedom, Immigration, and Pluralism in Flushing, Queens.* New York: Empire State Editions, 2016.

Trébor, Haynes. *The Flushing Remonstrance: The Origin of Religious Freedom in America.* Flushing, NY: State of New York, Distributed at Bowne House, 1957.

NEARBY SITE OF INTEREST

Main Street Station (7 Train)

Roosevelt Avenue and Main Street, Flushing, NY

The single largest interchange between bus and subway lines in North America, this station connects more than 20 city and Nassau County (Long Island) bus routes, the Long Island Rail Road, and the city subway system. Its narrow platforms are the result of private developers quickly seizing the bordering land when the station was approved in 1921.

Olde Towne of Flushing Burial Ground

46th Avenue and 164th/165th Streets, Flushing, NY. (forty minute walk, twenty minute bus ride)
Burial Site of African Americans and Native Americans.

3.11 Hindu Temple Society of North America (Ganesh Temple)

45–57 Bowne Street, Flushing, NY

Flushing is home to a number of Hindu temples, and others exist all over Queens and the rest of the city, but the Ganesh Temple holds special historical and religious significance to New York Hindus. Nestled into a third of an otherwise residential block, the Hindu Temple Society of North America (more commonly known as the Ganesh Temple) was the first of five traditional Hindu temples built in North America and the most prominent in the New York-New Jersey-Connecticut area.

Following the Hart-Celler Act's extensive changes to US immigration policy, the largest new immigrant group to arrive in Queens in the late 1960s came from South Asia. A core group of South Indian professionals settled in Flushing, and their success in the neighborhood helped attract more South Asian immigrants to the area. Other South Asian enclaves formed in Jackson Heights and Richmond Hill, Queens, as

Inside the Hindu Temple Society of North America, 2017. CREDIT: SCOTT DEXTER

well as parts of Manhattan and New Jersey. Hindu immigrants worshipped wherever they could—in homes, churches, and other places—until a small group gathered in the house of Dr. Alagappa Alagappan in Jamaica Estates in 1970 to plan for the construction of a traditional Hindu temple in Queens. Flushing was chosen to house the Ganesh temple for three reasons: nearly all Indian immigrants to the United States came through New York, and there was a strong Hindu community in the tristate area; it was within walking distance for many and accessible by public transit; and property for the temple was affordable. Today, the temple thrives as a place of worship and a community center, hosting weddings and a variety of activities. The Canteen restaurant, housed in its basement, serves some of the best Indian food in the city. The popular restaurant serves vegetarian food to about four thousand people a week, but during the Diwali season it feeds as many as ten thousand.

TO LEARN MORE

Hanson, R. Scott. *City of Gods: Religious Freedom, Immigration, and Pluralism in Flushing, Queens.* New York: Empire State Editions, 2016.

3.12 Lesbian Avengers

67–54 80th Street, Middle Village, NY

The grassroots Lesbian Avengers engaged in their very first action here in Queens at Middle Village Elementary School (P.S. 87) on September 9, 1992. That year, the school board representing this school and others refused to implement a new, multicultural curriculum called "Children of the Rainbow," an initiative undertaken by educators in the aftermath of the racist killing of Yusef Hawkins in Bensonhurst in 1989 (see **Howard Beach Riots**, p. 208). Hoping to teach children greater respect for diversity, the Rainbow curriculum included references to gay and lesbian families, and the school board rejected it for this reason.

In response, Lesbian Avengers' organizers carried a "TEACH ABOUT LESBIANS" banner and handed out lavender balloons to children and families on the first day of school with the words "Ask About Lesbians" printed on them. The action exemplified what would become the Avengers' signature guerilla activism and their media-savvy techniques, capturing the public's attention on local issues and affecting significant change.

The Avengers were founded by longtime activists Ana Simo, Anne-Christine d'Adesky, Anne Maguire, Marie Honan, Maxine Wolfe, and Sarah Schulman when meeting at the Lesbian, Gay, Bisexual, and Transgender Community Center of New York City in 1992 (see **Lesbian, Gay, Bisexual, and Transgender Community Center of NYC**, p. 117). Despite major successes among groups such as ACT UP (1987–1992) and Queer Nation (1990), a number of NYC lesbians and bisexual women recognized that women's issues were all too frequently ignored in these efforts, and, correcting that, sought to organize for issues specific to their gender. Using grassroots activism, the Lesbian Avengers "began as a direct action group focused on issues vital to lesbian survival and visibility."

Dozens of Lesbian Avengers' chapters were created in cities and towns internationally in the years to follow with their own agendas; the original incarnation of the NYC-based group disbanded in 1996. *The Lesbian Avenger Handbook: A Handy Guide to Homemade Revolution* was released as a way of helping others organize their own chapter or direct action group.

While ACT UP mostly targeted major urban locales and Queer Nation took to the city and suburbs, Lesbian Avengers spanned both while paying attention to heavily gendered spaces. Maxine Wolfe recalled, "We . . . do very visual actions, and we go to places where no one wants us to be." In their first year, the Avengers trained themselves to eat fire at their events and wore shirts that said "Be the bomb you want to throw!" and "We recruit;" these acts and

Alice Austen House action in Staten Island, 1994. CREDIT: SASKIA SCHEFFER

statements became their trademark. In 1993 alone, they held a skate-in at Rockefeller Center, holding hands and kissing; erected a statue of Alice B. Toklas next to her partner Gertrude Stein in Bryant Park, and followed with a Lesbian Waltz in the park; and rode the L train continuously one October evening to hand out literature to protest anti-gay and lesbian violence on the line.

In 1993 they also worked with ACT UP groups from Los Angeles and Philadelphia and Puss n' Boots in Los Angeles to create the first Dyke March in the United States to "demonstrate for lesbian rights and visibility." This first Dyke March preceded the 1993 March on Washington for Lesbian, Gay, and Bi Equal Rights and Liberation and took place in Washington, DC, with over twenty thousand marchers. Dyke March is still held annually in New York City without a permit on the Saturday before Pride, and San Francisco and other cities also hold annual

marches: "The New York City Dyke March is a protest march, not a parade. The March is a demonstration of our First Amendment right to protest and takes place without permits or sponsors" (Lesbian Avengers 2017). While always multi-racial and multi-class, the march became increasingly inclusionary of trans people, bisexuals, and gender non-conforming people in recent years.

—*Jen Jack Gieseking*

TO LEARN MORE

Cogswell, Kelly, Amy Parker, and Ana Simo, eds. n.d. *Lesbian Avenger Handbook, Ed 3*. Accessed August 28, 2020. http://www.lesbianavengers. com/handbooks/Lesbian_Avenger_ handbook3.shtml.

Baus, Janet, and Su Friedrich. n.d. *The Lesbian Avengers Eat Fire, Too*. Documentary. https:// www.youtube.com/watch?v=o4o0tZPETAc.

Lesbian Avengers. 2017. "An Incomplete History." Lesbian Avengers. http://www.lesbianavengers .com/about/history.shtml.

Mount Carmel Cemetery

83–45 Cypress Hills Street, Glendale, NY

Famed Jewish cemetery in the so-called "cemetery belt" on the Brooklyn-Queens border. Activist Bella Abzug, actor Jacob Adler, author Sholem Aleichem, socialist activist and writer Abraham Cahan, writer and performer Betty Comden, socialist politician Meyer London, Sam and Minnie Marx (of Marx Brothers fame), and countless other prominent Jews are buried here.

3.13 Store Front Museum

162–02 Liberty Avenue, Jamaica, NY

In 1971, the Store Front Museum opened its doors in Jamaica, Queens, with the intention of becoming an accessible center of culture rooted in Afrocentric philosophy. Established on a site designated for the eventual expansion of York College, the twelve-thousand-square-foot building was rented at a cost of five dollars a month. The museum hosted several major exhibitions and amassed a collection of art, books, photographs, and artifacts. It quickly expanded, opening the Paul Robeson Theatre and hosting Africa Festival, a two-day event on its outdoor mall that attracted thousands of visitors. The institution also organized workshops on Black ancestry and events for local businesses and professional organizations. The museum stood at this site for fifteen years before it was evicted by the City of New York.

The founding and short-lived success of the Store Front Museum was due in large part to founder Tom Lloyd, a Queens-born artist and social activist. From the late 1960s through the 1970s, Lloyd was part of the Art Workers' Coalition (AWC) where he worked alongside contemporary artists such as Faith Ringgold, Jacob Lawrence, and Raphael Montañez Ortiz (who founded El Museo del Barrio in East Harlem). The group's activism was aimed at making museums more democratic, and they staged several acts of protest at the Museum of Modern Art and the Metropolitan Museum of Art. In early 1969 the AWC made "13 Demands" of the MoMA, which included free admission, an area of the Museum dedicated to Black artists and under their direction, and, the third demand that "the Museum's activities should be extended into the Black, Spanish and other communities. It should also encourage exhibits with which these groups can identify."

When the Store Front Museum closed after several attempts to relocate to a permanent home, Lloyd donated the entirety of the museum collection to the Queens Library in Jamaica, within walking distance of the museum's former site.

—*Brandon Martinez*

King Manor Museum

150–03 Jamaica Avenue, Jamaica, NY

Colonial-era home of early abolitionist Rufus King.

Afrikan Poetry Theater (The Center for Culture)

176–03 Jamaica Avenue, Jamaica, NY

Community-based cultural institution founded in 1979 that hosts music performances, lectures, workshops, and a widely popular annual Kwanzaa celebration.

3.14 Rochdale Village

169–65 137th Avenue, Jamaica NY

Rochdale Village, still the largest housing cooperative in Queens, was also the largest housing cooperative in the world until the construction of Co-op City in 1971, as well as being a significant example of the city's efforts to racially integrate housing in the 1960s. Imagined by Robert Moses, developed by the United Housing Foundation (UHF), and funded by the Mitchell Lama program for affordable middle-income housing, its twenty buildings contain 5,860 apartments that house about twenty-five thousand residents. It operated two cooperative stores, a credit union, a pharmacy, and a cooperatively owned power plant that powered Rochdale and is still in operation today. At its height, Rochdale had more than 140 clubs, groups, fraternal orders, and other organizations.

From the mid-1950s through the 1960s a wide array of left and liberal social actors reached consensus that racial integration was the best solution to racial tensions. At the time Rochdale was conceived in 1959, South Jamaica was the third largest Black neighborhood in the city, almost entirely African American. Integration meant attracting white buyers to a Black community, and the developers worried that whites would not elect to move to one of the city's largest Black enclaves. At the same time, tensions in the city were building over racial discrimination in the building trade unions, and they coalesced at Rochdale. Hundreds of people were arrested at demonstrations at Rochdale in 1963 during its construction as protestors called for the construction industry to hire more minorities. Many future residents of Rochdale, both white and Black, participated in the demonstrations.

When Rochdale was completed in 1965, its residents were 85 percent white and 15 percent Black. While some whites were activists, committed to civil rights and racial justice, the vast majority were willing to try integration but were mostly motivated to live there for economic reasons. Rochdale's state funding made the apartments affordable for average New Yorkers, and it was the prospect of inexpensive housing, good schools, and a rich community that attracted whites to Rochdale. There were no racial

Students in music class in Rochdale elementary school, n.d. CREDIT: KHEEL CENTER FOR LABOR-MANAGEMENT DOCUMENTATION AND ARCHIVES, CORNELL UNIVERSITY

quotas at Rochdale as there were elsewhere, and the number of whites who elected to buy there surprised the UHF. Self-government was central in UHF cooperatives, and Rochdale's local governance was integrated—the first two people elected by residents to the Rochdale Village Board of Directors were Black.

But racial integration at Rochdale did not last. By 1969 many families—both Black and white—had left for the nearby suburbs. Crime was up, and Rochdale's new intermediate school that opened in 1967 never gained footing. The infamous 1968 teachers' strike fueled racial tensions (see **Junior High School 271**, p. 265). As more Black children were bused to Rochdale's schools, more white residents left. In the wake of white flight, new families in Rochdale were almost exclusively Black. By the late 1970s, the cooperative was only 20 percent white, and by the late 1980s, it was almost exclusively Black. It remains so today.

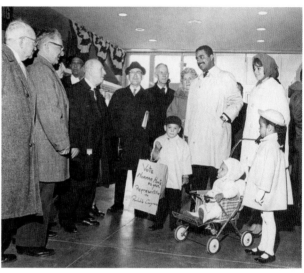

Resident campaigns for Rochdale Congress. CREDIT: KHEEL CENTER FOR LABOR-MANAGEMENT DOCUMENTATION AND ARCHIVES, CORNELL UNIVERSITY

TO LEARN MORE

Eisenstadt, Peter. *Rochdale Village: Robert Moses, 6,000 Families, and New York City's Great Experiment in Integrated Housing.* Ithaca, NY: Cornell University Press, 2010.

Freeman, Joshua B. *Working-Class New York: Life and Labor Since World War II.* New York: New Press, 2000.

NEARBY SITES OF INTEREST

Black Spectrum Theatre
177–01 Baisley Boulevard, Jamaica, NY
Founded in 1970, the theater brings productions focused on issues in the Black community to southeastern Queens and highlights Black directors, playwrights, performers, and designers.

3.15 Howard Beach Riots

Cross Bay Boulevard between 156th and 165th Avenues, Howard Beach, NY

Corruption in the NYPD, police brutality, the crack epidemic, and an economic crisis helped to aggravate existing racial tensions in New York City in the 1980s. White mobs murdered at least three Black men for being in white neighborhoods during this time: Willie Turks in Sheepshead Bay, Brooklyn, in 1982; Michael Griffith in Howard Beach, Queens, in 1986; and Yusef Hawkins in Bensonhurst, Brooklyn, in 1989.

Protesters outside of New Park Pizza in the wake of Michael Griffith's murder in Howard Beach, 1986. CREDIT: DITH PRAN/ *NEW YORK TIMES*/ REDUX

On December 20th, 1986, four Black men, Michael Griffith, Cedric Sandiford, Curtis Sylvester, and Timothy Grimes, went out for a drive through Queens. While on the Belt Parkway, the car started smoking, and the men stopped on Cross Bay Boulevard near Broad Channel. Curtis Sylvester stayed in the car, while the other three went to look for help. Meanwhile, three white teens from the neighborhood, Salvador DeSimone, Jon Lester, and William Bollander were driving DeSimone's girlfriend home from a party when they ran into the group. The teens used racial epithets and were cursed out in return. The white teens drove off, and the Black men went into the New Park Pizzeria to see if they could use a phone. Driving back to the party they'd left, the white teens spotted Griffith, Sandiford, and Grimes at the pizzeria. Arriving at the party, Lester was reported saying, "We should go back and kill them," A dozen white teens, armed with baseball bats and tree limbs joined Lester.

When the Black men spotted them, as they were leaving the pizzeria, they ran. Grimes got away, but the mob severely beat Sandiford and Griffith. At least six bystanders witnessed part of the Sandiford beating, and several called 911. As Griffith tried to escape the mob, he ran onto the Belt Parkway where an oncoming car killed him. Two days later, Jon Lester, Scott Kern, and Jason Ladone were arrested and charged with second-degree murder. The driver of the car that killed Michael Griffith was not charged.

On December 27, Reverend Al Sharpton led twelve hundred peaceful demonstrators along Cross Bay Boulevard. They were met with a small but significant counter demonstration, as neighborhood residents yelled out racist slurs. A year later, after a lengthy trial, Lester, Kern, and Ladone were convicted of second-degree manslaughter, and nine others were convicted on various charges.

In 2005, a similar incident occurred in Howard Beach when Nicholas Minucci, an

Italian American teen, severely beat Glenn Moore, a Black man, just a few blocks from the 1986 site of mob violence. (*Quotes are from Robert McFadden, "Black Man Dies After Beating by Whites in Queens."*)

TO LEARN MORE

Drury, Bob, and Charles J. Hynes. *Incident At Howard Beach*, 25th anniversary edition. Bloomington, IN: iUniverse, 2011.

McFadden, Robert D. 1986. "Black Man Dies After Beating by Whites in Queens." *New York Times*, p. A1, December 21, 1986.

3.16 Jamaica Bay Wildlife Refuge

175 Cross Bay Boulevard, Jamaica Bay, NY

At the Jamaica Bay Wildlife Refuge's Visitors' Center, you are at the center of Jamaica Bay, over twenty square miles of open water, saltmarsh, ponds, fields, and woods that crosses into both Brooklyn and Queens. Jamaica Bay is one of the most biodiverse places in the Northeast United States, supporting over 325 species of birds, 100 species of fish, and an unknown number of reptiles, amphibians, and mammals, all against the backdrop of the heavily urbanized coasts of Brooklyn and Queens. From the visitor center, you can follow nature trails to view a wide variety of flora and fauna, particularly birds, or take guided tours and boat trips.

Jamaica Bay has undergone numerous restoration projects to maintain biodiversity and water quality, which are constantly under threat. Jamaica Bay Park was established by the New York City Parks Department in 1953

after decades of serving as a repository for 50 million gallons of untreated sewage each day. After the 1972 Clean Water Act limited the flow of raw sewage into the environment, Gateway National Recreation Area was established as one of the first urban national parks, comprising sites in New Jersey, Staten Island, Brooklyn, and Queens. It includes the Jamaica Bay Wildlife Refuge, the islands of Jamaica Bay, Floyd Bennet Field, Jacob Riis Park, Fort Tilden, and the tip of Breezy Point.

While this was an important step in protecting the bay, in 2001 scientists discovered that about 50 percent of the land surface of salt marsh islands had disappeared in Jamaica Bay since 1900. If this rate of loss continues, marsh islands in the bay could disappear completely by 2045. Furthermore, Jamaica Bay receives most of its freshwater (223 million gallons per day) from the various Wastewater Treatment Plants surrounding it. The resulting presence of heavy metals, pharmaceuticals, and algae blooms can cause long-term damage to species living in the bay, as well as the people living in the surrounding communities of Marine Park, Mill Basin, Gerritsen Beach, Sheepshead Bay, Edgemere, Breezy Point, Bergen Beach, Canarsie, East New York, Far Rockaway, Broad Channel, and Howard Beach.

In response to these issues, in 2005, the NYC Department of Environmental Protection passed the Jamaica Bay Watershed Protection Plan, which includes strategies to help reduce pollution, improve water quality, and restore natural features for the diverse wildlife in and around the bay and its

(Above) A view of midtown Manhattan from Jamaica Bay. CREDIT: OLEKINDERHOOK, CC BY 3.0, WIKIMEDIA COMMONS

(Left) Houses in Broad Channel along Jamaica Bay. CREDIT: JOHN WALDMAN

neighboring communities. The continued implementation of this plan makes the bay a model of urban postindustrial resilience and sustainability.

—*Christopher Wassif*

TO LEARN MORE

"Jamaica Bay Wildlife Refuge." New York Harbor Parks, Jamaica Bay. November 30, 2014. http://www.nyharborparks.org/visit/jaba.html.

3.17 The People's Beach at Jacob Riis Park

157 Rockaway Beach Boulevard, Rockaway Park, NY

The People's Beach at Jacob Riis Park is one of New York's most beloved beaches. Its art deco bathhouse opened in 1932 and the boardwalk in 1937, and its close proximity to residential neighborhoods in South Brooklyn and Queens and access by bus

211

Voter registration at Riis Beach, 1971. CREDIT: LEONARD FINK ARCHIVE/LESBIAN, GAY, BISEXUAL, AND TRANSGENDER COMMUNITY CENTER

make it a popular summer destination. It has long been considered New York City's most LGBTQ-friendly beach, particularly the eastern edge; music and drag shows stretch back decades. Here is also where beachgoers have been enjoying the clothing optional section of the beach since the 1950s.

The relationship between police and LGBTQ beachgoers has almost always been tense, with harassment worse in some years than others. Nonetheless, Riis continues to be a beach home for the LGBTQ community, featuring events such as the Fat Femme Beach Day and Black Pride.

A summer day at Jacob Riis Beach, 2016. CREDIT: COURTESY OF THE NATIONAL PARKS SERVICE

Public Transportation

Joseph Raskin (2015) notes that "the 7 line's Main Street station [in Flushing Queens] is the biggest single interchange between local bus and subway lines in North America." This incredible fact illustrates the sheer scale of New York City's public transit system. With 230 route miles, and nearly 2 billion riders a year, the NYC subway is the fifth largest subway system in the world, and one of the oldest.

The newest subway station in Manhattan, 34th Street Hudson Yards, 2016. CREDIT: METROPOLITAN TRANSPORTATION AUTHORITY OF THE STATE OF NEW YORK—34 ST–HUDSON YARDS STATION, CC BY 2.0, WIKIMEDIA COMMONS

Given its density, it's not surprising that the idea of mass transit came relatively early to the city. By the early nineteenth century, horse trolleys crisscrossed the land and ferries traversed the rivers between New York and its neighbors in Brooklyn and Queens. Horse trolleys soon gave way to electric trolleys, and by 1867–1870 Charles Harvey opened the first Elevated Railway (known as "El" trains), creating north-south routes in Manhattan during the 1880s.

Political battles shaped decisions about opening the subway from the start. Real estate interests, safety concerns, and cost all factored into the vigorous debates about whether the city should have a subway at all. Neither the city, state, nor any private company wanted to risk financing an entire integrated system. Therefore, even though the subway was "owned" by the city, it was leased to private companies that operated it on long-term contracts—first the Interborough Rapid Transit Company (IRT; 1904), followed by the Brooklyn Rapid Transit Company (BRT, later BMT; 1911). The pri-

vate system was inadequately regulated, and its poorly trained, largely immigrant workforce put in long hours in dangerous and dirty working conditions. Seeking greater profits, owners expected speed and efficiency, and accidents resulted. Two of the worst in transit history occurred in the autumn of 1918. The first was a collision in the Bronx involving two trains, in which thirty people were injured and eighteen taken to the hospital. Less than a month later a BRT train on its way to Coney Island was speeding to make up for lost time and jumped the track at a sharp curve (now Franklin Avenue Shuttle at Prospect Park) killing ninety-three people and injuring one hundred more.

Whether and where more underground lines would be built or whether the El system would be expanded was also the subject of much debate and negotiation. Increased density in the city and the need for rapid expansion of the system, as well as a feeling that these private entities were reaping

The 1905 9th Avenue New York City Subway Derailment. CREDIT: UNKNOWN AUTHOR - ELEKTROTECHNISCHE ZEITSCHRIFT (GERMAN), NOV. 2, 1905, S. 1010, PUBLIC DOMAIN, WIKIMEDIA COMMONS

huge profits from taxpayers, led the city to develop its own system called the Independent Subway System (later IND), which opened its first line in 1932. But politicians, real estate developers, and small businesses were often at odds over the development of the subway. There were also significant tensions surrounding the expansion of mass transit outside of Manhattan. In Queens, the Bronx, and Brooklyn, communities fought for access to mass transit, but also for the expansion of the underground system (the more expensive option) instead of the El system, which people criticized for being unsightly, noisy, dirty, reducing property values, and putting small businesses out of work.

The public transportation system expanded in the late 1930s and 1940s when the city took over bus corporations in all five boroughs, a feat not fully completed until 2006. As of this writing, the MTA Regional Bus Operations has the largest fleet of municipal buses in the United States.

This expansion of the public system, however, was short-lived. When Robert Moses took over as chairman of the Triborough Bridge and Tunnel Authority, he directed transportation funding to the construction of new bridges, tunnels, and expressways—away from public transit, including the city's subway system and buses, thereby privileging white suburban communities over the multiracial, working-class city. Transit deserts emerged in parts of the Bronx, much of Queens, southeastern Brooklyn, and Staten Island. By the late 1960s, mass transit suffered from lack of funding and low ridership. The subway authority was forced to adopt a policy of "deferred maintenance" in 1956, and service predictably declined. Moses's biographer, Robert Caro (1974), argues that, given such priorities, "When Robert Moses came to power in New York in 1934, the city's mass transportation system was probably the best in the world. When he left power in 1968, it was quite possibly the worst."

Inadequate public funding and the resultant deferred maintenance continue to severely impact New York City transit. Trains and the signal system are old and outdated. Schedules and work safety rules have not been updated. Yet, fares have gone up nearly 50 percent over inflation since 1990. Improvements to the system have not kept pace with the needs of a growing city population. In 2010's, riders suggested that conditions on the train in terms of wait times, delays, and accidents reminded them of the 1970s, during the worst of the fiscal crisis, even though the New York State

Protest Posters Against Fare Hikes Made with Used Metro Cards, 2009. CREDIT: LATINOART JUAN CARLOS PINTO - OWN WORK, CC BY-SA 4.0, WIKIMEDIA COMMONS

budget had by then experienced years of surplus.

The completion of the first leg of the Second Avenue Subway in 2016 marked the first major expansion of the system in decades. A new station at Hudson Yards on the far west side of Manhattan followed. A new ferry system has been a bright spot along the East River, and another private/public partnership with Citibank has yielded the Citibike system, aided by hundreds of miles of bike lanes across the city. But these relatively innovative projects serve a primarily affluent and tourist ridership, as do the recent transformations of some subway stations to allow for more retail space, all while the basic system faces enormous challenges.

While the train cars and stations have never been cleaner, the COVID-19 pandemic has nearly destroyed the subway. In 2019, immediately pre-pandemic, the subways seemed to be improving slightly with the improvement of on-time rates on several key lines, a $7 billion plan to replace the system's 1930's signal system along six routes, and the promise of congestion pricing—a toll for driving below 60th Street in Manhattan—bringing millions of dollars to the cash strapped MTA. But ridership on the subway, buses, and commuter rails is a small fraction of pre-pandemic norms. For example, ridership on the subway and buses fell 90% in April 2020, represting a devastating loss of income for the MTA, at a time when the system has had to invest more money into cleaning and safety protocols.

Fights over public transportation remain as essentially political as they have been since the first horse trolleys. Groups like the Straphangers Campaign, Transportation Alternatives, and dozens of local community groups do what they can to pressure the city and the state to improve service and invest in underserved areas in need of transit support. The city's future lies in transit: but not everyone shares the same vision for what that future should look like, or for whom. (*Quotes are from Joseph Raskin,* The Routes Not Taken: A Trip Through New York City's Unbuilt Subway System, *and Robert Caro,* The Power Broker.)

TO LEARN MORE

Ballon, Hilary, and Kenneth T. Jackson. *Robert Moses and the Modern City: The Transformation of New York.* New York: W.W. Norton & Co, 2007.

Caro, Robert A. *The Power Broker: Robert Moses and the Fall of New York.* New York: Vintage, 1974.

Freeman, Joshua Benjamin. *In Transit: The Transport Workers Union in New York City, 1933—1966.* With new epilogue. Philadelphia: Temple University Press, 2001.

Raskin, Joseph B. *The Routes Not Taken: A Trip Through New York City's Unbuilt Subway System.* New York: Fordham University Press, 2015.

4

Brook-
lyn

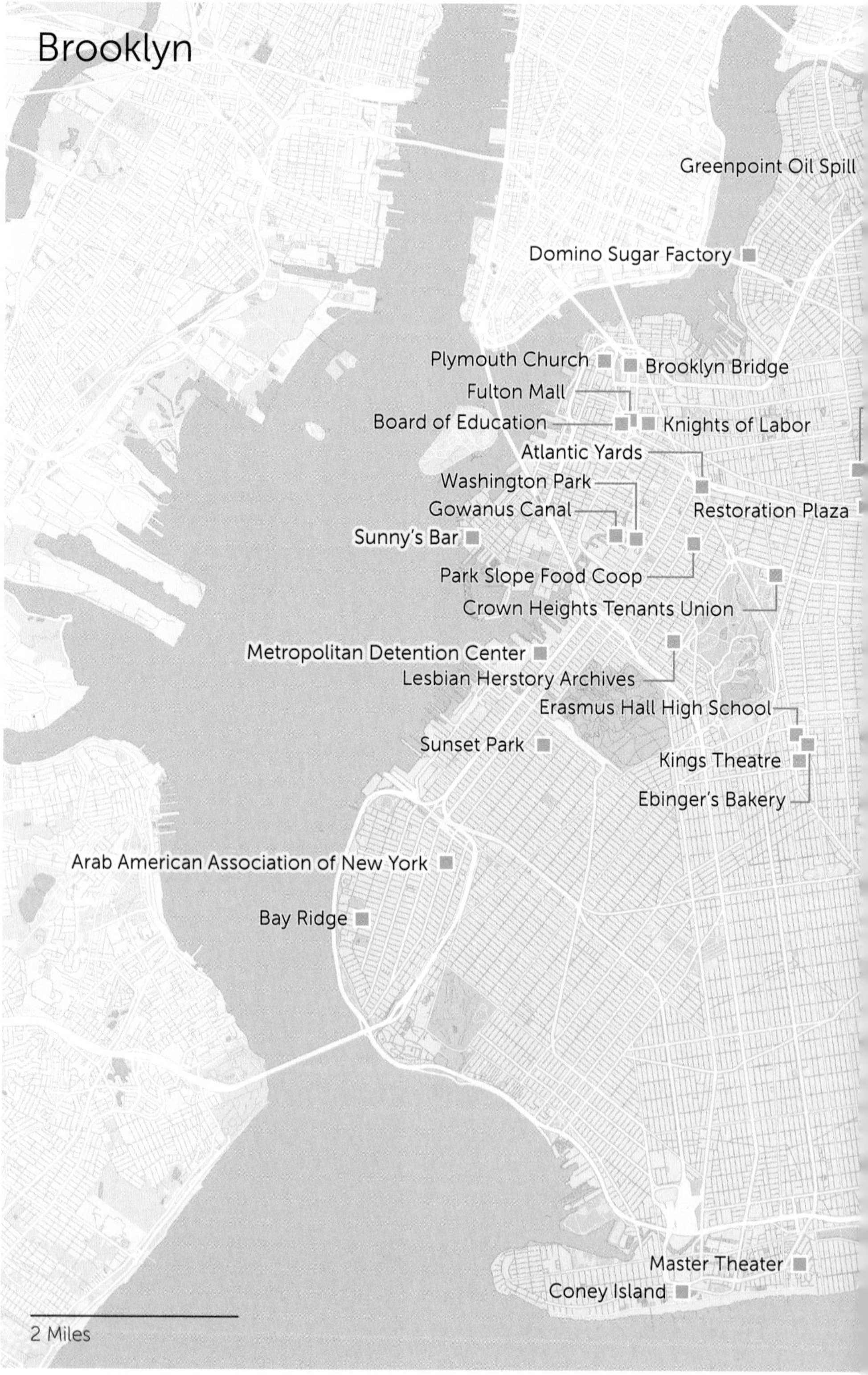

Brooklyn

Greenpoint Oil Spill

Domino Sugar Factory ■

Plymouth Church ■ ■ Brooklyn Bridge
Fulton Mall
Board of Education ■ ■ Knights of Labor
Atlantic Yards
Washington Park
Gowanus Canal
Sunny's Bar ■ ■ ■ Restoration Plaza

Park Slope Food Coop
Crown Heights Tenants Union

Metropolitan Detention Center ■
Lesbian Herstory Archives
Erasmus Hall High School
Sunset Park ■
Kings Theatre ■
Ebinger's Bakery

Arab American Association of New York ■

Bay Ridge ■

Master Theater ■
Coney Island ■

2 Miles

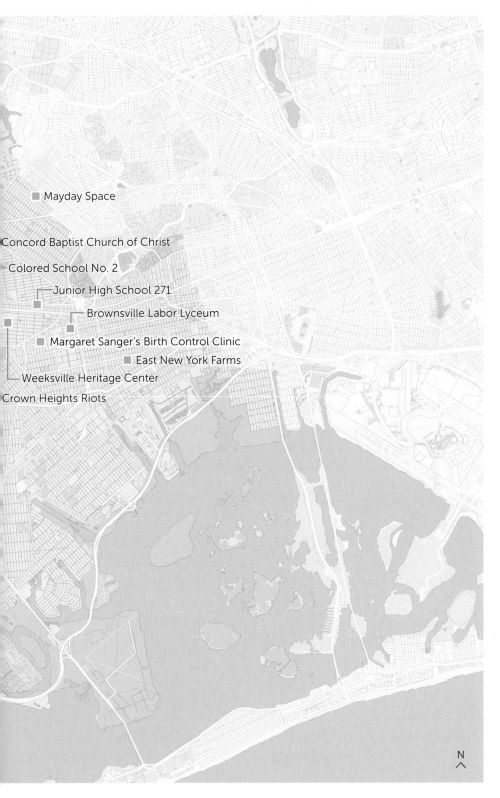

Mayday Space

Concord Baptist Church of Christ

Colored School No. 2

Junior High School 271

Brownsville Labor Lyceum

Margaret Sanger's Birth Control Clinic

East New York Farms

Weeksville Heritage Center

Crown Heights Riots

N

Introduction

THE FARMERS AND SLAVE OWNERS OF THE sleepy Dutch settlement of Breuckelen and the hipsters who have branded today's Brooklyn as the epicenter of cool planted their stakes in this borough, willingly or unwillingly, through the displacement of others. Streets and neighborhoods named by or after the Dutch abound: Conyne Eylandt (Coney Island), Lefferts, Flatbush, Dyker Heights, Red Hook. Few, however, hearken back to the days when the Canarsie tribe fished and hunted along its southern shore, or Chief Gouwane (Gowanus) led among the Lenape. The erasure of Brooklyn's past has taken a different form in recent decades. Now dissolving is Brooklyn's long association with New York's gritty industrialism, with its tough-talking, working-class white ethnics, and with the sprawling Black neighborhoods across its center. Gentrification, driven by real estate moguls and corporations looking for quick profits, as well as artists and professionals seeking relief from Manhattan's rent squeeze, is quickly changing the very character of this diverse, still largely working-class borough. Brooklyn is now the city's most populous borough with nearly 3 million inhabitants and would be the fourth largest US city if it were not incorporated into New York City. Brooklyn brands, arts, industries, authors—they all sell, making Brooklyn not only très chic, but also an artisanal capital of the United States. Brooklyn's cachet is quite recent (since the 2000s) and its history tells a different story,

providing context for the contemporary moment.

Brooklyn rose to prominence in the eighteenth and nineteenth centuries in large part because of the slave trade. One-third of the population of Kings County was enslaved at the beginning of the Revolutionary War and it continued to grow after American independence from Britain. Brooklyn soon became New York's "slaveholding capital." Many prominent Dutch and English families also lent their fortunes to banks that went on to underwrite the slave trade. Ships arriving at Brooklyn's seven miles of waterfront, from Red Hook to Williamsburg, delivered the products of enslaved people's labor, including cotton, sugar, tobacco, wheat, and grain, to hundreds of warehouses along the shore. From there, these products traveled across the city, or East to Europe, or inland. At the same time Brooklyn was home to one of the nation's strongest abolitionist movements and freed slave communities (see **Plymouth Church**, p. 233; and **Weeksville Heritage Center**, p. 249).

The rapid commercialization of Brooklyn brought shipbuilding, printing presses, slaughter houses, tanneries, oil, sugar refineries, and glass manufacturing to the docks of the East River. Italian, Irish, and Jewish immigrants moved to Brooklyn to work in all of these industries, as well as a newly established garment industry that in the 1920s was shifting from the Lower East Side. By the end of World War II, high rates of unionization helped turn these workers into a relatively economically secure group, also making Brooklyn a destination for working-class leisure, replete with baseball, beaches, and racetracks. Black workers, meanwhile, were often excluded from good union jobs and more often relegated to work as common laborers, domestic workers, sweepers, and porters. Doors opened for workers of color in unionized industries only as they were experiencing decline by the early 1970s, when deindustrialization had hit Brooklyn hard, particularly on the waterfront. It wasn't until the rise of the public sector unions that Black workers in Brooklyn, and the rest of the city, gained a serious foothold in unionized jobs. (Today in New York City, Black workers are more likely to be unionized than white.)

Throughout its history, Brooklyn's Black working and middle classes lived side by side in neighborhoods such as Weeksville, Fort Greene, Clinton Hill, Bedford and Stuyvesant Heights (today's Bed-Stuy), and Flatbush. Black professionals were drawn to these neighborhoods both because they were excluded from white neighborhoods and because they wanted to be immersed in urban Black cultural life.

Many neighborhoods in Brooklyn were redlined—denied mortgage credit—because of the relatively old housing stock and social mix of residents. A white working class with access to the GI Bill, cars, newly built expressways, and the Verrazzano Bridge fled neighborhoods such as Brownsville and Flatbush and moved to the Long Island suburbs, Staten Island, and New Jersey. Entire neighborhoods were abandoned. At the same time, the city built new public housing all over Brooklyn, fueling racial tensions and stoking more white flight.

Realtors took advantage of these racial animosities, encouraging white Brooklynites to sell their homes at discounted prices only to rent or sell them to people of color at exorbitant rates (a practice called blockbusting), fueling more white flight and new ghettoization. But, even though white flight was the predominant trend at the time, a small back-to-the-city movement was also taking hold. Revolting against the modern city with its dog-eat-dog, alienated, and impersonal culture, artists, writers, and other free-thinkers began to seek out neighborhood "authenticity" and diversity. By the late 1950s, white, middle-class professionals were buying brownstone houses in Brooklyn Heights, often returning them to their original, single-family grandeur. As Brooklyn Heights became too expensive, these new "Brownstoners" moved to neighboring areas, where they started block associations and created new neighborhood names, such as Cobble Hill, Carroll Gardens, Park Slope, and Prospect Heights.

The Brownstoners often lived in tension with other residents of these neighborhoods, which included white ethnics who had not fled for the suburbs, African Americans, and Puerto Ricans. Brownstoners then found themselves in a contradictory position. They were revitalizing neighborhoods from the grassroots by buying properties, renovating them, and encouraging their friends to do the same, thus contributing to the potential displacement of longer-term residents. At the same time, they were sometimes teaming up with some of these very same residents to fight urban renewal and encourage banks and realtors to begin to invest in their neighborhoods.

Despite the burgeoning revitalization of Brownstone Brooklyn, huge swaths of the borough continued to deteriorate in the 1970s and 1980s. Brownstoners were not interested in Crown Heights, Brownsville, Flatbush, and East Flatbush. Rather, the 1965 immigration act played a more central role in neighborhood change, as hundreds of thousands of immigrants from the Caribbean, Asia, and Latin America moved into these and other neighborhoods. Today Brooklyn has one of the largest Caribbean populations in the world, with Flatbush alone home to the largest concentration of Haitians outside of Haiti (officially known as "Little Haiti," as of 2020), who join their Jamaican, Trinidadian, Guyanese, and Bajan neighbors. Sunset Park is home to Puerto Ricans and Mexicans, among other Latina/o/x groups, and their Chinese neighbors in the city's second largest Chinatown; Brighton Beach and Sheepshead Bay house thousands of Russians and Eastern Europeans; Bay Ridge has a large and vibrant Arab and Muslim American community; and a little north, Kensington maintains a thriving Bangladeshi and Pakistani community.

Brooklyn has come full circle, with increasing white populations moving back to the borough as it has become a leading center of gentrification in the world. But gentrification has not been monolithic across Brooklyn neighborhoods. The gentrification of Williamsburg has differed from Cobble Hill, Carroll Gardens, and Park Slope, which also differs from Fort Greene, Clinton Hill, and Bedford-Stuyvesant –each process with its own character.

Williamsburg experienced gentrification in a way that is more familiar with the public's typical imaginary. As prices on the Lower East Side increased, artists looking for more space at affordable prices crossed the river along the L train route. In the heart of Puerto Rican, Polish, and Italian enclaves, new boutiques and art studios opened alongside cafés and award-winning restaurants. As a result, real estate values soared and sprawling developments were erected, especially along the waterfront, which despite some nice green spaces now mostly resembles a large midwestern office park. As Williamsburg became too expensive for the young people who'd recently put it on the hipster map, they moved to places like Greenpoint and Bushwick, which then began to gentrify in earnest.

Gentrification in Carroll Gardens, Cobble Hill, and Park Slope was fueled by the Brownstoners, and a significant number of middle-class Black New Yorkers joined whites looking for elegant homes at affordable prices in Fort Greene/Clinton Hill. Only more recently have real estate developers begun marketing these long-standing Black neighborhoods (along with Bed-Stuy) to white and affluent newcomers. Crown Heights, in the meantime, has faced the scourge of real estate investors whose business model rests on mass evictions: they profit by driving out rent-stabilized tenants and pricing the apartments at higher rates, often with little reinvestment in the buildings (see **Crown Heights Tenant Union**, p. 268).

Across the borough a key to gentrification has been convenient access to the subway system and city policies such as the lifting of zoning restrictions to facilitate the transformation of places for financial gain. Brooklyn has become known for its artisanal industries, high-tech start-ups, design firms, and entertainment industry. The former Navy Yard now houses 450 private firms (food processing, industrial design, film and TV production) employing over eleven thousand people, more than half with bachelors or advanced degrees. During the global COVID-19 pandemic, some of these Navy Yard industries became producers of hand sanitizer and personal protective equipment (PPE) for overwhelmed New York City hospitals. The former Pfizer factory in Williamsburg is a hub of the foodie industry; the industrial waterfront area of Sunset Park is now home to "Industry City," thirty-five acres of space for makers, artisans, and niche manufacturing; and Manhattan's famed "Silicon Alley" is rapidly shifting to downtown Brooklyn.

Yet gentrification has not taken hold of the entire borough. Many neighborhoods, especially those not close to a subway, have not experienced these levels of neighborhood change. Sheepshead Bay, Mill Basin, Gerritsen Beach, Bath Beach, Marine Park, and Dyker Heights, traditionally strongholds of white working-class ethnics, have grown more diverse with the perpetual influx of immigrants, but have not gentrified. Similarly, East Flatbush, Canarsie, and Flatlands remain predominantly working- and middle-class neighborhoods. Brooklyn is changing, but for now it is maintaining its diversity and, with that, its economic, political, and cultural vibrancy.

TO LEARN MORE

Freeman, Lance. *There Goes the 'Hood: Views of Gentrification from the Ground Up.* Philadelphia: Temple University Press, 2006.

Osman, Suleiman. *The Invention of Brownstone Brooklyn: Gentrification and the Search for Authenticity in Postwar New York.* New York: Oxford University Press, 2011.

Wilder, Craig Steven. *A Covenant with Color: Race and Social Power in Brooklyn.* New York: Columbia University Press, 2000.

■ ■ ■

Greenpoint

4.1 Greenpoint Oil Spill

Apollo Street between Norman and Meeker Avenues, Brooklyn, NY

Under these blocks lies the remnants of the greatest environmental disaster in NYC history and one of the largest oil spills on American soil—one-and-a-half-times larger than the *Exxon Valdez* spill in Alaska in 1989. To call this a spill is misleading—it is the product of something more like a constant leak of somewhere between 17 million and 30 million gallons of oil over a hundred years from ExxonMobil, Chevron/Texaco, and BP's nearby historic processing facilities

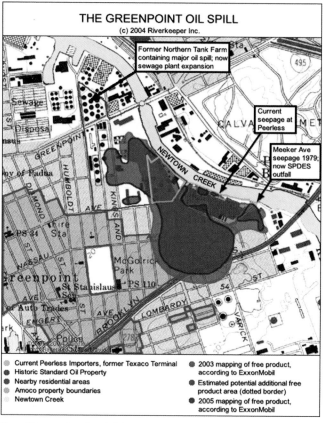

THE GREENPOINT OIL SPILL
(c) 2004 Riverkeeper Inc.

Former Northern Tank Farm containing major oil spill; now sewage plant expansion

Current seepage at Peerless

Meeker Ave seepage 1979; now SPDES outfall

- Current Peerless Importers, former Texaco Terminal
- Historic Standard Oil Property
- Nearby residential areas
- Amoco property boundaries
- Newtown Creek
- 2003 mapping of free product, according to ExxonMobil
- Estimated potential additional free product area (dotted border)
- 2005 mapping of free product, according to ExxonMobil

Map of Greenpoint oil spill, 2004. CREDIT: COURTESY OF RIVERKEEPER

into the soil and groundwater in Greenpoint. The result is a fifty-plus-acre underground petroleum plume beneath more than one hundred homes on three residential blocks that seeps into nearby Newtown Creek. The site remains highly contaminated and an ongoing threat to the ecosystem and human health in this long-standing Polish and Puerto Rican enclave. The oil spill, combined with other toxic pollutants from industry and city waste transfer facilities along Newtown Creek, makes Greenpoint among the most polluted neighborhoods in New York City. Residents have been organizing for decades

to fight for environmental cleanup and against the concentration of environmental and health hazards in the community.

Once a marshy area rich in fish and shellfish inhabited by the Canarsie people, Greenpoint was transformed by the Dutch and English colonizers, first into a trading post given its location along Newtown Creek, and then into an agricultural district. When the Long Island Railroad established a terminal at Greenpoint, heavy industry flocked to the area to take advantage of easy transport. Fertilizer, dye, glue, copper, and chemical plants, as well as dozens of refineries, including Charles Pratt's (of Pratt Institute) Astral Oil Works, set up along Newtown Creek. By 1875, more than fifty oil refineries lined the waterfront from Williamsburg to Greenpoint, making it one of the centers of oil refinery in the United States. In 1886, a "smelling committee" of neighboring residents formed to patrol Greenpoint, "sniffing out hot spots of pollution."

John D. Rockefeller's Standard Oil (later Mobil, and then Exxon) combined many of these refineries into the single, enormous Brooklyn Refinery. The Brooklyn Refinery burned in 1919 (perhaps intentionally for the insurance payout), spilling 110 million gallons of oil in the surrounding area. Because Brooklyn pumped its own drinking water until 1947, the oil moved away from the creek and into the neighborhood, filling in the areas where water had been pumped out. In 1950, gasoline leaking into the city's sewers exploded at Huron Street and Manhattan Avenue, blasting twenty-five manhole covers three stories into the air and shattering windows. Still, the oil pooling below the surface of the neighborhood went unacknowledged.

In 1978, a US Coast Guard helicopter patrol discovered a giant plume of oil in nearby Newtown Creek, and an enormous pool of oil underneath Greenpoint (see **Environmental Justice Tour** in chapter 6, p. 331). ExxonMobil would not take responsibility for the spill until 1989, beginning the cleanup in 1990 when it entered into consent orders with the state. ExxonMobil agreed to gradually remove the oil; the

state agreed to impose neither a deadline nor a fine.

In 2002, the chief investigator of Riverkeeper, an environmental group, discovered that a substantial part of Newtown Creek was coated in a one-quarter-to-one-half-inch-thick layer of oil, and that oil had seeped to varying depths underneath neighborhood properties. The group joined with Concerned Citizens of Greenpoint and local officials to push for faster cleanup, forming the Newtown Creek Alliance and suing ExxonMobil in 2004 under the Clean Water and Resources Conservation and Recovery Acts. The 2010 settlement brought $19.5 million to the Greenpoint Community Environmental Benefit Fund to help pay for green infrastructure and other environmental projects.

Altogether, BP, Chevron, and Exxon Mobil have removed more than 12 million gallons of oil from the creek. Still, a 2007 Riverkeeper analysis revealed that Greenpoint soil samples should have been classified as toxic waste given how "heavily contaminated with benzene and methane" they were. ExxonMobil's cleanup operation will take approximately twenty years. But local neighborhood groups, particularly the Newtown Creek Alliance, continue to work toward environmental remediation in this working-class (though gentrifying) community and along Newtown Creek (declared a Superfund site in 2010), and several mass tort lawsuits have been filed on behalf of Greenpoint residents for tens of millions of dollars in damages to quality of life and property. The impact of the remaining benzene and methane on residents' health has yet to be determined. (*Quote is from Steve Lerner,* Sacrifice Zones: The Front Lines of Toxic Chemical Exposure in the United States.*)

TO LEARN MORE

Angotti, Tom. *New York for Sale: Community Planning Confronts Global Real Estate.* Cambridge, MA: MIT Press, 2008.

Lerner, Steve. *Sacrifice Zones: The Front Lines of Toxic Chemical Exposure in the United States.* Cambridge, MA: MIT Press, 2010.

NEARBY SITE OF INTEREST

Astral Apartments
184 Franklin Avenue, Brooklyn, NY

These "model" apartments opened in 1886 as affordable housing for workers at the Astral Oil Works, run by Charles Pratt, who also endowed the Pratt Institute located in Clinton Hill. The relatively airy and well-appointed apartments were joined by a kindergarten and settlement house on the premises, as well as a branch of the Pratt library.

FAVORITE NEIGHBORHOOD RESTAURANTS

Christina's
853 Manhattan Avenue, Brooklyn, NY

Polish American restaurant with diner basics and Polish specialties, like pierogies, stuffed cabbage, and goulash.

Old Polish Bakery
926 Manhattan Avenue, Brooklyn, NY

One of the few remaining places in the neighborhood to try a variety of sweet and savory babkas.

Williamsburg

4.2 Domino Sugar Factory

Kent Avenue between S. 2nd Street and S. 3rd Street, Brooklyn, NY

On the heavily gentrified Williamsburg waterfront, one can still see remnants of the Domino Sugar empire, once expanding from South 2nd to Grand Streets. In the mid-nineteenth century, consumer demand for refined sugar catapulted the growth of the sugar industry, particularly on the East Coast. One of the biggest players in the industry was H.O. Havemeyer. As a result of intense competition among sugar refin-

The old Domino Building and new construction with the Empire State Building in the background, 2017.
CREDIT: SCOTT DEXTER

eries, Havemeyer thought it important to create a sugar trust comprised of various refinery owners to limit competition and control prices. The sugar trust, formed in 1887, under the name American Sugar Refining Company, combined eighteen East Coast refineries, including six refineries in Kings County (Brooklyn), the three largest of which were owned by the Havemeyer family (representing more than 50 percent of the trust's capacity for production). Upon consolidation, the trust immediately controlled over 80 percent of sugar production in the United States. By 1901 it controlled 95 percent of the sugar produced in the United States, much of which was produced at this Domino Sugar refinery, the largest one in the country.

Despite the Sherman Antitrust Act of 1890, which limited monopolies, Havemeyer continued to oversee a robust business by constantly innovating. He understood that the way to continue to make a profit in a cutthroat industry was brand loyalty. At a time when most sugar was sold in barrels with no attention to brands, Havemeyer introduced "Domino" sugar cubes, named for their shape. In its peak years, 1887–1914, the Domino Sugar Plant employed over three thousand workers.

Even with the dangerous working conditions, workers engaged in only two strikes in the entire history of the factory (1882–2004). They struck for higher pay in 1906 (the going rate was eighteen cents an hour) and lost. The next strike didn't occur until 2000, when workers once again protested low wages and poor working conditions at the factory.

In one of the longest strikes in US history, Domino's workforce picketed the factory for twenty months. In the end, the union settled for a mediocre contract that was not much better than the one offered to them before the strike. At that point Domino was no longer owned by the American Sugar Refinery Company, but by London-based Tate and Lyle, one of the world's largest sweetener producers. Shortly after the strike, the company decided to shut down the refinery.

In 2014 Creative Time, a public arts organization, commissioned Kara Walker to build a sculpture. *"A Subtlety, or the Marvelous Sugar Baby, an Homage to the unpaid and overworked Artisans who have refined our Sweet tastes from the cane fields to the Kitchens of the New World on the Occasion of the demolition of the Domino*

"A Subtlety, or the Marvelous Sugar Baby" by Kara Walker in the Domino Sugar factory, 2014. CREDIT: ADJOAJO - OWN WORK, CC BY-SA 3.0, WIKIMEDIA COMMONS

Sugar Refining Plant" debuted in May 2014. The sculpture, a woman with African features in the shape of a sphinx, measured eighty feet long by forty feet high. Ironically, Domino foods donated eighty tons of sugar for the piece. In July of the same year, the building was demolished and luxury condominiums were constructed on the site.

TO LEARN MORE

Ayala, César J. *American Sugar Kingdom: The Plantation Economy of the Spanish Caribbean, 1898–1934.* Chapel Hill: University of North Carolina Press, 1999.

Rugoff, Stephanie. 1970. "The Imperialist Role of the American Sugar Company." *NACLA Newsletter*, 1970.

NEARBY SITES OF INTEREST

Domino Park
300 Kent Avenue, Brooklyn, NY
A five-acre public park built on the former site of the refinery.

City Reliquary Museum
370 Metropolitan Avenue, Brooklyn, NY
A tiny, interactive storefront museum that tells an eclectic history of NYC through fascinating ephemera and artifacts, including old subway tokens, merchandise from the 1939 World's Fair, Jackie Robinson's portrait, and thousands of other items. This nonprofit hosts film screenings and block parties, as well as yearly festivals, including occasions such as Collectors Day and Bike Fetish Day.

Former Site of F&M Schaefer Brewing
Kent Avenue between 9th and 10th Streets, Brooklyn, NY
German immigrants to New York City popularized the lager beer, a clearer, lighter, and more sparkling beer than what was consumed at the time. Lagers were first introduced to the city by the Schaefer brothers in the 1840s, produced at this location for the first half of the twentieth century (most of the dozens of other Brooklyn breweries at the time operated along "Brewers Row" in Bushwick). When Schaefer closed in 1976 it left Brooklyn without a brewery for nearly a decade, when the microbrewery business took off in New York City, symbolized well by the nearby Brooklyn Brewery (79 N. 11th Street), whose own "Brooklyn Lager" is now sold internationally.

Acme Smoked Fish
30 Gem Street, Brooklyn, NY (open to the public only Fridays from 8 A.M. to 1 P.M.)
Wait in line on Friday mornings to get great deals on smoked fish at this long-standing family owned smokehouse, which started in Brownsville but moved to this location in Williamsburg in 1954.

FAVORITE NEIGHBORHOOD RESTAURANTS

Peter Pan Donuts and Pastry Shop
727 Manhattan Avenue, Brooklyn, NY
Open since the 1950s, this Greenpoint neighborhood donut and pastry joint doesn't disappoint. The shop basically looks the same way it did when it opened, and neighborhood residents wouldn't have it any other way.

Peter Luger Steakhouse
178 Broadway, Brooklyn, NY
Peter Luger's is the last remaining steakhouse opened by a German immigrant in the nineteenth century in New York City. Opened as Carl Luger's Cafe, Billiards, and Bowling Alley in 1887, the restaurant became an instant hit in the then mostly German neighborhood. The restaurant survived prohibition, two World Wars, and several economic crises, and continues to thrive today.

Bushwick and Boerum Hill

4.3 Mayday Space and Brooklyn Commons

176 St. Nicholas Ave, Brooklyn, NY

STARR BAR AND CAFÉ

214 Starr Street, Brooklyn, NY

BROOKLYN COMMONS

388 Atlantic Avenue, Brooklyn, NY

One of many activist spaces in New York City, Starr Bar in Bushwick, 2017. CREDIT: SCOTT DEXTER

Mayday and the Commons join a small but substantial list of places whose sole purpose is creating a space for a wide variety of movement groups to incubate their work. Most typically, groups repurpose other spaces for their regular gatherings and events. Taverns and bars, churches and synagogues, schools, restaurants, union halls, workers' centers, and community centers all serve as movement spaces. On occasion, groups have rented spaces for short- and long-term use: in the early 1970s, Vietnam Veterans Against the War had a storefront on Brooklyn's Fifth Avenue and also had offices at 17 East 17th Street in Manhattan, where other antiwar organizations had set up shop, too, like the Fifth Avenue Vietnam Peace Parade and the Student Mobilization Committee. It is frequently the case that related organizations have rented offices near each other, as when the Center for Constitutional Rights and the National Lawyers Guild were both at 853 Broadway. Occasionally, leftist groups have even owned real estate in New York. Most famous was the "Peace Pentagon" building at 339 Lafayette Street (Manhattan), formerly owned by the A. J. Muste Institute, which for decades served as a home to the War Resisters League, Global Revolution TV, Paper Tiger TV, and the Socialist Party USA (when Muste had to sell, these groups relocated to rental space at 168 Canal Street). The Communist Party still owns the building at 235 West 23rd Street in Manhattan, though it rents out many of its floors to businesses.

Mayday Space and Brooklyn Commons are two of the most recent of innumerable "movement spaces" created in New York City, where the movements of the city have met, hatched their plans, educated themselves, connected with each other, done their work, celebrated, and more. Some groups hold regular meetings, workshops, or classes in the spaces. Others hold occasional retreats or special events. Brooklyn Commons has a number of resident organizations, including the Brooklyn Filmmakers Collective, Families United For Racial and Economic Equality, *Jacobin* magazine, The Right to the City Alliance, *The Indypendent* (newspaper), and WBAI Radio, NYC's affiliate with the Pacifica chain of progressive radio stations. The Marxist Education

Project is one of its core tenants, which was itself founded when the Brecht Forum, New York City's preeminent left educational center since 1975, closed its doors in 2014.

Mayday Space is collectively managed by a group of long-time social justice activists, most of whom are deeply connected to local Bushwick community-organizing, including work against gentrification and for food justice. The Mayday founders appreciate that movements are not only fostered by work and organizing, but by community, culture, conviviality, and personal connections as well. To underscore this, Starr Bar and Café is their sister organization, which provides a social space with musical, dance, and spoken word programming for the community to enjoy. Its proceeds support the work of the community space. The Commons also has a café, located on its first floor, open during the day.

NEARBY SITE OF INTEREST

Bushwick Collective Murals
Troutman Street and St. Nicholas Avenue, Brooklyn, NY
Started by Bushwick native Joe Ficalora in 2013, the Bushwick Collective creates murals that adorn these and nearby streets in a vast volunteer public art project featuring dozens of artists who contribute to the outdoor gallery. The murals are loved for their breathtaking artistry but ambivalently embraced by the neighborhood, as their popularity is often seen as contributing to the neighborhood's rapid gentrification.

FAVORITE NEIGHBORHOOD RESTAURANT

Tortilleria Mexicana Los Hermanos
271 Starr Street, Brooklyn, NY
A tortilla factory, small cantina, and neighborhood favorite. The chorizo tacos are particularly delicious, served on warm tortillas right off the line.

Brooklyn Heights

4.4 Brooklyn Bridge

Tillary and Adams Streets, or Cadman Plaza, Brooklyn, NY

Along the crowded wooden walkway that allows pedestrians passage across the bridge are numerous plaques telling the story of the bridge's construction. Called "the 8th Wonder of the World" upon opening in 1883, the Brooklyn Bridge was the world's tallest and longest suspension bridge in its era, hailed a feat of modern engineering, and to this day remains an international architectural icon. Here on the Manhattan facing side of the tower closest to that borough is a sign acknowledging the work of one of the essential but, at the time, overlooked contributors to the bridge's completion, Emily Roebling. The role she played in executing the erection of the bridge is indelibly linked to the workplace illness associated with its construction, decompression sickness.

Suspension bridges were still experimental when John Roebling, Emily's father-in-law, initially drafted its plans and design. The unique crosshatching wires were not part of this original plan: horizontal cables were added when some of the initial suspension wires were found to be brittle, one of many contracting scandals that plagued the bridge's prolonged construction.

But quite possibly the greatest challenge in building the bridge was the initial work of creating the foundation. The bridge's two towers stand on caissons, enormous boxes built at the Brooklyn Navy Yard, which were lowered to the riverbed and filled with compressed air so that workers could dig the sediment below until the boxes reached bedrock. The weight of the towers being built on top of the caissons helped the structure sink at the same time that workers were digging inside. The work was incredibly difficult: dim, suffocating, smelly, dangerous—and poorly compensated. The laborers, mostly Irish and Italian immigrants, did not tend to stick with the awful work for very long, and as many as a hundred left their jobs each week. The most pervasive illness among workers in the construction of the bridge was "the bends," or decompression

sickness, until that point an unknown disease brought on by too-rapid decompression as one travels from high pressure depths to surface-area air pressure. In a rapid ascent dissolved nitrogen in the blood forms into bubbles, which first can affect one's joints (hence, "the bends" as the place where one is in pain), but also one's nervous system, with symptoms that can include paralysis, blindness, and cognitive impairment. In fact, this illness now associated with scuba-divers and astronauts is also known as "caisson disease," as these bridge workers were the first diagnosed. As workers dug further and further down to bedrock, the sicker they got when reaching the surface.

John Roebling was injured at the start of the bridge's construction and died from a resulting tetanus infection in 1869. His son Washington took over as chief engineer. Washington Roebling, who was at the job site every day, and in the caissons frequently, suffered his first attack of decompression sickness in 1870, forcing him to stay home for several weeks. He eventually recovered from this initial attack, but grew to be quite concerned about symptoms among workers. Ahead of his time in thinking about worker health and safety, Roebling implemented restrictions on the number of hours workers could be in the caissons and hired a physician on staff. Workers spent no more than two hours down, before coming up to the surface. They would rest for an hour, and then

Brooklyn Bridge during construction, n.d. Cadman Plaza, Brooklyn, NY. CREDIT: *BROOKLYN DAILY EAGLE* PHOTOGRAPHS, BROOKLYN PUBLIC LIBRARY, BROOKLYN COLLECTION

go back down. Ultimately over one hundred workers were sickened with the bends, and it wasn't until the early twentieth century that physicians recognized that a slower ascent to the surface mitigated the problem. In 1909 New York State became the first state to pass caisson-safety laws, to protect the "sandhogs," as the excavation workers were known, during the construction of the East River train tunnels.

Given the extraordinarily harsh working conditions, it is surprising that there is only one documented strike in the construction of the bridge, a failed effort by the sandhogs in 1872 to raise their pay. The dangers yielded a number of deaths in the construction of the bridge; estimates range between twenty and forty over the entire construction period.

The Brooklyn tower reached bedrock after forty-four feet, which was fortunate, because fewer workers were affected by the illness at that depth. The Manhattan caisson was a different story: the digging proved to be faster, but bedrock was much further down. On the Manhattan side, Roebling suffered his second attack, leaving him permanently disabled and unable to be at the work site or directly supervise the construction of the bridge for the remaining period. From 1872 to the completion of the bridge in 1883, Emily Roebling served as a liaison between Washington Roebling and the outside world, including to the staff of engineers, the trustees of the bridge company, and the media. More than simply relaying Washington's vision, Emily's advanced study of engineering meant that she explained and directed

Charles-Émile-Auguste Carolus-Duran (French, 1838–1917). *Portrait of Emily Warren Roebling*, 1896. Oil on canvas, 89 x 47 1/2 in. CREDIT: BROOKLYN MUSEUM, GIFT OF PAUL ROEBLING

the work. While fighting to maintain her husband's appointment to the position and public recognition for the bridge's construction, she in fact became surrogate chief engineer. Years later, in a letter to her son, she argued, "I have more brains, common sense, and know-how generally than any two engineers civil or uncivil that I have ever met, and but for me the Brooklyn Bridge would never have had the name of Roebling in any way connected with it! . . . Your father was for years *dead* to all interest in that work." Though unacknowledged in the first hundred years of the bridge's existence, for decades it has been recognized that the bridge could have never been completed without her efforts, brilliance, and political savvy. In addition to the plaque , a block of Columbia Heights where the Roebling house stood was renamed Emily Warren Roebling Way in 2018. *(Quote from* Heroes of New York Harbor *by Marian Betancourt, p. 74.)*

TO LEARN MORE

Betancourt, Marian. *Heroes of New York Harbor: Tales from the City's Port.* Guilford, CT: Globe Pequot Press, 2016.

McCullough, David. *The Great Bridge: The Epic Story of the Building of the Brooklyn Bridge.* Reprint edition. New York: Simon and Schuster, 1983.

Weigold, Marilyn E. *Silent Builder: Emily Warren Roebling and the Brooklyn Bridge.* Millwood, NY: Associated Faculty Press, 1984.

4.5 Plymouth Church

57 Orange Street, Brooklyn, NY

Plymouth Church stands as a reminder of Brooklyn's abolitionist history as one of only a handful of sites that is formally and nationally recognized for its role in the underground railroad, despite the fact that Plymouth was just one of many anti-slavery churches in the city of Brooklyn that agitated for slavery's end in the antebellum period. The others included Brooklyn's oldest Black church, Bridge Street AWME, Berean Baptist, Concord Baptist (see **Shirley Chisholm's Presidential Launch at Concord**

Baptist Church of Christ, p. 244), and Siloam Presbyterian (see **1964 School Boycott–Board of Education,** p. 239), all of which still exist today. Plymouth's prominence tells us a great deal about the priorities of historical memory and the politics of commemoration. Indeed, Plymouth's recognition was due, in large part, to the church's larger than life white pastor, Henry Ward Beecher (brother of Harriet Beecher Stowe, author of *Uncle Tom's Cabin*). He served Plymouth Church as its inaugural pastor from its inception in 1847 until his death in 1887. During his tenure, Beecher, a charismatic, fiery abolitionist, cemented Plymouth Church's reputation as a center of abolitionist activity.

In 1847, New England liberals living in the nation's first suburb of Brooklyn Heights invited thirty-four year old Henry Ward Beecher from Indianapolis to lead the new church. Within three years, the congregation increased to twelve hundred. Beecher stated to the building's architect "I want [the congregation] to surround me, so that I shall be in the center of the crowd, and have the people surge all about me." He achieved this metaphor in life and legacy. A savvy marketer, Beecher was seen regularly in local and national newspapers endorsing a range of commercial goods including lozenges, hay fever medicine, and soap.

But it was his dramatic anti-slavery sermons and scenes that made him a national public figure. In fact, it is alleged that the Fulton Ferry that usually shepherded passengers between the two separate cities of Brooklyn and Manhattan were called "Beecher's Boats" because of the large number of people who traveled on a Sunday to see the pastor. As sectional tensions grew in the United States after 1850, and as the Fugitive Slave Law allowed federal special commissioners to cross state lines and arrest any person of color suspected of being a fugitive, Plymouth Church became a site of increasingly complex scenes of emancipation. Between 1848 and 1863, Beecher conducted a series of performative fundraisers that resembled slave auctions. He invited young, enslaved women and girls to stand next to him at his church while he pled slavery's sin and the largely white congregation threw money in a plate as to buy their freedom.

But Beecher's activity only built on the work of Brooklyn's early free Black community which had long led and pioneered the anti-slavery struggle. The city of Brooklyn had deep-rooted ties to slave economies and a number of its churches were embedded in pro-slavery ideology. It was this very outrage that had led Black Brooklynites in 1818 to reject the sermons at Sands Street Methodist Church and form the African Methodist Episcopal Church nearby in what is now considered downtown Brooklyn (today the church is Bridge Street AWME and has since moved to Bedford Stuyvesant). This small community of activists formed their own institutions, including schools, churches, and mutual aid societies in order to combat the racism they faced. They would also buy land in what would become Weeksville to create oases of safety and refuge, as well as to establish the property ownership that free Black men (but not white men) needed for voting rights in New York (see **Weeks-**

ville Heritage Center, p. 249). Most of these churches often fundraised for the emancipation of enslaved Black people, sometimes with Beecher, even if they did not resort to some of Beecher's bravado.

Today, Plymouth Church and Beecher are well commemorated for their anti-slavery politics. A monument by John Quincy Adams Ward and Richard Morris Hunt in nearby Cadman Plaza opposite Brooklyn Borough Hall depicts the pastor standing tall while three children, one of them Black, kneel at his feet. The kneeling figures provide a reminder that often it is those at the bottom eager to tell their own story of bravery, struggle, and survival, even if our buildings and monuments do not always privilege their voices.

—*Prithi Kanakamedala*

NEARBY SITES OF INTEREST

Transit Workers Union Local 100
195 Montague Street, Brooklyn, NY

On December 20, 2005, New York City transit workers, members of the Transit Workers Union (TWU) Local 100 went on strike, effectively shutting down New York City in the middle of the Christmas shopping season. Public sector strikes have always been illegal in New York City, but the penalties for these strikes became enforceable with the passage of the Taylor Law in 1967. In addition to the lost wages and fines that individual strikers incurred, the TWU was fined $2.5 million, and the union president was sentenced to ten days in jail. Perhaps most importantly, the union temporarily lost automatic dues deduction, forcing them to make rounds and collect dues from members on a monthly basis. While the loss of an automatic dues deduction nearly bankrupted the local, they have fortunately rebounded and opened this spacious union hall at this site in Brooklyn Heights.

Sahadi's

187 Atlantic Avenue, Brooklyn, NY

Sahadi's opened at this location in 1948, by immigrants from Lebanon. The iconic Middle Eastern grocery store attracts visitors from all over Brooklyn for its delicious prepared foods, nuts, spices, coffee, and cheeses.

Damascus Bakery

195 Atlantic Avenue, Brooklyn, NY

Opened in 1930 by Syrian immigrants, Damascus Bakery has been serving pita, lahvash, flatbreads, savory pies, and baklava to Brooklyn residents ever since.

Downtown Brooklyn

4.6 Knights of Labor, District Assembly 75

407 Bridge Street, Brooklyn, NY

The cover of *Harper's Weekly* in February 1895, "The Strike in Brooklyn—Firing at the Mob," 1895. CREDIT: *HARPER'S WEEKLY*

On January 14, 1895, five thousand electric railway workers walked off their jobs, initiating a month-long strike that stopped the flow of traffic throughout the city of Brooklyn. They struck for a living wage, better working conditions, and a safer environment during an age of unsettling technological change and the "Great Depression" of 1893–1897. The action represented the largest railroad strike in Brooklyn's history and the first general strike among electric trolley-car workers in the United States. This site at 407 Bridge Street served as headquarters for the Knights of Labor, District Assembly 75, the union that represented the railway workers.

These workers were also among the last of the Knights to organize and win a strike.

While at their peak they had over 600,000 members, the Knights of Labor had seen their membership decline precipitously after the 1886 strikes for the eight-hour-day and the Haymarket Massacre in Chicago. The Brooklyn chapter of the Knights was one of the last remaining strong and militant locals of the organization.

Like other workers across the nation, Brooklyn's trolley workers had already organized in response to deteriorating working conditions. An earlier strike (1886) won them important victories, including protection from dismissal for union membership, a twelve-hour day, and a seniority system. But the railroad owners vowed to reverse those gains, and 1895 presented them with an opportunity to crush the workers and the Knights.

Brooklyn's railroad companies had recently consolidated their holdings (and hundreds of miles of track) into just a few companies, which promised to eradicate competition to save labor costs and profit from increased speed. As a state investigation later revealed, the companies had also issued "watered" (below par) stocks and bonds to fund the consolidation, as a way of reaping "very exceptional profits, and at the same time avoiding and evading certain responsibilities to the laws of this State." Evading the state's recently legislated Ten-Hour Law was among their maneuvers and a central issue of the strike.

Finding a loophole in the Ten-Hour Law, and with the national unemployment rate reaching 16 percent in 1894, Brooklyn's consolidated railroad companies refused to pay conductors and drivers while railroad cars sat idle, and instead used a greater number of "trippers" (those "paid by the trip" and on-call for twelve hours/day to meet the demands of rush-hour traffic), suspended or discharged employees at will (often for taking meals guaranteed under contracts), hired nonunion scabs to replace those suspended, and changed work schedules by increasing the number of trips workers had to undertake each day. Electrification made speedier trips possible and enhanced company revenues by allowing firms to run more of the large electric cars that could accommodate an expanding population of passengers. Accelerated speed also put the public at risk. Between 1892 and 1894, accidents

along the line increased, resulting in nearly one hundred fatalities. Those accidents, in turn, expanded idle time and increased stress among workers held responsible for safety.

The executive committee of the Knights of Labor brought these issues to the table in December 1894, but negotiations to execute a pending contract between employees of the roads and four railroad corporations—the Brooklyn Heights; Brooklyn, Queens County, and Suburban; Atlantic Avenue; and Brooklyn City and Newtown railroad companies—ultimately collapsed. Indeed, as the state investigation also revealed that company representatives never intended to negotiate. Neither freezing temperatures nor snowfall deterred the railroad workers from voting to strike. During the first days of the five-week standoff, the public generally sympathized with the cause, and the striking workers' wives and friends joined them on the picket line. Unfortunately, when the railroad companies hired replacements to break the line, skirmishes broke out. Ultimately, those skirmishes changed to riots involving strikebreakers, the strikers and their wives, a host of community members, and the local police.

In the meantime, the powerful forces of capital and state came together, in the form of Brooklyn's mayor, Charles Adolph Schieren. A merchant, banker, and friend to Brooklyn's railroad magnates, Schieren employed anti-union newspapers to build a case against the strikers and their wives, in a string of articles accusing both of inciting riots throughout the city. He then called upon the services of seventy-five hundred National Guardsmen, to patrol the streets, quell (or instigate) riots, end the strike, and deliver a final death blow to the Knights of Labor.

—Jocelyn Wills

TO LEARN MORE

Gerteis, Joseph. *Class and the Color Line: Interracial Class Coalition in the Knights of Labor and the Populist Movement.* Durham, NC: Duke University Press, 2007.

Henry, Sarah M. "The Strikers and Their Sympathizers: Brooklyn in the Trolley Strike of 1895." *Labor History* 32, no. 3 (1991): 329–353. https://doi.org/10.1080/00236569100890211.

NEARBY SITE OF INTEREST

Cave Canem

20 Jay Street, Suite 310-A, Brooklyn, NY

Persistent lack of racial diversity in New York's publishing and literary scenes has helped to foster cultural spaces focused on specific communities of color. Cave Canem began in 1996 as a collective committed to the representation and support of Black poets; today with hundreds of members, it hosts workshops, New Works reading series, and other programs, and is connected to various retreat centers for writers.

Fulton Mall, 2017. CREDIT: SCOTT DEXTER

4.7 Fulton Mall

Fulton Street between Smith Street and Flatbush Avenue Extension, Brooklyn, NY

Fulton Mall, the section of Fulton Street between Borough Hall and Flatbush Avenue, has been Brooklyn's retail hub since the 1880s, when the newly constructed Brooklyn Bridge began depositing arrivals to Brooklyn at Fulton Street and a nearby elevated train brought people from as far away as East New York. The development of the area as a full-fledged commercial district was anchored by the construction of a dry goods store, Abraham & Strauss (A&S), which eventually became a major department store. Its art deco building, which now houses a Macy's, still stands on Fulton Streets between Hoyt Street and Gallatin Place.

Many of the large, landmarked buildings on Fulton Street itself were built during the 1940s, when Fulton Street was consolidated as a major retail district through stores like A&S, Mays, Namm's, Woolworth's, and Schrafft's. As historians Woo and TenHoor note, it was hoped that department stores would make Fulton Street respectable: "They were seen as more than just respectable purveyors of physical goods, they also sold membership into society. Fulton Mall was more than just a place to make purchases, it was a place to go."

This sense of Fulton Mall as a "place to go," a connector of people as well as a consumer destination, stuck even as Brooklyn was transformed by redlining, white flight, disinvestment, and Black migration from the South between 1940 and 1970. The Irish, Italian, German, and Jewish immigrants that had thronged to Fulton Street left for suburbs, and the big department stores eventually followed them. But Fulton Street didn't collapse: in an impressive show of resourcefulness and entrepreneurialism, Black Americans and Caribbean immigrants, despite lack of access to capital, managed to keep Fulton Mall flourishing throughout decades when Brooklyn was plagued by disinvestment and speculation. At a time when racial prejudice made it stressful, if not dangerous, to shop in white stores in Manhattan or South Brooklyn, Fulton Mall provided a friendly environment and access to small businesses that catered to the tastes and needs of Black Brooklynites.

By the 1980s, Fulton Street, which the city had remade into "Fulton Mall" by blocking all traffic except buses, was once again a vibrant thoroughfare and the center of Black life in Brooklyn, memorialized by Spike Lee in *She's Gotta Have It*. Small businesses—fabric stores, barbershops, Caribbean food shops, wig stores, and Black bookstores—made the small streets connecting Fulton and Willoughby particularly lively. Many of Fulton's street department stores were subdivided and leased to smaller businesses. Often

these would be subdivided into "mini-malls," where six or ten vendors sold the latest sneakers, custom spray-painted clothing, and jewelry, including gold and silver and "fronts" for teeth. Even Junior's, at the corner of Dekalb and Flatbush, changed with the times. It added soul food to its Jewish deli menu and is worth a visit today for its cheesecake.

This eclectic mix of highly specialized small businesses, larger stores like Cookies (Brooklyn's only children's department store), and Fino Menswear and Shoes (which sold the zoot suits and hats worn in many of Brooklyn's Black churches), and the public culture of the space created the ideal environment for creative expressions. Fulton Mall was an important location for the development of hip-hop in Brooklyn. Much of this activity centered around record stores like Beat Street records, where artists would come to promote their albums, and the Albee Square Mall (Fulton and Albee Square).

As a rapper named Dezo says in the documentary *My Brooklyn*, "You had Big Daddy Kane, you had Biz Markie down here in the mall like every other day. These guys went to school down here, and sometimes on the corner you would see like a group of guys standing there, and they'd all be sitting there rhyming to each other. That was when the big chains was out, and everybody used to wear the big chains. The major jewelry shops who sold those chains were in the Albee Square Mall." The Albee Square Mall exists only in memory, and in songs like Biz Markie's "Albee Square Mall."

Even in its current iteration, in which global chain stores and high-rise luxury apartments predominate, a discerning visitor can find evidence of the area's more varied and distinct past. Street vendors along Fulton Street still sell books, Malcolm X speeches, and accessories (the "Belt Man" is particularly worth tracking down). On Livingston Street, which runs parallel to Fulton one block to the South, you can still find longtime independent businesses like Joyce Keihm's Hair Heaven, which sells wigs that the shop then styles for customers. Stur-Dee Health Foods, however, a pioneer since 1932 in advocating for diet and vitamins as a cure for illness and one of Brooklyn's few surviving family-owned health shops, has now permanently closed.

Despite its consistent commercial success, Fulton Mall has long been regarded as "failed" space. Extensive rezoning in 2004 paved the way for rapid gentrification of the area, including the displacement of over one hundred nearby stores (and counting). Whether the new Fulton Mall is an improvement over what was there before is in the eye of the beholder and dependent on one's sense of who the city is for and whose values it should reflect. Visiting, one can't help but ask the question Woo and TenHoor ask: "What would the area be like if the city had asked a different question over the years, rather than 'What's wrong with Fulton Street?'" (Quotes from Rosten Woo and Meredith TenHoor, Street Value: Shopping, Planning, and Politics at Fulton Mall; and Kelly Anderson and Allison Lirish Dean's documentary My Brooklyn.)

—Kelly Anderson

TO LEARN MORE

Anderson, Kelly (dir.), and Allison Lirish Dean (prod.). My Brooklyn (documentary). 2012. New Day Films. 85 minutes.

Woo, Rosten, and Meredith TenHoor. Street Value: Shopping, Planning, and Politics at Fulton Mall. New York: Princeton Architectural Press, 2010, 51, 33.

NEARBY SITES OF INTEREST

227 and 233 Duffield Street, Brooklyn, NY
These two homes have long been recognized by their owners and experts as stops on the Underground Railroad. Number 227, owned by Joy Chatel until her death in 2014, once belonged to the prominent abolitionists Thomas and Harriet Lee Truesdell. In 2021, after decades of protest and advocacy, the building finally received landmark status. Sadly the decision came too late to save 233 Duffield (now a building). The owners of these buildings believed their basements were used to house and feed people escaping slavery because they were close to Plymouth Church, a center of abolitionism in nearby Brooklyn Heights (see **Plymouth Church**, p. 233), and because their homes were connected by an underground tunnel.

4.8 The 1964 School Boycott–Board of Education

110 Livingston Street, Brooklyn, NY

Today a luxury condominium building, 110 Livingston was for decades home to the city's Board of Education, overseeing the city's public schools that serve more than a million youth. On February 3, 1964, New York City was home to the largest civil rights demonstration of the era. Nearly half a million students and teachers of color participated in a massive boycott of the city's

SCHOOL
BOYCOTT!
FREEDOM DAY   FEBRUARY 3, 1964

"I Don't Have A Good Integrated School"

JOIN THE ONE DAY BOYCOTT!

FOR INFORMATION CALL:

BRONX	BROOKLYN	QUEENS	MANHATTAN
LU 9-8409	UL 7-9200	JA 6-9070	AU 1-6333
JE 7-8270	ST 9-7050	RA 1-5855	Uptown MO 6-0400
			Lower East Side SP 7-9090

City Wide Committee for Integrated Schools

Flyer publicizing the 1964 public school boycott.
CREDIT: QUEENS COLLEGE LIBRARIES DEPARTMENT OF SPECIAL
COLLECTIONS AND ARCHIVES

public schools to dramatize the poor conditions in predominantly Black and Puerto
Rican schools and demand that city officials
construct a comprehensive plan for desegregation. Teachers, parents, students, activists,
and other community members demon-
strated at 300 of the city's 860 schools and
marched across the Brooklyn Bridge, ending
at this building. White backlash to this boycott caused the landmark federal Civil Rights
Act of 1964 to include language that effectively allowed New York City to maintain a
segregated system to this day.

For decades Black and Latina/o/x children attended overcrowded schools with
dilapidated facilities, less rigorous curricu-
lums, and less experienced teachers. Some
predominantly Black and Puerto Rican

schools were so overcrowded that they operated in shifts, with students receiving only
four hours of instruction each day, while
schools in some predominantly white communities were only half enrolled.

The school boycott grew out of the
decade-long struggle following the Supreme
Court's landmark *Brown v. Board* decision
ruling school segregation unconstitutional.
Grassroots organizers in New York pushed
to ensure the verdict was implemented
within the city's segregated and unequal
public schools. Reverend Milton Galamison,
a pastor at Siloam Presbyterian Church in
Bedford-Stuyvesant and local organizer,
spearheaded the effort. He gained momentum after building on the work done by Harlem activist and organizer Ella Baker, who
had established a multiyear campaign that
demanded improvements in faculty and
resources for public schools that educated
students of color. Her work led to the formation of Parents in Action, a multiracial
coalition of parents and activists fighting
educational discrimination. It also built on
the work of the Harlem 9, a group of mothers from Harlem who were charged with
negligence when they decided to keep their
children out of junior high schools 136, 139,
and 120 in 1958 to protest the city's segregated and unequal schools.

With this grassroots foundation in place,
Galamison had made previous attempts to
negotiate with city officials, but they maintained their lackluster approach to school
integration. Mass protest was needed.
Though the boycott was the largest civil
rights boycott of the era, many news sources

in New York opposed the demonstration. The *New York Times* published an editorial titled "No More School Boycotts" which framed the demonstration as "tragically misguided" and generalized all boycotts as "pointless," "dangerous," and "destructive" to the children of New York. Labeling those in charge of the boycott as "intolerable," they professed that concerning segregation in New York City schools, "there is no realistic way to alter the balance."

In response to the boycott, a group of ten thousand protesters, mostly white women associated with the largely white and female anti-desegregation organization Parents and Taxpayers gathered again at this building to march in the other direction across the Brooklyn Bridge to City Hall to oppose school desegregation. Coverage of this mother's march reached the halls of Congress just as legislation for the 1964 Civil Rights Act was being drafted. With the march in mind, Brooklyn Congressman Emanuel Celler created a loophole in Section 401B that defined "desegregation": "'Desegregation' means the assignment of students to public schools and within such schools without regard to their race, color, religion, or national origin. Desegregation shall not mean the assignment of students to public schools in order to overcome racial imbalance." Ultimately, the preferences of the white New Yorkers of Parents and Taxpayers would outweigh the weight of the February 1964 school boycott, and the Civil Rights Act itself would provide a way for northern cities like New York to avoid desegregation yet keep their federal funds. *(Quote from* New York Times *editorial board, "No More School Boycotts.")*

—Ethan Barnett and Jeanne Theoharis

TO LEARN MORE

New York Times. 1964a. "No More School Boycotts." *New York Times,* February 3, 1964, sec. Archives.

Taylor, Clarence. *Civil Rights in New York City: From World War II to the Giuliani Era.* New York: Fordham University Press, 2011.

4.9 Atlantic Yards

Intersection of Atlantic and Flatbush Avenues, Brooklyn, NY

The landscape at the corner of Atlantic and Flatbush Avenues in Brooklyn could be any US city or suburb. At the northeast, a mall featuring Applebee's, Target, and Chuck E. Cheese's rises. Across Flatbush, an enormous Modell's outpost sells everything from running shoes to squash rackets. And across from both, at the southeast corner of Atlantic and Flatbush, looms the architecturally arresting Barclays Center, a stadium financed by the London-based global financial services corporation Barclays. Year-round, the stadium hosts the Brooklyn Nets basketball team, as well as internationally acclaimed entertainers in grand style Almost none of this existed before 2003, when then-mayor Michael Bloomberg announced plans to redevelop the area, known as Atlantic Yards, with the help of the Empire State Development Corporation (ESDC) and Forest City Ratner, a Brooklyn-centric real estate company. At the time, Bloomberg was

Construction at Atlantic Yards, years after the space is claimed by eminent domain, 2017. CREDIT: SCOTT DEXTER

famously vocal about his desire to brand New York City as "a high-end product, maybe even a luxury product." Atlantic Yards was a twenty-two acre piece of that expensive puzzle, which also included the reinvention of Manhattan's Midtown West, the construction of the new Freedom Tower and its environs in lower Manhattan, and the mayor's bid for the city to host the 2012 Olympics. While all of these redevelopment plans were met with resistance, Bloomberg, the ESDC, Brooklyn Borough President Marty Markowitz, and Forest City Ratner principal Bruce Ratner were bombarded with unanticipated fury over Atlantic Yards.

The reasons for local defiance were legion. Over a thousand residents and businesses were at risk of displacement under the development plan, which would also bring high-rise buildings and increased traffic to a relatively low-density, residential neighborhood. Moreover, the early involvement of the ESDC meant that eminent domain could be deployed in the area, robbing the community of not only privately owned

properties but the right to refuse or even adjust the planned development through traditional modes of land use approval. At the same time, the city and state signaled its unwavering support for Ratner's plans by devoting over $300 million toward the project.

To many, it seemed that Ratner was handed unbridled control over the Atlantic Yards site. ACORN (Association of Community Organizations for Reform Now) and BUILD (Brooklyn United for Innovative Local Development), signed a "community benefits agreement" with Ratner, who promised to provide affordable housing to low- and moderate-income residents, job training, and jobs for construction workers of color through the Atlantic Yards development. Yet, ultimately, little of this agreement was delivered. Indeed, by early 2017, few of the promised "affordable" units had been constructed and the organizations that signed the original agreements with Ratner had dissolved.

The community benefits agreement signed by ACORN (along with BUILD) was drastically modified within a mere four months of its announcement: The promised public park became a private one; additional luxury condos were added to the portfolio, reducing the number of affordable units available; and office space, which was matched with new job investment in the area, was reduced by two-thirds. More than simply an example of collusion between a growth-oriented municipal government and a willing global real estate trust, the saga of Atlantic Yards revealed the variety of corrupt and cynical practices behind the city's escalating development plans. Investigative reporting in the local press revealed backroom deals between the Metropolitan Transit Authority, which owned the rail yard that was to become Atlantic Yards, and Forest City Ratner. Meanwhile, Forest City Ratner was found to be one of the top donors to ACORN at the same time ACORN was supposedly negotiating on behalf of local residents.

Yet the story is not only about powerful interests (literally) bulldozing the interests of ordinary Brooklynites. Despite attempts to divide the communities surrounding the project along racial and class lines, a diverse group of residents and business owners joined together in protest of the development. Groups such as Develop, Don't Destroy Brooklyn and UNITY (Understanding, Imagining, and Transforming the Yards) organized around different visions for their neighborhoods, hoping to preserve the people-focused streetscape, while allowing for new construction and investment to come in. Although the development, rebranded as "Pacific Park," eventually transformed

the built environment and introduced new, more affluent residents to the area, resistance and neighborhood alliances have also survived. This has been none more evident than in 2020 when the plaza in front of the Barclays Center served as a central organizing and protest hub for Black Lives Matter after the brutal murder of George Floyd in Minneapolis. Thousands of protestors occupied the plaza nightly protesting police brutality, racism, and inequality, and calling for defunding and abolishing the police. A hotspot of gentrification has once again turned into a hotspot of resistance. (*Quote is from Michael Bloomberg, in Diane Cardwell, "Mayor Says New York Is Worth the Cost,"* New York Times, January 8, 2003.)

—*Becky Amato*

NEARBY SITE OF INTEREST

BRIC
647 Fulton Street, Brooklyn, NY
At the heart of the "Brooklyn Arts District," close to the various theaters of the district's anchor institution, the Brooklyn Academy of Music, as well as the Mark Morris Dance Company, BRIC is Brooklyn's free culture space, with programming and galleries open to the public all week, free of charge. The space is home to Brooklyn's public access television channels and includes a media lab, classrooms, and editing suites for Brooklyn media makers; it also includes artist studios, performance spaces, and a café.

Brooklyn Commons
(see **Mayday Space and Brooklyn Commons; Starr Bar and Café**, p. 229)

Bedford-Stuyvesant

4.10 Shirley Chisholm's Presidential Launch at Concord Baptist Church of Christ

833 Gardner C. Taylor Boulevard (formerly Marcy Avenue), Brooklyn, NY

On January 25, 1972, in front of supporters and the press, Congresswoman Shirley Chisholm declared her decision to run for president of the United States here at Concord Baptist Church. This huge brick, gothic-inspired church was founded in 1847 and served as a beacon of hope and sanctuary for free and enslaved African Americans. So there is no question why it was chosen for the historic announcement of the first African American and first woman to run for the US presidency from a major political party. One could imagine that making this announcement in Washington, DC, would garner more national attention, yet Chisholm's decision to announce at Concord Baptist Church in her district of Bedford-Stuyvesant represented her determination to run as the "People's candidate." The economic disparities and political disenfranchisement that faced her district in the 1960s reflected those that impacted Crown Heights, the neighborhood that she grew up in, as well as other communities of color throughout the United States.

Chisholm started her political career in the New York Assembly (1965–1968), where she helped pass New York State's first unemployment insurance coverage for personal and domestic employees influenced by the many women within her district and throughout Brooklyn who were employed as domestics. In 1968 she became the first Black woman to be elected to Congress and the first Black congressional member to represent the newly drawn 12th Congressional District. Nationally, Chisholm's congressional election was also part of an unprecedented wave of Black political leaders who entered political office in the late 1960s due to gains made by the 1965 Voting Rights Act. Proclaiming that she was the "Unbought and Unbossed," candidate, her grassroots campaign attracted the district's Black and Puerto Rican constituents to vote against the status quo politics that ignored the district's problems with poverty, joblessness, police brutality, dilapidated housing, and inadequate public education. Chisholm's Congressional election, therefore, represented her constituents' hopes, as well as their distrust and frustrations with electoral politics.

In her presidential announcement she proclaimed, "I am not the candidate of black America, although I am black and proud. I am not the candidate of the women's movement of this country, although I am a woman and equally proud of that. I am not the candidate of any political bosses or fat cats or special interests. I am the candidate of the people of America. And my presence before you now symbolizes a new era in American political history." Operating as the People's candidate, she established broad-based alliances with multiracial coalitions, radical and moderate political organizations, and economic and working-class progressives around a liberal platform that

BRING U.S. TOGETHER

VOTE CHISHOLM 1972

UNBOUGHT AND UNBOSSED

Shirley Chisholm's Presidential Campaign Poster, 1972. CREDIT: [UNITED STATES: N.G. SLATER CORPORATION] PHOTOGRAPH, COURTESY LIBRARY OF CONGRESS

to back Chisholm, along with limited campaign funds, created significant obstacles for Chisholm to win the 1972 Democratic nomination. Nonetheless, Chisholm's campaign and her twenty-plus years of political office highlight her attempt to be a catalyst for substantive political change. Concord Baptist Church continues to be at the center of Black political life in Bedford-Stuyvesant.

—*Zinga Fraser*

TO LEARN MORE

"The Concord Baptist Church of Christ History." n.d. Accessed August 28, 2020. http://www .concordcares.org/about-us/history.
Shola Lynch Collection. Shirley Chisholm Project of Brooklyn Women's Activism of 1945 to Present. Brooklyn College Library Special Collections.

was against the Vietnam War, pro-choice, and advocated for increased funding to eradicate racial, gender, economic, and environmental inequalities. When congressional leaders tried to marginalize Chisholm by putting her on the House Agricultural Committee, she innovatively used her position to push for an expansion of the food stamp program.

Her legacy is alive today in the SEEK (Search for Education, Elevation, and Knowledge) program that still exists for students at SUNY and CUNY schools (passed while she was on the New York Assembly). Despite her efforts to create coalitions between second wave feminists, Black feminists, Black militants, liberals, and Black elected officials, the inability of white feminists and the Congressional Black Caucus

4.11 Restoration Plaza

1368 Fulton Street (between Brooklyn and New York Avenues), Brooklyn, NY

Restoration Plaza is the architectural embodiment of a community's aspirations. Built in the 1970s as the centerpiece of a nationally acclaimed experiment in neighborhood renewal, the sprawling complex in the heart of Bedford-Stuyvesant also harkens back to previous eras of industrial activity and civil rights activism.

For half a century, the site on Fulton Street housed the Sheffield Farms milk-bottling facility, which was the world's largest dairy-products plant when it opened in 1915. Elegant yet imposing, the building's white terra-cotta façade featured cow busts and milk-bottle reliefs—visible to this

Restoration Plaza, 2019. CREDIT: SUSAN DEVRIES FOR BROWNSTONER

day from the sidewalk below. The novelist Paule Marshall, who grew up nearby in the 1930s, recalled that as a child she used to visit Sheffield Farms and "stand for what seemed hours in front of its large picture window, watching the endless train of bottles being filled with milk from the mechanical udders." Awe turned to anger in the early 1960s, when protestors repeatedly converged on the site, led by the local Unity Democratic Club (whose members included rising political stars Thomas R. Jones and Shirley Chisholm) and the Brooklyn chapter of the Congress of Racial Equality (CORE). Pickets urged a boycott of Sealtest Dairy—which had taken over the plant's operations—on grounds that only 1 percent of the company's employees in the New York area were Black. The campaign extracted a promise from Sealtest to hire more minority workers. But the company closed up shop shortly thereafter—as did a distressing number of central

Brooklyn businesses in the 1960s. When riots broke out in July 1964 following the police shooting of a Harlem teenager, adjacent areas of Fulton Street sustained substantial property damage. The abandoned milk plant came to symbolize the problems facing the community—and the potential for change.

The Sheffield Farms site was purchased in 1968 by the fledgling Bedford-Stuyvesant Restoration Corporation, which grew out of a decade-long campaign by local activists to improve the quality of life in Bed-Stuy and neighboring Crown Heights. Both areas had experienced rapid capital flight since World War II, and large numbers of low-income Black migrants had moved in; by the 1960s, some 400,000 people lived in what was sometimes dubbed "America's largest ghetto." Rates of poverty, joblessness, and infant mortality in Bed-Stuy ranked among the highest in the city. Yet the area also featured leafy streets and beautiful brown-stones, which housed thousands of home-owning professionals.

Beginning in 1964, federal War on Poverty programs in Bed-Stuy aimed to stem juvenile delinquency, provide job training for unemployed dropouts, and send teen mothers back to school, while empowering poor people to transform their community. A coalition of local groups known as the Central Brooklyn Coordinating Council—led by block-level organizers such as Elsie Richardson—lobbied city and federal offi-cials for funds to undertake the physical revi-talization of the area. Among those swayed was Robert F. Kennedy, then the junior sena-tor from New York, who was seeking new solutions to urban problems as he mulled a presidential run in 1968. After touring the area with Richardson in early 1966, Kennedy was convinced to make Bed-Stuy the testing ground for a nationwide experiment in community-based economic development.

Restoration launched in 1967 with mon-ies from the War on Poverty and additional support from the Ford Foundation. Early efforts focused on restoring old brown-stones, sprucing up dilapidated blocks, and nurturing Black-owned businesses. Ken-nedy allies on Wall Street, including banker Benno Schmidt, Sr., helped amass a $70 mil-lion mortgage pool, which Restoration man-aged. Meanwhile, the corporation hired Arthur Cotton Moore, a Washington, DC architect, to reimagine the old Sheffield Farms plant, where hundreds of young, Black Brooklynites were hired and trained as laborers. Reopened in 1972, the building housed Restoration's corporate headquar-ters and several commercial tenants. The *New York Times* described it as "a stunning sky-lit, brick-lobbied office building flowing with lush green plants and decorated with paintings, photographs and sculpture by local artists."

A further revamping followed in 1975. Now sprawling across the entire stretch of Fulton Street between Brooklyn and New York Avenues, Restoration Plaza included 115,000 square feet of retail space, 60,000 square feet of office space, a 30,000-square-foot outdoor plaza, a low-income housing development, and an array of social-service agencies. Restoration's founding presi-dent, Franklin Thomas, hoped the complex would spark business development along Central Brooklyn's main commercial artery, but it was the 1979 opening of a Pathmark supermarket (now a Foodtown) in Resto-ration Plaza itself that made the biggest impact. The plaza also served as a focal point for the community's culture; ameni-ties included the Billie Holiday Theatre, the Skylight Gallery, and an ice-skating rink (the latter, unsurprisingly, has long since disap-peared). "Passing through the artful space," wrote sociologist Michael Harrington in 1978, "one can see an important fact: Urban decay is not inevitable."

And yet Restoration Plaza did decay over subsequent decades, as the corporation lost much of its federal funding and was forced to scale back its ambitious plans. A fresh round of renovations, begun in 2008, has slowly injected new life into the facility. An outdoor wall of fame, rendered on eight-foot-high panels of green glass, memorializes the unique coalition that gave birth to Restoration; honorees include local notables (Chisholm, Richardson, Jones, Thomas), and the outsiders who supported their efforts, including Kennedy, Schmidt, Jacob Javits, and John Doar. Across the street, newly minted Marcy Plaza hosts farmers markets each Wednesday and features a sidewalk mosaic (by artist Ellen Harvey) that incorporates hard-to-spot architectural details from eighteen historic buildings in the surrounding area. Interested visitors can look for clues on the stretch of Nostrand Avenue immediately north of Fulton Street, home to nineteenth-century gems such as the Renaissance and Alhambra apartment buildings (both by Montrose Morris) and the former Girls High School, the oldest public secondary building in the city. Or, one can head in the opposite direction from Restoration Plaza and stroll along the splendid residential blocks of Decatur and MacDonough Streets, in the Stuyvesant Heights Historic District. More than anything else, it is the persistence of such spaces—and of the Black community that has nurtured them for a half-century—that testifies to Restoration's past successes. As gentrification and displacement transform Central Brooklyn, it's a legacy well worth recalling. (*All quotes from Michael Woodsworth, The Battle for Bed-Stuy: The Long War on Poverty in New York City.*)

—*Michael Woodsworth*

TO LEARN MORE

Woodsworth, Michael. *The Battle for Bed-Stuy: The Long War on Poverty in New York City.* Boston: Harvard University Press, 2016.

NEARBY SITES OF INTEREST

Former Site of The East
10 Claver Place, Brooklyn, NY

Jitsu Weusi (Les Campbell), a former social studies teacher at JHS 271, and the African American Student Association created The East, an African-centered community education and arts organization in 1969. The East quickly became a neighborhood cultural hub and source of community empowerment, with a bookstore, jazz club, and restaurant all focused on Black self-determination. The East even housed an African-centered school named Uhuru Sasa Shule, which was established as a response to the lack of Black history in the public school system (see **Junior High School 271**, p. 251). The organization closed in 1986.

Notorious B.I.G. Mural
1091 Bedford Avenue, Brooklyn, NY

Mural depicting famed hip-hop artist the Notorious B.I.G. (Christopher George Latore Wallace, 1972–1997), known as a talented lyricist and for his Brooklyn pride. In 2017 the owner of the building threatened to take it down, but as a result of public outcry and community organizing, the mural remains. Other murals featuring B.I.G. dot the surrounding neighborhoods in Fort Greene, Bushwick, and Prospect Heights.

United Order of Tents
87 MacDonough Street, Brooklyn, NY
Black women's fraternity lodge.

FAVORITE NEIGHBORHOOD RESTAURANT

A&A Bake and Double and Roti Shop
1337 Fulton Street, Brooklyn, NY
Trinidadian shop for roti, doubles, aloo pie and other Caribbean favorites.

Weeksville

4.12 Colored School No. 2/P.S. 68/83/243

1634 Dean Street, Brooklyn, NY

The condos you see here were once the site of Colored School No. 2. "Colored Schools" started opening in Brooklyn in the 1820s. The first opened in Fort Greene in 1827, the second, in Weeksville in 1840, and the third in Williamsburg in 1879. The Weeksville school played a particularly important role in national debates over school integration. While Brooklyn was slow to integrate its student body, Colored School No. 2 was the first school to hire Black and white teachers, to teach Black and white students, and was the first school in which a Black woman, Maritcha Lyons, supervised white student teachers.

Colored School No. 2 opened in 1840 and in 1847 was led by Junius C. Morel, an abolitionist, journalist, and activist. By 1851 the school had forty students, twelve of whom were white. By 1869 nearly 50 percent of the school was white. At this point the Brooklyn school board intervened claiming that it was "unhealthy for Black and white students to have such an intimate relationship." The school board ordered that white students move to neighboring white schools. However, five years later, seventeen white students still remained.

In the 1890s, conflict emerged again over Colored School No. 2, now called P.S. 68. A new school opened with segregated floors. In the end, Black leaders on the Board of

Education such as T. McCants Stewart prevailed, and the Weeksville school became fully integrated. Over 120 years after these racial integration battles, the Weeksville school of today (now a few doors down at 1580 Dean) is deeply segregated. As of 2020 the school is 72 percent Black, 24 percent Latina/o/x, and 3 percent Asian. (*Quote is from Judith Welman's* Brooklyn's Promised Land.)

TO LEARN MORE

Wellman, Judith. *Brooklyn's Promised Land: The Free Black Community of Weeksville, New York.* New York: NYU Press, 2014.

NEARBY SITES OF INTEREST

Howard Colored Orphan Asylum

1550 Dean Street, Brooklyn, NY

The Orphanage opened in 1866 to meet the needs of the huge influx of Black women and children migrating to Brooklyn from the South. It also took in over twenty children displaced by the draft riots (see **Colored Orphan's Asylum/Draft Riots**, p. 107).

Bethel Tabernacle AME Baptist Church

90 Schenectady Avenue, Brooklyn, NY

Opened in 1847, it is considered to be the first Black church in Weeksville.

4.13 Weeksville Heritage Center

158 Buffalo Avenue, Brooklyn, NY

Beyond the cast-iron fence along Buffalo Avenue, four landmarked, wood-frame houses recall the nineteenth-century community of free, Black landowners called Weeksville. Neighborhood activists selected these houses for preservation in 1968, protecting them from urban renewal efforts reshaping the neighborhood. Weeksville residents William Harley, Joseph Haynes, Patricia Johnson, and Delores McCollough worked with amateur historian Jim Hurley, the local Boy Scout troop, and countless others to document fading memories of this community, landmark its structures,

Hunterfly Row Houses at Weeksville Heritage Center, 2009. CREDIT: ANONITECT (TALK), WIKIPEDIA COMMONS

and begin the project of preserving the story of Weeksville. The historic houses opened for public tours in 2005 and the new cultural center opened in 2014.

The first known reference to Weeksville as a distinct place appears in the 1839 Brooklyn Directory, where James Weeks is listed in "Weeksville, Bedford." By 1800 one in three Black people in New York State were free (about ten thousand people), but most were unable to vote because they didn't own property worth $250. Slavery in New York came to an end in 1827, and by the 1830s, Black men such as Henry C. Thompson and stevedore James Weeks, the settlement's namesake, began purchasing property in Brooklyn's eastern district, in part because land ownership guaranteed access to the franchise. Weeksville first appeared on maps of Brooklyn's rural Eastern District in the 1840s and '50s. The "hamlet," as a school superintendent described it in 1850, "consist[ed] of some thirty or forty colored families;" and was dotted with small, neat, white houses.

Weeksville's population tripled in its first fifteen years, growing from 165 residents in 1840 to 521 by 1855. In that time, the community established the Bethel AME Church in 1848, Colored School No. 2, where Junius C. Morel served as principal, the Howard Colored Orphanage, the Berean Baptist Church, and Zion Home for the Aged, where New York's first Black female physician, Susan Smith McKinney Steward practiced medicine. Weeksville was also an important site of safety for Black New Yorkers escaping the draft riots in 1863.

Though Weeksville disappeared from area maps by the 1860s, its hills and valleys remained home to a relatively autonomous Black community for another thirty years. Developers plotted the eastward extension of the city's street grid, but never built the roads until the turn of the twentieth century, after the opening of the Brooklyn Bridge. And even as the area finally absorbed new inhabitants, long-established institutions like the Weeksville school remained strong.

Over the following several decades, the village attracted Black migrants from the Caribbean islands and the US South, in addition to European immigrants fleeing the crowded conditions in Lower Manhattan. As its population expanded, the name Weeksville gave way to Bedford-Stuyvesant. Widely known as one of the nation's largest Black enclaves, this area was actually home to a mixed-race community for the first half of the twentieth century, until the neighborhood was redlined, devalued, and the federal government subsidized white suburbanization in the 1940s.

—*Amy VonBokel*

TO LEARN MORE

Wellman, Judith. *Brooklyn's Promised Land: The Free Black Community of Weeksville, New York.* New York: NYU Press, 2014.

Weeksville Heritage Center, www.weeksville society.org.

FAVORITE NEIGHBORHOOD RESTAURANT

Tropical House Baking
267 Schenectady Avenue, Brooklyn, NY
Caribbean bakery known for fresh beef and chicken patties.

United Federation of Teachers on Strike in 1968 in front of Junior High School 271. CREDIT: CHARLES FRATTINI/*NEW YORK DAILY NEWS* ARCHIVE VIA GETTY IMAGES

Ocean Hill / Brownsville

4.14 Junior High School 271

1137 Herkimer Street, Brooklyn, NY

Junior High School 271 was ground zero for the Ocean Hill-Brownsville schools crisis of 1968, one of the most racially divisive events in the modern history of New York. The controversy helped create a long-standing rift between oft-allied progressive Black and Jewish communities in the city and paved the way for Jewish New Yorkers to be more incorporated into the "white" ethnic then-majority of the city.

In 1968 JHS 271 served a segregated Black and Latina/o/x student population in a community coping with the effects of white flight, discriminatory housing and lending policies, and economic disinvestment. A year before, the New York City Board of Education began an experiment in community control of education in Ocean Hill-Brownsville in response to the failure of plans to desegregate its schools. The local school board elected by area residents soon clashed with the union representing the city's public school teachers, the overwhelmingly white United Federation of Teachers (UFT), over its personnel powers.

Junior High School 271 in 2019. CREDIT: SCOTT DEXTER

On May 9, 1968, the local school board terminated nineteen white educators in the Ocean Hill-Brownsville district, including Fred Nauman, a JHS 271 science teacher and UFT chapter chair. The UFT responded with a series of citywide teachers' strikes in the fall of that year aimed at both the reinstatement of Nauman and his white colleagues and the removal of the local school board. The strikes were charged with racial and class venom. The city's outer borough middle-class white population lined up behind the UFT. Black and Latina/o/x New Yorkers and Manhattan-based white political, business, and cultural elites backed the Ocean Hill-Brownsville local school board.

JHS 271 remained open most days in the face of the UFT strikes, staffed by an integrated group of young, left-leaning "replacement" teachers. They introduced an innovative curriculum that featured instruction in Black history and culture and an alternative pedagogy based on child-centered "affec-

tive" learning philosophies. During the UFT strikes, JHS 271 was the scene of almost daily confrontations between white unionists and local school board supporters as racial invective flew and police struggled to keep the two sides apart. The UFT strikes ended in November 1968 with the forced return of Nauman and the terminated teachers to JHS 271 and the other Ocean Hill-Brownsville schools. The local school board was later dissolved and the Ocean Hill-Brownsville community control experiment discontinued.

The Ocean Hill-Brownsville crisis left a residue of racial and class bitterness that affected electoral politics, labor relations, municipal budgeting, housing policies, and educational governance in New York for the rest of the twentieth century. The strike and win by the UFT made the union more centralized and powerful than ever before, but it also had the detrimental effect of radically isolating the union from community partners and parent concerns. It could be argued that neither the union nor public education in New York have recovered from these rifts; contemporary struggles over testing, teacher accountability, and charter schools remain haunted by the long-time institutional isolation of community, union, and parents.

JHS 271 was later designated an intermediate school, serving grades 6 through 8 until 2008, when it was closed by the city. Its building now houses the Ocean Hill Collegiate Charter School and the Eagle Academy for Young Men at Ocean Hill.

—*Jerald Podair*

TO LEARN MORE

Brier, Stephen. n.d. *The UFT's Opposition to the Community Control Movement.* Jacobin.

Podair, Jerald. *The Strike that Changed New York: Blacks, Whites, and the Ocean-Hill Brownsville Crisis.* New Haven: Yale University Press, 2004.

School Colors, https://www.schoolcolors podcast.com/.

4.15 Brownsville Labor Lyceum

219 Sackman Street, Brooklyn, NY

The Brownsville Labor Lyceum was the beating heart of Brownsville's intellectual community and radical politics from the turn of the twentieth century through the 1930s. During this period Brownsville had over one hundred thousand residents, 80 percent of whom were Jewish. The neighborhood boasted over forty synagogues. Brownsville was a quintessential, working-class Jewish neighborhood. These were largely "Jews without money," as writer Mike Gold from Manhattan's Lower East Side would say. And, like Mike Gold, a fair

number of them were communists. Even before the Lyceum opened, workers were active in Brownsville's unions. The Knights of Labor organized garment workers there as early as 1885, and in 1908 over eight hundred garment workers went on strike against local firms. By 1917 the International Ladies Garment Workers Union (ILGWU) had more than twenty-five hundred Brownsville members.

The Lyceum served as headquarters for the Socialist Party, as well as a number of labor unions and worker societies such as the Workmen's Circle. (The Communist Party, meanwhile, met in numerous branches across the neighborhood, including at 207 Stone St, now Mother Gaston Boulevard.) The Lyceum was also home to the Socialist Sunday School which sought to "coun-

The Brownsville Labor Lyceum in 1940. CREDIT: COURTESY OF NYC MUNICIPAL ARCHIVES

teract the overly individualistic, competitive, nationalistic, militaristic, and anti–working-class schemes that appear prevalent in public schools and other aspects of capitalist culture."

When the Lyceum was rebuilt after a fire in 1917, the new building included a library, bowling alleys, a pool, billiard and recreation rooms, and an auditorium. Historian Wendell Pritchett notes that the Lyceum was also famous for its courses and weekly lectures that covered topics ranging from "Fundamentals of Socialism" to "Advanced English" and "The International Labor Movement." Labor leaders like A. Philip Randolph of the Brotherhood of Sleeping Car Porters and Socialist politicians like Norman Thomas gave lectures there. Brownsville was also home to two libraries, a Carnegie library (see **Stapleton Carnegie Library**, p. 307) that had the largest circulation of any library in Brooklyn until 1940, and the first Children's Branch in New York City.

In 1919 the Brownsville Lyceum was raided in what became the Palmer Raids. Socialist leaders were arrested for violating the Alien and Sedition Acts, which made it easier to deport noncitizens who were deemed dangerous and criminalized critics of the federal government. While those arrested were not found guilty, Prichett explains that the "goal of this action was to weaken the party and scare away supporters." While the Socialist Party lost power in the 1920s due to expulsion from the state assembly and the gerrymandering of the district, the American Labor Party was very active in Brownsville throughout the Great Depression. *(Quotes are from Wendell Pritchett, Brownsville, Brooklyn.)*

TO LEARN MORE

Pritchett, Wendell E. *Brownsville, Brooklyn: Blacks, Jews, and the Changing Face of the Ghetto.* Chicago: University of Chicago Press, 2002.

4.16 Margaret Sanger's First Birth Control Clinic

46 Amboy Street, Brooklyn, NY

In a former building at this site, on October 16, 1916, Margaret Sanger, a Socialist birth control activist and nurse, opened the first birth control clinic in the United States. The clinic was a bold move in birth control activism, serving as a direct challenge to the anti–birth control Comstock Law (1873), the "Act for the Suppression of Trade in, and Circulation of, Obscene Literature and Articles for Immoral Use." The law, named after the New York State based US Postal Inspector and anti-vice activist Anthony Comstock who championed it, was used to prosecute those who distributed birth control information or devices. Sanger believed direct action was the appropriate challenge to the law and picked Brownsville as the site of the first clinic after meeting five women from the neighborhood who had shared with her the dire circumstances brought on by their incapacity to plan their families. Each had a more tragic story than the last, detailing chronic poverty, sickly children, abortions gone wrong, and the fear of yet another mouth to feed. Sanger scouted a suitable location in Brownsville the very next day. For weeks before opening

(Left) Women and babies waiting outside of the Sanger Clinic in 1916. CREDIT: COURTESY OF LIBRARY OF CONGRESS, LC-USZ62–138888

(Below) The building that replaced the Sanger clinic, 2019. CREDIT: SCOTT DEXTER

the clinic, Sanger and her colleagues hung flyers in English, Yiddish, and Italian in shop windows along Pitkin Avenue and posted notices in local papers. They read, "Mothers! Can you afford to have a large family? Do you want any more children? If not, why do you have them? Do not kill, Do not take life, but Prevent. Safe, Harmless Information can be obtained of trained Nurses at 46 Amboy Street . . . All Mothers Welcome." Once open, the clinic gave women a short lecture on their reproductive system and instructions for the use of contraceptives. News of the clinic spread through word-of-mouth, and it was a wild success, serving about four hundred women in its first ten days. On the 10th day the police shut the clinic down, arresting Sanger, her sister (a registered nurse) and a translator. Sanger was released the following day and reopened the clinic on November 16th, but was arrested again. She opened it once more on November 18th, but the police forced the landlord to evict Margaret Sanger and the clinic closed for good. Her trial began in

January 1917 and she was sentenced to thirty days in the Queens Penitentiary. The case that followed her arrest led to the Crane decision in 1918, which allowed married women to use birth control for "therapeutic reasons." Following this decision, in 1936 the courts allowed physicians to distribute birth control across state lines. And finally in 1965 the Supreme Court allowed married couples to use birth control without restrictions. Birth control was not wholly legalized in the United States until 1972.

Margaret Sanger founded the American Birth Control League in 1921. The organization advocated for reproductive health research, education, legislative work, sterilization "of the insane and feebleminded," and international chapters. It changed its name to Planned Parenthood Federation of America in 1942. Today, Planned Parenthood has health centers in each of the five boroughs and over six hundred nationwide, serving 2.4 million people annually.

While Sanger was successful in promoting reproductive health, her ideas were greeted with mixed responses from a variety of groups, including disabled people and their families and some in the Black and Latina/o/x communities. Sanger herself had a complicated and deeply problematic relationship with eugenicists in the early twentieth century, at times trying to convince them that birth control was important to achieve their goals of "racial betterment," and at other times critiquing their anti–birth control views. Planned Parenthood has denounced Sanger's most controversial beliefs, practices, and associations. In June 2020, Planned Parenthood of New York removed her name from the Manhattan clinic because of her connection to the eugenics movement. (*Quotes are from the Margaret Sanger Flyer,* Mothers! *and Dorothy E. Roberts,* Killing the Black Body.)

TO LEARN MORE

"Margaret Sanger Papers Project," New York University, https://sangerpapers.wordpress.com

Roberts, Dorothy. *Killing the Black Body: Race, Reproduction, and the Meaning of Liberty.* Vintage, 1998.

Sanger, Margaret. *The Autobiography of Margaret Sanger.* Dover Publications, 2004.

East New York

4.17 East New York Farms!

613 New Lots Avenue, Brooklyn, NY

The 3-train south to the end of the line will bring you to East New York, Brooklyn, a low-income, predominantly Black community. Out the subway car window, the view generally consists of public housing complexes, run-down multistory apartment buildings, discount retail stores, and vacant lots. But at the approach to the last stop, New Lots Avenue, the view opens to community gardens, urban farms, and a farmer's market. On the right side of the train car, you'll find a four-story apartment building with a mural emblazoned across its side that reads "East New York Farms!" in bright orange. The mural stands in front of the half acre ENYF! Youth Farm, where teenage interns are rotating the compost bins, pulling weeds, tending to the bees, giving tours of the farm to residents, and watering rows and rows of cucumbers, okra, bitter melon, swiss chard, garlic, and tomatoes.

Adjacent to the Youth Farm is Schenck Avenue, which is generally full of parked vehicles and livery car drivers that wait

A group of young people learning about urban farming, 2014. CREDIT: COURTESY OF EAST NEW YORK FARMS!

for their next fare. But on Saturdays from June to November the area is turned into a lively farmers market and social space for East New Yorkers. The parked vehicles are replaced with tent-covered stalls, picnic tables, and a performance stage. Wandering the market, you will see upstate farmers selling sweet corn, squash, and watermelon, local gardeners selling produce, soups, and hot sauces, and the ENYF! youth interns selling tomatoes and hot peppers. Caribbean vendors sell patties, sweet bread, and plantain chips as well as curried goat with sides of mac and cheese, rice and peas, and stewed greens. If you are lucky you will arrive on one of the days ENYF! hosts a special event celebrating the people and food of East New York, from the hot pepper and bitter melon festivals to poetry slams, afro battles, and Caribbean dancing contests.

Across and down the street, the farmers market is surrounded by New Visions Garden, Triple R Garden, and Hendrix Garden, formerly vacant land that is now full of raised beds overflowing with collards, callaloo, bush peas, malabar spinach, dasheen, and green pumpkins. In these spaces, community gardeners, hailing from the Caribbean, South Asia, West Africa, and Latin America, assert their identities and maintain familial histories by growing food for themselves and the community that they cannot obtain in their local grocery stores, and by distributing the rich surplus through formal and informal means to extended family, neighbors, co-workers, strangers, and regular customers.

This bustling network of community gardens and urban farms in this corner of Brooklyn is the hub of the food justice organization East New York Farms!, which emerged out of a three-year participatory planning project in 1998 to combat social, economic, and ecological disinvestment in the area by linking assets (gardeners, gardens, and youth) with needs (fresh produce, land tenure, and youth jobs) in order to build a community food economy in East New York. Today, the organization has six full-time staff and operates a farmers market and farm stand, a thirty-plus-member youth program, several urban farms, and networks with over thirty food producing community gardens, all in an effort to utilize food as a community mobilization strategy to build a more just and sustainable world.

—*Justin Sean Myers*

NEARBY SITE OF INTEREST

African Burial Ground Square
Corner of Livonia and Barbey Streets, Brooklyn, NY
One of at least four sites of graves of formerly enslaved people in New York City.

Red Hook

4.18 Sunny's Bar

253 Conover Street, Brooklyn, NY
Located across the street from what was once one of the busiest ports in the world, Sunny's bar is dark and kitschy, its shelves lined with art, collectibles, and booze. The bar (formerly known as John's Restaurant and Bar) has been in operation since the 1890s, when Red Hook was developing as a thriving dockside neighborhood. At its peak in 1950, Red Hook was home to over ten thousand mostly Irish and Italian longshoremen and their families. Sunny's was one of 40 bars/restaurants in the neighborhood, but because it was closest to the docks it enjoyed special success and stability. In one of Brooklyn's roughest neighborhoods, the bar was witness to mob violence, deaths,

and salty longshore culture. Longshore work was difficult, dirty, and dangerous. In the early days, workers participated in the "shape up" system, in which workers were selected on a daily basis for the backbreaking work of loading and unloading the ships. This once took place dockside, and was later moved to the union hiring hall, but in neither case was the extreme competition for work settled. Indeed, the foremen operated with exclusive control, and corruption and nepotism ruled. Eventually the Waterfront Commission took over the hiring hall, generating jobs through a computerized system.

Containerization, introduced in the 1960s, left the Red Hook docks behind. This system of intermodal transport uses standardized shipping containers that can be more efficiently loaded and unloaded directly onto ships, docks, and trucks. Container ships need deeper waters and sufficient truck transport. As a result of containerization most of the work on the docks was shifted to larger docks in New Jersey. This led to significant job loss in Red Hook. The population in the 1980s dropped to a mere thirty-five hundred. Yet, Sunny's bar remained open, lucky to have at least a few locals come in every day. By the late 1980s and early 1990s the neighborhood began to attract artists, lured by cheap rents and ample space, and Sunny's became known as an "authentic," "old school" neighborhood bar among the new arrivals and their friends.

Sunny officially took over the bar after his uncle John Balzano's death in 1996, but long before that he was opening and closing the bar once a week. When the liquor license for the bar expired in 1996, Sunny decided to hold Friday night parties. A three dollar donation got you a drink, and customers kept their own tabs and paid up at the end of the night. The parties were a big hit and attracted all sorts of characters. Tim Sultan describes the scene in his book on Sunny's:

Sunny's Bar, Red Hook, 2017. CREDIT: SCOTT DEXTER

"There was the neighborhood firebrand, John McGettrick, possessor of a mustache that extended to his knees when unwound . . . He could often be found talking to a pigtailed, bearded glassblower named Pete, who had once lived on a restored Hudson river boat moored at the end of the street before moving into a tar-paper house without plumbing around the corner."

In 2000 the bar was shut down for operating without a liquor license. At that point Sunny could have retired, but he didn't want to let the neighborhood down, so he got a liquor license and reopened to much acclaim. The bar thrived until Superstorm Sandy hit in 2012, when the flood helped knock out its electricity for months. The neighborhood rallied, and through multiple fundraising efforts Sunny's was able to open and stay open. Despite Sunny's death at age eighty-one in 2016 and various family disputes over the buildings, the bar continues to be a cornerstone of the community. (*Quote is from Tim Sultan's "Sunny's Bar,*

A Spiritual Holdout in Red Hook," New York Times, *February 19, 2016,)*

TO LEARN MORE

Sultan, Tim. *Sunny's Nights: Lost and Found at a Bar on the Edge of the World*. New York: Random House, 2016.

NEARBY SITE OF INTEREST

Waterfront Museum
290 Conover Street, Brooklyn, NY
A museum commemorating the history of the docks.

Gowanus

4.19 Gowanus Canal

From the Harbor in Red Hook through Gowanus to Boerum Hill

The nation's busiest industrial canal is now a Superfund site in one of Brooklyn's hippest neighborhoods. Named for the leader of the Canarsie band of the Lenape, Gowanus Bay

Bay Oil delivery trucks along the Gowanus,
with Gowanus Houses in the background, n.d.
CREDIT: KEN GOULD

Whole Foods on the Gowanus Canal, n.d.
CREDIT: KEN GOULD

was once a tidal inlet of saltwater marshland.
The construction of the 1.8 mile Gowanus
Canal, completed in 1869, created one of the
nation's first planned industrial development
districts. Coal gas manufacturing plants;
sulfur producers; cement works; paper mills;
and paint, ink, and chemical plants lined the
canal where mostly working-class European
immigrants lived and worked, subjecting
them to toxic industrial pollution and routine flooding.

In the late nineteenth century, local population growth outstripped sanitation planning
in Brooklyn. When the borough constructed
the first municipal sewer system in the United
States, it drained human waste directly from

affluent uphill brownstone neighborhoods
like Cobble Hill to the open sewer in working-class Gowanus. In 1911, calls for remediation led to a publicly funded "flushing tunnel" that connected the head of the canal to
New York Harbor. Flushing the canal with
seawater reduced the stench and the accumulation of raw sewage and industrial efflu-
ent, though dredging was still necessary.

Industry boomed along the Gowanus
until shipping shifted from the Brooklyn
waterfront to New Jersey following World
War II (see **Sunny's Bar**, p. 258). No longer
used, Brooklyn's waterfronts fell into decay.
In 1955, the Army Corps of Engineers suspended regular dredging of the canal, and

in the early 1960s, the flushing tunnel broke down. As the waterfront deteriorated, the city constructed new public housing nearby—first, the Gowanus Houses in 1948, and then, the Wyckoff Gardens community in 1966.

With the canal no longer vital to the city's economy, the city proved financially and politically uninterested in repairing the canal's cleansing mechanism. Meanwhile, the city's sewer system combined raw domestic and industrial sewage with stormwater, and major rain and snow events caused the sewers to overflow into the city's waterways (called Combined Sewer Overflows, or CSOs). As in Newtown Creek (see **Environmental Justice Tour**, p. 330), raw sewage mixed with the remnants of industrial toxins and pollution from the industries that remained active, especially during storms, exposing the neighborhood's largely poor and working-class residents to environmental and health hazards.

By the 1990s, the gentrification of brownstone Brooklyn picked up steam, and rising housing costs on higher ground in the surrounding neighborhoods of Park Slope, Carroll Gardens, and Boerum Hill led would-be gentrifiers to seek out cheaper housing in Gowanus. As the Gowanus ecosystem attracted higher-income people, the flushing tunnel was reconstructed in 1998. But the rush to redevelop Gowanus hit a bump in 2010 when the US Environmental Protection Agency designated the Gowanus Canal a Superfund cleanup site. Remediation began in 2020 and is expected to take up to twelve years to complete, at an estimated cost of $300 million to $500 million. CSOs still drain raw sewage into the canal during every major rain event, and gentrification of the neighborhood continues relatively unabated.

—*Ken Gould and Tammy L. Lewis*

TO LEARN MORE

Gould, Kenneth A., and Tammy L. Lewis. *Green Gentrification: Urban Sustainability and the Struggle for Environmental Justice*. New York: Routledge, 2017.

NEARBY SITES OF INTEREST

Gowanus Batcave
3rd Avenue and 1st Street, Brooklyn, NY
This former transit power station from 1896 operated until the 1950s. It stood abandoned until it was occupied by punk rock squatter communities and graffiti artists in the early 2000s. In 2012 the building was acquired by Powerhouse Environmental Arts Foundation and a renovated arts space is to open in 2021.

4.20 Washington Park

Corner of 3rd Avenue and 1st Street, Brooklyn, NY

At the corner of 3rd Avenue and 1st Street in Brooklyn's Gowanus neighborhood, an otherwise nondescript wall offers a remarkable connection to Brooklyn's extraordinary baseball history—a stark reminder of the sport's long standing labor struggles between players and owners.

Although the Dodgers are practically synonymous with baseball in Brooklyn—and their 1957 departure emblematic of the borough's once waning fortunes—the municipality has played an oversized role in the sport's development and evolution. Central to the

Washington Park, Brooklyn, flag raising, April 1915. CREDIT: [BAIN NEWS SERVICE] COURTESY OF LIBRARY OF CONGRESS

professionalization and commercialization of the sport in the 1850s and 1860s, Brooklyn was home to a number of important "firsts" including the first enclosed, paid admissions stadium (Union Grounds, 1862), championship dynasty (the Brooklyn Atlantics), and paid superstar player (Jim Creighton). Most significant, of course, was the location of baseball's integration, when Jackie Robinson took the field for the Dodgers on April 15, 1947.

The surviving stretch of wall, which extends about a third of the way down the block, was associated with the last of three stadia that stood in the vicinity. All three were named Washington Park for their proximity to the major encounter of the Battle of Brooklyn (1776). The first ballpark was built in 1883 and located on the opposite side of 4th Avenue (now a public park named Washington Park). Within the park is the reconstructed Old Stone House, which played a critical role in the battle and inspired the

name of the stadium. In later years, the Old Stone House served as a team clubhouse. The second stadium (1898) stood on the site of the surviving wall, between 3rd and 4th Avenues and 1st and 3rd Streets. It was home to Brooklyn's National League franchise, which in 1913 moved to the newly built Ebbets Field (of Dodger fame). In 1914 the commercial baking magnate Robert B. Ward purchased the dilapidated ballpark to house the Brooklyn franchise of the new Federal League. Ward invested $300,000 in rebuilding the stadium, which he had enclosed with a thirteen-foot-high enclosure wall. Ward named his team the Tip-Tops after a popular brand of bread sold by his company.

The upstart Federal League sought to challenge the monopoly of the two major leagues, the National (begun in 1876) and the American (1901). To recruit established players to its cause, it forewent the notorious reserve clause—a system by which teams essentially "owned" the rights to their players for life. Players had little leverage in regards to their salaries or contract terms, and could be blacklisted by owners for challenging the status quo. Though the new league's motivation was largely financial, it nevertheless constituted a significant endorsement of players' rights.

The Federal League lasted only two seasons, unable to attract any top-flight talent to its eight teams. The Tip-Tops managed only fifth and seventh place finishes, failing to draw the attendance hoped for. The stadium itself was subsequently used for a variety of sports and activities. It appears that the surviving wall—originally a portion of the left centerfield enclosure circuit—may have been incorporated into a warehouse around this time. In 1925, the Brooklyn Edison electric company purchased the site, demolishing what remained of the stadium in 1926.

It was not until the early 2000s that interest in the wall was sparked after Con Edison revealed plans to demolish it. Appeals to the company succeeded, and Con Edison ultimately preserved a section. Though generally (and erroneously) believed a piece of Dodger history, the association with the labor-friendly Federal League is noteworthy—and admirable—as well.

Other remains of Brooklyn's storied baseball history include the well-preserved clubhouse of the famed Brooklyn Excelsiors, one of the city's early successful teams (133 Clinton Street) and the original flagpole from Ebbets Field (demolished in 1960), re-erected in front of the Barclays Center in 2012. The site of Ebbets Field is now occupied by the Ebbets Field Apartments (1720 Bedford Avenue), originally built as part of the Mitchell-Lama housing program.

—*Lucas Rubin*

NEARBY SITES OF INTEREST

New York City Public Bath House #7
227 4th Avenue, Brooklyn, NY
Public health concerns led to the establishment of public bath houses throughout New York City, particularly in poor and working class neighborhoods in the late nineteenth and early twentieth centuries. Bathhouse no. 7 was particularly important to Brooklynites because it was the most ornate and the only one with a plunge pool. Today the building houses a Blink gym.

Interference Archive
314 7th Street, Brooklyn, NY
This volunteer-run archive and program space documents, exhibits, and supports movements mobilizing for social transformation. It features an exhibit space and an open stacks archival collection with pamphlets, posters, flyers, audio recordings, and other materials associated with social movements. Its programming includes exhibitions, talks, workshops, publications, and "propaganda art" parties where visitors are encouraged to share and make work (especially in relation to ongoing progressive campaigns and movements).

Park Slope

4.21 Park Slope Food Coop

782 Union Street, Brooklyn, NY
The Park Slope Food Coop (PSFC), located at 782 Union Street, is the nation's largest worker-owned cooperative of its kind and one of New York City's best-known

Park Slope Food
Coop, 2017. CREDIT:
SCOTT DEXTER

progressive institutions. From humble beginnings, the PSFC has grown, if reluctantly,
into an enormously successful financial
enterprise: as of 2019, total membership
exceeds eighteen thousand and annual revenues reach $50 million. It serves as a local
incubator of other food co-ops, and as a
national and international model for worker-
owned cooperative enterprises.

The PSFC was established in 1973 in association with the Mongoose Community
Center, an activist organization whose programming embodied an array of contemporary leftist causes including feminism,
vegetarianism, and war resistance. The
nascent co-op subleased a ten-by ten-foot
second floor space from the Mongoose at
782 Union Street, and began operating with
seven donated refrigerators in February of
that year.

In 1973 the PSFC reorganized itself along
the lines of its present form: households
paid a scaled membership fee, all members
were required to work mandatory shifts, and
oversight was delegated to various committees. This basic form—most notably, the universal work requirement—has remained a
core organizational and philosophical principle of the co-op, investing each member
with a sense of shared purpose and collective success. (The COVID-19 global pandemic forced the co-op to halt mandatory
shifts for the first time in its history.)

Over the next four decades, the PSFC
would experience continuous (if episodic)
growth. The business model became retail
in orientation, and the hours of operation repeatedly expanded. By 1985, it was
open daily. Expansion was physical, as well.
In 1978, following the demise of the Mongoose, the co-op leased all of 782 Union
Street, which it purchased outright in 1980.
At present, PSFC contains about six thousand square feet of cramped shopping space
spread across what had been three independent buildings.

Growth in the PSFC's membership and physical space was not without consequences, nor without some resistance. Many members felt that the heightened numbers eroded the strong sense of community, and the increased space allowed a deviation from the co-op's emphasis on natural foods: the initial purchase of 782, for instance, permitted sales of housewares and, controversially, snack items and sweets.

Though first and foremost a communitarian venture shaped around wholesome, affordable, and environmentally conscious food, the PSFC has a long history of activism. The membership has approved a number of boycotts and has also banned items from use (such as plastic water bottles in 2008). Even the sale of ethically sourced meats was controversial, with assent to their sale only reached nearly thirty years after the co-op's founding. Boycotts have included grapes from Chile in the early 1970s (in protest of Augusto Pinochet); items from Colorado in 1995 (in response to anti-gay legislation); and, notably, all Coca-Cola Company products (2004, on a host of concerns). More recently, the co-op membership has engaged in vigorous and highly publicized debate about removing Israeli products from its shelves.

The building at 782 Union Street also maintains an interesting and somewhat ironic connection with Park Slope's earlier history. One of the property's first owners was Robert Pinkerton, the East Coast principal of the Pinkerton Detective Agency. The Pinkertons were infamous for their union-busting activities, especially in the mining and railroad industries. On the evening of April 10, 1904, the police broke up a cock-fighting ring at 782 Union Street, which was then Pinkerton's stable. The story proved scandalous, as many in the crowd were believed to be the scions of Brooklyn's most upstanding families. The American Society for the Prevention of Cruelty to Animals became involved, lobbying for maximum punishment, but wealth and privilege proved formidable opponents, and those present both retained their anonymity and suffered little consequence. Some seventy years later, Pinkerton's ghost has been long since exorcised.

—*Lucas Rubin*

NEARBY SITES OF INTEREST

1960 Plane Crash
Intersection of 7th Avenue and Sterling Place, Brooklyn, NY

This corner represents the deadliest commercial airplane disaster until 1968, killing 134 people. The crash was instrumental in the organization and eventual unionization of air traffic controllers.

Montauk Club
25 8th Avenue, Brooklyn, NY

The landmarked Montauk Club (25) is the only surviving Victorian-era social club in Brooklyn, its magnificent headquarters designed by Francis Kimball after Venice's Ca' d'Oro. Its longevity can be partially attributed to a more democratic disposition; Jews were counted among its earliest members.

Community Bookstore
143 7th Avenue, Brooklyn, NY

A cozy store that lives up to its name, since 1971 this store has offered a meticulously curated selection of everything you'd want to read, with a garden, great children's section, and a pet cat to boot.

Lesbian Herstory Archives, 2020. CREDIT: SASKIA SCHEFFER

4.22 Lesbian Herstory Archives

484 14th Street, Brooklyn, NY

The Lesbian Herstory Archives, the largest archive for, by, and about lesbians in the world, is located here in the Park Slope neighborhood of Brooklyn. In 1974, lesbian activist Joan Nestle began to collect lesbian documents, journals, newsletters, books, photographs, letters, videos, and ephemera in the home she shared with her then partner and co-activist, Deb Edel, at 215 West 92nd Street, apartment 13A, in Manhattan. The Lesbian Herstory Archives (LHA, or the Archives) released its first newsletter the following year. For the first ten years, the LHA ran solely on donations and volunteer work, and Nestle and Edel, and eventually others, carried materials from the archives and eventually created a slide show to share more fragile materials. Judith Schwarz, one of the first lesbian historians, began to organize the LHA, and activist Georgia Brooks created the LHA's first Black Lesbian Studies group. From the mid-1980s until 1992, the LHA Coordinating Committee ran a fundraising collection to purchase a building for the collections. The brownstone in Park Slope, Brooklyn, opened in June 1993.

The founders of LHA specifically placed it in Park Slope because it had been a place for lesbian, bisexual, and queer women to gather since the 1970s. Park Slope includes and included many other lesbian spots like the Rising Café and Bar and the Cattyshack bar and club, and lesbian-friendly places like the Park Slope Food Coop (see **Park Slope Food Coop**, p. 263), feminist bookstores, and the Women's Martial Arts / the Center for Anti-Violence Education.

The Archives holds fast to their politics to remain independently funded and run by lesbians alone. Like most radical archives, the Archives is completely volunteer-run and organized by "coordinators" who collect, save, and store these documents and ephemera. Every lesbian is welcome to come and coproduce the Archives once they have taken part in an orientation. Each "Archivette"—an LHA term for coordinators as well as the more come-and-go volunteers—uniquely aids and takes part in producing findings; only a handful of coordinators have possessed professional archival or library training. As women's and gender studies scholar Rachel Corbman describes in her genealogy of the Archives, thousands of volunteers and tens of thou-

Lesbian Herstory Archives, 2020. CREDIT: SASKIA SCHEFFER

closet on the second floor, and the multigenerational T-shirt collection is in the built-in wardrobe nearby. Visitors are encouraged to take a tour to navigate the mass of exciting and powerful artifacts and documents.

The LHA maintains an active website (http://lesbianherstoryarchives.org/), which includes their open hours. It is best to email or call ahead to confirm an opening, or try to attend one of their many events.

—*Jen Jack Gieseking*

sands of visitors have helped to build the LHA over the years.

Collections are easily accessible to visitors. Beyond Nestle, Edel, Schwarz, and Brooks, a key member of the LHA was Mabel Hampton, (1902–1986; see **Mabel Hampton's Former Apartment**, p. 81). She volunteered weekly until her death, and served as a mentor and oral historian of the Harlem drag balls and the Harlem Renaissance. Her extensive collection of 1950s lesbian pulp paperbacks remains on display. Maxine Wolfe, who helped to found the Lesbian Avengers, (see **Lesbian Avengers**, p. 204) was also a long-term Archivette and collected most of the LGBTQ organizational records, which may be the largest and most diverse such collection in the United States. The LHA remains a key site for LGBTQ research for scholars, activists, historians, and interested parties around the world. Original versions of works by Audre Lorde and Adrienne Rich can be found in the back

TO LEARN MORE

Corbman, Rachel. "A Genealogy of the Lesbian Herstory Archives, 1974–2014." *Journal of Contemporary Archival Studies* 1, no. 1 (2014). https://elischolar.library.yale.edu/jcas/vol1/iss1/1.

Gieseking, Jen Jack. "Useful In/Stability: The Dialectical Production of the Social and Spatial Lesbian Herstory Archives." *Radical History Review* 2015, no. 122 (2015): 25–37. https://doi.org/10.1215/01636545-2849504.

Gieseking, Jen Jack. *A Queer New York: Geographies of Lesbians, Dykes, and Queers.* New York: NYU Press, 2020.

FAVORITE NEIGHBORHOOD BAR

Ginger's Bar
363 5th Avenue, Brooklyn, NY
The last remaining lesbian bar in Park Slope, a casual, dive-y bar.

Crown Heights

4.23 Crown Heights Tenant Union

Ronald McNair Park, Eastern Parkway and Washington Avenue, Brooklyn, NY

This park sits at the western end of the neighborhood of Crown Heights, which stretches east to Utica, north to Atlantic Avenue and south to Empire Boulevard. Starting from here, you might walk to dozens of buildings in this neighborhood that have been organized by the Crown Heights Tenants Union (CHTU, locations listed on their website). With 70 percent of New York City's housing comprised of rental units, the city has among the longest, strongest, and most creative tenants' movements in the country. As a result, New York is one of a handful of states with rent control laws, and the city holds the largest number of shared-equity housing cooperatives in the country—nearly one-third of privately owned housing units are co-ops. (By comparison, nationwide less than one-third of households are rentals, and cooperatives are less than 1 percent of housing units.)

The city's tradition of "rent control" began with World War II–era federal controls, which severely limited landlords' ability to raise rents and provided tenants with protections regarding eviction. New York's strong labor and other left-leaning movements pushed for their continuation after federal regulation ended. New Yorkers also engaged in rent strikes, particularly in 1963–1964, as a way to force landlords to properly maintain their units. Over time, rent controls were incrementally lifted. Rent control ended for all new rentals beginning in the 1970s; as a result, only twenty-two thousand rent-controlled units remain as of 2020, among a mostly poor and elderly population. The vast majority of formerly controlled rental units have passed into "rent stabilization," in which annual rent increases are overseen by a state board. Since the 1990s, various laws have limited stabilization, including laws that allow landlords to raise the rent when tenants leave, when they "improve" the building, when rents reach a certain level, or when tenants' income reaches a certain threshold. These changes caused hundreds of thousands of units to be lost over the years, and as of 2020 nearly 1 million rent-stabilized apartments remain, housing 2.4 million city residents. Maintaining, enforcing, and expanding the remaining protections are some of the core projects of the city's current tenants' rights movement, including CHTU.

Like many Brooklyn neighborhoods, Crown Heights is undergoing residential displacement as it gentrifies. The neighborhood has long been a mixed-income, mostly West Indian and African American community. With substantial numbers of multiunit buildings interspersed with single-family homes and duplexes, thousands of residents live in buildings protected by the rent control and rent stabilization laws. As new residents move into the neighborhood, innovative nonprofit and grassroots groups have tapped into unusual interracial and cross-class solidarity to maintain tenant protec-

Crown Heights Tenant Union in action, 2014.
CREDIT: COURTESY OF THE URBAN HOMESTEADING ASSISTANCE BOARD

tions and, in some cases, to empower tenants to purchase buildings for cooperative ownership.

CHTU emerged out of the Occupy Wall Street movement. Occupiers from the neighborhood sought to root the grassroots democracy and critiques of inequality emblematic of Occupy in practical, community-based organizing. They began a Crown Heights Assembly to illuminate neighborhood concerns and figure out how they might collectively address them. Most of the Crown Heights occupiers were new to the neighborhood, disproportionately white, younger, and middle class.

But meetings between the long-term residents and the new residents helped them discover common problems. Landlords in the neighborhood were harassing and evicting long-term renters, letting buildings fall into disrepair, deregulating units wherever they could, and charging young tenants exorbitant prices. By the summer of 2013 the work of the Assembly had become the

work of organizing tenant unions, which joined together the small number of buildings in the neighborhood that were already organized with other newly organized buildings. Together they drafted "contract demands," including a five-year rent freeze, a right to repairs, an affirmation of the rights of current residents to stay, as well as rights to organize, fair renovations and building conditions, access to rent history, fair late penalty policies, fair leases, and protections for elderly and disabled tenants.

CHTU also works with the Urban Homestead Assistance Board (UHAB), whose focus is educating tenants about their rights and helping tenants to transform their buildings into tenant-owned cooperatives. Since the early 1970s, UHAB has helped create over sixteen hundred housing cooperatives across the city, and their programs range from UHAB University (for tenants seeking to create co-ops) to educating and organizing tenants against predatory speculators seeking to "flip" buildings by forcing out low-rent tenants and deregulating the units, driving up the rents.

By 2011, flipping was widespread in Crown Heights. Some landlords offered long-term tenants modest buyouts so they could be renovated and thus taken out of rent stabilization. Others cut off hot water or conducted loud construction on adjoining walls. Tenants in multiple buildings complained of noise, freezing apartments, ceilings caving, and vermin swarming. The CHTU has worked with UHAB to maintain and coordinate over forty tenants' associations to confront the most egregious landlords, using tactics such as marches, rallies, and demonstrations, as well as lawsuits and rent strikes, to win repairs, prevent evictions, and support each other as tenants. CHTU has also run campaigns to otherwise curb gentrification in the neighborhood, including a plan to stop the city from selling the Bedford Union Armory (1579 Bedford Avenue) to private condominium developers.

Most notably, the CHTU, UHAB, and other city tenants' rights' groups, including the venerable Metropolitan Council on Housing, won a historic rent freeze in 2015 and 2016; there had previously never been a single rent freeze under the board. In 2017, indigent city tenants facing eviction also won the right to city-funded lawyers to represent them in housing court—the first in the country to do so. Most impressively, in 2019 nearly all parts of a Tenants Bill of Rights were passed into state law, greatly strengthening tenant protections: for all renters statewide, it meant limiting the size of security deposits, extending time for ten-

ants to fix lease violations and challenge evictions, and extending the time that landlords must notify tenants of eviction. Other elements of the rent laws that have contributed to the loss of stabilized units in NYC since the 1990s were also eliminated or substantially changed, including most of the legal practices used by Crown Heights landlords to force out their rent-stabilized tenants.

—With Bronte Walker

TO LEARN MORE

Crown Heights Tenant Union, https://crown heightstenantunion.org/.
Met Council on Housing, https://www.met councilonhousing.org/.
UHAB Urban Homesteading Assistance Board, https://www.uhab.org/.

NEARBY SITE OF INTEREST

Franklin Park Reading Series
618 St. John's Place, Brooklyn, NY
At the bar and restaurant Franklin Park, this free event each second Monday evening of each month is known for its mix of emerging and internationally recognized authors.

4.24 1991 Crown Heights Riots

Corner of Utica Avenue and President Street, Brooklyn, NY

Late in the summer of 1991, a car accident at this corner sparked ongoing ethnic, racial, and religious tensions between the West Indian, African American, and Hasidic Jewish communities in Crown Heights. One of the cars in Lubavitcher Hasidic Rebbe Menachem Schneerson's motorcade jumped the sidewalk, killing seven-year-old Gavin

Police disperse crowds during the height of tensions in Crown Heights in 1991. CREDIT: ANGEL FRANCO/*NEW YORK TIMES*/REDUX

Cato and injuring his cousin Angela Cato, children of Guyanese descent. The incident tapped into long-standing feelings among Black Crown Heights residents that Black lives held less value in the community. Later that same evening, Yankel Rosenbaum, an orthodox Jewish PhD student visiting from Australia, was stabbed and killed by a Black teenager nearby. Riots would last several days.

Interpretations of these events and the riots as a whole vary significantly depending on who you ask. For Black residents of Crown Heights, the riots expressed anger and frustration at city disinvestment in the neighborhood since the 1970s' fiscal crisis, leading to poor schools and services, criminalization, and abusive landlords. It was what Jesse Jackson termed a "social accident of American apartheid," pointing to the structural racism that Black residents experienced. The Hasidic community perceived the car accident as a tragedy—nothing more. However, they experienced the stabbing of Yankel Rosenbaum and the looting

and other physical and verbal attacks on the Jewish community as anti-Semitism. In fact, many in the Hasidic community felt that Black residents were using the language of racial inequality as an excuse to engage in a pogrom. As anthropologist Henry Goldschmidt points out, "rather than beneficiaries of racial inequality, Jews in Crown Heights see themselves as victims of religious bigotry." And while a majority of Black residents condemned the violent stabbing of Rosenbaum, they tended to downplay any accusations of anti-Semitism.

At the time of the riots, New Yorkers had recently elected their first Black mayor, David Dinkins, with the expressed intention of uniting a fractured city. However, both Black and Jewish New Yorkers felt that Dinkins handled the riots poorly. This perception played a major contributing role in the election of Republican Rudolph Giuliani in 1993, who ushered in a new era of intensive policing and increased criminalization of the Black community. In 2020, the Black

Lives Matter movement began to reshape these community dynamics once again when members of the Hasidic community in Crown Heights and elsewhere organized protests in solidarity with their Black neighbors and the BLM movement. Geoffrey Davis, a Black community organizer who began an anti-violence group after the 1991 riots, joined the chants of the solidarity protest, remarking, "This was a message to young African Americans, who had never seen this sort of thing before, that some Hasidic Jews do care about their lives. Now that's powerful." (*Quote from Emily Wax-Thibodeaux, "Young Hasidic Jews Protest in Support of Black Neighbors, Challenging History of Racial Tensions," Washington Post, June 19, 2020.*)

—*With Katy Coto-Batres*

TO LEARN MORE

Goldschmidt, Henry. *Race and Religion among the Chosen People of Crown Heights*. New Brunswick, NJ: Rutgers University Press, 2006.

Shapiro, Edward. *Crown Heights: Blacks, Jews, and the 1991 Brooklyn Riot*. Waltham, MA: Brandeis University Press, 2006.

FAVORITE NEIGHBORHOOD RESTAURANT

Gloria's Caribbean Cuisine
764 Nostrand Avenue, Brooklyn, NY
A standout Trinidadian spot, with varied delicious choices for roti fillings, and a rich oxtail stew.

Sunset Park

4.25 Brooklyn Metropolitan Detention Center

80 29th Street, Brooklyn, NY

Sunset Park's Metropolitan Detention Center (MDC) is the largest detention facility in the United States. It has an inmate population of up to three thousand men and women, and a maximum-security unit designed to contain dangerous, violent, or escape-prone inmates. MDC inmates have cases pending in the United States District Court for the Eastern District or are serving brief sentences. Despite community protests that the MDC represented a "slap in the face" for a neighborhood overburdened by noxious land uses, Sunset Park's MDC, initially a two-building compound, was constructed in 1993 at 29th Street and 3rd Avenue, a corner of then-largely empty Bush Terminal, a huge complex of industrial warehouses along the neighborhood's waterfront. A second facility was opened in 1999 to house inmates who have already been sentenced but are waiting for transfer to a permanent facility.

As the neighborhood site of the federal MDC, Sunset Park holds particular significance in the post 9/11 treatment of Arab and Muslim Americans and political prisoners. Through several months of 2002, weekly protests organized by human and immigrant rights organizations took place outside the MDC facility to call attention to the detainment of eighty-four Arab and South Asian immigrants without cause, and the subse-

The Metropolitan Detention Center, 2017. CREDIT: SCOTT DEXTER

and Reverend Al Sharpton—served sentences between forty and ninety days.

Although women make up less than a tenth of the MDC inmate population, media coverage has exposed substandard conditions, mistreatment of female inmates (including those who are pregnant), sexual assault, and rape there. In May 2017, major media outlets including the *New York Times* reported that two MDC supervisors

quent hardships on their families and communities. Referred to as Brooklyn's "Abu Ghraib," Sunset Park's MDC was the subject of a 2003 US Department of Justice (DOJ) investigation. Findings of widespread abuses of immigrant detainees are documented in a DOJ Office of the Inspector General report. In June 2015, a divided three-judge federal panel of the US Court of Appeals allowed a long-standing 2002 lawsuit filed by eight, mostly Muslim, immigrant detainees against several high-ranking Bush administration officials to move forward, but in 2017 the Supreme Court reversed the lower court's decision.

In 2001, four prominent NYC political leaders were jailed at the MDC for trespassing on military property in protest of the US Navy's bombing of the Puerto Rican island of Vieques. The "Vieques Four"—Roberto Ramirez, chairman of the Bronx Democratic Party, City Councilman Adolfo Carrion Jr., New York State Assemblyman Jose Rivera,

and one corrections officer were charged with repeated incidences of sexual assault and rape of nine female inmates. These same MDC supervisors were responsible for educating subordinates about their duties under the 2003 Prison Rape Elimination Act. These news accounts augment the substandard and abusive conditions documented in a 2016 National Association of Women Judges report that found MDC's small female inmate population kept in windowless rooms with little access to air and light, poor food quality, and lacking medical services. During a cold spell in late January 2019, inmates were without heat or electricity for over a week. The COVID 19 pandemic has only worsened the already dismal conditions at the MDC. In December 2020, fifty-five inmates tested positive for COVID-19. A report from the Federal Defenders of New York indicates that sick inmates are not receiving adequate medical attention, corrections officers are not properly wearing masks, sanitation is substandard, and there is not contact tracing at the facility.

—*Tarry Hum*

NEARBY SITES OF INTEREST

Center for Family Life
443 39th Street, Brooklyn, NY
Community social service organization that also helps to incubate worker owned cooperatives.

4.26 Sunset Park

41st to 44th Streets, 5th and 7th Avenues, Brooklyn, NY

Sunset Park sits at the second highest point in Brooklyn after Battle Hill in nearby Greenwood Cemetery, lending it spectacular views of the upper New York Harbor including the Statue of Liberty, Staten Island, New Jersey, and the Manhattan skyline. The park's development began in 1891 to serve the neighborhood's then-largely Scandinavian and Irish immigrant population.

In his role as the commissioner of the New York City Department of Parks, Robert Moses redesigned Sunset Park in 1935 to accommodate a large public swimming pool (see **Thomas Jefferson Pool**, p. 83) and a bathhouse designed in a neoclassical/Art Deco style. The improvements to Sunset Park were part of the massive Works Progress Administration capital construction program. As in many NYC neighborhoods of color, quality recreational space is limited. Even with a twenty-five-acre park, the neighborhood is still lacking in open space— a per- capita measure indicates less than an acre of open space for every thousand residents. Sunset Park therefore provides critical public space to build community among its racially and ethnically hyper-diverse population. It is a vital space for recreation, exercise, and family activities. On any given day, weather permitting, there will numerous Asian and Latina/o/x park users dancing, doing Tai Chi, playing dominoes or mahjongg, picnicking, and celebrating birthdays. In addition to recreational activities, Sunset Park is a site for community organizing and engaging in dialogue with the neighborhood's multiple publics.

As an example, for a few years (2012–2013), a collective of volunteers, Rice and Dreams: A People's Kitchen, prepared home-cooked meals that they served in Sunset Park, weather permitting. During the other months, Rice and Dreams served meals at a local church, St. Jacobi Lutheran Church. The goal of Rice and Dreams was "(T)o bring neighbors and friends together around meals that heal us from the inside out, and also work toward positive change in our world that will heal us from the outside in." Around the same time, Occupy Sunset Park formed and was widely known as one of the most active neighborhood-based groups in the Occupy movement. Occupy Sunset Park's social justice actions, community education, and organizing events often took place in the park.

Numerous luxury commercial and residential developments in the area bely the escalating pace and scale of the neighborhood's gentrification, perhaps most prominently displayed in the adaptive reuse and redevelopment of Sunset Park's extensive industrial infrastructure along the waterfront. In spring 2017, a neighborhood resi-

Asian and Latina/o/x
families Occupy
Sunset Park, 2012.
CREDIT: TARRY HUM

dent lined Sunset Park's 5th Avenue entrance with more than a dozen flags of Latin American countries and handwritten signs with messages such as "Our Community Is Not For Sale" and "Sunset Park Unite".

—*Tarry Hum*

TO LEARN MORE

Hum, Tarry. *The Making of a Global Immigrant Neighborhood. Brooklyn's Sunset Park*. Philadelphia: Temple University Press, 2014. Nearby Sites of Interest

NEARBY SITES OF INTEREST

Alku and Alku Toinen
816 and 826 43rd Street, Brooklyn, NY
New York City's first cooperative apartment buildings, developed by Finnish socialists. In 1916, sixteen families contributed five hundred dollars each to purchase a lot on 43rd Street between 8th and 9th Avenues and built a four-story apartment building. In subsequent years, twenty additional housing cooperatives were established near Sunset Park.

Greenwood Cemetery
500 25th Street, Brooklyn, NY
Greenwood has served as a green oasis to New Yorkers since it opened in 1838, and for many years it was one of the country's most popular tourist attractions because of its great beauty and views. Among many prominent writers, artists, and politicians buried there is the grave of John Matthews, an immigrant from England known for having invented the apparatus to dispense carbonated water, therefore setting off the first craze for seltzer in the country. Greenwood has tours of his grave and many others on Wednesdays and Sundays. Reservations are encouraged.

Brooklyn Banya
602 Coney Island Avenue, Brooklyn, NY
In nearby Kensington, this Russian bathhouse, also known as a "shvitz" (in Yiddish), is where one can go to sweat it out and sample some Slavic fare during breaks from the sauna.

FAVORITE NEIGHBORHOOD RESTAURANTS

Pacificana
813 55th Street, Brooklyn, NY
A popular dim-sum palace, serving Cantonese favorites since 2004.

Nieves Tia Mimi
4711 5th Avenue, Brooklyn, NY
Tia Mimi has been serving nieves (ice cream/sorbet) at this spot for over twenty years.

Flatbush

4.27 Erasmus Hall High School

911 Flatbush Avenue, Brooklyn, NY

Over its two centuries of existence, Erasmus Hall High School has been emblematic of the shifting fortunes of New York City's schools. Referred to as the "mother of high schools," Erasmus Hall Academy was founded as a private institution for higher learning in 1786 by Reverend Walter Livingston and Senator James Vanderbilt and was the first secondary school in New York to be chartered by the Board of Regents. The school received generous contributions from Alexander Hamilton, Aaron Burr, and Peter Lefferts, and the land on which it was constructed was donated by the Flatbush Dutch Reformed Church (890 Flatbush Avenue) on the condition that it would always remain a high school.

Erasmus High School, ca. 1930s; courtyard with original building. CREDIT: *BROOKLYN DAILY EAGLE* PHOTOGRAPHS, BROOKLYN PUBLIC LIBRARY, BROOKLYN COLLECTION

Erasmus opened its doors in 1787 to twenty-six men in the Dutch neighborhood of Flatbush. By 1801 it started accepting women and an official "female department" was opened in 1826. As the Erasmus Chronicles documents, "The young misses are occupied in reading, writing, arithmetic, geography and such other studies as promise to render them useful and ornamental members of society." The school was successful and by 1860, hundreds of students paid tuition of two hundred and fifty dollars a year. By the end of the nineteenth century, however, enrollments had dropped. As of 1874 education had become compulsory between the ages of eight and four-

teen (a law not strictly enforced until 1901) and the city had begun to open free public high schools. Flushing High School was the first public high school to open in Queens in 1875; Central Grammar School was the first high school to open in Brooklyn in 1878, and its rapid expansion led to the opening of Girls High School in 1886 and Boys High School in 1892. In 1896, two years before the full geographic consolidation of New York City, Erasmus Hall was turned over to the public system and renamed Erasmus Hall High School. Members of the New York Education Board stated at the time, "a good system of High Schools is of vast civic importance. The diffusion of a High School education leads directly to independent thinking. Independent thinking leads to independent conduct. Independent conduct leads to independent voting and to independence in the discharge of all the duties of citizenship." The expansion of a free and public education was seen as imperative to a successful democracy.

Erasmus High School, 2017. CREDIT: SCOTT DEXTER

dled with crime and low test scores. The New York City Board of Education closed the school in 1994 and turned it into the Erasmus Hall Educational Campus, hosting five smaller schools. Today, these five schools are all examples of extreme segregation in the New York City school system. (*Quotes are from* Chronicles of Erasmus Hall.)

TO LEARN MORE

Boughton, Willis, Eugene W. Harter, Brooklyn (New York, NY), and Erasmus Hall High School. *Chronicles of Erasmus Hall.* Brooklyn, NY: General Organization, Erasmus Hall High School, 1906.

NEARBY SITES OF INTEREST

Flatbush Dutch Reformed Church
890 Flatbush Avenue, Brooklyn, NY
Founded in 1654, this is the oldest continuously running religious institution in New York City. The Church played an important role in establishing Erasmus Hall Academy (across the street) and in serving as the school's religious institution.

Flatbush Town Hall
35 Snyder Avenue, Brooklyn, NY
In 1873 the town of Flatbush voted down a proposal to become part of the City of Brooklyn. As an independent town, citizens felt that Flatbush needed to have a Town Hall for civic business. The building was completed in 1875 and housed police headquarters and a courthouse. The town's independence, however, was short-lived, as Flatbush and the rest of Brooklyn were incorporated into New York City in 1898. Today the building is occupied by a public school serving children with special needs.

Erasmus High flourished, enrolling over three thousand students by 1910, requiring additional infrastructure and buildings. The façade seen today was built at this time, though the original Academy building can still be seen in the courtyard of the newer buildings. By 1934, with over eight thousand students, Erasmus was bursting at the seams. The school continued to grow, but by the 1960s and '70s, the demographics of the school had dramatically changed from working-class white to Black and Puerto Rican.

By the late 1980s Erasmus Hall High School was considered a failing school rid-

Congress of
Racial Equality
Boycott of
Ebinger Bakery in
1962. CREDIT: BOB
ADELMAN ESTATE

4.28 Ebinger Baking Company Boycotts

2207 Albemarle Road, Brooklyn, NY

This is the former site of one of the major truck depots of the Ebinger Baking Company, which opened its first store in Flatbush in 1898. It is also the site of a 1962 civil disobedience in protest of Ebinger's discriminatory hiring practices. Ebinger was once a household name in New York City, famous for its German pastries and later for its Brooklyn Blackout cake, which has been adapted by scores of Brooklyn bakeries since. By the time of its closing in 1972 it was the largest retail bakery on the East Coast, with sixty-seven stores across Brooklyn, Queens, Staten Island, and Long Island. But Ebinger's had a troubled history. In the 1930s, the bakery was accused of Nazi affiliation and of discrimination against Jews. By the 1950s most of its clientele was Jewish, though the bakery staff did not reflect this; as Brooklyn's demographics shifted

after World War II, the bakery's clientele increasingly became Black and Puerto Rican, yet they were rarely hired. Some Black Americans worked as janitors or as low-level employees in the bakery division, but no Black or Puerto Rican women were hired as "Ebinger Girls" in the retail stores, or as high-level bakery staff or managers. As a result, the Congress of Racial Equality (CORE), along with Operation Unemployment, targeted the Ebinger Baking Company for their jobs campaign to combat urban employment discrimination. Their goal was to push Ebinger's to hire more people of color in its retail stores, bakery, and truck depots. This campaign established the Brooklyn Chapter of CORE as one of the one of the most radical in the country, even inspiring students at nearby Erasmus High School to form their own chapter (see **Erasmus Hall High School**, p. 276).

The campaign was defined by repeated betrayals on the part of Ebinger's, and escalating tactics on the part of CORE. After an initial approach and negotiation, Ebinger agreed to hire six Black women in sales. The company then did nothing. At that point CORE moved to boycott Ebinger's, hosting picket lines at key locations every Saturday, including at its first store at 1110 Flatbush Avenue. Though there were too many picket lines and too few volunteers, Ebinger was once again forced to negotiate. Again, the company agreed to hire African Americans. This time, they agreed that Black women would receive three of every five available positions for an indefinite period. Yet months passed and Ebinger's did nothing to hire more Black and Puerto Rican workers. CORE once again had to escalate with more picket lines, this time with a petition from the community promising not to purchase Ebinger's products until discriminatory practices changed. Despite this community pressure, the bakery still did not capitulate.

It was not until seven members of CORE went to Ebinger's truck depot here and blocked morning deliveries on August 25, 1962, that Ebinger's finally negotiated in earnest. But implementing the nondiscrimination policy proved to be much more difficult than anticipated. In the end, Ebinger's was forced to hire more people of color, but the company still found ways to discriminate. It remained majority-white until it closed in 1972. At the time of this writing, the site is home to CubeSmart Self Storage, but if you look above the entrance, you will still see the building's original name.

—*With Ethan Barnett*

TO LEARN MORE

Purnell, Brian. *Fighting Jim Crow in the County of Kings: The Congress of Racial Equality in Brooklyn.* Lexington: University Press of Kentucky, 2013.

4.29   Kings Theatre

1027 Flatbush Avenue, Brooklyn, NY

In the midst of the Great Depression, Kings Theatre offered an inexpensive opportunity for working-class Brooklynites to enjoy an escape from the hardships of their daily lives. The majestic Loew's theater opened September 7, 1929, a short seven weeks before the stock market crash of "Black Tuesday." Thousands came to the opening (tickets cost between twenty-five and sixty cents), which featured the live stage show *Evangeline* starring Dolores del Rio, Hollywood's first famous Mexican actress. Kings Theatre, with a seating capacity of over three thousand, was one of five Loew's "Wonder Theatres" in the New York metropolitan area. The

Kings Theatre restored and reopened, 2015. CREDIT: JIM HENDERSON, OWN WORK, CC BY SA 3.0, WIKIMEDIA COMMONS

others included Loew's 175th St Theatre (4140 Broadway in Manhattan), Loew's Paradise Theatre (2403 Grand Concourse in the Bronx), Loew's Valencia Theatre (165–11 Jamaica Avenue in Queens), and Loew's Jersey Theatre (54 Journal Square in Jersey City). All of these others currently serve as churches. In its heyday, the actors and stagehands lucky to work at Kings could make use of an exercise room and a basketball court in its basement, which hosted an inter-theater basketball team.

By the 1950s the theater was deteriorating, unable to attract sufficient crowds or compete with multiplexes that could show more than one movie at a time. By the 1970s the theater was no longer showing feature films, and shortly after the 1977 New York City blackout, it closed, remaining so until 2015. In 2010, New York City identified Kings Theatre as a potentially lucrative entertainment venue in the heart of a rapidly gentrifying Flatbush, and chose the ACE Theatrical Group to rebuild and run the theatre. The renovations cost over $90 million. The theater features musical and theatrical performances, lectures, comedy jams, and graduations. Diana Ross was the opening day performer in 2015.

NEARBY SITE OF INTEREST

Sears Roebuck and Co.
2307 Beverley Road, Brooklyn, NY
Sears came to Flatbush in 1929, just weeks before the stock market crashed. The store could be seen all over the neighborhood because of its elegant art deco tower that simultaneously served as advertisement and hid the water tower.

As part of its commitment to the neighborhood, the store built a large auditorium that seated 650 people on the third floor and was available to local Brooklyn civic, church, and philanthropic organizations for free.

Bay Ridge

4.30 Arab American Association of New York

7111 5th Avenue, Brooklyn, NY

On a stretch of 5th Avenue in Bay Ridge, among the Irish pubs, hookah bars, bodegas, Arab/Middle Eastern grocery stores, and cell phone shops, one will find a nondescript storefront with Arabic writing on the awning, community bulletins and flyers taped in the window, and a glass door front that lets light into the open-spaced lobby. This is the office of the Arab American Association of New York (AAANY), a nonprofit organization founded not long after the events of September 11, 2001, and the ensuing tide of Islamophobia that gripped the country. It has served the local Arab community ever since, both Muslim and Christian, with services ranging from adult education, youth development, and legal and immigration services, to college counseling and youth community organizing. To many Arab Americans, it is an oasis in a city that often fails to acknowledge their longtime local existence and contributions, let alone address their needs.

The AAANY has also become an important hub for advocacy and civic engagement. In recent years, it has been central in defend-

Offices of the Arab American Association of New York, 2017. CREDIT: SCOTT DEXTER

backlash as familiar tensions periodically erupted into incidents of violence. In the fall of 2015, when across the country racial tensions were flaring as a result of the murders of Michael Brown in Ferguson, Missouri, and Eric Garner in nearby Staten Island, a young Muslim woman who wears the hijab was attacked at a bus stop on Fort Hamilton and 86th Street. This and other non-reported incidents served as a breaking point for many in the community, both Arab and non-Arab, Muslim and non-Muslim. The community rallied and responded by organizing a march on Martin Luther King's national holiday that began at the site of the attack and proceeded up the 5th Avenue corridor, cutting across town to the Salam Arabic Lutheran Church on 4th Avenue and 80th Street.

ing the community against NYPD surveillance and led the push to get the city to recognize the Muslim holy days of Eid al-Fitr and Eid al-Adha on the public school calendar. The evolution of the organization's purpose—from providing social services to fostering civic engagement and building political power for its base—was a gradual but necessary one, as Islamophobia never dissipated. The Arab American population continued to grow, with immigrants coming from Syria, Egypt, Lebanon, Palestine, and Yemen, among other countries, many fleeing war or just seeking improved economic conditions like the waves of immigrants before them. The AAANY stands out not just for its local reach but also for its national profile, representing the largest concentration of Arab Americans in the country outside of Dearborn, Michigan. With this growth, however, came a predictable

From that moment—the attack itself and the action that followed—the community began to create and build intergroup bonds. The election later in the year of Donald Trump, who ran on an explicit platform of anti–Black/Brown racism, Islamophobia, xenophobia, and right-wing nationalism, reopened wounds for many in the community and emboldened bigots nationwide. In the fall of 2016, a white male verbally assaulted a female Muslim off-duty police officer as she dropped her son off in Bay Ridge. The officer, one of the few who wear a hijab while on duty, was accosted by the man who ranted about ISIS and threatened to cut her head off. On hearing of this assault, the community once again rallied, and a follow-up march was organized. Since then, the MLK Day March has become an annual tradition in the neighborhood.

Civil rights activist Linda Sarsour, known nationally as one of the co-organizers of the historic Women's March on Washington, DC, was for a long time the executive director of the AAANY. Sarsour was a fierce advocate for the organization and for the community despite often-virulent pushback and personal attacks against her. In 2017, the Arab American community supported the campaign of Reverend Khader El-Yateem, a Lutheran pastor who ran for City Council. Had he won, he would have been the first Palestinian to hold a seat on the New York City Council.

—*Danielle Bullock, David Farley, and Alan Aja*

TO LEARN MORE

Aja, Alan A., and Alejandra Marchevsky. 2017. "How Immigrants Became Criminals." *Boston Review*, March 16, 2017. https://bostonreview .net/politics/alan-aja-alejandra-marchevsky -how-immigrants-became-criminals.

Apuzzo, Matt, and Adam Goldman. *Enemies Within: Inside the NYPD's Secret Spying Unit and Bin Laden's Final Plot against America*. New York: Simon & Schuster, 2013.

4.31 Mortgage Lending in Bay Ridge

Housing on 77th Street between Colonial Road and Narrows Avenue, Brooklyn, NY

Bay Ridge was the only neighborhood in Brooklyn that received the federal government's highest rating for mortgage credit after World War II, ensuring the neighborhood's relative affluence in the following decades. Housing that was built leading up to and during this period can be seen on blocks like 77th Street between Colonial Road and Narrows Avenue.

In the wake of the Great Depression, the federal government began to insure and issue mortgages with the goal of helping average Americans own homes. In the course of determining the financial risk of these new activities, federal agencies graded neighborhoods in American cities based on their social composition on a scale of A ("Best," coded green); B ("Still Desirable," coded blue); C ("Definitely Declining," coded yellow); and D ("Hazardous," coded red). Neighborhoods with more than nominal shares of Black or Latina/o/x residents or immigrants, or of older housing or rental housing, were given grades C and D—what came to be known as "redlined," or considered too risky for investment. Financial institutions followed this federal guidance and largely withheld credit from redlined communities, fueling their economic decline.

Only twelve areas in all of New York City received a green—or "best"—designation, marking them profitable for investment. In Riverdale and Fieldston in the Bronx; Washington Heights and the neighborhoods just

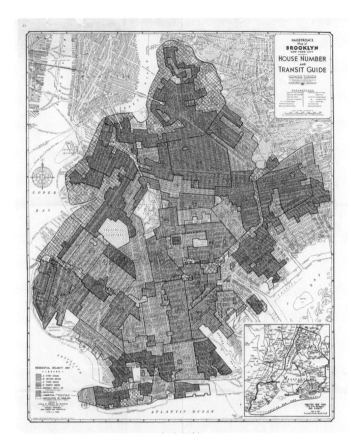

Home Owners Loan
Corporation map of
Brooklyn 1935–1940.
CREDIT: MAPPING
INEQUALITY

east of Central Park in Manhattan; Randall
Manor, Silver Lake, Grymes Hill, and Todt
Hill on Staten Island; Forest Hills in Queens;
and parts of Bay Ridge, in Brooklyn, credit
flowed freely. These parts of Bay Ridge—
the area from 74th to 86th Streets between
Ridge and Shore Roads, and along the western shore of Brooklyn—were "greenlined"
for investment because of their relatively
homogenous population (principally Irish
and British), new housing, and lack of low-
income families, Black residents, and immigrants. Meanwhile, a full 83 percent of the
Bronx, 65 percent of Manhattan, 89 percent of Queens, 82 percent of Staten Island,

and 76 percent of Brooklyn were labeled as
"Definitely Declining" or "Hazardous."

The redlining of large areas of American
cities after World War II made them virtually unable to compete with new suburbs
for investment. Limited mortgage lending
meant a decline in homeownership, a dwindling tax base, and the resulting decline of
city resources and services. While the federal government financed the growth of
majority- (and in many cases, almost exclusively) white suburbia, its neighborhood rat-
ings system triggered the economic decline
of countless urban neighborhoods, including in Brooklyn.

FORM 8
10-1-37

AREA DESCRIPTION - SECURITY MAP OF _____ New York City, N.Y.

1. AREA CHARACTERISTICS:
   a. Description of Terrain.   Slightly rolling with slope toward Bay.

   b. Favorable Influences.   Shore Road Drive landscaped. Harbor view. Main section restricted and zoned. Lawns & gardens. Away from noise and heavy traffic.

   c. Detrimental Influences.   None

   d. Percentage of land improved 90 Res. 90%; e. Trend of desirability next 10-15 yrs. Static

2. INHABITANTS:
   a. Occupation Business executives and professional ; b. Estimated annual family income $ 7500-25,000
   c. Foreign-born families 20 %; Irish & British predominating; d. Negro No ; %
   e. Infiltration of No ; f. Relief families No
   g. Population is increasing ; decreasing ; static Yes

3. BUILDINGS:

	PREDOMINATING 90 %	OTHER TYPE 5 %	OTHER TYPE %
a. Type	1 family 6-12 rms	2-family 5-7 rms	
b. Construction	Brick-stucco-frame	Brick-frame	
c. Average Age	18 Years	15 Years	Years
d. Repair	Good	Good	
e. Occupancy	100 %	100 %	%
f. Home ownership	95 %	90 %	%
g. Constructed past yr.	2 or 3	None	
h. 1929 Price range	$ 18,000-25,000 100%	$ 16,000-20,000 100%	$ 100%
i. 1935 Price range	$ 10,000-15,000 58 %	$ 9,500-14,000 65 %	$ %
j. 1938 Price range	$ 10,500-16,000 62 %	$ 10,000-14,500 68 %	$ %
k. Sales demand	$ Fair	$ Poor	$
l. Activity	Poor	Poor	
m. 1929 Rent range	$ 100 - 200 100%	$ 80 - 125 100%	$ 100%
n. 1934 Rent range	$ 75 - 125 67 %	$ 60 - 80 68 %	$ %
o. 1938 Rent range	$ 80 - 135 72 %	$ 70 - 100 83 %	$ %
p. Rental demand	$ Good	$ Good	$
q. Activity	Fair	Good	

4. AVAILABILITY OF MORTGAGE FUNDS: a. Home purchase Ample ; b. Home building Ample

5. CLARIFYING REMARKS: 5% high class apartments principally along shore - 2-6 rms at $20-23 per room. An area of substantially built homes adaptable to future modernization to place them on a competitive basis with new offerings. New high school proposed for Crescent Athletic Club property between 83rd and 85th St. at Shore Rd.

6. NAME AND LOCATION Bay Ridge, Brooklyn SECURITY GRADE A AREA NO. 1
   ASSESSED VALUES: 110% of market value.

Home Owners Loan Corporation's description of Bay Ridge 1935-1940. CREDIT: MAPPING INEQUALITY

Redlining became officially illegal under the Fair Housing Act of 1968, but the legacy of decades of neglect remained, and informal discriminatory practices continued relatively unabated. Like other cities, New York lost population and industry after World War II and suffered years of fiscal crisis and deterioration. But even during this time, relatively affluent neighborhoods like Bay Ridge, Fieldston, and Forest Hills survived and thrived, largely due to the legacy of the investment in them following World War II.

TO LEARN MORE

"Mapping Inequality." n.d. Digital Scholarship Lab. University of Richmond. Mapping Inequality: Redlining in New Deal America. Accessed August 28, 2020. https://dsl .richmond.edu/panorama/redlining/.

NEARBY SITE OF INTEREST

Owl's Head Park
Colonial Road and 68 Street at Shore Road, Brooklyn, NY
A 150-foot tunnel under this park represents the only attempt to connect Staten Island to the city's subway system. Begun in 1912 by one of the private subway companies, the line under the bay to Staten Island was never finished due to political opposition and limited funding (see **Public Transportation**, p. 213).

FAVORITE NEIGHBORHOOD RESTAURANT

Tanoreen
7523 3rd Avenue, Brooklyn, NY
Celebrated Middle-Eastern restaurant, in the neighborhood since 1999.

Brighton Beach

4.32 ## Master Theater
1029 Brighton Beach Avenue, Brooklyn, NY
New York City is home to the largest Russian and Russian-speaking population in the Western Hemisphere, mostly concentrated in Brighton Beach just east of Coney Island and in nearby Sheepshead Bay. Brighton Beach Avenue is home to numerous groceries, restaurants, clubs, and stores that cater to Russian-speaking immigrants. The Master Theater (previously the Millennium Theater) sits along this stretch, regularly featuring Russian and former Soviet performers. Russian-speaking New Yorkers have flocked to see renowned performers like Tamara Gverdtsiteli, "the Russian Edith Piaf," violinist Vladimir Spivakov, and violist Yuri Bashmet at this neighborhood institution.

Brighton Beach's history initially made it an attractive destination for Russian Jewish immigrants. Unlike its immediate neighbors (Coney Island and Manhattan Beach), Brighton Beach was relatively friendly to the city's Jewish population from its inception. As Brighton Beach developed into an entertainment center, Jewish people from the Lower East Side, Brownsville, and East New York began to move to the area, establishing strong cultural and political institutions, including Democratic clubs and neighborhood improvement groups. They were later joined by Russian and European Jewish immigrants escaping Nazism and fascism in the 1930s and 1940s. Brighton Beach still houses the largest concentration of

Holocaust survivors in New York City. The neighborhood began to change to cater to the new population: the Brighton Beach Music Hall converted to a Yiddish theater in 1918, and developers began to build large apartment buildings to respond to the growing demand for the neighborhood. The private, members-only Brighton Beach Baths opened in 1907 and remained popular until it closed in 1994, when it was the oldest remaining beach club in the city. At its peak, it had twelve thousand members that enjoyed three swimming pools, tennis handball courts, areas for playing cards, and a stage that hosted a revolving cast of borscht belt comics.

Brighton Beach Avenue, home to the largest Russian enclave in New York City. CREDIT: ALEXANDER KLYUCH - USER: (WT-SHARED) AKLYUCH AT WTS WIKIVOYAGE - OWN WORK, WIKIPEDIA COMMONS

The neighborhood grew overcrowded while continuing to welcome throngs of summer beachgoers, and infrastructure suffered during the 1970s fiscal crisis. Yet, as Soviet immigration policies shifted, Soviet Jews arrived in such numbers that Brighton Beach became known as "Little Odessa" reinvigorating the neighborhood. Newcomers from former Soviet territories continued to come to Brighton Beach in the wake of the Soviet Union's collapse in the 1990s and to new enclaves all over the city, particularly on the south coast of Staten Island, the Bronx's Riverdale, and Forest Hills in Queens. Businesses catering to the new arrivals opened up along Brighton Beach Avenue, including what was then the Millennium Theatre, which began featuring live performances in 1996 as the Russian-speaking population grew dramatically.

While Russian-speaking immigrants enlivened Brighton Beach from its midcentury deterioration, it is immigrants from Central Asia that represent the new wave of settlement and investment in the neighborhood. Rising real estate values and the new condominiums that crowd the beach threaten the bustling community, but many of the neighborhood's anchoring businesses and institutions, including the Master Theater, remain wedded to the neighborhood and to serving and entertaining Russian-speaking New Yorkers. *(Quotes are from Robin Pogrebin "A Theatre Tied by Heartstrings to the Old Country," New York Times and Michael Immerso, Coney Island: the People's Playground,)*

TO LEARN MORE

Immerso, Michael. *Coney Island: The People's Playground.* New Brunswick, NJ: Rutgers University Press, 2002.

Pogrebin, Robin. 2012. "A Theater Tied by Heartstrings to the Old Country." *New York Times*, March 11, 2012, sec. Arts. https://www .nytimes.com/2012/03/12/arts/millennium -theater-in-brighton-beach-as-link-to-old -country.html.

NEARBY SITES OF INTEREST

Brighton Bazaar

1007 Brighton Beach Avenue, Brooklyn, NY
The preeminent Russian supermarket, famous for its buffets and wide selection of Russian and Eastern European treats.

Oceana Condominiums

75 Oceana Drive E., Brooklyn, NY
Former site of the Brighton Beach Baths.

Coney Island

4.33 Coney Island

South of Surf Avenue to the Boardwalk and Atlantic Ocean, Brooklyn, NY

One of New York City's most magnificent beaches, Coney Island has long been a site of contrast between the prerogatives of wealth and the leisure demands of New York's working people. But unlike much of today's city, working people still have the advantage. While there have been amusements of all sorts in Coney Island since the 1800s, the people's history of Coney Island really starts on May 1, 1920, the day the train fare was cut from a dime to a nickel, creating a boom in people going to the beach. But Coney Island wasn't yet a beach for the people. Up and down the shore of Coney Island, private bathhouses, each owning their fenced-off section of sand, lay in wait ready to give access to sun, surf, and fun times—for a price of course. While a 1921 law capped this price at two dollars, this still represented about a day's wages for a typical garment worker just to take their family to the beach.

The uproar over the situation led the New York State legislature—pushed by Brooklyn Borough President Edward Riegelmann—to pass laws to make the beach public and pour almost $4 million (about $60 million in today's currency) to improve and open the shore and construct the famous boardwalk. On August 13, 1922, the *New York Times* headline read, "War on our

Coney Island beachgoers in 1900. CREDIT: COURTESY OF LIBRARY OF CONGRESS, LC-DIG-GGBAIN-08402

Bath Barons! Coney Profiteering Beach Hogs Vanquished!" The boardwalk (later named for Riegelmann) was finished and the beaches opened to the public.

The old Luna Park at night, 1906. CREDIT: SAMUEL H. (SAMUEL HERMAN) GOTTSCHO (1875–1971). MUSEUM OF THE CITY OF NEW YORK. 54.77.6

One could now walk almost two miles unobstructed down the beach, from Ocean Parkway to West 37th street, at least if you were white. While the Green Book for Negro Travelers mentioned Coney Island as a destination from its first national edition in 1937, and buses with Black amusement-seekers would drive in from as far away as Baltimore and Washington, DC, in common practice segregation on the beaches and other areas plagued Coney Island until the 1960s.

Of the three great amusement parks first built there, Dreamland burned down in 1911, the original Luna Park closed in 1946, and Steeplechase closed in 1964. Since then, Coney Island has had to endure continuing battles against the forces of high-end development—emerging with wounds, but surviving. The most recent was in the 2000s, when one failed development plan called for Las Vegas–style resorts on Surf Avenue. Another was in the 1960s after Steeplechase Park closed, when developer Fred Trump sought to create a "Miami Beach in Brooklyn" by building luxury high-rise apartments. Denied the zoning change he needed, out

of spite he arranged a party for guests to destroy the stained glass façade of the Steeplechase Park Pavilion. Other losses include the old Thunderbolt roller coaster—made famous by the movie Annie Hall—which was demolished in 2000, and the rotating Astro Tower observation deck, a victim of Superstorm Sandy in 2012.

The landmarks that remain have had to fight. The oldest active roller coaster in the world, the Cyclone (West 10th and Surf Avenue) was expected to be demolished in the 1970s before being renovated. The Parachute Jump, a 250-foot-tall decommissioned thrill ride relocated from the 1939 World's Fair called the "Eiffel Tower of Brooklyn" (West 16th and the boardwalk) almost fell victim to Fred Trump's offer to demolish it, even after being declared a city landmark along with the Cyclone and Deno's Wonder Wheel (West 12th between Bowery Street and the boardwalk) in the late 1980s.

As much as the place itself, the practices of Coney Island have kept some of the best of the city's working-class traditions of fun alive, and created many new ones as well. It is difficult to imagine Manhattan hosting a hot dog eating contest (July 4th), sandcastle competition (mid-August), handball tournament (usually late July or early August), beard and moustache competition (first Saturday in September), crowning an official representative through a burlesque pageant (Miss Coney Island Burlesque Beauty Pageant, September), or putting on a parade where anyone is invited as long as they make a passable attempt to dress like a mythical sea creature (Mermaid Parade, June, usually the closest Saturday to the summer solstice). If you visit in winter, you could also take a plunge into the Atlantic with the Polar Bear Club on New Year's Day. At Totonno's Pizzeria (1524 Neptune Avenue), the water still comes in paper cups and the pizza on paper plates despite winning awards from everyone from Zagat's to the James Beard foundation. And the fabled corner candy store? There's still one on Surf Avenue (Williams Candy Shop, 1318 Surf Avenue), open for the last seventy-five years. The history, traditions, and culture of Coney Island is helped kept alive by the Coney Island History Project, a nonprofit in operation since 2004, (3059 W. 12th Street) and can be explored directly at the Coney Island Museum (1208 Surf Avenue).

Celebrity has graced Coney Island from time to time, although never too fancy a version. Woody Guthrie lived down at 3520 Mermaid Avenue and Arlo Guthrie was born there, although the old house has long been demolished and replaced with a senior housing development. But the folk heroes of Coney Island—the people still talked about by the residents and regulars—are people like Vic Hershkowitz, a New York City firefighter and one-wall handball legend who used to dominate the Coney Island handball courts (West 5th street north of the Boardwalk), Robert "Mr. Lou" Williams, a nursing home manager who was a father figure to countless people, including future NBA stars Stephon Marbury and Sebastian Telfair, on the basketball courts of the Surfside Gardens projects (W. 32nd Street between Mermaid and Surf Avenues), and shipyard worker Jerry Bianco, who decided to build his own submarine meant to salvage a sunken Italian cruise ship. Its launch unsuccessful, the bright yellow contraption was abandoned in Coney Island Creek—the wreck can still be seen by crossing the creek to the tip of Calvert Vaux Park on the northern shore.

In contrast to the New York City of today, where it seems as if the upper classes are pushing people further and further out, Coney Island is the opposite—the amusements, businesses, and everyday life extends two and a half miles through its heart. Walking the boardwalk, you'll pass Soviet army veterans back from a daily swim, kids practicing their skateboard tricks, families from all over the boroughs pushing strollers and taking in the sights. Only on the ends—in the upper-crust Manhattan Beach on the eastern end of the peninsula, and the gated community at the western end known

Coney Island's Luna
Park today, 2019.
CREDIT: PENNY LEWIS

as Sea Gate—do the rich have a foothold.
Coney Island, for this reason, still remains a
"paradise of the proletariat."

—*Moses Gates*

TO LEARN MORE

Coney Island History Project: A wealth of
historic photographs, maps, documents,
and videos, including over two hundred oral
histories. http://www.coneyislandhistory.
org. For current happenings, visit the Coney
Island USA website (http://www.coneyisland
.com), which also runs the Coney Island Museum
and puts on the annual Mermaid Day parade.

Denson, Charles. *Coney Island: Lost and Found.*
Berkeley, CA: Ten Speed Press, 2004.

Frank, Robin Jaffee, Charles Denson, Josh Glick,
John F. Kasson, and Charles Musser. *Coney
Island: Visions of an American Dreamland, 1861–
2008.* New Haven: Yale University Press, 2015.

Immerso, Michael. *Coney Island: The People's
Playground.* New Brunswick, NJ: Rutgers
University Press, 2002.

Parascandola, Louis, and John Parascandola, eds. *A
Coney Island Reader: Through Dizzy Gates of Illusion.*
New York: Columbia University Press, 2014.

**FAVORITE NEIGHBORHOOD
RESTAURANTS**

Williams Candy
1318 Surf Avenue, Brooklyn, NY
Opening in 1936, Williams candy has been a favorite for candied apples, caramel popcorn, and
cotton candy ever since. In the summer the shop
sells more than four thousand apples a week.

Nathan's Famous
1310 Surf Avenue, Brooklyn, NY
With a three hundred dollar loan, Polish immigrant
Nathan Handwerker opened Nathan's Famous in
1916. Legend has it that the first hot dog eating contest occurred that same year, but it wasn't until
1972 that the famous 4th of July hot dog eating
contest was official and recorded. Today the hot
dog eating contest is as popular as ever.

Totonno's Pizza
1524 Neptune Avenue, Brooklyn, NY
Opened in 1924 by Italian immigrants from Na-
ples, Totonnos is said to be the oldest, family-run,
continuously operated pizzeria in the country.
Surviving two fires and Superstorm Sandy, at this
writing the neighborhood awaits its post-COVID
reopening.

Bridges, Tunnels, and Expressways

There is no New York City without the dozens of bridges, tunnels, and roadways that knit its islands of Manhattan, Long Island, and Staten Island together and into the US mainland. Indeed, prior to the consolidation of the five boroughs into the city of New York in 1898, there were only a few ways to cross the waterways that flow in, around, and through the city. As the cities and towns that would eventually become New York City grew in the nineteenth century, ferries transported people over the Hudson and East Rivers and New York Bay. A few small bridges dotted the region, crossing various waterways and tributaries, until the Brooklyn Bridge became the first fixed crossing of the East River, linking Brooklyn and Manhattan in 1883 (see **Brooklyn Bridge**, p. 230).

The five boroughs were officially consolidated into New York City in 1898, but physical consolidation happened piecemeal with each new bridge and tunnel constructed afterward. The city's earliest bridges, like the Macombs Dam, Washington, and Third Avenue Bridges, linked Manhattan to some of its earliest (1873) annexations in the Bronx across the Harlem River. Following the Brooklyn Bridge in 1883, the toll-free Williamsburg, Manhattan, and Queensboro Bridges opened in 1903 and 1909, respectively, transporting New Yorkers by foot and trolley across the East River to Brooklyn and Queens.

Consolidation brought tunnels, too. In 1908 the Joralemon Street Tunnel became the first under the East River, carrying subway cars from the southern tip of Manhattan to Brooklyn Heights, the nation's first suburb. That same year, the Uptown and Downtown Hudson Tubes began carrying people by subway under the Hudson River between lower Manhattan and Jersey City, New Jersey. The Steinway Tunnel began shuttling New Yorkers from Long Island City, Queens, under

Toll Plaza at the Throgs Neck Bridge that links the Bronx and Queens over the East River. CREDIT: COURTESY OF MTA BRIDGES AND TUNNELS SPECIAL ARCHIVE

Bridges and Tunnels

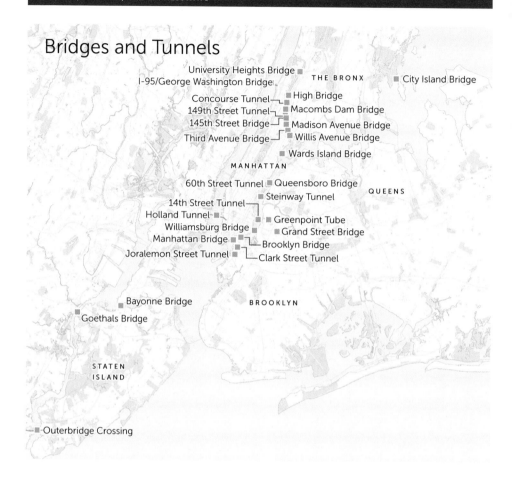

University Heights Bridge
I-95/George Washington Bridge
THE BRONX
City Island Bridge
Concourse Tunnel — High Bridge
149th Street Tunnel — Macombs Dam Bridge
145th Street Bridge — Madison Avenue Bridge
Third Avenue Bridge — Willis Avenue Bridge
Wards Island Bridge
MANHATTAN
60th Street Tunnel — Queensboro Bridge
QUEENS
Steinway Tunnel
14th Street Tunnel
Holland Tunnel
Williamsburg Bridge — Greenpoint Tube
Manhattan Bridge — Grand Street Bridge
Brooklyn Bridge
Joralemon Street Tunnel — Clark Street Tunnel
Bayonne Bridge
BROOKLYN
Goethals Bridge
STATEN
ISLAND
Outerbridge Crossing

the East River to Manhattan in 1915, and the Clark Street Tunnel to Brooklyn Heights followed suit in 1919. Scores of New Yorkers moved to the burgeoning neighborhoods surrounding these new transit links along the East and Hudson Rivers in Brooklyn, Queens, and Jersey City, New Jersey. They included workers, mostly immigrants, commuting to work in Manhattan, as well as the city's wealthiest residents, many of whom preferred new suburbs, like the Bronx's Fieldston, Forest Hills in Queens, and Brooklyn's Flatbush, over living in crowded Manhattan.

While the city's early era of bridge and tunnel construction largely facilitated the transport of people by foot and mass transit to and from Manhattan, some remarkable early projects integrated car travel into the metropolis. The fifty-cent Holland Tunnel between lower Manhattan and Jersey City opened to great fanfare in 1927—the world's first continuous underwater tunnel designed for cars. A year later, three bridges—the Goethals, Outerbridge, and Bayonne— opened within three years that linked Staten Island's western shore not to the rest of the city of which it had been a part for nearly

Expressways

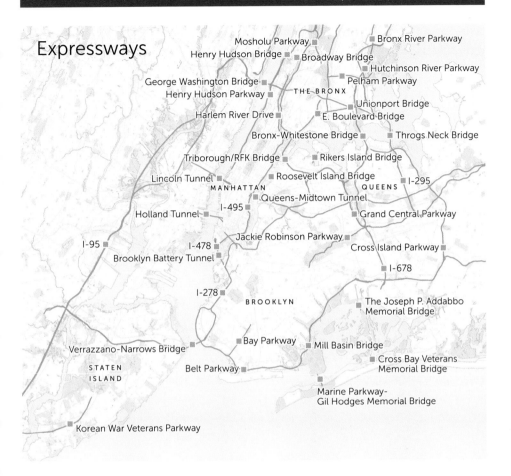

Mosholu Parkway
Bronx River Parkway
Henry Hudson Bridge
Broadway Bridge
Hutchinson River Parkway
George Washington Bridge
Pelham Parkway
Henry Hudson Parkway
THE BRONX
Unionport Bridge
Harlem River Drive
E. Boulevard Bridge
Bronx-Whitestone Bridge
Throgs Neck Bridge
Triborough/RFK Bridge
Rikers Island Bridge
Lincoln Tunnel
Roosevelt Island Bridge
I-295
MANHATTAN
QUEENS
Queens-Midtown Tunnel
Holland Tunnel
I-495
Grand Central Parkway
Jackie Robinson Parkway
I-95
I-478
Cross Island Parkway
Brooklyn Battery Tunnel
I-678
I-278
BROOKLYN
The Joseph P. Addabbo
Memorial Bridge
Bay Parkway
Mill Basin Bridge
Verrazzano-Narrows Bridge
Cross Bay Veterans
STATEN
Belt Parkway
Memorial Bridge
ISLAND
Marine Parkway-
Gil Hodges Memorial Bridge
Korean War Veterans Parkway

thirty years and had no physical connection to, but to Bayonne, Elizabeth, and Perth Amboy, New Jersey, by car. When the "great gray" George Washington Bridge opened in 1931, it carried four lanes of traffic over the Hudson River from upper Manhattan to Fort Lee, New Jersey, with room to expand to eight lanes—laying the foundation for its current status as the most heavily traveled automobile bridge in the world. All of these early projects linked parts of New York City with New Jersey, but even the Queensboro Bridge included four car lanes when it opened a generation earlier in 1909.

If this era of bridge and tunnel construction knitted the five boroughs and parts of New Jersey together for people to get around primarily (but not exclusively) by foot, trolley, and subway, when planner Robert Moses rose to power in the 1920s and 1930s, he wove New York City into much of the rest of suburban and semi-rural New York, New Jersey, and Connecticut by car. He spent the Bridge and Tunnel Authority's money to build new roads that would carry people in and out of the city rather than on maintaining and expanding the mass transit that got most New Yorkers from point A to point B across the boroughs. Overwhelmingly, perhaps exclusively, bridge and tunnel construction under Moses's leadership facilitated car travel rather than walking or mass transit. And over more than thirty years, Moses linked his new toll bridges and tunnels, which included the Alexander Hamilton, Bronx-Whitestone, Cross Bay, Gil Hodges Memorial, Henry Hudson Memorial, Triborough, Throgs Neck, and Verrazzano Bridges and the Hugh L. Carey (previously Battery) Tunnel, to a giant network of highways, expressways, and parkways that he snaked through the city to Long Island and Westchester County (see map).

This new auto-transit network first laid the plan for and then propped up a regional landscape fundamentally shaped by racial and economic segregation. To begin, the new network of bridges, tunnels, and roadways thrust people with cars and the money for tolls out of the city to new, affordable, spacious suburbs, most of which, like the famous Levittown development on Long Island, barred Black people and other people of color from owning homes there through restrictive covenants. Indeed, beginning in late 1940s and 1950s and well into the 1970s, the new expressways transported waves of white New Yorkers and those with relative means who wanted to flee the city and its new public housing developments, its rapidly declining mass transit, its racial animosities, and its rising crime, to the region's new suburbs—and they took their tax revenues with them. They included some of the wealthiest New Yorkers, who fled Manhattan for Westchester county, Connecticut's

gold coast, and Long Island's north shore, as well as members of the city's middle and working classes, who left Brooklyn and Queens for Long Island, Staten Island, and suburban New Jersey.

In the pre–Robert Moses era, New York's elite lived in close proximity, in relative terms, to the groups and circumstances they largely defined themselves against—Black people and other people of color (including to some extent Jews, Italians, and those groups racialized as nonwhite), immigrants, and poverty. But Moses's expressways, alongside the expanded commuter rail system, could catapult them and the middle classes to places as physically distant from the city as they could reasonably commute, where the city and its discontents could stay literally out of sight and out of mind. One way in which Moses helped to realize this vision of the suburbs as exclusively white was by protecting Jones Beach on Long Island from city dwellers by ensuring that some of the roads leading to this beloved beach would have overpasses that blocked the heights of city buses.

The Moses-era bridges, tunnels, and expressways took people, money, goods, and services to the suburbs of Westchester, Long Island, New Jersey, and Connecticut. But for those who remained in the five boroughs by choice or circumstance during this era of mass suburbanization, Moses's expressways also increased social segregation within the city. They physically isolated communities like Red Hook, cut off from the rest of Brooklyn by the Brooklyn-Queens Expressway, and Hunts Point, blocked from the rest of the Bronx by the Bruckner Expressway. This physical isolation continues to contribute to school segregation, limited job access, environmental racism, disparate policing, and poor health outcomes in these communities. The Staten Island Expressway similarly divides the island's North and South Shores, a boundary that has been at times compared to the Mason-Dixon line. Its construction prompted massive investment in the Mid-Island and South Shore. Coupled with the redlining of much of the North Shore, including Tompkinsville, Stapleton, Clifton, and Port Richmond, and the strategic placement of public housing in those very same places, the expressway continues to constitute a de facto boundary between the island's largest concentrations of Black, Latina/o/x, immigrant, and low-income residents on its North Shore and its majority-white, middle-class, and affluent South Shore (see **Staten Island** introduction, p. 300).

Today, the city's bridges, tunnels, and expressways are some of the most traveled in the world. Despite being home to the busiest mass transit system in the Western Hemisphere, the city has the second most congested traffic in the world, surpassed only by Los Angeles. Gentrification and the widespread relative affordability of cars have pushed many New Yorkers to drive for daily commutes. Car travel is often the only reliable and timely means of transport between affordable neighborhoods, which largely lie in places without subway stations in the outer boroughs and in parts of Long Island and New Jersey. This trend that has been amplified by the COVID-19 pandemic with more New Yorkers buying cars and moving to suburban communities. Almost half (45 percent) of New Yorkers own cars and about one-quarter commute by car, but the percentage is much higher in Queens and Staten Island.

5

Staten Island

Staten Island

Amazon Warehouse ■

Willowbrook State School ■

Freshkills Park ■

Sandy Ground ■

Spanish Camp ■

■ Lenape Burial Ridge/Conference House Park

1 Mile

Staten Island Ferry

Tompkinsville Park

Stapleton Carnegie Library

Stapleton Union American
Methodist Episcopal Church

Verrazzano Bridge

N

Introduction

IN 1993, STATEN ISLANDERS VOTED two-to-one to secede from New York City. The secession movement was the culmination of decades of tensions between Staten Island and the rest of the city. Ultimately nothing came of the vote, as it required approval of the Democrat-controlled State Assembly to move forward. But the movement brought into focus the island's peculiar sort of existence as a "suburb trapped in a global city," as political scientists Daniel Kramer and Richard Flanagan describe it. The island tends toward suburban politics and sensibilities while being subject to city policies and politics. Its relationship with the rest of New York City is fraught in other ways as well, having been the city's literal dumping ground for much of its history, playing host to quarantine hospitals in the middle of the nineteenth century and, for the second half of the twentieth, the largest garbage landfill in the world (see **Freshkills Park**, p. 314).

Staten Island is often misrepresented as uniformly suburban, but tensions between the older urban industrial core on the island's North Shore and the newer suburban communities radiating outward toward the southern and western shores in fact belie this characterization. At the same time, changing immigration patterns make the island a far more dynamic corner of a global city than its popular portrayals as a homogenous, conservative outpost suggest.

Staten Island is the borough most geographically distant from the rest, closer to New Jersey than to New York. There remain only two means of transport from the island to the rest of the city: the Staten Island Ferry, which crosses the New York Bay between the St. George Terminal on the northern shore of the island and the Whitehall Terminal on the southern tip of Manhattan; and the Verrazzano Bridge, which connects Staten Island to Brooklyn by car. Staten Island is the only borough that is not connected to the city's subway system.

Travel to New Jersey, however, is much easier. Three bridges—the Outerbridge Crossing, the Goethals Bridge, and the Bayonne Bridge—connect the island to Perth Amboy, Elizabeth, and Bayonne, New Jersey. All three were constructed in the 1920s to facilitate travel to New Jersey more than thirty years before the Verrazzano Bridge linked Staten Island to the rest of New York City (Brooklyn) by car in 1964. As a result, the island is in many ways culturally and politically closer to New Jersey than to the rest of New York City.

Relative cultural, material, and geographic isolation from the rest of the city helped fuel Staten Island's drive toward political secession. Often dubbed "the forgotten borough" by residents and outsiders alike, it is the whitest, most suburban, and most politically conservative borough. Indeed, at 63 percent of the population, Staten Island is the only borough with a non-Hispanic white majority. Staten Islanders have the highest median income, homeownership rates, and car ownership rates in New York City. Close to 70 percent of Staten Islanders own their own homes, compared to about 30 percent citywide, and Staten Island's car ownership rate is 82 percent—nearly double the citywide rate.

Despite these features that make Staten Island relatively unique, dynamics that are present in the rest of the city are at work here as well. The island is segregated. Its northern shore, bordering the Staten Island Ferry terminal, contains the oldest and densest neighborhoods, and is home to the largest concentrations of people of color on the island. The Mid-Island and South Shore, on the other hand, are primarily suburban, and remain the whitest, wealthiest parts of the island. But while Staten Island houses the fewest immigrants of all the boroughs—only 21 percent of its residents are foreign born—it has seen the largest recent growth in the immigrant population in the city. The foreign-born population on the island increased by more than 35 percent in the decade between 2000 and 2010. Over a third of the foreign-born population is European, primarily Italian, Russian, and Polish. Another third is Asian, primarily Indian, Pakistani, Chinese, Taiwanese, Korean, and Filipino. The final third is Latina/o/x, primarily Mexican. Notably, new immigrants live all over the island, with 27 percent on the North Shore, 28 percent in the Mid-Island, and 16 percent on the South Shore, with European immigrants concentrated on the South Shore and those from Latin America on the North Shore. Like the rest of the boroughs, Staten Island is ever-evolving.

Long before Staten Island became part of New York, it was occupied by three tribes of the Lenape Nation: the Raritans, Hackensacks, and Tappans. Staten Island may be the borough with the greatest number of Lenape archeological sites (see **Lenape Burial Ridge/Conference House Park**, p. 320). The first known European contact with the island was by the Italian explorer Giovanni da Verrazzano, for whom the Verrazzano Bridge is named. The Dutch tried to colonize the island multiple times upon their conquest of present-day New York City, but the Lenape drove the settlers off the island over the course of three Dutch-instigated wars between 1641 and 1655. Dutch settlement was not successful until 1661, more than thirty-five years after the Dutch established Fort Amsterdam in Manhattan (see **National Museum of the American Indian [Fort Amsterdam]**, p. 170).

Dutch, Walloon, and French Huguenots established the first permanent colonial settlement on Staten Island near present-day Old Town on the island's eastern shore, followed in 1820 by twenty free Black people that established what would become the oldest community of formerly enslaved Black people in North America, on the opposite side of the island (see **Sandy Ground**, p. 316). Abundant shellfish, particularly oysters, sustained the Lenape, and later provided the foundation for the island's economy. Most of Staten Island's oldest communities lie along its eastern waterfront, where sail charters and then private ferry services in the nineteenth century connected the island's successful commercial centers like Stapleton with Manhattan. Until 1964, residential and commercial development on the island was limited primarily to the old waterfront neighborhoods on the northern and eastern shores served by ferry and the Staten Island Railway and, after 1930, on the western shore near the bridges to New Jersey.

Shell fishery and oyster cultivation were the island's major industries until Proctor and Gamble opened its East Coast manufacturing and distribution center at Port Ivory in 1907. The North Shore of Staten Island quickly became a manufacturing center, due to its strategic location on the Kill Van Kull, a shipping channel that provides the primary access for container ships to the Port Newark-Elizabeth Marine Terminal, the busiest port in the eastern United States. Local factories produced soap, steel, commercial foods, chemicals, paint, metal, textiles, tools, and building materials. Many of these factories have since closed, but the North Shore is still the city's busiest working waterfront, with marine and container terminals, including the Howland Hook Marine Terminal, docks, and shipyards. While health care and retail have become two of Staten Island's largest industries, one in three residents commutes to Manhattan for work.

The construction of the Verrazzano Bridge and Staten Island Expressway in 1964 singularly transformed Staten Island into the largely suburban, socially segregated patchwork of communities it remains today (see **Verrazzano-Narrows Bridge** p. 310). As the new bridge and expressway facilitated car travel, previously undeveloped parts of the island between its hamlets, particularly on central and southern parts of the island, devel-

oped quickly into new suburban tracts. Residential construction on the island boomed just as a housing crisis in Brooklyn, right across the Verrazzano, reached a boiling point.

Brooklynites, particularly Italian Americans, migrated to Staten Island en masse, especially from neighborhoods bordering the Brooklyn side of the Verrazzano like Bay Ridge and Bensonhurst. While the rest of New York City's population declined precipitously during the fiscal crisis of the 1970s, Staten Island's population boomed. Between 1960 and 1980, the population increased by 60 percent. Staten Island still has the largest per capita population of Italian Americans of any American county.

But with the development of central and southern parts of Staten Island came disinvestment from the North Shore, including Tompkinsville, Stapleton, Clifton, and Port Richmond. Much of the northern and eastern shores of the island had already been redlined in the postwar period because of their age, density, and relative diversity. Meanwhile, the city strategically placed new public housing developments in these very same places. At the same time, the opening of the Staten Island Mall on the mid-island in 1973 put local businesses along shopping corridors like Port Richmond Avenue out of business. Property values fell and long-time residents moved away.

Today, the island's North Shore communities remain the most impoverished on the island. The Stapleton Houses, once home to several members of the famed hip-hop collective the Wu-Tang Clan, make up the largest public housing development on the island. Other public and low-income housing complexes are concentrated nearby. Crime was notoriously high in the 1980s around these communities, and the area became a hotbed of "quality of life' policing efforts in the decades that followed (see **Tompkinsville Park**, p. 306). The North Shore also faces staggering levels of environmental toxicity, playing host to at least twenty-one EPA-identified contaminated sites over 5.2 square miles, all of which are within seventy feet of homes and apartment buildings.

Contending with these challenges are some of the island's largest immigrant groups, including Mexicans, Liberians, and Sri Lankans. Park Hill/Clifton is home to the largest Liberian community outside of Liberia in the world. Ruth Perry, the first female president of Liberia and of any contemporary African nation, lived in Clifton before returning to Liberia to serve as its leader in the mid-1990s. Neighboring Tompkinsville is home to one of the largest Sri Lankan communities outside of Sri Lanka in the world, as well as a growing Mexican community. Sri Lankan businesses dot Victory Boulevard, including several famed Sri Lankan restaurants.

While Staten Island is ever-changing, its voters remain more conservative relative to the rest of the city. It is a Republican base in citywide elections; two of its three City Council representatives are Republican. In 2016 and 2020 it was the only New York City borough in which the majority of residents voted for Donald Trump (57 percent both years), and Trump carried Staten Island by more than 15 percent—the largest margin since the 1988 election of George H. W. Bush. In fact, Staten

Islanders have voted for a Republican for president in four of the past ten national elections. But the island is far from a Republican stronghold. The majority of registered voters in Staten Island are, in fact, Democrats: 45 percent, compared to 29 percent Republicans, and 20 percent Independents. Nationally, it is considered a "swing" county.

But Staten Islanders across the political spectrum do tend to unite over their "forgotten" status, which puts them at underdog odds against the larger city that, to their mind, time and again acts upon them without consultation. In turn, Staten Islanders on the whole have a long history of resistance to New York City and the state. The fierce resistance of Staten Islanders has manifested in other Not In My Back Yard (NIMBY) movements, for example. Residents have famously resisted "overdevelopment," including stopping planner Robert Moses's attempts to build highways across the island and succeeding in blocking the construction of one of the largest planned communities in the world on the South Shore in the 1970s. Somewhat paradoxically, the legacy of these protests has been increased traffic and haphazard, unplanned, chaotic real estate development all over the island. (*Quotes are from Kramer and Flanagan's* Staten Island.)

TO LEARN MORE

Kramer, Daniel C, and Richard M Flanagan. *Staten Island: Conservative Bastion in a Liberal City*. Lanham, Md.: University Press of America, 2012.

■ ■ ■

St. George

5.1 Staten Island Ferry

1 Bay Street, Staten Island, NY

There are two means of transport from Staten Island to the rest of New York City: the Verrazzano Bridge, which requires a car and a toll, and the Staten Island ferry. The free ferry connects commuters from Whitehall Terminal near Battery Park at the south end of Manhattan—a newly renovated, major transit hub—to St. George at the northeastern end of Staten Island. It is part of the city's vast public transportation network. The ferry carries about seventy thousand passengers a day a five-mile distance every thirty minutes, twenty-four hours a day. It is also popular with tourists, as the ride offers some of the best views of the New York harbor, Statue of Liberty, and Ellis Island. Edna St. Vincent Millay's 1922 poem about the ferry, "Recuerdo," captures some of the romance that ferry travel continues to hold for visitor and native alike in the city: 'We were very tired, we were very merry—/ We had gone back and forth all night on the ferry." But for most Staten Islanders, their commuter travails are anything but romantic.

Early transport from Staten Island to Manhattan was in the form of sail charters, followed by steamboats. Staten Island's northern shore was dotted with piers that docked competing private ferry services. One of these private ferry services, owned by Daniel D. Tompkins of the Richmond Turnpike Company, would eventually become what is now the Staten Island ferry.

It changed ownership several times during the late nineteenth century until two accidents that caused hundreds of deaths and injuries propelled the City of New York to take over ferry service from Staten Island to Manhattan in 1905, commissioning five new ferries. The fleet now includes nine.

But the city never linked the vast subway system that connected the other four boroughs with Staten Island. An attempt was made in 1912, when one of the then-private operators of the New York City subways dug 150 feet of the beginnings of a tunnel from Brooklyn to Staten Island before funding stalled. The mayor, governor, Port Authority, and the city's Transit Commission all opposed the project, and it halted in 1925, although the tunnel still remains under Owl's Head Park in Bay Ridge, Brooklyn.

So while the subway system grew throughout the other four boroughs in the early decades of the twentieth century, Staten Islanders could rely only on ferry services like this one and others that connected the island with New Jersey to the west. The railway that ran the whole of the island did not link to other parts of the city or region (now the Staten Island Railway). The opening of the Verrazzano Bridge and Staten Island Expressway in 1964 made driving the preferred mode of travel on the island. Lack of integrated public transit on Staten Island has made it one of the most traffic-congested parts of the country, and Staten Islanders have some of the longest commutes in the nation.

Ferry service is free—a result of agitation on the part of Staten Islanders, who are the

Staten Island Ferry, 2017. CREDIT: SCOTT DEXTER

wealthiest of New York City residents on average. The ferry's fare was initially twenty-five cents in 1817, but by 1897 and the city's takeover in 1905, the fare was five cents. It was not raised until 1972, when it cost ten cents before being raised to twenty-five cents in 1975 during the city's fiscal crisis and again to fifty cents in 1990. The fare hikes contributed to a growing sentiment on the part of Staten Islanders that they received disproportionately fewer public services but contributed more to the city's coffers. Rudy Giuliani ran his 1993 mayoral campaign partly on making the Staten Island Ferry free and delivered on his promise in 1997.

TO LEARN MORE

Ballon, Hilary, and Kenneth T. Jackson. *Robert Moses and the Modern City: The Transformation of New York*. New York: W. W. Norton & Co., 2007.

Staten Island Ferry, https://www.siferry.com/.

NEARBY SITES OF INTEREST

Former site of New York Marine Hospital ("Quarantine")

Along St. Mark's Place, Staten Island, NY

More than a hundred years before Ellis Island was established, officials inspected immigrants on board their ships and sent anyone with contagious diseases to a twenty-building compound referred to as "Quarantine" just south of what is now St. George's terminal. When New York State proposed expanding the quarantine station in 1858 as immigration to the city increased, Staten Island residents burned it to the ground in what would come to be known as the "Quarantine War."

Staten Island Museum

75 Stuyvesant Place, Staten Island, NY

New York City's only general interest museum. Exhibits focus on connections between natural science, art, and history.

FAVORITE NEIGHBORHOOD
RESTAURANT

New Asha

322 Victory Boulevard, Staten Island, NY

One of a number of affordable and delicious Sri Lankan spots in Tompkinsville and St. George.

Tompkinsville

5.2 Tompkinsville Park

45 Victory Boulevard, Staten Island, NY

Staten Island has often represented a refuge from "city problems" for its mostly white and middle-class residents. Over the last several decades, however, it has also served as a refuge for a growing number of poor nonwhite residents who are also seeking out safer and lower-cost spaces from other parts of the city. This latter population has centered mostly around the North Shore of Staten Island, encompassed by the 120th Precinct. The Tompkinsville section includes large public housing developments, older single-family homes, and a central business district with small three-story buildings with shops, clustered around Tompkinsville Park.

In recent years, Tompkinsville Park has been a center of disorder for some within the community. Large numbers of people socialize there, including some who are intoxicated or using drugs, giving it the local nickname of "Needle Park." Within and near the park people are able to buy alcohol and drugs often in the proximity of local businesses. At the same time, Tompkinsville is currently experiencing redevelopment pressure. Across the street from the park is a new high-rise residential development called "The Pointe at St. George," where two-bedroom apartments cost $500,000.

Local residents report that with the new development has come increasingly intensive policing focused on the low-level disorder in the park. Arrests and harassment have become more common in keeping with the NYPD's emphasis on using the "broken windows" theory to frame this low-level policing as part of a strategy of fighting serious crime.

The "broken windows" theory was developed in 1982 but didn't become popular until it was embraced by urban conservatives such as the Manhattan Institute, which encouraged then mayoral candidate Rudolph Giuliani to make it a central feature of his first campaign. The theory claims that if police aggressively enforce minor disorderly behavior, this will create a climate of lawfulness that will translate into lower serious crime rates and improved neighborhood vitality. In practice, however, it is often used as a justification for displacing poor people from public spaces in the interest of improving commercial and real estate values.

On July 17, 2014, a squad of NYPD plainclothes and uniformed officers was engaged in such enforcement. They had been told to crack down on a variety of disorderly behaviors including the sale of loose cigarettes by local street vendor Eric Garner. Officers approached Garner, whom they had arrested and ticketed numerous times before, and attempted to place him under arrest. Garner expressed his deep frustration at being the target of constant police harassment and refused to cooperate, saying,

"Every time you see me, you want to mess with me. I'm tired of it. It stops today. Why would you . . . ? Everyone standing here will tell you I didn't do nothing. I did not sell nothing. Because every time you see me, you want to harass me. You want to stop me [garbled] selling cigarettes. I'm minding my business, officer, I'm minding my business. Please just leave me alone. I told you the last time, please just leave me alone."

While saying this he placed his hands in the air and refused to submit to being handcuffed. In response Officer Daniel Pantaleo grabbed him around the neck and shoulder and pulled him to the ground to place him under arrest. While on the ground, officer Pantaleo continued to have Garner in a choke hold, while several other officers piled on top of him. During this scrum, Garner repeatedly said, "I can't breathe," in a raspy voice. Despite his pleas, officers continued to remain on top of him until he stopped breathing. After a delay, officers called an ambulance, but the EMTs failed to take immediate life-saving action. Garner was eventually transported to the hospital where he was pronounced dead on arrival.

The entire interaction was caught on video by local resident Ramsey Orta, who released it to the media creating a firestorm of protest as part of the emerging Black Lives Matter movement. A major march led by family members of those killed by police, the Reverend Al Sharpton, and community and union leaders took place on August 23rd, 2014, and started in Tompkinsville Park. Garner's daughter, Erica Garner, became a leading voice for police account-

ability calling for major reforms in police training and use-of-force policies, as well as accountability for the officers involved. She died of a heart attack at the end of 2017. Daniel Pantaleo was fired from the NYPD and stripped of his pension due to his use of the chokehold, and his sergeant supervisor was required to rescind vacation days to avoid a public tribunal.

Meanwhile, Eric Garner's dying words, repeated scores of times by other Black men killed by the police in subsequent years, were once again echoed by George Floyd in Minneapolis in 2020 as he too was killed by police following a minor infraction. This time, the Black Lives Matter movement spread globally, and among other reforms won so far by this movement was the banning of choke holds, one part of a set of NYPD accountability measures enacted in 2020.

—*Alex Vitale*

TO LEARN MORE

Vitale, Alex S. *City of Disorder: How the Quality of Life Campaign Transformed New York Politics.* New York: NYU Press, 2008.

Vitale, Alex S. *The End of Policing.* New York: Verso, 2018.

Stapleton

5.3 Stapleton Carnegie Library

132 Canal Street, Staten Island, NY

The Stapleton Library, opened in 1907, is one of the sixty-seven original Carnegie libraries that form part of the New York City Public Library System (NYPL), which includes branches in Manhattan, Bronx, and Staten

Stapleton Carnegie Library, 2017. CREDIT: SCOTT DEXTER

Island. Brooklyn (BPL) and Queens (QPL) have separate library systems developed before New York City incorporated these boroughs in 1898. While the central library of the NYPL (476 5th Avenue in Manhattan) was not completed until 1911, many of the branch libraries, including Stapleton, were opened years before.

Carnegie libraries are architecturally distinguished, many of them designed by the most prominent architecture firms of the turn of the last century, including McKim, Mead & White, as well as Carrère & Hastings, who were known for their Beaux-Arts style and who were the designers of this branch. Carnegie libraries boast tall ceilings and large, often arched windows, allowing for ample natural light in their interiors. They often include grand wooden staircases and large solid wooden desks for study.

Before the development of NYPL, a multitude of private institutions made up the public library system. Among the most important were the Free Circulating Libraries, which included a number of branches, plus the singular branches of the Astor Library and the Lenox Library. In 1886, former governor Samuel J. Tilden bequeathed $2.4 million to the establishment of a public library system for New York City, but unfortunately, after a lengthy court battle between Tilden's heirs, only about $400,000 of this money went to the library system. Meanwhile, the Astor and Lenox libraries were having financial difficulties. The trustee in charge of Tilden's funds devised a plan to merge these organizations into a new entity, the New York Public Library (1895). Its first proposals entertained the creation of the greatest reference and research library in the world. But it soon became clear that a truly public library needed to give access to a wide range of citizens, not only scholars. Amid this debate over the nature of "public," in 1901 steel magnate Andrew Carnegie, one of the world's richest men, offered the NYPL $5.2 million to build a branch library system, the equivalent of around $160 million today. In exchange, the City of New York would have to agree to allocate taxpayer money to maintain and expand the collections of the branch libraries, thereby securing public support of a public library system in perpetuity. Carnegie's incentivizing of the construction essentially forced a merger between the Free Circulating Libraries already in existence with the newly created circulation department of the NYPL. Today, its operating budget is over $150 million, including the separate Brooklyn and Queens systems. (New York City was not the only beneficiary of Carnegie libraries. He was responsible for creating over 1600 libraries across the country.)

Carnegie libraries are costly to maintain, to have the required refurbishment for new technologies, and to be accessible to the disabled. This branch recently added a more modern wing and renovated its interiors. One of the unique characteristics of the Stapleton Library is its neighborhood oral history project, "Stapleton Speaks," which documents Stapleton history through interviews with residents; it is available online and in the library.

TO LEARN MORE

Glynn, Tom. *Reading Publics: New York City's Public Libraries, 1754–1911.* New York: Empire State Editions, 2015. http://site.ebrary.com/id/10987127.

The New York Public Library, https://www.nypl.org/.

NEARBY SITES OF INTEREST

Tappan Park
Bay Street between Canal and Water Streets, Staten Island, NY
Among the oldest parks on Staten Island, former center of village of Edgewater.

Waterfront Park
455 Front Street, Staten Island, NY
Newly redeveloped waterfront esplanade replacing old navy facilities.

5.4 Stapleton Union American Methodist Episcopal Church

49 Tompkins Avenue, Staten Island, NY

Founded in 1801, the Stapleton Union American Methodist Episcopal Church (AME) is the oldest African American church on Staten Island and one of four Black congregations on the island established before 1900. The church received membership in the Union Church of Africans Conference in 1838 under the leadership of Reverend Isaac Barney, who is buried at the Stapleton Union AME church. The church survived the draft riots of 1863 (see **Colored Orphan's Asylum/ Draft Riots**, p. 107), though some members' homes did not, and it lived on through three buildings at the same location.

Inside the Stapleton Union American Methodist Episcopal Church, 2017. CREDIT: SCOTT DEXTER

The Stapleton Union AME church still has a very active congregation that operates a food pantry and a soup kitchen that provides more than fourteen thousand meals a year. The Union AME church is an anchor within the larger Stapleton community, a majority Black and increasingly Latina/o/x neighborhood that houses the largest public housing project on Staten Island (Stapleton Houses). The neighborhood has struggled in recent decades to attract investment, and Stapleton Union AME represents the longevity of Black communities on Staten Island.

NEARBY SITES OF INTEREST

Audre Lorde Residence

207 St. Paul's Avenue, Staten Island, NY
From 1972 to 1987, Black lesbian, writer, feminist, and professor Audre Lorde lived here with her family. The corner of St. Paul's and Victory Boulevard is now called "Audre Lorde Way."

Sri Lankan Arts & Cultural Museum NY

61 Canal Street, Staten Island, NY
The world's first museum dedicated to Sri Lankan arts and culture outside of Sri Lanka, the museum was founded in 2017 by Julia Wijesinghe, the daughter of Sri Lankan immigrants to Staten Island, when she was eighteen years old.

Alice Austen House/Museum

2 Hylan Boulevard, Staten Island, NY
Alice Austen was one of the earliest female photographers in the United States. Breaking away from Victorian tradition she was fiercely independent, extraordinarily prolific, and the first woman on Staten Island to drive a car. She shared this home with her lifelong partner Gertrude Tate.

Park Hill Market

160–180 Park Hill Avenue, Staten Island, NY
Vendors sell traditional foods and goods in this summertime open-air market in the heart of "Little Liberia."

The Verrazzano-Narrows Bridge with Brooklyn in the distance, 1964. CREDIT: COURTESY OF MTA BRIDGES AND TUNNELS SPECIAL ARCHIVE

5.5 Verrazzano-Narrows Bridge

At a span of 4,260 feet, the Verrazzano-Narrows Bridge that connects Staten Island to Brooklyn remains the longest suspension bridge in the Americas. It serves as a gateway to the New York harbor and ports of New York and New Jersey. Two decks each carry six lanes of traffic over the Narrows of New York Bay. Around 200,000 vehicles cross the Verrazzano every day—the only connection by car from Staten Island to the rest of the city—at a cost ranging from five-dollars-and-fifty cents for Staten Island residents to seventeen dollars for travelers without a New York E-ZPass. The bridge generates about $1 million a day in revenue.

First conceived of in the 1920s but finally constructed in the early 1960s and opened in 1964, the naming of the bridge became one site in the broader struggle over the position of Italian Americans in New York's racial and ethnic order. In 1959, the Italian Historical Society of America proposed to then-governor Nelson Rockefeller that the bridge be named after Giovanni Da Verrazzano, whom they argued was the first European to enter New York harbor in 1524. A Newark man had suggested naming the bridge connecting Manhattan to Fort Lee, New Jersey, after Verrazzano thirty years before, but conventional wisdom at the time taught that it had been the British Henry Hudson who entered the harbor "first" in 1609, not Verrazzano nearly a century earlier, and the bridge was named for George Washington.

The Staten Island Chamber of Commerce expressed their strong opposition to naming the bridge after Verrazzano, advocating instead for the "Staten Island Bridge." The Italian Historical Society of America called Verrazzano the "first white man to explore the area"—a statement indicative of the wider appeals of Italian Americans to be included in America's broad and ever-changing "white" racial category. But the Staten Island chamber of commerce called Verrazzano "a foreigner who made a navigational mistake." They questioned the general agreement of historians that Verrazzano probably was the first European to enter New York harbor: "There is doubt that Verrazzano ever sailed up New York harbor." They claimed that the name Verrazzano was too difficult to pronounce or spell, and "few people have ever heard of it." And in a 1959 letter to Governor Rockefeller, the chamber reminded him that the majority of the people on the island usually, but not always, voted Republican.

But, ultimately, the Italian Historical Society of America (IHSA) successfully lobbied Rockefeller to name the bridge after Verrazzano. At a 1959 meeting, IHSA member Dr. Salvatore Rosolia said, "They want to name it the Staten Island Bridge, Harbor Bridge, Liberty Gate, Brooklyn-Richmond Bridge, Pauw Bridge, and the Heart Break Bridge, or Rice Pudding Bridge—but not Verrazzano. I have nothing against these names. I'm fighting one point—the way they're fighting the name Verrazzano." Even after the IHSA won the bridge-naming battle, the press still often referred to the bridge as the more generic "Narrows Bridge." And pre-Verrazzano Staten Islanders began to call the bridge the "guinea gangplank," a bigoted reference to the large numbers of working-class Italian Americans who moved from Brooklyn to Staten Island in the decades following the bridge's opening. Staten Island continues to have the largest population of Italian Americans, per capita, in the United States.

TO LEARN MORE

Kramer, Daniel C., and Richard M. Flanagan. *Staten Island: Conservative Bastion in a Liberal City.* Lanham, MD.: University Press of America, 2012.
Talese, Gay, Bruce Davidson, and Lili Rethi. *The Bridge.* New York: Harper & Row, 1964.

Bulls Head

5.6 Willowbrook State School

2800 Victory Boulevard, Staten Island, NY

The successful struggle against deplorable conditions at the Willowbrook State Developmental Center during the 1970s was a major catalyst in the movement for disability rights. Legal actions taken in the wake of public exposure and parental lawsuits grew into multiple rulings that extended the rights of people with disabilities. The nationwide practice of "deinstitutionalization" of the mentally disabled, and the shift toward outpatient systems, including group homes and halfway houses, stems from these rulings.

Willowbrook opened in the 1940s as a home that was intended to serve mentally disabled children. The sprawling, steepled red-brick institution consisted of an imposing cross-shaped building that rose six stories, set in green, manicured grounds. By the 1960s, its patient population was six thousand, two thousand people higher than its maximum capacity. The young residents were malnourished, overcrowded, living in filth with little regular care or habilitation. Some were shackled to beds or kept in solitary confinement for long periods. New York senator Robert Kennedy visited the center in 1965 and described conditions there as a "snake pit." Doctors at the facility described it as a "warehouse" for the mentally disabled. But despite the attention and some briefly maintained changes, conditions at Willowbrook continued to be inhumane.

Willowbrook State School, now part of CUNY College of Staten Island, 2017. CREDIT: SCOTT DEXTER

In addition to this attention from politicians, the problems of large scale institutionalization of the mentally ill and disabled had been raised by some scholars and artists, such as Erving Goffman in his classic *Asylums*, published in 1961, and Ken Kesey's novel *One Flew Over the Cuckoo's Nest* (1961), which had been adapted for Broadway as well. The rights-based and freedom-oriented movements of the 1960s further raised consciousness about the oppressive nature of total institutions. It was in this climate that a 1972 investigative report aired on ABC news graphically depicting the miserable lives of the Willowbrook residents, which finally generated sufficient attention for meaningful change. The parents of the patients filed a class action lawsuit arguing that the center had violated the constitutional rights of their children. The media sustained its attention on the school. A consent decree issued as a result of the lawsuits mandated a higher quality of care, specifying the many ways in which such care should be improved, including all aspects of health care, privacy, cleanliness, and education. In what was a significant advance against the "warehousing" ideology that such institutions normally upheld, the ruling also specified that the care should prepare their residents for "life in the community at large." These precedents, and the public uproar following the media expose, helped lead to the nation's first federal disability rights laws, including the Developmental Disabilities Assistance and Bill of Rights (1975), and the Civil Rights of Institutionalized Persons Act (1980).

Deinstitutionalized care and the social supports it demands have not received the funding they deserve, and today's crisis in city jails, where thousands of impoverished mentally ill and disabled adults are held, stems in part from the underfunded mandate that the rulings of the 1970s created. But the overall effect of the changes wrought in that time, for both the lives of many of the formerly institutionalized and the public consciousness of the rights of the mentally disabled, has been overwhelmingly positive. Although Willowbrook was not finally closed until 1987, it had only a few hundred patients at the end of its tenure. Today the buildings are part of the campus of the College of Staten Island, CUNY.

TO LEARN MORE

Goode, David. *A History and Sociology of the Willowbrook State School*. American Association on Intellectual and Developmental Disabilities, 2013.

5.7 Amazon Warehouse Walkout

546 Gulf Avenue, Staten Island, NY

The COVID-19 pandemic highlighted the hidden, critical labor of essential workers,

Amazon worker's strike during the coronavirus pandemic over unsafe working conditions at the distribution center on Staten Island, 2020. CREDIT: COURTESY OF MAKE THE ROAD

many of whom work in warehouses, grocery stores, meatpacking, and agriculture. The Staten Island Amazon warehouse is one of the largest urban fulfillment centers in the country, representing a growing industry of low-wage jobs on Staten Island.

On March 30, 2020, over a hundred workers at this Amazon warehouse (named JFK8) walked out because Amazon refused to shut down the facility after learning a worker tested positive for COVID-19. Instead, the company asked the worker to keep the information quiet. Health and safety concerns have been ever present at this three-thousand-worker facility since its opening in September 2018. The walkout follows earlier organizing efforts at the warehouse with support from labor and community groups in New York City.

Chris Smalls, one of the worker leaders of the protest, feared that the virus would spread at this warehouse, unless the company took urgent measures to prevent it. Workers demanded that the warehouse be temporarily closed for disinfecting and pushed to be compensated while the facility was shut down. Amazon fired Smalls almost immediately after the walkout, and despite a massive outpouring of support for Smalls from unions, politicians, and the community at large, he was not reinstated. In May, one of the workers at the JFK8 facility died of COVID-19, lending legitimacy to the claims of so many workers that Amazon was not protecting them adequately. In June of 2020, several legal groups filed a lawsuit against the Amazon Staten Island facility, arguing that the company had put both workers and their families at risk.

The walkout at the Staten Island facility came after similar efforts in Queens in early March 2020 where workers distributed a petition over paid leave and working conditions, including a lack of personal protective equipment. Soon after, Amazon announced that employees diagnosed with COVID-19 or forced to quarantine would receive two weeks of paid leave.

Organizing by workers at Amazon comes at the tail of the efforts by activists, community groups, unions, and progressive politicians in New York City to push back against a deal that included $3 billion in city and state subsidies to help Amazon establish its second national headquarters (HQ2) in Long Island City, Queens. The coalition rightfully argued against corporate welfare for one of the world's largest and wealthiest corporations. While Governor Andrew Cuomo and Mayor Bill DeBlasio expected it to be a done deal, the massive backlash from the community forced Amazon to withdraw its proposal from New York City and move it to Northern Virginia.

TO LEARN MORE

Alimahomed-Wilson, Jake, and Immanuel Ness, eds. *Choke Points: Logistics Workers Disrupting the Global Supply Chain.* London: Pluto Press, 2018.

Arden Heights, Travis, and New Springville

5.8 Freshkills Park

Freshkills Park, Staten Island, NY

Freshkills was once the largest landfill in the world, a dumping ground for 10 million tons of New York City's garbage per year. Built in 1947 as a temporary solution to the stream of waste produced by mid-twentieth-century New York City, Freshkills stayed open until 2001. In that time, the site grew to

Dumping Landfill at Freshkills, 1973. CREDIT: CHESTER HIGGINS, COURTESY OF NATIONAL ARCHIVES, PHOTO NO, 412-DA-5861

Aerial View of Freshkills Park, 2018. CREDIT: ALEX MACLEAN AND NEW YORK CITY PARKS DEPARTMENT

nearly three-and-a-half square miles, roughly three times the size of Central Park. Due to "mounding," the layering process used for a landfill's vertical expansion, Freshkills was also quite tall, with its four mounds rising between 90 and 225 feet. Though the idea that the dump could be seen from the moon was an urban myth, it was undoubtedly a blight of grotesque proportions.

Modern landfills like Freshkills were imagined as efficient and clean solutions to the problem of garbage. City planners viewed the ecologically diverse salt marshes they destroyed as "worthless" land. The layering and maintenance of the fill could provide new land for parks, highways, and commercial infrastructure, it was argued, and Staten Island politicians accepted the landfill assignment in the context of such development being promised for its west side. But Freshkills was never a boon for the community. The stink of the dump hovered over and beyond its borders, spreading stench and its particulates for miles around. Rats and

feral dogs roamed the area. As the air pollution and ash disposal created by incineration in other parts of the city came under greater scrutiny in the 1960s and other landfills reached capacity, Freshkills absorbed more and more of the garbage, until it was taking in millions of tons of garbage each year.

Garbage has always been a flashpoint for power struggles in the city. A century before, pigs had supplemented the underdeveloped sanitation systems of New York City. Efforts of elites to rid the city of free roaming pigs were met with resistance by working-class communities for whom the pigs represented a modicum of food security independent of employment, as well as the only reliable garbage consumers for their neglected neighborhoods. Many poor New Yorkers worked as "ragpickers," scavenging rags for paper, bones for handles, buttons, soap, sugar refinement, and more. By the end of the nineteenth century, the city was incinerating its waste in numerous city plants and individually in apartment buildings, as well as dumping it on Rikers Island and other areas out of the city's center. The city closed its last waste incinerator in 1994. To this day, historically impoverished neighborhoods like the South Bronx, Greenpoint/Williamsburg, Sunset Park, and Red Hook remain the areas of concentrated waste transfer, but all of New York City's garbage is now exported to landfills in New York State, Pennsylvania, Virginia, and South Carolina.

TO LEARN MORE

Ascher, Kate. *The Works: Anatomy of a City.*
  London: Penguin Books, 2007.
McNeur, Catherine. *Taming Manhattan:*
  Environmental Battles in the Antebellum City.
  Cambridge, MA: Harvard University Press, 2014.
Rogers, Heather. *Gone Tomorrow: The Hidden Life*
  of Garbage. New York: New Press, 2006.
Steinberg, Ted. *Gotham Unbound: The Ecological*
  History of Greater New York. Reprint edition.
  New York: Simon & Schuster, 2015.

NEARBY SITE OF INTEREST

Staten Island Mall

2655 Richmond Avenue, Staten Island, NY
Opened in 1973 to serve the burgeoning population of Staten Island, the island's only indoor shopping mall contributed to the commercial decline of the North Shore and is one of the island's largest transit hubs.

Rossville

5.9 Sandy Ground

1538 Woodrow Road, Staten Island, NY
The community of Sandy Ground in southwestern Staten Island's present-day Rossville neighborhood is the oldest community established by free Black people in North America, and the oldest continuously settled free Black community in the United States. Known at other times as Harrisville and Little Africa, a 1963 fire destroyed much of the community, but the Sandy Ground Historical Society, museum, and library works to preserve materials related to the history of the community. The museum holds the largest collection of African American culture and history on Staten Island, provides educational tours and workshops, and raises money for archaeological work in the area.

Free Black people from Maryland's eastern shore established the settlement of Sandy Ground—named for its poor quality soil—in the mid-1820s. Fleeing laws that restricted the rights of free Black people in Maryland, around twenty families trekked to Staten Island. In February of 1828, Captain John Jackson was the first Black man to purchase land in Richmond County (now Staten Island.) The original community around the intersection of Bloomingdale and Woodrow Roads grew as freed and escaped enslaved people from Virginia and Delaware and Black families from New York, New Jersey, and Connecticut arrived. Many of these original settlers were skilled in oyster harvesting, a major component of Staten Island's economy during the nineteenth century. Prince's Bay, a prime site of oyster harvesting, was within walking distance of Sandy Ground. Other residents of Sandy Ground

Sandy Ground Historical Society, 2017. CREDIT: SCOTT DEXTER

grew fruits and vege-
tables; still others were
skilled blacksmiths.

Residents of Sandy
Ground established the
Zion African Method-
ist Episcopal Church
(now the Rossville AME
Zion Church) in 1850.
One of four Black con-
gregations on the island
founded before 1900,
nearby Rossville AME
Zion Church still houses

House on left and Mount Zion AME church on right on Bloomingdale Road in Sandy Ground, 1927. CREDIT: PERCY LOOMIS, COLLECTION OF HISTORIC RICHMONDTOWN

an active congregation (see **Stapleton Union American Methodist Episcopal Church**, p. 309). The church became an important meeting point for the community as the area became a significant stop on the Underground Railroad. Captain Jackson may also have used the ferry boat he owned to ferry people escaping slavery across the Kill van Kull from New Jersey to Staten Island. In addition to Sandy Ground, the Livingston area on Staten Island may have also housed stops on the Underground Railroad, as a group of prominent abolitionists lived there.

About 150 African Americans lived in Sandy Ground by 1880, and by 1900 it had about 200 residents from 50 families. But when the city banned oystering in the polluted harbor in 1916, an economic decline began in the community as many left the area, although some families did remain, finding other work. But a 1963 fire destroyed much of what remained of the old Sandy Ground community, and many of the remaining families who could not afford

to rebuild moved away. At the same time, developers began to buy up large lots of land in the area.

Ten families descended from Sandy Ground's original settlers still live in the community. While Sandy Ground was designated a state and historical landmark in 1974 and 1982, the community still contends with the infringement of development as the Sandy Ground Historical Society in particular works to uncover and preserve the community's rich history.

TO LEARN MORE

Sandy Ground Historical Society, https://www .nyc-arts.org/organizations/341/sandy-ground -historical-society.

NEARBY SITES OF INTEREST

Rossville African Methodist Episcopal Zion Church

584 Bloomingdale Road, Staten Island, NY
One of four African American churches on Staten Island built before 1900, an important site on the Underground Railroad.

St. Joseph's Church

16 Poplar Avenue, Staten Island, NY

The oldest Roman Catholic church still standing on Staten Island.

Annadale

5.10 Spanish Camp/Former Site of Dorothy Day's Home

457 Poillon Avenue, Staten Island, NY

You can hear the sound of the water from here, next to the entrance of what is now marked as "Central Park East Estates." This spit of land on Raritan Bay used to be known as Spanish Camp, founded by Spanish Anarchists in 1923. Dorothy Day, the radical Catholic who founded the Catholic Worker movement, lived her final days at two small beach bungalows here on Staten Island's South Shore.

Day had long been drawn to Staten Island. She was living here when she converted to Catholicism in 1927, and she was baptized at the Church of Our Lady Help of Christians on the island. She established a Catholic Worker farm at 469 Bloomingdale Road (now gone) and is buried in Resurrection Cemetery (361 Sharrott Avenue).

Yet Day's life was defined by the fast pace of urban centers, in particular Manhattan, a world away from the bucolic surroundings of Spanish Camp. She spent years as a radical journalist, writer, and activist, living downtown, a comrade and friend to many of the most prominent writers of the day and involved in the most central struggles, from women's right to vote to supporting the Industrial Workers of the World and other labor struggles. She was involved with socialism, communism, and anarchism before her conversion to Catholicism, and many of the teachings of those radical traditions infused her life's work (especially anarchism and pacifism).

Day struggled with combining her evolving religious commitments with her social

Dorothy Day at her cottage in Spanish Camp on the shore of Staten Island, 1974. CREDIT: ROSE MORSE

justice activism. She described her turn toward individual, personal work as a move toward appreciating that she and others were the subjects of history, who, through good works, could change the world. The *Catholic Worker* paper, named as a direct challenge to the Communists' *Daily Worker*, was always sold for one cent. It explained its vision in its first issue, hawked at 1933's May Day rally (see **Union Square Park**, p. 113):

> For those who are sitting on park benches in the warm spring sunlight. For those who are huddling in shelters trying to escape the rain. For those who are walking the streets in the all but futile search for work. For those who think that there is no hope for the future, no recognition of their plight—this little paper is addressed. It is printed to call their attention to the fact that the Catholic Church has a social program—to let them know that there are men of God who are working not only for their spiritual but for their material welfare.

With Peter Maurin, Dorothy Day began the Catholic Worker as a rejection of the common stipulations that to be radical was to be atheist, on the one hand, and that Catholicism was not oriented toward improving the material lives of the poor, on the other. As lay people, Day and Maurin sought to live according to the ideals of service and poverty they saw at the heart of Catholic teachings. To do this, they relinquished their earthly possessions, and they created, lived, and served within the hospitality houses they established in their work. These houses were staffed entirely by volunteers and paid through donations, and they were places

where the homeless and destitute could find a meal, clean clothes, and someone to speak with. Unlike their urban communities, Catholic Worker communal farms, like the former one on Bloomingdale Road, were places of work and study.

Day balanced intensely urban and rural lives, but preferred the rural and Staten Island's shore most of all. Her bungalows came close to being marked as historical landmarks in 2001, but a real estate developer illegally bulldozed them before the commission was able to decide. The site remains undeveloped, but also not landmarked. Half completed mansions, and the remains of some surviving cabins can be found on the eighteen-acre property, along with a pond and wetlands that had made this a beautiful natural retreat. As of this writing, Catholic Worker's Maryhouse, which served food and provided showers and clothes for women at 55 East 3rd Street in Manhattan since the 1970s, is closed; St. Joseph House, providing hospitality for men, and the *Catholic Worker* newspaper are still housed at 36 East 1st Street in Manhattan and they remain open, as do over one hundred other hospitality houses and a number of farms in the United States.

TO LEARN MORE

Barrett, Wayne. 2001. "The Story of the Demolition of Spanish Camp and the Dorothy Day Cottage." *Village Voice*, May 2–8, 2001.

Coles, Robert. *Dorothy Day: A Radical Devotion.* Cambridge, MA: Da Capo Press, 1989.

Miller, William. *Dorothy Day: A Biography.* New York: Harper Collins, 1984.

Tottenville

5.11 Lenape Burial Ridge/ Conference House Park

298 Satterlee Street, Staten Island, NY

The Lenape Burial Ridge is one of the few surviving archeological sites dating from the Native American society that made this region its home before European colonialism. It is in the park on the cliffs of Wards Bluff overlooking Raritan Bay. This is the southernmost point in New York State.

When people first settled on Staten Island, it was at the edge of the massive Laurentides ice sheets that, during the extended period known as the Wisconsin glaciation, covered all of modern day Canada and much of the northern United States. From today's Staten Island a floodplain extended another seventy miles out into what is today the Atlantic Ocean; it was only with the melting of the glacier and the rising of the seas that this area became an island at the mouth of the great Hudson River. Oyster shell middens—towering piles of shells that dotted the New York landscape—were discovered along the shore here from around five thousand years ago, indicating sustained settlement from that time forward, though evidence of native peoples living here extends back twelve thousand years. The original people of the New York City region called themselves Lenape, or "the real people."

The Lenape were part of the greater Algonquin peoples related by a root language and other political connections; those in what would become New York City shared a common culture and language, Munsee, connecting groups that spanned from today's Delaware, through New Jersey and along the Hudson River, and across Long Island. Many of the regional and local place names, most notably Manhattan, Raritan Bay, Canarsie, Rockaway, Jamaica, and Connecticut, are adapted from the Munsee dialect. The Raritans lived in southern Staten Island, where, like their fellow Lenape in Mannahatta, they moved with the seasons to various camps around the island, a rotation based on hunting, fishing, gathering, and farming conditions. Wards Point, a landmarked area in the Conference House Park, was one such camp, which over time appears to have become a major settlement. Artifacts discovered in the area, including pottery and weapons, indicate a long history of trade and contact with other Lenape across the coast and up the river. Tulip trees, towering hardwoods still prevalent across the city, can be seen in this park and were the preferred wood for the canoes that the Lenape used for travel.

The Dutch began to colonize the island in earnest in 1630 and fought three wars (the Pig, Peach, and Whisky) with the Lenape before settling a treaty in 1661. Like other treaties with indigenous peoples, it is unlikely that the terms of the agreement were understood by both sides to mean exactly the same things; certainly, the Lenape did not agree to the European notion of ownership, as they held the land to be common, but over time they did learn about private property and often used the concept to their advantage

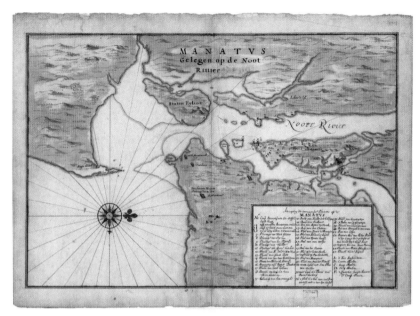

Seventeenth-century Dutch map of Staten Island. CREDIT: COURTESY OF THE LIBRARY OF CONGRESS

in their dealings with the Dutch and others. But no advantage held: in addition to wars, the Lenape had been devastated by contact with Europeans, with at least fourteen epidemics killing thousands from 1633 through 1702. Reduced from perhaps twenty thousand people across the region to three thousand by the early eighteenth century, the remaining Lenape left the land they'd lived in for millennia. Local Raritans were last recorded on the island in the early 1700s. The loss of their people, elders, and land nearly shattered their religion and culture, one survivor from a century later explained, "No one can have visions because the earth is no longer clean." Now known as the Delaware, they moved west alongside other native peoples—Oklahoma, Wisconsin, and Ontario, Canada, eventually became the primary homes of their descendants.

This burial ridge was first re-discovered in 1858 and has been the subject of multiple archeological excavations, including by the American Museum of Natural History. Archeology buffs today wander the woods on the bluffs in the park looking for evidence of the sites. Conference House Park is named for a failed peace conference between the British and the Americans held at the site in 1776, attended by Benjamin Franklin, among others. (*Quote is from Betsy McCully's,* City at the Water's Edge.)

TO LEARN MORE

Grumet, Robert S., and Daniel K. Richter. *The Munsee Indians: A History.* Norman: University of Oklahoma Press, 2009.

McCully, Betsy. *City at the Water's Edge: A Natural History of New York.* New Brunswick, NJ: Rivergate Books, an imprint of Rutgers University Press, 2007.

6

Thematic Tours

Chinatowns Tour
Manhattan, Brooklyn, Queens

With nine distinct ethnic Chinese enclaves (four in Queens, three in Brooklyn, and two in Manhattan), New York City has the largest ethnic Chinese population in the United States. The broader metropolitan area hosts the largest ethnic Chinese population outside of Asia.

Chinese immigrants first moved to New York City in the early 1800s. Most worked as sailors on ships trading between the United States and China, while others came as a result of increasing racial discrimination on the West Coast of the United States. As the economy tightened and the railroad work that brought many Chinese immigrants to the United States dried up, these workers faced more persistent discrimination across the country. This culminated in the Chinese Exclusion Act of 1882, which all but eliminated Chinese migration to the United States until 1965. The Exclusion Act forced not only Chinese immigrants but American-born Chinese out of smaller towns and into larger cities. As Peter Kwong noted, "The shift of Chinese into these urban ghettos was not voluntary." These were not like the immigrant ghettos of Italians, Jews, or Poles, which tended to disappear as each group integrated into American society. Rather, they were segregated areas where the Chinese were meant to stay. The segregation was maintained by the exclusion of Chinese from the larger labor market. While from the outside it might appear that ethnic Chinese "self-segregated" to be with others like themselves, "Chinatowns" were created out of political, economic, and social policies and practices. The communities have been maintained by some of these same structures, and also transformed by newer developments such as the rise of Taiwanese, Chinese, and Asian American capital investment into these areas.

This tour takes you to the three largest ethnic Chinese enclaves in the city: lower Manhattan; Sunset Park, Brooklyn; and Flushing, Queens.

MANHATTAN

Start your day in Manhattan Chinatown, the oldest Chinatown in the city. Begin at **COLUMBUS PARK** (67 Mulberry Street, see p. 164) to watch the neighborhood wake up. Columbus Park was historically the center of New York's infamous Five Points slum, known for its violence and corruption (see **Five Points/Columbus Park**, p. 164). From here, you can walk north along Elizabeth Street past the **5TH PRECINCT** of the New York Police Department. In 1975 police abuse stemming from this precinct sparked the largest demonstration in Chinatown to that point, when over ten thousand neighborhood residents marched from Mott Street to City Hall demanding justice against ongoing harassment and the beating of Peter Yew, a twenty-seven-year-old engineer from Brooklyn. Next walk to bustling **CANAL STREET,** the heart of Chinatown's tourist

Manhattan Chinatown Tour

Museum of Chinese in America
Broome St
Delancy St
Canal St
Lafayette St
Baxter St
Mulberry St
Mott St
Elizabeth St
Bowery
Chrystie St
Grand St
Eldridge St
Allen St
Walker St
Centre St
Hester St
Fifth Precinct
Canal Street
Silver Palace Restaurant
Canal St
CAAAV
Columbus Park
Chinese Theater
Confucius Plaza
Van Line
East Broadway Mall
East Broadway
Chinese Theater
Henry St
Chinese Theater
Manhattan Bridge
Madison St

drag, including shopping and street vendors. If time permits, walk to the **MUSEUM OF CHINESE IN AMERICA** (215 Centre Street, New York, NY) founded in 1980 as a community public history project by historian John Kuo Wei Tchen and activist Charles Lai to promote a better understanding of the Chinese American experience. Next walk to the **FORMER SITE OF THE SILVER PALACE RESTAURANT** (50–52 Bowery, New York, NY, see p. 166), now a luxury hotel, but previously the first unionized restaurant in Chinatown organized by the Chinese Staff and Workers Association in 1978. In 1993 it was the site of one of the labor movement's most epic battles when the restaurant's owners locked out workers for over seven months. Eventually the workers were hired back, but the restaurant went bankrupt in 1995. Just down the

block **CONFUCIUS PLAZA** (17 Bowery) represents the first initiative to provide affordable housing to Chinatown's growing immigrant population. The developer of this 762 unit project, the DeMatteis Organization, refused to hire Chinese or other minority construction workers. Asian Americans for Equality, one of the oldest political organizations in Chinatown, led a six-month campaign protesting the construction site until the developer finally agreed to hire workers of color. Head to the former sites of these **CHINESE THEATERS** (5–7 Doyers, 11 East Broadway, and 75–85 East Broadway). The first of these theaters opened on Doyers Street in 1893 serving the important cultural function of showing movies in Chinese. It closed in 1911, but created a path for the opening of other Chinese theaters in the neighborhood.

(Also worth a stop on the block is the **NOM WAH TEA PARLOR** at 13 Doyers which has been serving dumplings since 1920.) Notable theaters include the Sun Sing (75–85 East Broadway), formerly the Florence, which originally opened its 980 seats in 1911, but did not feature Chinese opera and Chinese movies until the 1940s and '50s. The Pagoda (11 East Broadway) opened its 492 seats in 1964 and showed Chinese films with English subtitles until the late 1980s. None of these theaters remain today.

East Broadway serves as an invisible dividing line between Chinatown and Little Fuzhou. In the late 1980s and 1990s a large new wave of Chinese immigrants came from Fujian Province. These predominantly working-class Fujianese and Mandarin-speaking immigrants first settled in Manhattan Chinatown, traditionally dominated by Cantonese-speaking immigrants, but discrimination and language barriers pushed them to the margins of Chinatown along East Broadway, now known as Little Fuzhou. Walk to **CAAAV** (55 Hester Street), the Coalition of Asian Americans Against Violence, to see the site of impressive community organizing and building power among low-income Asian immigrants and refugees. Double back to the **EAST BROADWAY MALL** (88 East Broadway, New York, NY). Here you have two choices, you can take a van line at the **MALL** to Sunset Park Chinatown or you can walk back to Canal Street and take the N train to 62nd Street and 8th Avenue in Brooklyn.

SUNSET PARK, BROOKLYN

Rising rents and gentrification in the 1990s as well as language barriers and discrimination pushed recent Fujianese immigrants to Brooklyn's 8th Avenue with its burgeoning commercial strip, garment jobs, and relatively low-cost housing. After Flushing, this is New York City's second largest Chinatown. Conveniently near the train station, you can stop at the **FEI LONG MARKET** (6301 8th Avenue, Brooklyn, NY). At over twenty-two thousand square feet, Fei Long might be the largest Asian market and food court in the five boroughs. The project, owned by the Guiffre family and financed by the Bank of China, highlights the role of Chinese capital and ethnic banks in the development of Brooklyn's Chinatown. The supermarket and food stalls cater to the Fujianese immigrant population, but also carry wide varieties of dried goods, snacks, fish, meats, and every type of Chinese fruit and vegetable imaginable. The food stalls serve classic dishes such as xiao long bao (pork soup dumplings) and congee (rice porridge). Most recently, community leaders and the community board approved a pagoda-like arch to symbolize Brooklyn's little Fuzhou.

Next, walk to **LUCKY ZHANG'S FAMILY GROCER** (5606 8th Avenue, Brooklyn, NY). As Fujianese immigrants started flocking to Brooklyn for affordable housing, Lucky Zhang's Family Grocer became the clearinghouse navigating the neighborhood's housing options. At all hours of the day and into the early evening a crowd can be seen milling around outside of Lucky Zhang's looking through handwritten advertisements

Brooklyn Chinatown Tour

on the wall. In addition to being known for more affordable housing, Sunset Park also became known in the 1990s for its garment sweatshops that moved production from Manhattan Chinatown. You can walk to the now closed **CHINESE STAFF WORKERS ASSO-CIATION** (5411 7th Avenue, Brooklyn, NY) outpost that opened in response to rampant sweatshop conditions reported to the Chinese Staff and Workers Association main office in Manhattan Chinatown. The Brooklyn location was at the center of produc-

ing a new model of worker organizing. On June 18, 1995, several hundred demonstrators marched down 8th Avenue in Brooklyn to protest poor working conditions and low wages and demand union recognition and back wages. Their material gains from the demonstration were limited: some employers paid back wages the night before the demonstration out of fear and others received "letters from the Workers Center" to pressure them into improving working conditions. The more substantial win came in the form of empowerment and confidence from the workers mobilizing themselves and advocating on their own behalf.

If it is a nice day you can stroll to **SUNSET PARK** (7th Avenue and 42nd Street, Brooklyn, NY, see p. 274), with views of Manhattan and the gentrifying waterfront in Sunset Park. The park is an important recreational area for Latina/o/x, Arab, and Asian families in this multiethnic neighborhood. From here walk back to 8th Avenue to the **BROOKLYN CHINATOWN VAN STOP** (8th Avenue between 61st and 62nd Streets, Brooklyn, NY), where you can take a van back to Manhattan Chinatown or continue onto Flushing Chinatown. Fujianese entrepreneurs developed this informal van transportation industry as a popular, cheap, and sometimes quicker means of transportation between Manhattan, Brooklyn, and Queens Chinatowns. The van service is convenient, reliable, and comfortable. It allows immigrant workers to live in more affordable locations such as Sunset Park, but work in Manhattan Chinatown or the various Chinatowns in Queens. This kind of "shadow transportation" industry is not exclusive to Chinatown; it also exists in other parts of New York City not well served by subways, such as Flatbush Avenue in Brooklyn, Eastern Queens, and the Bronx.

FLUSHING, QUEENS

In contrast to both Manhattan and Sunset Park, which cater to working-class immigrants, Flushing Chinatown is decidedly middle class. The first Chinese immigrants moved to Flushing as employees of the United Nations, originally headquartered in Long Island. It was not until the 1970s, however, that Flushing established itself as one of the largest ethnic Chinese enclaves in New York City. Taiwanese who migrated to the United States in large numbers after the 1965 Hart-Celler Act did not settle into Manhattan's Chinatown due to poor housing stock, working-class culture, and the dominance of Cantonese speakers in the enclave. Instead, these largely well-educated migrants settled in Flushing. Today, Flushing Chinatown—also known as Little Taipei—has more ethnic variation, including immigrants from Fujian Province and Hong Kong, as well as from neighboring countries such as Korea. As a result, the main drag in Flushing, Main Street, has a very different feel than Canal Street in Manhattan or 8th Avenue in Brooklyn.

From Main Street walk to the **FLUSHING COMMONS** (138–35 39th Avenue, Flushing, NY). This project exemplifies redevelopment efforts in Flushing, Queens. Robert Moses sold the land to the Department of Transportation, which constructed the first municipal parking lot. In 2013 the lot was sold to the F&T group, an international development corporation led by Taiwanese-born Michael Lee and the Rockefeller Development Corporation. The Flushing Commons project, financed by the F&T group, includes luxury condominiums, a town square, a YMCA, commercial space, and a parking lot. While the median home in Flushing costs about $697 per square foot, one-bedroom apartments in Flushing Commons are expected to start at $800 a square foot.

Flushing Chinatown Tour

Northern Blvd

Taiwan Center

37th Ave

Main St

Flushing Commons

Union St

39th Ave

Flushing–Main Street Subway Station

Roosevelt Ave

Kissena Blvd

Sanford Ave

41st Ave

Golden Shopping Mall

Merchants on nearby Main Street are concerned about rising rents and how the project will impact them. Community groups have protested the lack of affordable housing in the neighborhood's redevelopment process.

Next walk to the **TAIWAN CENTER** (137–44 Northern Boulevard, Flushing, NY), the first Taiwanese community center established by Taiwanese Americans through private donations. Finally, Flushing has many different fantastic dinner options; try any number of

food stalls at the **GOLDEN SHOPPING MALL** (41–28 Main Street, Flushing, NY). (*Quotes are from Peter Kwong's,* The New Chinatown.)

TO LEARN MORE

Hum, Tarry. *Making a Global Immigrant Neighborhood: Brooklyn's Sunset Park.* Philadelphia: Temple University Press, 2014.

Kwong, Peter. *Chinatown, New York: Labor and Politics, 1930–1950.* New York: New Press, 2001.

Kwong, Peter. *The New Chinatown.* New York: Hill and Wang, 1996.

Environmental Justice Tour

Kenneth A. Gould, Tammy L. Lewis, and Emily Tumpson Molina

Environmental injustice occurs in places where environmental burdens, such as exposure to toxins or to unwanted land uses like landfills and waste treatment facilities, disproportionately affect poor, working-class, and people of color. Injustices of this sort rest on housing segregation, which is prevalent in Brooklyn. Housing segregation also concentrates environmental amenities, such as clean air, parks, and bike paths, in more advantaged communities. In Brooklyn, community activism has been central to the fight for access to environmental amenities and against the unequal distribution of environmental health hazards. This tour takes you through the Brooklyn neighborhoods of Greenpoint, Williamsburg, Gowanus, and Brooklyn Heights by bike, foot, and subway.*

* Rather than taking the subway, you may choose to bike from Domino Sugar Factory along the waterfront to Brooklyn Bridge Park, and then on to Gowanus. Consult the bike path and CitiBike station maps for routes and stations for switching bikes.

GREENPOINT

Make your way to the Nassau Avenue stop on the G train. Exit the station at the corner of Manhattan and Nassau Avenues, and walk four blocks east along Nassau Avenue to Newel to pick up a Citi Bike on the corner (if you prefer, you can also walk). You are in the heart of Greenpoint, a long-standing Polish enclave. Greenpoint and nearby East Williamsburg contain a large concentration of environmental and health hazards from industry and city facilities for waste transfer, wastewater treatment, and previously, incinerating trash. A massive oil spill, toxic contamination from dry cleaning industries under a thirty-block stretch, a busy segment of the Brooklyn-Queens Expressway, and the largest concentration (38 percent) of waste transfer stations in the city all converge in roughly two square miles. The residents of this (until recently) working-class, immigrant neighborhood have organized over the decades for cleanup of oil and other toxic materials and for the equal distribution of city waste facilities across the boroughs.

Bike or walk eleven blocks down Nassau Street and make a right on Apollo Street. You are now above the **GREENPOINT OIL SPILL** (see **Greenpoint Oil Spill**, p. 223). The residents of these homes and neighboring blocks live atop the remnants of the greatest environmental disaster in New York City history—the Greenpoint oil spill, one-and-a-half times larger than the 1989 *Exxon Valdez* spill in Alaska. From the late 1800s through World War II, between seventeen million and thirty million gallons of oil leaked from the BP, Chevron, and Exxon Mobil refineries along nearby Newtown Creek (the next stop on this tour). This area remains contaminated with benzene and methane, and residents have organized to file lawsuits against the oil companies for damages and faster remediation.

Follow Apollo Street for one block and make a left on Meeker Avenue for four blocks to its end at Gardner Avenue. From

Environmental Justice Tour

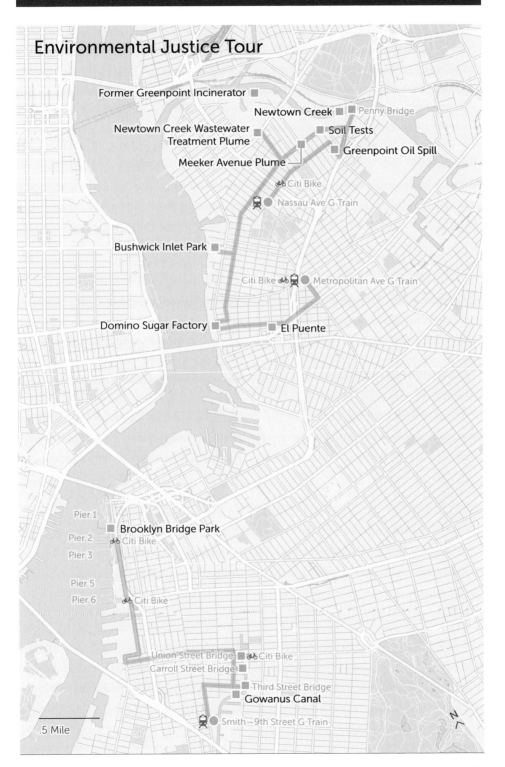

Former Greenpoint Incinerator

Newtown Creek ■ Penny Bridge

Newtown Creek Wastewater Treatment Plume ■ Soil Tests

Greenpoint Oil Spill

Meeker Avenue Plume

Citi Bike

Nassau Ave G Train

Bushwick Inlet Park

Citi Bike ■ Metropolitan Ave G Train

Domino Sugar Factory ■ El Puente

Pier 1

Brooklyn Bridge Park

Pier 2 ■ Citi Bike

Pier 3

Pier 5

Pier 6 ■ Citi Bike

Union Street Bridge ■ Citi Bike

Carroll Street Bridge

Third Street Bridge

Gowanus Canal

Smith–9th Street G Train

.5 Mile

here you will need to walk straight ahead to **PENNY BRIDGE** along **NEWTOWN CREEK**. You will see that Penny Bridge is no longer a bridge—only a concrete barrier along the creek. Built in 1894, Penny Bridge once linked Greenpoint, Brooklyn, to Sunnyside and Maspeth, Queens, for a one-cent toll. As industry grew along the banks of Newtown Creek—notice the industry that remains on both sides of the water—city officials demolished Penny Bridge to accommodate heavier shipping traffic. To replace it, the city constructed the Kosciuszko Bridge in 1939, which was demolished in 2017 to construct the new Kosciuszko Bridge that you can see to your right.

This is where the Greenpoint oil spill was initially discovered by the Coast Guard in 1978, where they noticed a large plume of oil in the creek in front of you. The area that you are standing on makes up about a half-acre of city-owned land that went neglected for decades, used as a dumping ground for waste of all sorts. The Newtown Creek Alliance—a community group dedicated to cleaning and restoring Newtown Creek—is working to transform the area into green space for local workers and residents.

Dividing Brooklyn and Queens, **NEWTOWN CREEK** was declared a Superfund site in 2010. It is among the most polluted waterways in the United States. The East River feeds the creek, where water mixes with oil and other pollutants, raw sewage, and garbage. Its bottom is lined with "black mayonnaise"—a decades-old conglomeration of oil, raw sewage, and varied industrial waste that includes arsenic, polychlorinated biphenyls, and concrete, animal, and nuclear waste.

Oil refineries became concentrated along the creek in the late nineteenth and early twentieth centuries, joined by sugar refineries, copper wiring plants, canneries, hide tanning plants, and other heavy industry. Little to no government regulation meant that these industries could dispose of whatever they wanted in the creek, despite citizen protests at the time. The city added to the area's pollution by building a trash incinerator and sewage treatment plant along the creek, to your left about a mile up the creek. In addition, the city's combined sewer overflow (CSO)—combining raw domestic sewage, storm water, and industrial wastewater—drains untreated raw sewage into the creek when it rains (see **Gowanus Canal**, p. 259). The Environmental Protection Agency has just (as of 2019) finished its remedial investigation and feasibility study of the creek and has named the City of New York, BP, National Grid, ExxonMobil, Phelps Dodge Refining Corporation, Chevron, ConEd, AMTRAK, the LIPP, Shell Oil, SimsMetal, and others as potentially responsible parties. Cleanup is planned for the coming years.

Make your way back on Meeker for one block. Make a right on Bridgewater Street. Follow Bridgewater for one block to make a slight left on Norman Avenue. Exxon Mobil's tests of the soil under this intersection of Bridgewater, Norman, and Apollo show potentially explosive concentrations of methane and toxic levels of benzene, a known carcinogen. Continuing down Norman, at Kingsland Avenue you are above the **MEEKER AVENUE PLUME** of toxic chlorinated solvents in the soil and groundwater, caused by irresponsible dumping and manufacturing processes by dry cleaners and metalworking businesses. Discovered during monitoring of the Greenpoint oil spill, the plume is considered a significant threat to the public health and environment.

Continue to bike on Norman. As you cross over Humboldt, look to your right. About three blocks down Humboldt is the **NEWTOWN CREEK WASTEWATER TREATMENT PLANT**, which operates guided tours a few times a year to teach the public about New York City's water infrastructure (they are also open by appointment). The Wastewater Treatment Plant borders the former **GREENPOINT INCINERATOR**, shut down in 1994 because of community pressure. The homes that surround this industrial zone always attracted immigrants to work; first the Irish, then Italians, and most recently, Polish newcomers. Without political clout, much of the neighborhood was mostly resigned to living with the "Greenpoint stink" of concentrated pollution. But residents began organizing in the 1980s, fed up with the petrochemical odor along Newtown Creek. Six Greenpoint women, including Irene Klementowicz, organized the Concerned Citizens of Greenpoint to pressure regulators for faster cleanup of the Greenpoint oil spill and to shut down the Greenpoint incinerator that processed waste from across the five boroughs. While the incinerator has been closed for decades, Greenpoint and neighboring East Williamsburg are home to nineteen waste transfer stations (WTS) that hold almost 40 percent of New York City's waste. Tractor-trailers transport more than

4 million tons of waste through the neighborhoods annually, bringing additional pollution to the community. O.U.T.R.A.G.E., a coalition of more than twenty community groups in the neighborhoods, works to pressure officials to more equitably distribute WTS throughout the city.

Head west on Norman Avenue, which will turn into Wythe Avenue.

WILLIAMSBURG

Make a right on N. 10th Street and ride one block. On your left, you will come up on the six acres of green space that is all that has been realized of **BUSHWICK INLET PARK**—a soccer field and park building. This makes up a small piece of a twenty-eight-acre park promised to this community in a 2005 waterfront rezoning plan. The Greenpoint-Williamsburg waterfront has been a focal point of efforts to convert brownfield sites into waterfront parks, greenways, and high-density luxury condominiums. Williamsburg and Greenpoint have distinct histories, but they are unified through a waterfront redevelopment vision. In 2003, Mayor Bloomberg announced a rezoning plan that would pave the way for a sweeping redevelopment of the Greenpoint-Williamsburg waterfront—a planned "green gentrification" project that would couple an array of public green amenities (parks, ball fields, esplanades, and bike paths) with huge imposing massive luxury housing developments. A coalition of community leaders and activists demanded affordable housing as a bulwark against displacement, and more green space, including the planned twenty-eight-acre

Bushwick Inlet Park. Notice the warehouse behind you (if you are facing the park; to the right if you are facing the water). This eleven-acre parcel was in dispute for years, because without public ownership of it, the residents of Williamsburg and Greenpoint would essentially be walled off from access to the waterfront by luxury towers from the Williamsburg Bridge (if you are facing the water, to the left) and Newtown Creek (to your right). The city finally bought this land for $160 million in 2016.

Continue south along the bike path on Kent. As you bike south on Kent for twelve blocks, you are on the edge of gentrified "hipster" Brooklyn, though you may not be able to tell from the office-park feel of the strip today. In the 1960s and '70s, the offshoring of American industry deindustrialized portions of the Brooklyn waterfront. Williamsburg's deindustrialized spaces became the vortex for the hipster gentrification that made greening the waterfront attractive to developers and the city. At the corner of S. 2nd and Kent you'll see what is left of the former **DOMINO SUGAR FACTORY**—a massive new development site (see **Domino Sugar Factory**, p. 226). This eleven-acre waterfront site, home to the Domino Sugar plant from 1856 to 2004, was initially slated to remain industrial and commercial. However, the 2005 rezoning discussed earlier allowed for residential development. The property was sold in 2012 for $180 million to a developer planning luxury housing towers. After community outcry, developers revised their plan to add 60 percent more publicly accessible open space, including a public park along the waterfront and a public square at the refinery building (a turn toward the water will bring you to that Domino Sugar Park).

Bike south on Kent (with the water on your right) to make a left on S. 3rd Street. Bike east on S. 3rd Street for about seven blocks. Crossing over Roebling Street, **EL PUENTE** is on the block to your right. Founded by former Young Lord Luis Garden Acosta in 1982 (see **Young Lords' Garbage Offensive**, p. 84), this community organization has worked tirelessly for environmental justice in this (until recently) Latina/o/x enclave. They successfully worked to limit the activities of a radioactive and hazardous waste storage facility nearby, organized with local Hasidic Jews to ward off the construction of a fifty-five–story trash incinerator in Williamsburg, and conducted a community asthma study conceived and carried out by students at nearby El Puente Academy—in addition to many other victories related to health, safety, and quality of life in the neighborhood.

Follow S. 3rd under the Brooklyn-Queens Expressway and make a left on Borinquen Place. Follow Borinquen for five blocks and make a left on Union Avenue. Head four blocks north and make a left on Metropolitan Avenue. If you are biking, drop your Citi Bike off on this block of Metropolitan Avenue (on the north side of Metropolitan between Union and Rodney).

Hop on the G train at the Metropolitan Avenue station at the corner of Union and Metropolitan. Take the G train headed south toward Coney Island and get off at the Smith and 9th Street subway stop.

GOWANUS

Standing on the Smith and 9th Street platform, you are atop the highest subway station above ground level in the world. Look out the platform window at the Gowanus Canal as it empties into Gowanus Bay. Notice the scrap metal recovery facility, the oil storage tanks, the concrete plant, and the Gowanus Expressway beyond that. Walk down the stairs and head north on Smith Street past Public Place, a brownfield site the city has held for decades. Make a right on 3rd Street and walk three blocks to reach the **GOWANUS CANAL** (see p. 259).

The **3RD STREET BRIDGE** that crosses the Gowanus was completely submerged during Superstorm Sandy in 2012. The storm pushed a thirteen-foot storm surge up the canal, sending sewage-laden waters over the banks, up the streets, and into the residential, industrial, and commercial spaces of the neighborhood. Floodwater spread out more than a block on either side of the canal turning the area between Bond and Nevins Streets into a five-foot-deep lake. Power outages took the pumping station offline for thirty-three hours, causing 13 million gallons of sewage to discharge into the floodwaters that covered the neighborhood. As you look north up the canal, the Wycoff Gardens public housing projects are the closest tall buildings toward the east, and the Gowanus Houses are the closest tall buildings to the west—both built to house the city's poor and working classes as the waterfront fell into decay.

Walk back west from whence you came, and turn right on Bond Street. Go three blocks to Carroll Street and turn right again to go to the **CARROLL STREET BRIDGE**. This retractable bridge was built in 1889, and it is one of four such bridges remaining in the United States. Look at the southeast bank of the canal from the Carroll Street Bridge and you can see a CSO pipe. If there has been heavy rain lately, you will see (and smell) the untreated sewage entering the canal from this ancient brick-lined infrastructure.

Walk back to Bond Street, and make a right. Walk two blocks to Union Street. Turn right again toward the **UNION STREET BRIDGE**. Looking north from the Union Street Bridge you can see the end of the canal and the pipes that connect to the flushing tunnel.

Continue on the Union Street Bridge, crossing the Gowanus to get a Citi Bike at Nevins Street. Ride back over the Union Street Bridge, make a right onto Bond Street and then a left onto Sackett Street. Stay on this for just under a mile until you get to the T at Van Brunt Street where you will turn right and get on the bike path that takes you north along Columbia Street. Ride along the path to Atlantic Avenue (less than half a mile) where you can leave the bike or continue on the bike along the path and pass through Brooklyn Bridge Park to the next bike station at Pier 2 (about three-quarters of a mile more).

BROOKLYN HEIGHTS

Guides to **BROOKLYN BRIDGE PARK (BBP)** focus on its sustainability features. It was constructed using salvaged materials and includes native species, recycled storm water, composting, and green roofs. The park also boasts numerous recreational amenities. You will enter the park at Atlantic Avenue, which is near Pier 6, the southernmost end. BBP covers eighty-five acres and extends 1.3 miles north along the piers, under the Brooklyn Bridge, and ends just past the Manhattan Bridge. Ride or walk to Pier 5, the soccer field.

Fifteen years ago this was the site of abandoned warehouses. BBP was conceived in the 1980s, park construction started in 2008, and it continues as we write in 2021. Take a 180-degree turn away from the water and observe the neighborhood on the bluff, above the Promenade. This is the historic district of Brooklyn Heights, among the wealthiest, most educated, and whitest communities in Brooklyn. BBP increased the already astronomical property values here. The abandoned piers could have become many things—the Port Authority considered public housing, a resort hotel, athletic fields, and manufacturing. The president of the Brooklyn Heights Association (BHA), an investment banker, argued for a resort that "would cater predominantly to the Wall Street market." The BHA historically fought off unwanted land use before, such as the Brooklyn-Queens Expressway, hidden under the Promenade at great expense, and low-income housing. City planners, however, opted for public access to the waterfront. In the end, local residents used their social capital to lobby the city to ensure that it would be transformed into an environmental amenity rather than a locally unwanted land use.

The park was constructed with funding from both the city and state, but it's now required to be economically self-sufficient. Residential buildings, including ground-floor commercial space, were constructed to generate revenue, including One Brooklyn Bridge, a warehouse that was converted into luxury condominiums across from Piers 5 and 6, and new (as of 2019) townhomes across from Pier 1 that sell for a minimum of $2 million.

Either bike or walk northward from the soccer fields. Each pier is dedicated to a different theme. Pier 6 has playgrounds, beach volleyball, and food concessions. Pier 5 has a soccer field and picnic areas; Pier 4 is a beach; Pier 3 is a greenway; Pier 2 offers basketball, bocce, roller-skating, and fitness equipment; and Pier 1 is a place for a stroll and food. Brooklyn Bridge Park Conservancy hosts music, outdoor movies, and waterfront workouts in the summer. You can take a free tour or a kayak ride, and park officials estimate that an average summer weekend brings 119,000 visitors.

TO LEARN MORE

Gould, Kenneth A., and Tammy L. Lewis. *Green Gentrification: Urban Sustainability and the Struggle for Environmental Justice*. New York: Routledge, 2017.

7 Train Tour: Immigration in Queens

NOTE: This tour will likely take you a full day. Bits and pieces can be done in shorter time.

Queens houses some of the most diverse neighborhoods in the United States. Nowhere is this more evident than on the 7 train from Long Island City to Flushing, which was designated one of "16 National Millennium Trails" by the White House Millennium Council in 1999. "The International Express," as it was named, takes us around the world in just five miles. This tour takes us through several ethnic enclaves in Queens that have been continuously transformed by different waves of immigration over the decades. Our trip begins in Long Island City and will end at the Main Street–Flushing stop in one of the largest Chinatowns in the world (see **Chinatowns Tour**, p. 324).

Make your way to the 7 train's **COURT SQUARE** stop in Long Island City to begin your day. Once an industrial neighborhood lined with commercial bakeries and factories, Long Island City has been gentrifying since the early 2000s with high-rise buildings dotting the waterfront views. Nonetheless, the area continues to serve a large immigrant population.

Walk one block north from the Court Square stop on 23rd Street and make a right on Court Square. Walk one block to see the City University of New York's law school, one of the leading public interest law schools in the country, which houses the **CUNY LAW SCHOOL IMMIGRANT AND NON-CITIZEN RIGHTS CLINIC** (2 Court Square, Long Island City, NY). CUNY's public interest law program was one of the first in the country to host a free immigration clinic in the community. The clinic has grown dramatically and now, through the CLEAR project, provides free legal assistance to all CUNY students and their families as well as "know your rights" training in schools, workplaces, and community organizations throughout the city.

Walk back to the train and take the 7 to the **52 STREET** stop. Get off and walk north on 52nd Street to make a left on Skillman Avenue. Make a right on any street between 50th and 44th Streets to see **SUNNYSIDE GARDENS** (see p. 192), the first planned garden community in the United States. Sunnyside Gardens provided an affordable alternative to crowded Manhattan where working- and middle-class people could purchase apartments and small homes among swaths of green space for the better part of the twentieth century. Until the 1960s, residents were largely white European ethnics, including Irish, Germans, Czech, and Dutch. Since the 1980s, Sunnyside Gardens has grown increasingly diverse as new Korean, Colombian, Chinese, Turkish, and Filipino residents have joined the community.

Make your way back to 52nd Street. Walk south on 52nd Street, past the 52nd Street–Lincoln Avenue station, until you get to Queens Boulevard, which is the northern border of **CALVARY CEMETERY**. With more than 3 million interred, Cavalry is the largest cemetery in the United States (in terms of burials). This area borders the Woodside neighborhood. Initially a predominantly German hamlet, Woodside became 80 percent Irish by the 1930s. Until recently, it was known to house the largest Irish community in Queens. During the epidemics of influenza, cholera, and tuberculosis in the 1850s, Cavalry hosted fifty burials a day, half of which were poor Irish children under the age of seven. Ninety percent of the headstones in Old Calvary cite Irish places of birth. Notably, Annie Moore Schayer (1874–1924), the first immigrant to have come through Ellis Island, is buried at Calvary (section 20, range 3, plot F, grave 13). Annie migrated to the United States from County Cork, Ireland, and soon after her arrival in New York City she married a German immigrant and had eleven children. Since the 1990s the neighborhood has experienced significant migration from Latin America and Asia, particularly the Philippines. As with Sunnyside, recent Irish immigrants have also settled in Woodside.

Walk back to the 52nd Street stop to get back on the 7 train to the **69 STREET** stop. Walk south on 69th Street to the former site of the **BAYANIHAN FILIPINO COMMUNITY CENTER** (4021 69th Street, Woodside, NY). In the heart of "Little Manila," the Bayanihan Filipino Community Center (a project of the Philippine Forum) opened in 2008 serving the extensive Filipino community in Woodside. The center housed domestic workers' rights programs, typing and computer classes, youth leadership programs, and monthly health and legal clinics. Unfor-

7 Train Tour: Immigration in Queens

CUNY Law School
Sunnyside Gardens
Calvary Cemetery

tunately, due to the rising cost of rents in the area, the center was forced to close in 2014. As of 2018, the location has been taken over by a Pentecostal church. Despite the center's closing, community organizing continues to thrive in Little Manila with organizations like Gabriela NYC, Migrante NYC, Damayan, and Anakbayan. Instead of a physical location, these grassroots organizations have found other places to meet, such as churches, members' homes, and workplaces.

Turn around to walk north on 69th Street to make a right on Roosevelt Avenue. Notice the 7 train traveling above you as you walk two-and-a-half blocks to **DESIS RISING UP AND MOVING (DRUM)** (72–18 Roosevelt Avenue, Jackson Heights, NY). Founded in 2000, DRUM is located in the heart of Jackson Heights, sometimes referred to as "Little India," but it serves South Asian and Indo-Caribbean communities all over Queens, and it is one of the first membership-based organizations to represent South Asian immigrants. Their programing includes

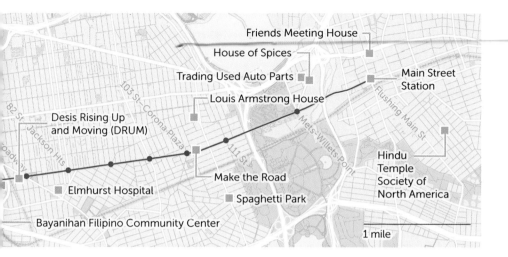

Friends Meeting House

House of Spices

Trading Used Auto Parts

Louis Armstrong House

Main Street Station

Desis Rising Up and Moving (DRUM)

Hindu Temple Society of North America

Make the Road

Elmhurst Hospital

Spaghetti Park

Bayanihan Filipino Community Center

1 mile

racial and immigrant justice campaigns, a South Asian worker center, youth empowerment, global justice, and legal and community services. DRUM played an especially important role in the aftermath of 9/11 to help and protect South Asians from racist attacks.

Historically, Jackson Heights was a planned garden community for middle and upper middle-class New Yorkers to raise their families. Given restrictive covenants excluding Jews and Catholics (until the 1940s) and discrimination against African Americans (until 1968), Jackson Heights was a typical white, semi-suburban neighborhood. New South Asian immigrants moved to the neighborhood beginning after the passage of the 1952 Immigration and Naturalization Act, which permitted skilled workers to migrate to the United States. A second wave of South Asian migration occurred in the 1970s and represented a more heterogeneous group with a wider range of socioeconomic status. Some settled in Jackson

Heights, but many settled in other parts of Queens. As immigrants moved in, white flight gained momentum.

At present, the South Asian population of Jackson Heights is shrinking as many people have migrated into more suburban neighborhoods, but Indians, Bangladeshis, Pakistanis, Nepalese, and Tibetans still make up a sizable proportion of the community. At the same time, the neighborhood's restaurants and Indian supermarkets continue to attract South Asians from across the five boroughs. The neighborhood also has a sizable Latina/o/x population that has grown since the 1970s, mostly comprised of South Americans (Colombians, Ecuadorians, and Argentinians).

Get back on the 7 train at the **74 STREET– BROADWAY** stop at 74th and Roosevelt Avenue. Take the train to the **82 STREET–JACKSON HEIGHTS** stop. Walk south on 82nd Street, and make a right on Baxter Avenue. One block up is **ELMHURST HOSPITAL CENTER** (79–01 Broadway, Elmhurst, NY).

Prior to World War II, this community was almost exclusively Jewish and Italian. Beginning in the 1980s, it has become one of the most diverse zip codes in the world. Residents hail from more than 150 countries, most commonly from places in Asia and Latin America. Elmhurst Hospital Center is the second oldest municipal hospital in New York City (the first is Bellevue in Manhattan). Long known for its trailblazing in serving poor New Yorkers, the hospital currently participates in an UndocuCare program with New York Lawyers for the Public Interest, which provides low-wage undocumented immigrants with access to health care. Given the extraordinary diversity of this community, the hospital's doctors are well trained in global infectious diseases, making it easier for them to diagnose illnesses that are typically no longer seen in the United States, like tuberculosis and malaria. Patients and caretakers at Elmhurst Hospital speak over 150 languages. The hospital was particularly hard hit during the COVID-19 pandemic because of the severity of the April 2020 peak of the illness in New York City and the lack of coordination between public hospitals. One doctor described the situation as "apocalyptic."

Get back on the 7 train at the 82 Street–Jackson Heights stop. Take the train to **111 STREET**. Walk west on Roosevelt Avenue until you reach **MAKE THE ROAD NEW YORK** (104–19 Roosevelt Avenue, Corona, NY; opening 2021)**,** a labor and community center started in 1997 in Brooklyn. Make the Road's model was unique for its time because it combined the traditional services of community organizations (legal aid, social services) with a model of bottom-up organizing intended to build power (legislative, strikes, direct action). As a multi-issue, multiethnic, multigenerational organization, Make the Road works on a variety of issues including workplace rights, LGBTQ advocacy, immigrant rights, health care, and housing.

Walk east and make a left on 108th Street. Walk four blocks north to 37th Avenue. Make a left. Make a right on 107th Street to see the **LOUIS ARMSTRONG HOUSE** (34–56 107th Street, Corona, NY; see p. 197). Historically, this neighborhood (Corona) was Italian and Italian American, its name deriving from the Italian word for crown. During the 1940s, the neighborhood experienced a significant influx of Black Americans, including prominent musicians, athletes, and civil rights leaders. While Black people had always had a presence in Queens since its colonization, the Great Migration increased the Black population in New York City by 66 percent and doubled in Corona during the 1940s. As Harlem became increasingly crowded, Black New Yorkers sought refuge in Corona and other Queens neighborhoods that offered space and quality housing.

Louis Armstrong and his wife Lucille moved to Corona in 1943, where they quickly became an important part of the community. The house was occupied by the famed musician until his death in 1971, and his wife continued to live there until her death in 1983. In 2003 the house was turned into a wonderful museum, recreating the life of the Armstrongs in the neighborhood.

Make your way back to 108th Street, this time walking south to cross over Roosevelt Avenue (where the 111 Street train stop is). Walk ten blocks south to **SPAGHETTI PARK** (William F. Moore Park at 108th Street and 51st Avenue, Corona, NY). This park is home to one of New York City's few bocce ball courts. While Corona is no longer a majority Italian neighborhood, Italian Americans from the neighborhood and elsewhere still come to the park to enjoy a game of bocce ball. Italian restaurants and the famed Lemon Ice King border the park.

The neighborhood began to house Dominicans in the 1950s, given the deepening economic crisis in the Dominican Republic at the time. Today, the neighborhood is predominantly Latina/o/x, with especially large numbers of Dominicans, Colombians, Ecuadorians, Peruvians, and Mexicans. In the 1990s, with a new influx of Latina/o/x immigrants coming to the neighborhood, racial tensions escalated. In 1996, Manuel Mayi Jr., a Queens College honor student, was beaten to death with baseball bats by three young white men who caught him spraying graffiti on a local Italian restaurant. The men were not convicted, but Mayi's family and community members remember him every year by gathering and marching at Spaghetti Park.

Head back to the 111 Street stop, and ride the 7 train one stop to the **METS–WILLETS POINT** stop. Willets Point has long been an industrial neighborhood next to Citi Field, where the New York Mets play. The neighborhood is currently being rezoned for development, with likely residential con-struction to come. Walk east on Roosevelt Avenue to 126th Street.

Make a left on 126th Street and a right on Willets Point Boulevard. You are now in the so-called "Iron Triangle," the industrial part of Corona. Notice the plethora of auto body and repair shops. Make a left on 127th Street. **TRADING USED AUTO PARTS** (127–02 35th Avenue, Corona, NY) is an example of one of dozens of auto body parts and repair shops that employ thousands of immigrant workers. While the Iron Triangle is zoned as an industrial area, a new rezoning plan includes construction of a mall, hotel, and housing.. It threatens the many body shops in the neighborhood, and owners and activists have been campaigning against it. After various stalls, a hotel was approved in February 2018, but as of 2020 the site is being redeveloped for affordable housing.

Double back on 127th Street to Willets Point Boulevard. This time, make a left on Willets Point. The Indian Spice wholesaler **HOUSE OF SPICES** (127–40 Willets Point Boulevard, Flushing, NY) is the largest employer in Willets Point. House of Spices employs several hundred immigrants to package and distribute spices across the five boroughs. Mr. Soni, an Indian immigrant from Kerala, opened it as one of the first stores dedicated to Indian food products in 1970.

Make your way back to the **METS–WILLETS POINT** stop, and get back on the 7 train to its final stop at **FLUSHING–MAIN STREET**. This bustling subway stop represents the largest single interchange between buses and subways in North America, serving over 19 million riders annually. It is a relatively small station, because it was never intended to be the end of the line, but rather one more stop in a subway system that planned to extend about three more miles, all the way to Little Neck Bay. An extension required other competing rail lines to cooperate. They refused, so Main Street in Flushing became the end of the line. As a result, the neighborhoods between Flushing and Little Neck Bay (Bayside, Bay Terrace, and Little Neck) had no access to subway transportation and remained majority-white for decades.

End your day in **FLUSHING**, New York's third-largest Chinatown (see also the **Chinatowns Tour**, p. 324). Flushing has long been known as a center of religious tolerance and diversity. Head to the nearby **FLUSHING FRIENDS MEETING HOUSE AND JOHN BOWNE HOUSE** (137–16 Northern Boulevard, Flushing, NY; see p. 201) to learn about the history of religious pluralism in Queens. Or finish at the **HINDU TEMPLE SOCIETY OF NORTH AMERICA** (45–57 Bowne Street, Flushing, NY; see p. 203), the first traditional Hindu temple built in North America, which thrives as a place of worship and community center and houses the famed Canteen restaurant in its basement.

TO LEARN MORE

Tonnelat, Stéphane, and William Kornblum. *International Express: New Yorkers on the 7 Train*. New York: Columbia University Press, 2017.

Wall Street: Capitalism and Protest Tour

From the beginning, lower Manhattan was conceived by its European colonizers as a real estate deal and source of wealth in global trade, and it served from its start as an outpost for labor's oppression and exploitation, as well as a strategic bulwark in the defense of international capital. Manhattan's history has been one of northern expansion, as its more affluent residents moved again and again to distance themselves from the congestion, filth, and poverty of the crowded city. But the business of business remained downtown, and, as such, this neighborhood has long served as a flashpoint for protest and resistance, sometimes violent. The sites along the tour highlight the literal and symbolic centrality of the city's premier business district to the centuries-old system of global capitalism, and the frequent challenges that have been brought to its doorsteps.

FRAUNCES TAVERN (54 Pearl Street, New York, NY) first opened its doors in 1719. This corner of Pearl and Broad would have been on the water at the time, bounded by the East River, whose oysters gave Pearl its name, and the Broad Street channel, a narrow inlet that extended another quarter mile inland. Fraunces Tavern was notable for its role in the Revolutionary War, where its proprietor Samuel Fraunces (whom some historians argue was a Black man of West Indian descent) likely served as a spy for the

Wall Street: Capitalism and Protest Tour

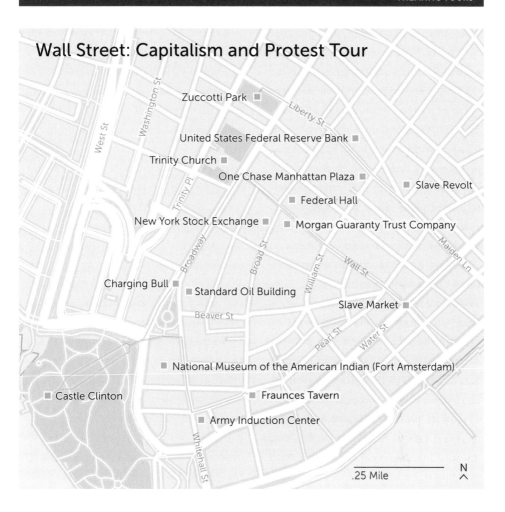

rebels while New York was under British control, and whose cozy rooms served as the site of George Washington's farewell address to his army in 1783. Centuries later, this historical significance helped make it a symbolic target of the Fuerzas Armadas de Liberación Nacional Puertoriquena (FALN, or Armed Forces of Puerto Rican National Liberation), who in 1975 planted a bomb on the second floor of a neighboring building, killing four men at the Tavern. The FALN was a Puerto Rican nationalist group that claimed responsibility for over one hundred bombings in the United States between 1974 and 1983, seeking to draw attention to the US colonization of Puerto Rico and the cause of independence.

Head west down Pearl to Whitehall Street. Before turning right, note the glass tower along Whitehall that fills the block on the south side of the street from Pearl to Moore. This glass façade covers what had once been the imposing, fortress-like tower of the **ARMY INDUCTION CENTER** (39 Whitehall

Street, New York, NY). For the duration of the Vietnam War, until it closed in 1972, antiwar protesters regularly gathered on Whitehall Street to protest the draft. In December 1967 as part of the second round of "Stop the Draft Week" protests that year, 264 people were arrested there in the early morning hours for "sitting-in" at the entrance to the building as it opened to inspect potential draftees. Poet Allen Ginsberg and pediatrician and war opponent Benjamin Spock were among those arrested; Tuli Kupferberg of the band The Fugs was one of two protesters charged with resisting arrest.

Walking north on Whitehall, you will come to an enormous Beaux Arts building on the west side of Whitehall at Bridge. Continue to the building's entrance in the plaza at the base of Broadway, across from the Bowling Green. This is the **NATIONAL MUSEUM OF THE AMERICAN INDIAN** (1 Bowling Green, New York, NY; see p. 170), standing in the footprint of what was once **FORT AMSTERDAM**. Beyond its initial service as a defense against the indigenous people honored there today, the area of the museum and Bowling Green was home to one of the Revolutionary War era's most famous of anti-British protests. Five days after the passage of the Declaration of Independence, a copy of the document was read aloud in what was then New York's Commons, today's City Hall Park, to General George Washington and his colonial troops, who used the Commons as their parade grounds. After hearing the Declaration, some of New York's pro-Revolutionary citizens who had joined the soldiers celebrated in the

streets, and a contingent of citizens and soldiers made their way down Broadway to the Bowling Green. A towering massive lead statue of King George III on horseback stood here, in front of what was by then known as Fort George, so named for the British monarchs but at the time under the control of the colonial army. The crowds, including many enslaved and free Black people, dismantled the statue, and over forty-two thousand bullets were made out the spoils. (Parts of the statue were, however, saved by British-supporting Tories, and among those parts preserved is the horse's tail, part of the permanent collection of the New York Historical Society.)

To the right, **BATTERY PARK/CASTLE CLINTON** (see p. 172) has been home to many public protests, including in recent years a nearly spontaneous rally and march of tens of thousands of New Yorkers during the first weeks of Donald Trump's presidency in opposition to the xenophobic and anti-Muslim immigration policies proposed by his administration. The march passed Trinity Church to the north, burial place of one of the United States' most famous immigrants, Alexander Hamilton. Walking north on Broadway, across from the "CHARGING BULL" sculpture that celebrates the muscular enthusiasm of a "bull market" upturn, you will find the entrance to **STANDARD OIL BUILDING** (26 Broadway, New York, NY; see p. 169), the original corporate home to the company that accelerated the carbon age and made John D. Rockefeller the world's richest man. For weeks during the spring of 1914, anarchists and socialists including Upton Sinclair led silent pickets outside these doors in protest of the company's killings of Colorado mine workers and their families in what became known as the "Ludlow Massacre."

Continuing north on **BROADWAY**: Much of this borough-spanning avenue was initially created by the Lenape natives and known as the Wickquasgeck Trail. Here, along its southern expanse, it nearly abutted the Hudson River when the Dutch first arrived. Almost one-third of the land of lower Manhattan is landfill, including nearly all of the streets here west of Broadway, the whole of Battery Park, and much of what lies east of Pearl and Water. The island's expansion began in earnest in the late eighteenth century, when "water lots" were sold for development; the final great expansion took place with the building of the former World Trade Center, whose foundational detritus became the land on which Battery Park City now rests. The value of land in New York City is such that even natural limits have been made fungible.

At Wall Street, turn east away from **TRINITY CHURCH** (89 Broadway, New York, NY). The **NEW YORK STOCK EXCHANGE** (11 Wall Street, New York, NY) has been cordoned off from any meaningful public approach since the terror attacks of 9/11/2001. But it has often served as an alluring site for spectacular dissent. In 1967, antiwar activist Abbie Hoffman pulled off his first successful "guerrilla theatre" protest in the Exchange, having entered with fellow pranksters for a tour, and then, from the visitor's gallery, showering the trading floor with dol-

lar bills. The traders' scramble for the loot made the "Marxist zap" against greed headline news around the country. More strategically, two decades later, members of ACT-UP (Aids Coalition To Unleash Power) entered the Exchange to protest price gouging of AIDS medicines. They chained themselves in at the opening of the day on September 14, 1989, dropping a banner reading "SELL WELLCOME" from the balcony, and successfully stopped the trading. Burroughs Wellcome, the principal owner of the AIDS medicine AZT, subsequently lowered the price of the drug.

Facing the Stock Exchange is **FEDERAL HALL** (26 Wall Street, New York, NY), which marks the site of the first government of the United States. On May 8, 1970, it was the gathering spot for antiwar protesters who came at lunch to memorialize the killing of four students at Kent State University in Ohio at the hands of the National Guard. Construction workers from the World Trade Center site were encouraged to take their lunch break to confront the protesters. Joined by other Wall Street workers, the construction workers attacked the antiwar protesters and marched uptown toward City Hall, where they punched out any "longhairs" they saw, including many students at nearby Pace University. This demonstration came to be known as the "Hard Hat riot," and served as a lasting symbol of class divisions between white workers and progressive social movements. In the case of the war, such symbolism was inaccurate and unwarranted, as a majority of workers

345

opposed the Vietnam war and condemned the riots at the time.

Across the street from Federal Hall, further east along Wall Street, is another temple to finance: the now-shuttered **MORGAN GUARANTY TRUST COMPANY** (23 Wall Street, New York, NY), former headquarters of J. P. Morgan's sprawling banking empire. On September 16, 1920, a horse-drawn wagon was parked outside a little before noon. As the bells of Trinity Church rang at midday, the wagon exploded, ultimately killing thirty-eight people. The bomb's maker was never caught, though investigations at the time and since point toward an Italian anarchist named Mario Buda, whose likely motive was opposition to the arrest of fellow anarchists and Italian immigrants Nicola Sacco and Bartolomeo Vanzetti months before. Sacco and Vanzetti had been accused of robbery and murder; within the year they had been found guilty after a trial that stood out for its fraudulent and prejudicial nature. Their arrest, conviction, and eventual execution in 1927 marked the culmination of the oppressive frenzy of the first "Red Scare" in the United States. The limestone façade of the building still bears pockmarks from the explosion.

Continue down Wall Street to Water. In 1711 this was the site of the city-created **SLAVE MARKET** (see p. 169) at what was then the waterfront Wall Street slip.

In 1712, the event that the white Europeans hoped the slave market might forestall occurred, at our next stop on the tour along **MAIDEN LANE**, two blocks north along Water. It was somewhere along this street, on what was then the outskirts of the city, that twenty-three enslaved Africans and at least one free Black person planned a revolt. Most of those enslaved were newly arrived from what is now Ghana. Historians believe they were familiar with the practices of West African slavery, which was significantly less oppressive and murderous than the form that had been developing in the British colonies. Together they set fire to the house of a baker who owned two enslaved people and ambushed the white colonists who came to put out the fire. The revolt was put down after nine whites were killed; twenty-one Black people were killed in retribution through brutal means, including being burned alive and hung by chains. Afterward, more laws were passed to further constrain the movement and rights of enslaved and free Black people, including laws that authorized violent treatment from owners, discouraged the freeing of any Black individuals, and barring free Black people from owning land in New York City.

Walking two blocks west across Maiden Lane, take Liberty Street at the fork (where Maiden Lane continues along the north side of the green triangular park). On the southwest corner at William Street is **ONE CHASE MANHATTAN PLAZA** (28 Liberty Street, New York, NY; see p. 168), the headquarters for J. P. Morgan Chase Bank, the largest bank of the United States. Chase has been a frequent target of protest over the decades. For example, it was here on March 19, 1965, that the Students for a Democratic Society organized a protest of three hundred demonstrators against Chase's extensive financial support for South Africa's brutal and oppressive system of Apartheid in South Africa.

Continue west along the Liberty Street backside of the fortress-like façade of the behemoth landmarked headquarters of the **UNITED STATES FEDERAL RESERVE BANK** (44 Maiden Lane, New York, NY), which occupies the whole of the block from William to Nassau. The Fed serves as the central bank for the United States and, as such, oversees monetary policy: among other things, the decisions made behind these walls directly implicate the protest cycles on the surrounding streets. Case in point: In two more blocks, Liberty opens onto Broadway and a park, whose eastern edge displays a tall red sculpture. This privately owned public space, **ZUCCOTTI PARK**, was home to the Occupy Wall Street (OWS) encampments of the fall of 2011. Hundreds of Occupiers were joined daily by thousands of supporters at this site, protesting as part of the "99%" rallying against Wall Street's "1%." From here OWS conducted daily marches across Wall Street, to the Federal Reserve, to Chase Plaza, to the charging bull. OWS's critique of inequality and the erosion of democracy was not limited to New York City, or even the United States. Hundreds of occupations spread to dozens of countries. Here is a good place to end the tour, from the staging ground of the latest movement to rise against the power of Wall Street's corporate titans, imagining the echoes from their chants and contemplating the future of protest at the heart of global capital: "We Are the 99%." "All Day. All Week. Occupy Wall Street!" "Whose streets? Our streets! Whose city? Our city!"

TO LEARN MORE

Fraser, Steve, and Mark Crispin Miller. *Wall Street: America's Dream Palace*. New Haven: Yale University Press, 2009.

Frohne, Andrea E. *The African Burial Ground in New York City: Memory, Spirituality, and Space.* Syracuse, NY: Syracuse University Press, 2015.

Jezer, Marty. *Abbie Hoffman: American Rebel*. New Brunswick, NJ: Rutgers University Press, 1993.

Jones, Thai. *More Powerful Than Dynamite: Radicals, Plutocrats, Progressives, and New York's Year of Anarchy*. New York: Bloomsbury USA, 2014.

Lewis, Penny. *Hardhats, Hippies, and Hawks: The Vietnam Antiwar Movement as Myth and Memory*. Ithaca, NY: ILR Press, 2013.

Recommended Reading

Algarín, Miguel, and Bob Holman. *Aloud: Voices from the Nuyorican Poets Cafe.* New York: Macmillan, 1994.

Anbinder, Tyler. *Five Points: The 19th-Century New York City Neighborhood that Invented Tap Dance, Stole Elections, and Became the World's Most Notorious Slum.* New York: Simon and Schuster, 2001.

Anbinder, Tyler. *City of Dreams: The 400 Year Epic History of Immigrant New York.* New York: Houghton Mifflin Harcourt, 2016.

Angotti, Tom. *New York for Sale: Community Planning Confronts Global Real Estate.* Cambridge, MA: MIT Press, 2008.

Ascher, Kate. *The Works: Anatomy of a City.* London: Penguin Books, 2007.

Baker, Kevin. *Paradise Alley.* New York: Harper Perennial, 2006.

Baker, Kevin. *The Fall of A Great American City: New York and the Urban Crisis of Affluence.* Westport, CT: City Point Press, 2019.

Baumann, Jason, Edmund White, and New York Public Library, eds. *The Stonewall Reader.* New York: Penguin Books, 2019.

Ballon, Hilary, and Kenneth T. Jackson. *Robert Moses and the Modern City: The Transformation of New York.* New York: W.W. Norton, 2007.

Bloom, Nicholas Dagen, and Matthew Gordon Lasner, eds. *Affordable Housing in New York: The People, Places, and Policies That Transformed a City.* Princeton, NJ: Princeton University Press, 2005.

Bloom, Nicholas Dagen. *Public Housing That Worked: New York in the Twentieth Century.* Philadelphia: University of Pennsylvania Press, 2009.

Blush, Steven. *New York Rock: From the Rise of The Velvet Underground to the Fall of CBGB.* New York: St. Martin's, 2006.

Brash, Julian. *Bloomberg's New York: Class and Governance in the Luxury City.* Athens: University of Georgia Press, 2011.

Burrows, Edwin G., and Mike Wallace. *Gotham: A History of New York City to 1898.* Oxford University Press, 1998.

Caro, Robert A., and Robert A. Caro. *The Power Broker: Robert Moses and the Fall of New York.* Alfred A Knopf Incorporated, 1974.

Chang, Jeff. *Can't Stop Won't Stop: A History of the Hip-hop Generation.* St. Martin's Press, 2007.

Chauncey, George. *Gay New York: Gender, Urban Culture, and the Makings of the Gay Male World, 1890–1940.* New York: Basic Books, 1994.

Chisholm, Shirley. *Unbought and Unbossed.* Take Root Media, 2010.

Dávila, Arlene. *Barrio Dreams: Puerto Ricans, Latinos, and the Neoliberal City.* Berkeley: University of California Press, 2004.

Delany, Samuel R. *Times Square Red, Times Square Blue.* New York: NYU Press, 2001.

Duberman, Martin. *Stonewall: The Definitive Story of the LGBTQ Rights Uprising That Changed America.* Revised edition. New York: Plume, 2019.

Eisenstadt, Peter. *Rochdale Village: Robert Moses, 6,000 Families, and New York City's Great Experiment in Integrated Housing.* Ithaca, NY: Cornell University Press, 2020.

Enck-Wanzer, Darrel. *The Young Lords: A Reader.* New York: NYU Press, 2010.

Fernandez, Johanna. *The Young Lords: A Radical History.* Chapel Hill: University of North Carolina Press, 2020.

Fink, Leon, and Brian Greenberg. *Upheaval in the Quiet Zone: 1199/SEIU and the Politics of Healthcare Unionism,* Second Edition. Urbana: University of Illinois Press, 2009.

Fitch, Robert. *The Assassination of New York.* New York: Verso, 1993.

Fraser, Steve, and Mark Crispin Miller. *Wall Street: America's Dream Palace.* New Haven: Yale University Press, 2009.

Freeman, Joshua Benjamin. *In Transit: The Transport Workers Union in New York City, 1933–1966.* Oxford: Oxford University Press, 1989.

Freeman, Joshua B. *Working-Class New York: Life and Labor Since World War II.* The New Press, 2001.

Freeman, Joshua B. *City of Workers, City of Struggle. How Labor Movements Changed New York.* New York: Columbia University Press, 2019.

Freeman, Lance. *There Goes the 'Hood: Views of Gentrification from the Ground Up.* Philadelphia: Temple University Press, 2006.

Frohne, Andrea E. *The African Burial Ground in New York City: Memory, Spirituality, and Space.* Syracuse, NY: Syracuse University Press, 2005.

Galusha, Diane. *Liquid Asset: A History of New York City's Water System.* Fleischmanns, NY: Purple Mountain Press, 2006.

Gandy, Matthew. *Concrete and Clay: Reworking Nature in New York City.* Cambridge, MA: MIT Press, 2002.

Gieseking, Jen Jack. *A Queer New York: Geographies of Lesbians, Dykes, and Queers.* New York: NYU Press, 2020.

Gilfoyle, Timothy. *City of Eros: New York City, Prostitution, and the Commercialization of Sex, 1820–1920.* New York: Norton, 1992.

Glickman, Toby, and Gene Glickman. *The New York Red Pages: A Radical Tourist Guide.* Greenwood, 1984.

Gonzalez, Evelyn. *The Bronx.* New York: Columbia University Press, 2004.

Gould, Kenneth A., and Tammy L. Lewis. *Green Gentrification: Urban Sustainability and the Struggle for Environmental Justice.* New York: Routledge, 2017.

Greenberg, Miriam. *Branding New York: How a City in Crisis Was Sold to the World.* New York: Routledge, 2008.

Gregory, Steven. *Black Corona: Race and the Politics of Place in an Urban Community.* Princeton, NJ: Princeton University Press, 1998.

Gryvatz Copquin, Claudia. *The Neighborhoods of Queens.* New Haven: Yale University Press, 2007.

Hanson, R. Scott. *City of Gods: Religious Freedom, Immigration, and Pluralism in Flushing, Queens.* New York: Empire State Editions, 2006.

Harris, Leslie M. *In the Shadow of Slavery: African Americans in New York City, 1626–1863.* Chicago: University of Chicago Press, 2004.

Hodges, Graham Russell Gao. *David Ruggles: A Radical Black Abolitionist and the Underground Railroad in New York City.* Chapel Hill: University of North Carolina Press, 2010.

Hum, Tarry. *The Making of a Global Immigrant Neighborhood: Brooklyn's Sunset Park.* Philadelphia: Temple University Press, 2014.

Jackson, Kenneth T., and New-York Historical Society. *The Encyclopedia of New York City*. New Haven: Yale University Press, 2010.

Jonnes, Jill. *South Bronx Rising: The Rise, Fall, and Resurrection of an American City*, Second Edition. New York: Fordham University Press, 2002.

Jones, Thai. *More Powerful Than Dynamite: Radicals, Plutocrats, Progressives, and New York's Year of Anarchy*. New York: Bloomsbury USA, 2014.

Kayton, Bruce. *Radical Walking Tours of New York City*. Seven Stories Press, 2016.

Krinsky, John, and Maud Simonet. *Who Cleans the Park? Public Work and Urban Governance in New York City*. Chicago: The University of Chicago Press, 2017.

Kramer, Daniel C, and Richard M Flanagan. *Staten Island: Conservative Bastion in a Liberal City*. Lanham, Md.: University Press of America, 2012.

Kwong, Peter. *Chinatown, New York: Labor and Politics, 1930–1950*. Monthly Review Press, 1979.

Kwong, Peter. *Forbidden Workers: Illegal Chinese Immigrants and American Labor*. New York: New Press, 1998.

Kwong, Peter. *The New Chinatown*. Macmillan, 1996.

Main, Thomas J. *Homelessness in New York City: Policymaking from Koch to de Blasio*. New York: NYU Press, 2006.

Maier, Mark H. *City Unions: Managing Discontent in New York City*. New Brunswick, NJ: Rutgers University Press, 1987.

Martinez, Miranda. *Power at the Roots: Gentrification, Community Gardens, and the Puerto Ricans of the Lower East Side*. Lanham, MD: Lexington Books, 2010.

McNeil, Legs, and Gillian McCain. *Please Kill Me: The Uncensored Oral History of Punk*. 20th Anniversary edition. New York: Grove Press, 2016.

McNeur, Catherine. *Taming Manhattan: Environmental Battles in the Antebellum City*. Cambridge: Harvard University Press, 2014.

Mele, Christopher. *Selling the Lower East Side: Culture, Real Estate, and Resistance in New York City*. Minneapolis: University of Minnesota, 2000.

Mitchell, Joseph. *Up in the Old Hotel and Other Stories*. New York: Vintage Books, 1996.

Moody, Kim. *From Welfare State to Real Estate: Regime Change in New York City, 1974 to the Present*. New York: The New Press, 2007.

Moss, Jeremiah. *Vanishing New York: How a great city lost its soul*. New York: Dey St, 2017.

Nahshon, Edna, ed. *New York's Yiddish Theater: From the Bowery to Broadway*. New York: Columbia University Press, 2016.

Newfield, Jack and Wayne Barrett. *City For Sale: Ed Koch and the Betrayal of New York*. New York : Harper & Row, 1988.

Nevius, Michelle, and James Nevius. *Inside the Apple: A Streetwise History of New York City*. Simon and Schuster, 2009.

Orleck, Annelise. *Common Sense and a Little Fire: Women and Working-Class Politics in the United States, 1900–1965*. Chapel Hill: University of North Carolina Press, 1995.

Osman, Suleiman. *The Invention of Brownstone Brooklyn: Gentrification and the Search for Authenticity in Postwar New York*. Oxford University Press, 2011.

Osofsky, Gilbert. *Harlem, the Making of a Ghetto: Negro New York, 1890–1930*, Second Edition. Chicago: Elephant Paperbacks, 1996.

Phillips-Fein, Kim. *Fear City: New York's Fiscal Crisis and the Rise of Austerity Politics*. Metropolitan Books, 2017.

Plunz, Richard. *A History of Housing in New York City*. Revised edition. New York: Columbia University Press, 2006.

Pulido, Laura, Laura R. Barraclough, and Wendy Cheng. *A People's Guide to Los Angeles*. University of California Press, 2012.

Raskin, Joseph B. *The Routes Not Taken: A Trip Through New York City's Unbuilt Subway System*. New York: Fordham University Press, 2015.

Reaven, Marci and Steve Zeitlin, eds. *Hidden New York: A Guide to Places That Matter.* New York: Rivergate Books, 2006.

Rosenzweig, Roy, and Elizabeth Blackmar. *The Park and the People: A History of Central Park.* Ithaca, NY: Cornell University Press, 1992.

Smith, Neil, Don Mitchell, Erin Siodmak, JenJoy Roybal, Marnie Brady, and Brendan P. O'Malley, eds. *Revolting New York: How 400 Years of Riot, Rebellion, Uprising, and Revolution Shaped a City.* Athens: University of Georgia Press, 2018.

Soll, David. *Empire of Water: An Environmental and Political History of the New York City Water Supply.* New York: Cornell University Press, 2003.

Solnit, Rebecca, and Joshua Jelly-Schapiro. *Nonstop Metropolis: A New York City Atlas.* Volume. 3. University of California Press, 2016.

Sorkin, Michael. *Variations on a Theme Park: The New American City and the End of Public Space.* New York: Macmillan, 1992.

Starecheski, Amy. *Ours to Lose: When Squatters Became Homeowners in New York City.* Chicago: University of Chicago Press, 2006.

Steinberg, Ted. *Gotham Unbound: The Ecological History of Greater New York.* Reprint edition. New York: Simon & Schuster, 2005.

Su, Celina. *Streetwise for Book Smarts: Grassroots Organizing and Education Reform in the Bronx.* Ithaca, NY: Cornell University Press, 2009.

Sze, Julie. *Noxious New York: The Racial Politics of Urban Health and Environmental Justice.* Urban and Industrial Environments. Cambridge, MA: MIT Press, 2007.

Taylor, Clarence. *Civil Rights in New York City: From World War II to the Giuliani Era.* New York: Fordham University Press, 2010.

Vitale, Alex S. *City of Disorder: How the Quality of Life Campaign Transformed New York Politics.* New York: NYU Press, 2008.

Wallace, Mike. *Greater Gotham: A History of New York City from 1898 to 1919.* Oxford University Press, 2017.

Walsh, Kevin. *Forgotten New York: Views of a Lost Metropolis.* Harper Collins, 2006.

Wellman, Judith. *Brooklyn's Promised Land: The Free Black Community of Weeksville, New York.* New York: NYU Press, 2014.

Whitehead, Colson. *The Colossus of New York : a City in Thirteen Parts.* New York Recorded Books, 2003.

Wilder, Craig Steven. *A Covenant With Color: Race and Social Power in Brooklyn 1636–1990.* Columbia University Press, 2000.

Woodsworth, Michael. *The Battle for Bed-Stuy: The Long War on Poverty in New York City.* Boston: Harvard University Press, 2016.

Young, Greg and Tom Meyers. *The Bowery Boys: Adventures in Old New York: An Unconventional Exploration of Manhattan's Historic Neighborhoods, Secret Spots, and Colorful Characters.* Ulysses Press, 2016.

WEBSITES

Bowery Boys, https://www.boweryboyshistory.com/

CUNY Digital History Archive, https://cdha.cuny.edu/

Ephemeral New York, https://ephemeralnewyork.wordpress.com/

Forgotten New York, https://forgotten-ny.com/

Interference Archive, https://interferencearchive.org/

Lesbian Herstory Archives, https://lesbianherstoryarchives.org/

Mapping the African American Past (MAAP, Columbia University), https://maap.columbia.edu/

NYC LGBT Historic Sites Project, https://www.nyclgbtsites.org/

The New York Times, https://nytimes.com

Place Matters, https://placematters.net/

Vanishing New York, http://vanishingnewyork.blogspot.com/

Acknowledgments

Writing this work proved to be a much longer project than we'd anticipated, spanning three presidencies, two mayoralties, and one pandemic. We knew from the start that no three people could do justice to a people's guide for a city as vast, complex, and heterogeneous as New York. So, critically, this project is the result of much collaboration, consultation, and conversation. We shared our proposal for the book, and our first ideas, with an advisory committee of New York experts and activists who helped us draw up the initial list of sites for the guide, and they generously shared their ideas about people we might speak with as we wrote up the sites, or who might write entries themselves. While we have written the bulk of the book ourselves, we are deeply fortunate to include multiple site entries from New York City scholars, writers, and students (credits follow each entry), some of whom also served in that original advisory group. We are equally fortunate to have worked with numerous students and colleagues who provided research for particular entries (credits also follow each entry). In addition to this and our own research, our work draws on the work and insights of other sociologists, historians, geographers, anthropologists, urban planners, and community and labor activists. Most sites are followed by a short bibliography for readers interested in learning more. A full list of recommended readings can be found at the back of the book.

Our advisors included Alan Aja, Becky Amato, Gianpaolo Baiocchi, Kevin Baker, Eve Baron, Jessica Blatt, Naomi Braine, Steve Brier, Caitlin Cahill, Melissa Checker, Zaire Dinzey-Flores, Josh Freeman, Lance Freeman, Jen Jack Gieseking, Miriam Greenberg, Tarry Hum, Phil Kasinitz, Alyssa Katz, Lize Mogel, Leith Mullings, Susan Saegert, Celina Su, and Chloe Tribich. The late Peter Kwong was also a passionate contributor to our initial meeting, and his work has deeply influenced this book. We are pleased and grateful to share entries written by Alan Aja, Becky Amato, Kelly Anderson, Ethan Barnett, Danielle Bullock, Karisa Butler-Wall, Wendy Cheng, Sara Evans, David Farley, Zinga Fraser, Josh Freeman, Sarah Fuller, Moses Gates, Jen Jack Gieseking, Ken Gould, Tarry Hum, Steven Johnson, Prithi Kanakamedala, Alyssa Katz, Tammy Lewis, Arianna Martinez, Brandon Martinez, Elena Martínez, Miranda Martinez, Lize Mogel, Justin Sean Myers, Jerald Podair, Lucas Rubin, Jeanne Theoharis,

Alex Vitale, Amy VonBokel, Christopher Wassif, Jocelyn Wills, Michael Woodsworth, and Cookie Woolner. Many of our literary nearby sites of interest came to us from our colleague Celina Su, who shared her extensive knowledge of literary New York. Many students and colleagues also helped us to research the book and contributed to specific entries: Xhoana Ahmeti, Ethan Barnett, Naomi Braine, Harry Corin, Katy Coto Batres, Sarah Fuller, Jamila Gandhi, Liat Halpern, Brian Lewis, Brandon Martinez, Laura Peñaranda, Thomas Powers, Lucy Pugh, Carly-Jo Rosselli, Julieta Salgado, Luisa Santos, Dana Steer, Jack Suria Linares, and Bronte Walker. Marco Castillo helped to standardize all of the references in the manuscript.

A number of guidebooks, websites, and blogs share objectives similar to ours, and we acknowledge our debt and appreciation, and urge our readers to read and explore them as well. The blog, "Forgotten New York," lovingly details places "the tourists never see" and its book version *Forgotten New York* by webmaster Kevin Walsh tells five borough snapshot histories from a native's perspective. "Ephemeral New York," another robust blog written by Esther Crain, has for over a decade chronicled pieces about the city's past. Greg Young and Tom Meyers's *Bowery Boys* blog is an indispensable guide to New York history, and they are perhaps more well known for their podcast of the same name; they too have a book, *The Bowery Boys Adventures in Old New York. Inside the Apple: A Streetwise History of New York City* by Michelle and James Nevius is another wonderful historical guide to Manhattan. Another book, more rooted in the present than the others, that we love and hope to complement here is *Hidden New York: A Guide to Places That Matter* by Marci Reaven and Steven J. Zeitlin, which provides historical and ethnographic essays about thirty-two places across the boroughs. This work continues on the lively, crowdsourced

"Place Matters" website to which we happily send anyone interested in a people's New York. Similarly, other websites mark important historical and political themes across sites in New York City's five boroughs, including the NYC LGBT Historic Sites Project and Columbia University's MAAP: Mapping the African American Past. The tour books closest in theme and site selection to the People's Guide APGTNYC are Bruce Katyon's *Radical Walking Tours of New York City* and the regretfully out-of-print *New York City Red Pages* by Toby and Gene Glickman. Finally, a book whose creativity, clarity, and commitment to alternative geography we celebrate is Rebecca Solnit and Joshua Jelly-Schapiro's *NonStop Metropolis: A New York City Atlas*.

Finally, a number of individuals and institutions provided essential support to our efforts. We were lucky to receive the support of the Urban Democracy Lab at NYU, under the leadership of Gianpaolo Baiocchi and Becky Amato, who gave us space for the advisory board meetings and provided delicious breakfasts for those meetings. Ruth Milkman generously provided space and sustenance for retreats at critical points in the manuscript's development; we are grateful for her friendship. The project has been financially supported by two grants from the PSC-CUNY labor-management support fund, a CUNY book completion grant, the CUNY School of Labor and Urban Studies, the Tow Foundation, the Ethyle R. Wolfe Institute for the Humanities at Brooklyn College, and the Mellon Transfer Research Program at Brooklyn College. Scott Dexter, our friend and former colleague at Brooklyn College, provided many of the outstanding photos we use in the book, and, later, our colleague Stephanie Luce at the School of Labor and Urban Studies brought her keen eye to further shots. We are deeply grateful to them both. John Emerson exhibited extraordinary patience with our team while designing and refining the maps for the project; we are in his debt for the extraordinary work he did.

We have been lucky to work with numerous archivists and librarians who helped us with our research and photo acquisitions: at CUNY, NYU's Tamiment, Schomburg, the Brooklyn Public Library, the New York Public Library, and the Brooklyn Historical Society. Special thanks to Linden Anderson, Jr. (Schomburg Center), Rebekah Burgess (NYC Parks), Caitlin McCarthy (LGBT Center), Lauren Robinson (Museum of the City of New York), and Saskia Scheffer (Lesbian Herstory Archives). Many other individuals and organizations generously granted permission to use images, and they are listed with photo credits. The book would not have been possible without them.

Anonymous reviewers for the press were critical interlocutors for the project, and their feedback helped us to see it with new eyes and make what we hope were improvements following their strong advice; all weaknesses of the book remain our own. Wendy Cheng, Laura Pulido, and Laura Barraclough, the Peoples Guide Series editors, were essential guides to us a well, and their insights, questions, and comments have made this a much better book. All of the *People's Guides* teams have provided camaraderie as we have collectively undertaken our projects. Our University of California Press editor Kim Robinson has helped steer this project over its gestation, always with patience and generosity. Francisco Reinking, Summer Farah, Lynda Crawford, and Robert Sauté brought their expert eyes to the production and text in the book's final stages.

Last, but far from least, we would like to express our love and extend particular thanks to our families (Ted, Emilio, Steve, Clara, Eleanor, Devin, Talia, and Marco) for supporting us in our endless writing, countless meetings, weekend trips away, and constant book-talk. We dedicate this book to our children, and all of their peers: the newest New Yorkers born to it or arriving today, who are already contributing to, and who will continue to shape and create the vital, people's New York.

—*Carolina, Penny, and Emily*
New York City, 2021

Credits

and Public Domain: https://commons.wikimedia.org/w/index.php?curid=605458

Page 170 (2.54): http://digitalcollections.nypl.org/items/510d47d9–9d46-a3d9-e040-e00a18064a99

Page 172 (2.56): Permission was sought but due to archives being closed and unreachable, we were unable to clear formal permission. The author and press will be glad to do so if and when contacted by the copyright holder of third party material.

Page 188 (3.2): https://commons.wikimedia.org/w/index.php?curid=6994021

Page 191 (3.4-1) https://commons.wikimedia.org/w/index.php?curid=20785006

Page 211 (3.16-1): https://commons.wikimedia.org/w/index.php?curid=54816342

Page 213 (3.18-1): https://commons.wikimedia.org/w/index.php?curid=43198171

Page 214 (3.18-2) https://commons.wikimedia.org/w/index.php?curid=3266770

Page 215 (3.18-3): https://commons.wikimedia.org/w/index.php?curid=8188225

Page 227 (4.2-2): https://commons.wikimedia.org/w/index.php?curid=74356705

Page 245 (4.10): https://www.loc.gov/item/2014646807/

Page 250 (4.13) https://commons.wikimedia.org/w/index.php?curid=17980389

Page 262 (4.20): https://www.loc.gov/item/2014698771/

Page 283 (4.31-1): https://dsl.richmond.edu/panorama/redlining

Page 284 (4.31-2): https://dsl.richmond.edu/panorama/redlining

Page 286 (4.32): https://commons.wikimedia.org/w/index.php?curid=23237617

Index

Founded in 1893,
UNIVERSITY OF CALIFORNIA PRESS
publishes bold, progressive books and journals
on topics in the arts, humanities, social sciences,
and natural sciences—with a focus on social
justice issues—that inspire thought and action
among readers worldwide.

The UC PRESS FOUNDATION
raises funds to uphold the press's vital role
as an independent, nonprofit publisher, and
receives philanthropic support from a wide
range of individuals and institutions—and from
committed readers like you. To learn more, visit
ucpress.edu/supportus.